Voices of
American

Voices of
American Muslims

23 Profiles

Linda Brandi Cateura

Breaking a long silence since 9/11,
23 American Muslims from all levels of society
speak up about Islam,
our nation, 9/11, its effects on their lives,
and their hopes for the future.

Introductory essay by *Professor Omid Safi*
Department of Islamic Studies,
Colgate University

HIPPOCRENE BOOKS
NEW YORK

25/6807

Also by Linda Brandi Cateura
Growing up Italian
Catholics USA: Will They Survive?
Protestant Portraits
Oil Painting Secrets from a Master

Book design by Acme Klong Design, Inc.
Jacket design by Ronnie McBride.

For information, address:
HIPPOCRENE BOOKS, INC.
171 Madison Avenue
New York, NY 10016

ISBN 0-7818-1054-X
Cataloging-in-Publication Data available from the Library of Congress.
Printed in the United States of America.

To

Glynne Robinson Betts
who gave me the idea for this book,
as well as her moral support.

I also acknowledge a debt
to her young grandson,
known to me only by name, who nonetheless
spurred the desire to write this book,
so that his generation may grow up knowing
more about Muslims than ours did.

PREFACE

This is a book about people of Muslim ancestry living in America today and known as American Muslims. Their families emigrated from many different countries and their religion, Islam, is practiced worldwide. Some who appear here were born in America, others are naturalized, and some may not yet be naturalized.

The author wishes to thank all twenty-three persons who consented to be interviewed, and thereby subjected themselves to innumerable calls and demands. Their cooperation was deeply reassuring. She remains forever appreciative of their willingness to talk and, very simply, *to give of themselves* to the extent shown here.

And, not lastly, thanks to Anne Kemper, the editor at Hippocrene Books who recognized the possibilities of the subject and to Priti Gress and Sophie Fels, who helped carry it through to complete satisfaction.

INTRODUCTION
by Linda Brandi Cateura

I am a Roman Catholic, born and bred. But that hasn't kept me from being curious to learn about other faiths in America, such as Judaism and the various denominations of Protestants. Yet I shamefacedly admit that up until September 11, 2001, I knew very little about Islam, the third great monotheistic religion, and about American Muslims. Frankly, very few of my friends, of whatever religion, did either.

I did, however, have one small point of contact with Muslims. Living in Brooklyn Heights, in New York City, I was aware of a community of people called Muslims who had small businesses on its fringes, the merchants and storekeepers on Atlantic Avenue, from whom we had been buying Middle Eastern foods for years. They were friendly and exuded a kind of warmth not found among storekeepers generally. I used to see a few women dressed in black garb with scarves wound around their heads, walking quickly down the street, as if not to be seen. But outside of this, the word, Muslim, meant little.

What added to the anonymity was the complete disregard of Muslims and their religion, Islam, in our studies at school. I was an attentive student, read the catechism, took courses in American and European history (including some coverage of religion). Strange to say, nowhere that I remember was the Koran mentioned, or the religion of Islam itself. Some years ago, when Salman Rushdie's life was threatened after he wrote a book that offended some believers in the Koran, the references were an unknown world and I could not figure out what all the fuss was about.

ISLAMIC STORES along Atlantic Avenue in Brooklyn are a mecca for Muslims seeking spiritual guidance and material goods. Behind the storefronts (above), on shelves, encased in glass, or piled high on tables and floors are prayer rugs, African black soap, shea butter, body oils, scents, kufis (caps for men), hijabs (head scarves for women), jilbabs (long dresses or coats), jewelry, books, copies of the Koran, disks, tapes, figs, Mecca cola, black seed (for nutrition), halal meats, fresh and frozen vegetables, cleansers, plus many other items. Fertile Crescent is a typical store. (Photo courtesy of Henry Cateura.)

Suddenly on September 11, the word Muslim struck us with astounding force. Not alone for the disaster itself, but for what has followed. The fury of Americans was not only directed toward the perpetrators, the murderers themselves, but toward all American Muslims. Not only was our government rounding up Muslims who were under suspicion, but also innocent Muslims throughout the country were being verbally attacked and victimized by other Americans. Locally, storeowners on Atlantic Avenue were being picketed. Loyal customers in the community were quick to respond, joining a peace march of Muslims and non-Muslims alike and marching through the streets on behalf of peace and mercy. Prayer vigils, comprising Jews, Christians, and Muslims, were held on the Promenade overlooking New York Harbor (directly across from the Twin Towers site). These groups memorialized the dead victims, and some pleaded for tolerance toward the grand majority of American Muslims who were not involved in the attack.

What has made this situation even more serious is that American Muslims for a long period remained relatively silent. The silence has aggravated a bad situation. Some of the reasons for the silence make sense. Muslims have few organized, socially minded organizations and these were mainly unprepared, without proper technology and sufficient office help, to respond to the media. When they did speak, with releases and letters roundly condemning the attacks, the media, ever in search of new and momentous news, largely, in effect, put the response aside. It should also be pointed out that there is an underlying tendency of immigrant groups (into which category the majority of American Muslims fall) to remain silent in the public arena. Their English is not good, their social contacts are perforce minimal, and they tend to focus on themselves. In a sense, loyal American Muslims have become secondary victims of the dreadful holocaust.

American Muslims are a silent mass in our country. In our erroneous image, the women walk around silently in head scarves and long gowns, and the men who usually wear Western-style dress are less recognizable. They seem a strange populace outside the experiences of America's melting pot and religious multiplicity. They are not part of the country's accepted Judeo-Christian montage, but a group that performs prayer ritual in a ramshackle mosque or solitary park. Many of us do not really know them and have not stopped to pay attention.

It is hoped that this book will help rectify the situation. In an effort to present a more balanced picture of American Muslims, I have interviewed twenty-three people in all walks of life who were willing and able to talk, and break the silence. They are verbal, outspoken and intelligent. Every one of them was eager and anxious to express his/her views and to voice the patriotism that each feels for America, and the anguish and occasional anger many experienced at the American response of incriminating innocent American Muslims after 9/11. The interviewees were deliberately chosen from different occupations and levels of society. They tell stories recreating the many worlds of Islam and a few look back to extraordinary experiences they had prior to their arrival in America.

What is most revealing about this group is that the people are so different one from another. If anything, they prove that not *all* Muslims are alike and that not all Muslims are Arabs (a common notion). They are of diverse ethnicities and backgrounds and represent many nations, including Indonesia, Egypt, Ghana, Palestine, Syria, Bangladesh, Pakistan, and Turkey. They are part and parcel of all areas of our national life, including the professions of medicine, law, education, business, finance, the armed forces, the media, writing, and the police. They are as infatuated with America as you or me, anxious to be known as loyal to what America represents, as any other immigrant or resident on these shores. Geographically, the interviewees cover many different areas: from Pasadena to New York City, from Detroit and Denver to Silver Spring, Maryland, from El Paso to Alaska. Both American-born Muslims and immigrants are included. They are delighted at the opportunity to appear on these pages.

Along the way, readers will ascertain facts about Islam itself, a religion unknown to many Americans. To better acquaint readers with Islamic beliefs and practices that may be unfamiliar to them, I offer the following, gleaned from two years of research and reading:

In Arabic, the word "Islam" means "submission to the will of God," or "having peace with God." The word "Muslim" is derived from "Islam," just as "Christian" is derived from "Christ" and "Jew" from "Judah." Place an *m* before "Islam" and you get a close approximation of the word "Muslim" with a minor change of vowel.

Muslims comprise one of the world's three great monotheistic (the belief in one God) religions, the other two being Judaism and Christianity. Islam was revealed by God in the Koran after Judaism and Christianity were established on earth, and is considered by Muslims to be a *continuation and update* of divine revelation of the Bible. But unlike the Bible, the Koran, according to Muslim belief, is the pure, direct word of Allah, untouched by intermediaries. It was revealed in the Arabic language to Muhammad, a prophet. Muslims believe in the same prophets that Jews and Christians do, and believe that Jesus is also a prophet, but not divine.

A word about the often-heard criticism that the Koran promotes conflict and war against non-Muslims. To see for myself, I bought a copy of the Koran in the Abdullah Yusuf Ali translation. With the aid of a guidebook, I found passages in which the Koran promotes interfaith tolerance, peaceful religious coexistence and unity, as long as the adherents of other faiths are peaceful toward Muslims. These passages follow. Please keep in mind that the Islamic reference to "People of the Book" refers to Jews and Christians.

> Say: O People of the Book! [Jews and Christians]. Come to
> common terms as between us and you: that we worship none

but Allah; that we associate no partners with Him; that we erect not, from among ourselves, Lords and patrons other than Allah. And if then they turn, say ye: Bear witness that we at least are Muslims [in the sense of bowing to Allah's Will]. (Al-i-'Imran 3/64)

And dispute ye not with the People of the Book, except in the best way, unless it be with those of them who do wrong but say, 'We believe in the Revelation which has come down to us and in that which came down to you; our God and your God is One; and it is to Him we submit (in Islam). (al-'Ankabut 46)

The following passages from the Koran further illustrate the advocacy of peaceful coexistence:

Say: We believe in God and that which was revealed unto us
And that which was revealed unto Abraham, and Ismail, and Isaac, and Jacob, and the tribes, and that which Moses and Jesus received,
And that which the Prophets received from their Lord.
We make no distinction between any of them and unto Him we surrender.
(Koran 2:136)

Behold, We have created you all out of a male and female, and have made you into nations and tribes, so that you might come to know one another…This community of yours is one single community,
since I am the Sustainer of you all: remain, then, conscious of me.
(Koran 49:13, 23)

Today, there are over one billion Muslims in the world, including a variety of races, nations, and cultures. The United States has from 5 to 7 million. The largest number, totaling 180 million, live in Indonesia and 18 percent are found in the Arab world. The remainder reside in many parts of Asia and Africa and are also found in smaller numbers in Russia, North and South America, and Europe. They differ from other monotheists in their form of worship and dress. Muslims sometimes perform their prayer ritual publicly, although this is not common in America. Their robes and head wrappings also set them apart from the world's predominantly Western or national garments. In the United States, the majority of Muslims wear Western clothing.

The basic Islamic beliefs are:

Belief in one God
Belief in the Angels
Belief in God's revealed books, Old and New Testaments and the Koran
Belief in the Prophets and Messengers of God
Belief in Heaven and Hell
Belief in the Day of Judgment
Belief in divine predestination

The Five Pillars of Islam (which each believer is expected to perform) are:

A testimony of faith (*shahada*)
Daily prayer (*salat*)
Giving support to the needy (*zacat*)
Fasting during the month of Ramadan
Performing hajj, a pilgrimage to Mecca, once in a lifetime

Since I was not seeking only people of unusual accomplishment and status in this book, I tried very hard to include "average-type" Muslims. By average, my mental image was an ordinary kind of Muslim, with medium or minimal education, a housewife, or someone having an ordinary job such as cabdriver, mail carrier, or dishwasher. Some of the "average" people I approached were unwilling to talk. The "average" people I succeeded in interviewing were unusual and interesting. Aisha Kareem, the nurse who seemingly fit the bill of "average," turned to be a woman of extraordinary background and intelligence. The "average" cabdriver, Zaki Hanafy, had been a lawyer in Cairo and is a devoted reader of the United States

COMMUNITY DINNER AT RAMADAN, 2003: Getting together during Ramadan are members of both the American Muslim and non-Muslim communities in New York City. In an effort to draw the two groups together, men and women gathered to break the day's fast and listen to speakers. Ramadan is the ninth month in the Islamic calendar and celebrates the occasion when the Angel Gabriel appeared to Prophet Muhammad and began revealing the word of the Holy Koran. It is a month of obligatory fasting, with one meal only taken each day. In the photo, Muslim women, wearing hijabs and jilbabs, check in guests. (Photo courtesy of Henry Cateura.)

Constitution. Amira al-Sarraf, who sounds like an "average housewife," is a graduate of the University of California-Berkeley and daughter of the founder of the prestigious Islamic Center of Southern California, and sister of Laila al-Marayati, ex-president of the Muslim Women's League. If these people in your lights turn out to be far from average, please absolve me. From my experience, the average is elusive, or can't be found, or refuses to talk. The possible exceptions are the students Aumrita Choudhury and Yuseph Sleem, who can be considered "average" by virtue of their being students.

Further bits of background: The book is based on interviews done either person-to-person or on the telephone. The question /answer form has been maintained in roughly half of them. In the others, the text has been carefully gleaned from the answers and fashioned into narratives. Readers are asked to keep in mind that since the writing of the book, some changes in professional status and jobs may have occurred.

The speakers' English renderings of Arabic terms were as varied as the interviewees themselves. When Arabic is transliterated into the Latin alphabet, there are no definitive spellings or standard Western pronunciations for these words. And then there were a few people, like Al-Haaj Ghazi Y. Khankan, who were careful to preserve as much as possible of the Arab sound and Arab titles. Witness the use of his choice of full Arabic name and title. Generally, I have used spellings that can more easily be recognized by American readers, such as Koran for Qu-raan, and so on.

Along with many chapters are photographs of the subject. They were either provided by the subject, or taken by the author's husband. They may help dispel the stereotypical image of Muslims—bearded men wearing kufis and women in hijabs and long dresses. Rather, they show how Muslims in the United States *do* dress—men in business suits, blue jeans, sneakers, women either wearing, or not wearing, hijabs and dresses that usually fall just below the knees (very few wear burkas or gowns).

With the reader thus advised, kindly pick up this volume, *Voices of American Muslims*, and get acquainted with your Muslim neighbors. Take off your overcoat of preconceptions, join our get-together, have a drink (sorry, no alcohol, Muslims don't drink; have coffee, Coke, or juice), relax, and listen.

American
Muslims

Past Legacy, Present Realities, and Future Challenges

by **Omid Safi**, Colgate University
Editor, *Progressive Muslims: On Justice, Gender, and Pluralism*
(Oxford: Oneworld, 2003)

American Muslims? Muslim Americans? Americanized Muslims?

American Muslims form the fastest growing religious block of citizens in America. In 1970, there were a scant hundred thousand Muslims in America. By 2003, accurate estimates put the number at more than 6 million. This sixty-fold growth in slightly over thirty years represents a phenomenal achievement. In spite of this growth, the presence of Muslims in America is one that is not adequately studied. This volume hopes to open a new chapter in that conversation, introducing you to the voices and perspectives of different Muslims in America.

What is new about this volume? It is that it brings together the voices of many different American Muslims, female and male, Sunni and Shia, immigrant, African American and white, scholar and imam, taxi-driver and activist, high school students and writers, in one volume. It allows American Muslims to speak for themselves. What is fascinating about these voices is that here Muslims talk about their own reality, their challenges, their hopes and dreams and loves and joys. September 11 casts its dark and terrible shadow over all of us, but the Muslims in this volume refuse to allow that event to be something that defines our existence. We all have to respond to that tragedy, but we had nothing to do with it. We were no more responsible for that tragedy than most Americans were responsible for Timothy McVeigh or the shootings at Columbine. And we will not live out the rest of our days apologizing for something we did not do. We all, Muslim and non-Muslim, have a responsibility to respond to that tragedy in compassion, justice, and pluralism toward all of humanity.

In the light of September 11, it seems that every aspect of talking about Islam and Muslims in America is touched with controversy. Even the terms we use to talk about these 6 million human beings who are American and Muslim are not uncontested. Language is a powerful tool, and the words we choose reveal a great deal about our hidden and not-so-hidden presuppositions. How does one refer to the approximately 6 million Muslims who call America home? If we call them American Muslims, are we implying that they are part of the global Muslim community first, and then qualified by being American (as distinct from their fellow Egyptian, Iranian, Pakistani, Indonesian, etc., Muslims)? That surely describes the identity of some. Do we refer to them as Muslim Americans? That choice would seem to highlight the American-ness of these citizens, and then qualify them as being Muslim (as distinct from their Christian, Jewish, and other neighbors). Far less satisfactory are terms like "Muslims in America," which has the perhaps unintended result of suggesting that there are Muslims in America but not really of it.

A very common way of talking about Islam in America has been through the framework of "Americanization of Islam." This whole notion is that of "Muslim" and "American" as separate and perhaps opposing categories. There are a number of problems with this initial assumption of separation. Given that approximately 35 percent of the Muslim population of America is African American, there is no question of "Americanization" for them: They are already, and have been, fully American. These are American citizens whose ancestors were stolen and brought over to this country, in many cases decades if not centuries before the majority of the waves of European immigration to the United States. The titles of popular volumes on North American Islam (such as *Muslims on the Americanization Path*[1]) reveal the identification of Islam with immigrant Islam, and a bypassing of the participation and contribution of African-American Muslims. That is deeply problematic, to say the least, and deeply hurtful and offensive to our African American sisters and brothers. Secondly, one could point to the fact that Muslims were present in the very early period of American history: there is now good evidence to suggest that Columbus's ships included some navigators of Muslim background. During some periods of slavery, somewhere as high as one-third of all the slaves stolen from Africa and brought to America in the inhumane transatlantic slave trade were from Muslim backgrounds. The number of Muslim slaves exceeded two million.[2] Sadly, plantation slavery systematically wiped away that religious heritage. A more continuous identity can be traced to the Muslims who have migrated to this country in the past hundred years. That number has drastically increased with the changes in the 1965 Immigration and Naturalization Act.[3] In other words, the presence and participation of Muslims in America goes back much further than most would suspect.

[1] Yvonne Yazbeck Haddad and John L. Esposito, Muslims on the Americanization Path (Oxford: Oxford University Press, 2000).
[2] Sylviane A. Diouf, Servants of Allah: African Muslims Enslaved in the Americas (New York: New York University Press, 1998), 48.
[3] Diana Eck, A New Religious America: How a "Christian Country" Has Become the World's Most Religiously Diverse Nation (New York: HarperSanFrancisco, 2001), 1-7.

African-American, Immigrant, Sufi, and Progressive Muslim Communities

There are four main current trends within North American Islam, and these do overlap to a great extent. These are not sectarian divisions, and many individuals and communities move with ease and grace between and among these various trends. Yet it might serve as a convenient starting point to talk about African-American Islam, immigrant Islam, Sufi Islam, and progressive Islam in contemporary America.

Islam returned as a significant aspect of African-American identity in the early period of the twentieth century. The movement was traced to the mysterious W. D. Fard, who appeared in Detroit. He trained Elijah Poole to be his disciple, bestowing the name Elijah Muhammad upon him. For a period of almost fifty years, Elijah Muhammad led what was then known as the Nation of Islam. Many immigrant Muslims have retrospectively objected to the association of the term Islam with this movement, as they have perhaps correctly pointed out that the Nation of Islam had little in common with the global practices and teachings of Muslims. Indeed the racial teachings of Elijah Muhammad, perceiving of whites as the incarnation of evil (embodied in the so-called "Jacob's Experiment," a mythical doctrine that held that white people were the result of a scientific experiment gone terribly wrong!) can best be seen as a mirror of the racist Christian teachings of the late nineteenth/early twentieth century that saw the white man as the highest embodiment of humanity, and all other races—specifically blacks—as belonging to an inferior category. Significant developments took place in the 1960s, under the leadership of Malcolm X, who reconnected with the broader Muslim *umma* (the global community of Muslims), and performed the Islamic pilgrimage to Mecca. There, seeing black and white, yellow and brown Muslim females and males performing the pilgrimage, Malcolm came to radically transform his views, moving to the universal brotherhood and sisterhood that has been a hallmark of Islamic teachings.[4] Sadly, Malcolm was assassinated soon after. Nonetheless, after the passing of Elijah Muhammad in 1973, the overwhelming majority of African-American Muslims crossed over to mainstream Sunni Islam under the leadership of Elijah's son, W. D. Muhammad. It is one of the great ironies of American Islam that the statistically insignificant following of Louis Farrakhan continues to garner so much media attention, while the overwhelming majority of mainstream African-American Muslims get bypassed in media coverage. That fact is probably not accidental, and connected to the way in which the media generally choose to focus on sensationalist events dealing with Islam.

There has been significant immigration to America for about a century now, although the immigration both increased and became more diversified

[4] For a powerful telling of this narrative, see The Autobiography of Malcolm X (New York: Grove Press, 1965).

post-1965, due to the changes in the immigration laws. Whereas before this point the majority of the Muslims who immigrated to America came from the eastern shores of the Mediterranean (Lebanon, Syria, etc.), post-1965 saw massive numbers of South Asians, Iranians, and other Muslims moving permanently to the United States. Indeed, it is fair to ask the question as to whether or not the label "immigrant" adequately describes these communities any longer. After all, many of their descendants have been born and raised here. In many cases they speak English and culturally, aesthetically, and linguistically fit only in the North American context. They identify first and foremost as Americans. By comparison, we rarely consider people to be "immigrants" whose grandfathers came from Irish or Eastern European Jewish backgrounds. How many generations of Muslims will have to live in America before they are considered simply and fully American? This is not to say that they must forget about cultural, linguistic, aesthetic, and even political connections with their ancestral homes, but simply to point out that the term "immigrant Muslim" can hang over the heads of people like a permanent weight, as if they are in the limbo of not yet having achieved full citizenship or in the purgatory of being "guests" but not citizens.

The above two phenomena (African-American Islam and immigrant Islam) have been well studied by a number of scholars. Lesser known, however, are two of the very creative areas of North American Islam: Sufi Islam and progressive Islam. There have been Muslim mystics (called Sufis) in America for over a century, going back to the time of Hazrat Inayat Khan who brought the teachings of the Chishti order of India to the West.[5] Sufis represent those Muslims who emphasize even more than other Muslims the intimacy of God with humanity, the importance of love as the primary mode of human-to-human relationship, and the possibility of realizing the presence of God inside one's own heart. The work of Hazrat Inayat Khan continued through the work of his son Pir Vilayat Khan, and his grandson Pir Zia Inayat Khan, culminating in the creation of the Sufi Order International. The Sufi Order has been the largest of Sufi organizations in the West, and a leading example of a wide-ranging engagement with other spiritual, psychological, and aesthetic traditions.[6] One has to also mention here the pioneering work of Bawa Muhaiyaddeen, who established a Fellowship in Philadelphia. This multifaith, multiracial community that has survived his earthly demise is a great example of the pluralistic teachings of Sufism in practice. Bawa's shrine, built outside of Philadelphia, is the first major Sufi shrine established in North America, and has since become a site of pilgrimage for many devotees.[7]

[5] For a comprehensive overview, see Pir Zia Inayat Khan, ed. A Pearl in Wine: Essays on Life, Music, and Sufism of Hazrat Inayat Khan (New Lebanon, NY: Omega Publications, 2001).
[6] http://www.sufiorder.org/.
[7] http://www.bmf.org/main.html.

In more recent years, almost every single significant Sufi group with a global presence has established a center in America.[8] These include the Persian groups Nimatullahis,[9] the Turkish-American groups such as the Mevlevi Order of North America[10] and the Mevlevi Order,[11] and other groups such as the Haqqani-Naqshbandis.[12]

The last significant component of Islam in America is that of progressive Islam. This is a movement that reaches across both scholarly and grassroots Muslim communities. This represents a newer facet of Muslim identity, one that takes a critical and engaged stance vis-à-vis both Islam and modernity. Self-describing progressive Muslims are usually Muslims who wish to engage the broad spectrum of all practices and interpretations marked as Muslim, and subject all of them to critical scrutiny to see how they pass the test of consistency, social justice, gender equality, and religious pluralism. Likewise, progressive Muslims are likely to hold both Muslim regimes and the United States accountable for their justice and injustice. For example, progressive Muslims have stood up to Wahhabism, Taliban, and Saddam Hussein in the Muslim majority world, and to the United States' holding of prisoners in Guantanamo Bay, and civilian causalities in Iraq and Afghanistan. Some of the better-known examples of progressive Muslims are Shirin Ebadi, the recent Nobel Peace Prize-winning Iranian activist, and Muslims in America such as Ebrahim Moosa, Amina Wadud, Asma Barlas, Farid Esack, Omid Safi, Kecia Ali, and others. These types of Muslim voices, fusing activism and scholarship, are being heard more often and more clearly these days. The most convenient place to access a sample of their work is in the recently edited volume *Progressive Muslims: On Justice, Gender, and Pluralism*.[13]

One of the important ways in which these Muslims are organizing is on the Internet. One can witness the creative work on a page such as Muslimwakeup![14] There are two Listservs for progressive Muslims that bring together hundreds of Muslims in the United States (and beyond), which pursue socially progressive goals and means. These lists are: the Network of Progressive Muslims (http://groups.yahoo.com/group/npmuslims/) and Progressive Muslims Network (accessible at: http://www.progressivemuslims.com).

As mentioned previously, it is important to realize that these divisions are not permanent and eternal ones, and that there is a great deal of overlap among them. For example, many progressive Muslims have been deeply

[8] A great resource for Western Sufi groups can be found at:
http://www.uga.edu/islam/sufismwest.html
[9] http://www.nimatullahi.org/
[10] http://www.hayatidede.org/
[11] http://www.sufism.org/
[12] http://www.naqshbandi.org/
[13] Omid Safi, ed. Progressive Muslims: On Justice, Gender, and Pluralism (Oxford: Oneworld, 2003).
[14] http://muslimwakeup.com/index.php.

inspired by the ethical teachings of Sufism, and a major mainstream immigrant Muslim organization, MPAC (Muslim Public Affairs Council), held its 2003 annual convention under the theme of "Progressive Islamic Thought and Human Rights."[15] There are a number of African-American teachers who are involved in both Sufism and progressive thought.

The rapid rise in the number of Muslims in America is due to both the immigration of Muslims from South Asia and the Arab world to the U.S. and the mass conversion of many Americans (largely African Americans) to Islam. Yet when one compares American Muslims to other religious groups with similarly large populations, there is a noticeable gap in representations of Islam in popular culture—aside from the unending focus on "terrorism." Virtually the only times that Islam comes up in the popular media are to somehow "explain" the real motivations of some terrorist group, or to talk about oppression of women. If one were to believe these media representations, one might conclude that Islam has no spiritual offerings save that of justifying violence and misogyny. Yet one has to ask the question: if that were the case, why would over a billion human beings on this planet call themselves Muslim? It is the ability of Islam, just like every other religious tradition, to offer guidance to humanity.

The most frequent comparison made by American Muslims themselves, one filled with admiration and envy, is with the American Jewish population. Any and all comparisons with American Jewry are filled with admiration for their political clout, envy for their civic institutions, outrage at the support of the U.S. government for Israel, and hope for achieving exactly the same level of prominence. Being wary of charges of anti-Semitism (and not always innocent of them), American Muslims usually voice these comparisons inside the Muslim community.

By now, many scholars of religion, such as Diana Eck, have noted that numbering at 6 million, there are as many American Muslims as American Jews, more Muslims than Episcopalians, and more Muslims than Presbyterians.[16] Looking at the bastion of mainstream culture, TV shows, one is hard pressed to find a single regularly occurring Muslim character. There is no shortage of Muslims on TV, but most occasions are in the context of either terrorism or political leaders of other countries. Both of these reinforce the stereotype of Muslims as quintessentially "other," fundamentally different from "us" Americans.[17] One is hard-pressed to think of a single Muslim intellectual, artist, or musician who is nationally known at the level of ABC, CNN, NBC, or CBS. The only American Muslims that most Americans would be able to name come from the realm of sports: Muhammad Ali, Hakeem Olajuwon, Kareem Abdul-Jabbar, etc. There are no Muslim journalists (apart from the

[15] see http://www.mpac.org.
[16] Diana Eck, A New Religious America, 2–3.
[17] The classic study here is Edward Said, Covering Islam: How the Media and the Experts Determine How We See the Rest of the World (New York: Random House, 1981, reprint Vintage Books, 1997).

half-Iranian Christiane Amanpour who does not self-identify as a Muslim) on these TV programs. In short, American Muslims are in the society, but have almost no representation in terms of popular culture aside from negative stereotypes such as terrorists and foreign despots.

When there are Muslims who show up in TV, they appear as "obviously Muslim," with a singularly religious identity that does not reflect the multiple and fractured identities of most Muslims today. The women almost invariably wear a conservative type of hijab, and the males are typically conservative, immigrant, bearded, and speak with an accent. Going back to the analogy with Judaism, it would be similar to having only ultra-Orthodox Jews on TV, rather than a full spectrum that would cover everything from Orthodox to Conservative and Reform. That great marker of humanity, humor, is uniformly lacking from Muslim subjects on TV. Muslims on TV experience grief or outrage, but almost never joy or laughter. Also absent from media depictions are the delicious wit and affectionate sarcasm for which so many real live Muslim cultures are known. When we laugh not at someone but with them, we have experienced their full humanity. The humanity of American Muslims will be acknowledged when we come up with our own successful and widely distributed version of Adam Sandler's "Hanukkah Song"! That project and others similar to it will have to take place alongside the daily struggle to achieve things like social justice and gender equality.

Political Participation

It is one of the great ironies of American political life that some 72 percent of American Muslims voted for George W. Bush in the 2000 elections,[18] only to see the Bush regime impose the most severe erosion of civil liberties in recent American history and initiate a hostile and potentially unending "war on terrorism" almost exclusively on Muslim populations all over the world. The assault on civil liberties, which affected Muslims in America more directly than other Americans, began with the so-called PATRIOT Act, passed hastily and without any opposition after September 11.[19]

For American Muslims, including this author, it is hard not to think of these days as open season on Muslims. Internationally, one sees the continued occupation, oppression, and bloodshed of Muslims in Afghanistan, Iraq, Palestine, Gujarat, Kashmir, Chechnya, and elsewhere. Domestically the situation is more of intimidation than outright violence, but it is hard to overestimate the amount of pain that the vile Islamophobia of the media causes American Muslims. Virtually every mention of Islam in the mainstream news is tied to fanaticism, in a way that is simply unparalleled when it comes to discussions of Christianity, Judaism, Hinduism, or Buddhism. It seems that in our age, it is

[18] http://www.beliefnet.com/story/54/story_5402_1.html.
[19] Very useful here is Bill Moyer's interview with the head of the Center for Public Integrity, at http://www.pbs.org/now/transcript/transcript_lewis2.html. For the ACLU's evaluation of the PATRIOT Act, see http://www.aclu.org/SafeandFree/SafeandFree.cfm?ID=12126&c=207.

no longer acceptable to make blanket statements about any other religious, ethnic, or sexual group. One can imagine the outrage that would be heard if a TV personality talked about how "all Jews are xx, or "all blacks do xx," but for some reason it is still acceptable to have so-called experts make blanket assertions about "Muslims believe" and "Islam teaches" without being challenged by anyone. That ends now. We owe it to our own selves to hold all of us, including the media, to a higher standard. We need to do this not just for the sake of American Muslims, but for the dream of justice and pluralism that is America itself.

Muslims have not been an active force in American politics. It is fair to say that no other group with over 6 million members in American society is so politically fragmented and ill organized.[20] While one is beginning to see the formative stages of development of Muslim PAC (political action committee) groups, there are still a number of substantial challenges ahead. The first is overcoming the divide between immigrant and African-American communities. It remains to be seen how much unity can be forged between the immigrant Muslim population in America and the African-American Muslim population. There are profound class divisions between the two, which often dictate communal, social, and political participation: immigrant Muslims tend to be middle and upper class, African-American Muslims middle and lower socioeconomic class. The second challenge is that of investing in American political structures; this is a particular problem for immigrant Muslims. Many came to this country for the same reasons that other immigrants have: the pursuit of a better life and the promise of freedom. Yet at least the first-generation immigrants have often looked back toward their origins as their real "homes," and have not fully invested monetarily and emotionally in American political and civic structures. Many immigrant Muslims have led lives of political neutrality and passivity, seeing their primary mission as that of providing for their families. There are, however, signs that this political lethargy is beginning to change in the charged post–September 11 environment, particularly among the second-generation immigrant Muslims.[21] The foremost leader of African-American Muslims, Warith Deen Muhammad, is a conservative Republican who has been criticized by many progressive Muslims for being uninterested in engaging the critiques of American foreign and domestic policy. Progressives realize that one has no hope of transforming a society along the lines of justice without participating in it and remaining engaged with it. Passivity is no longer an option, if it ever was, for American Muslims.

[20] http://www.beliefnet.com/story/50/story_5010_1.html.
[21] Rachel Zoll, AP religion writer, "U.S. Muslims Lobbying for Civil Rights," June 8, 2003. The article can be accessed at: http://www.newsday.com/news/nationworld/nation/wire/ sns-ap-american-muslims,0,2912861.story?coll=sns-ap-nation-headlines.

Education

As previously mentioned, there are currently no credible institutions of higher learning for the training of Islamic scholars in the United States, although organizations such as Zaytuna are moving in that direction. There are ongoing conversations about a Crescent University to be established outside New York City. Many of the leading scholars of Islam in America, such as Seyyed Hossein Nasr and John A. Williams, are involved in this ambitious project. It seems clear that this is a necessary step in the further evolution of an American Islamic identity, especially if it can be conducted in a way that does not lead to further ghettoization of American Muslims.

American Muslims, like other Americans, are drawn into the controversies over the teaching about religion in education systems. A vivid recent example was the University of North Carolina controversy in which a translation of the Koran (by American scholar Michael Sells) was chosen for a summer reading program. Bill O'Reilly, the controversial Fox News commentator, compared the Koran to Hitler's *Mein Kampf*. The state legislature threatened to cut off funding to the University.[22] These struggles are not confined to university curricula, and in some ways, the most widespread impact will come from revising junior-high and high-school offerings. The founder of the Council for Islamic Education, Shabbir Mansuri, recalls how he became involved in these struggles. His daughter's eighth-grade social-studies textbook included sections on every major world civilization. Whereas the chapter on every culture began with a picture of a historical figure, the chapter on Islam was introduced by a picture of a camel![23] This dehumanizing depiction of Muslims is so widespread that it will take a massive engagement with the system to transform it.

Is this an "American Islam"? Beyond the "Americanization of Islam" Model

One of the more hotly debated aspects of the emerging forms of Islam in America revolves around the issue of whether they represent a distinctly American form of Islam. The question is a complicated one, and like many complicated questions, the answer has to be simultaneously a "yes" and a "no." The argument in favor of it typically states that the values and institutions of the American political and social landscape transform all religious denominations within her borders, and in this case Islam too is developing in its distinctly American form in the same way that previous religious traditions (most distinctly Conservative Judaism) have.

This is particularly the case for progressive and Sufi understandings of Islam. The Sufis by nature have tended to lead the way in many pluralistic conversations, exploring the boundaries of aesthetic, spiritual, and literary meeting points between and among traditions. Likewise, one has to admit that

[22] For this controversy, see
    http://www.haverford.edu/relg/sells/UNC_ApproachingTheQur'an.htm.
[23] As conveyed in the video Islam in America, produced by the Christian Science Monitor.

there are elements of American civic culture and religious life that have helped create the space in which progressive Islam has flourished. The emphasis on pluralism in progressive Islam emerges in the context of engagement with pluralistic Christian perspectives, such as that of Diana Eck at Harvard. It also is indebted to the liberation theology of figures as wide ranging as Gustavo Gutiérrez,[24] Leonardo Boff,[25] and Rebecca S. Chopp.[26] These are important Christian thinkers who have put justice back in the forefront of Christian theology. The concern for gender equality, likewise, has been nurtured by many feminists in the West who have dared to envision societies in which men and women (and transgendered people) live side-by-side in justice. The emphasis on nonviolence, so important to many progressive Muslims including the present author, does not emerge without the wisdom of Martin Luther King, Jr., Gandhi, and His Holiness the Dalai Lama.[27] The peace activism of progressive Muslims has emerged through friendship and solidarity with many Jewish, Christian, and secular peacemakers.[28] Blessed are the peacemakers, in this and every age.

Furthermore, from a practical perspective, virtually all the face-to-face conversations among this particular group of progressive Muslims have taken place in America. Many of us have faced harassment in Muslim countries for opening a Pandora's box of questions about interpreting texts, rethinking gender constructions, and pursuing democracy.[29] Furthermore, many progressive Muslim leaders have either received our training in Islamic studies in the West, or are employed in Western academic institutions. It has to be acknowledged that part of our critical approach to the study of Islam is indebted to the Western, secular study of religion. Friendships with and mentoring by many generous and kind Western scholars of Islam, such as Bruce Lawrence, Carl Ernst, Michael Sells, Marshall G. S. Hodgson, Wilfred Cantwell Smith, Annemarie Schimmel, and more, have illuminated our understanding of Islam and indeed humanity. At a more technical level, we are indebted to Western cultures not just for the technology of e-mails, phone calls, and video-teleconferencing, but even more importantly for the much-cherished freedom of speech that enables us to undertake such difficult conversations openly. In all these important ways, we acknowledge that the American landscape is an important canvas upon which this understanding of Islam is being painted.

[24] Gustavo Gutiérrez, A Theology of Liberation (Maryknoll, NY: Orbis Books, 1988).

[25] Leonardo Boff, Introducing Liberation Theology (Maryknoll, NY: Orbis Books, 1987).

[26] Rebecca S. Chopp, Praxis of Suffering: An Interpretation of Liberation and Political Theologies (Maryknoll: Orbis Books, 1986).

[27] For a Muslim engagement with these figures, see Omid Safi, "The Times They Are A-changing—A Muslim Quest for Justice, Gender Equality, and Pluralism," in Progressive Muslims, 1–29.

[28] One could begin here by looking at the groundbreaking spiritual work of global justice undertaken by the Fellowship of Reconciliation (FOR): http://www.forusa.org/.

[29] A number of progressive Muslim thinkers all over the world, such as Abdolkarim Soroush, Nasr Abu Zayd, Saad Eddin Ibrahim, Farish A. Noor, and others have faced the wrath of Muslim governments.

Yet it would be a clear mistake to somehow reduce the emergence of progressive Islam to a new "American Islam." As the list of participants in the Progressive Muslims project above clearly demonstrates, we represent the global Muslim spiritual community (umma), with roots in places as far as Malaysia, South Asia, Iran, Turkey, Lebanon, South Africa, Canada, and the USA. Furthermore, it has to be acknowledged that when it comes to actually implementing a progressive understanding of Islam in Muslim communities, particular communities in Iran, Malaysia, and South Africa lead—not follow—the United States. Many American Muslim communities—and much of the leadership represented in groups such as ICNA,[30] ISNA,[31] CAIR[32]—are far too uncritical of Salafi and Wahhabi extremist tendencies that progressives oppose. Lastly, and this is quite important, almost all progressive Muslims are profoundly skeptical of nationalism, whether American, Arab, Iranian, or otherwise. Indeed, we see nationalism as one of the great ills of human societies in the past two hundred years. While we acknowledge that the freedoms and opportunities in America have helped us consolidate this progressive understanding of Islam, we do not wish to have this project become a nationalistic commodity that can then be exported along with jeans and hamburgers all over the world.

Our identities, like identities of all human beings, are complicated, multi-faceted, and nuanced. In this regard, we share the fracturing of our identities with post-colonial subjects. We are gendered human beings that are racially, sexually, and socio-economically diverse, spiritually Muslim, and in solidarity with all oppressed peoples of the world. Some of us occasionally find some loose sense of affiliation with the highest ideals of America without wishing to be collapsed into the pigeonhole of flag-waving nationalists. It is perhaps an all-too-easy dichotomy, but I would venture a guess that one might be able to describe many such American Muslims as being patriotic in the sense of wanting to hold America responsible for reaching her highest and loftiest ideals without being nationalistic in the sense of identifying first and foremost with the citizens of one nation-state over and above identification with all of humanity. It is that type of a spiritual patriotism that one finds in Martin Luther King, Jr., who calls us to place ourselves with other social critics, and recognize America as the "dream, a dream as yet unfulfilled"[33] and bring about that fulfillment.

[30] Islamic Circle of North America: http://www.icna.com/.
[31] Islamic Society of North America: http://www.isna.net/.
[32] Council on American-Islamic Relations: http://www.cair-net.org/.
[33] Martin Luther King, Jr., "The American Dream," in James M. Washington, ed., The Essential Writings and Speeches of Martin Luther King, Jr. (HarperSanFrancisco, 1986), 208.

Conclusion:
What Does the Emergence of Islam Mean for America?

It is safe to say that the engagement of Islam with America is now entering its critical age. In the next two generations, both Islam and American society at large will change to accommodate one another. At the heart of this dance is a central set of questions: will America be an ostensibly Judeo-Christian country, whereby other religious communities are merely tolerated? Progressive Muslims have pointed out that the term "tolerance" has its origin in medieval toxicology and pharmacology, dealing with how much foreign substance and poison a body can tolerate before it dies. For Muslim progressives, as indeed other pluralistic human beings, there has to be a higher calling than merely *tolerating* those different from us until it kills us! Our challenge is to push America toward what Diana Eck and others tell us it has already become, the "most pluralistic nation on earth." This America will be more than merely "Abrahamic," since even that wonderful umbrella that brings together Jews, Christians, and Muslims still leaves out our Hindu, Buddhist, Taoist, Jain, Sikh, Zoroastrian, Wiccan, atheist, and agnostic friends.

Will this America be one that truly believes in the equal protection of all human beings before the law, or rather will it target disempowered racial, religious, and ethnic minorities? Will civil rights be seen as necessary sacrifices in an ongoing "war on terrorism," or will they be seen as the very foundation of what is worth saving about America itself? Will immigrant and African-American Muslims realize that in every civilization where Islam has flourished it has done so through the interaction of timeless spiritual teachings and timely cultural contexts? Will the highest and most humanistic elements of American culture be blended along into the collage of Islamic values? These are open-ended questions, and the answers, as Bob Dylan tells us, "are blowing in the wind."

Omar Abu-Namous

A leading imam's response to terrorism

> *The murderers (terrorists) are an isolated group of persons who are very parochial, with narrow understanding. ...They read the text of the Holy Koran and form an understanding, so narrow, as if you would peek through a peephole and think you had a view of the whole room inside. No, you would have a very small view of the room.*
>
> *To a great extent, Muslim men—those who are religious and are practicing—keep themselves from having sex before marriage, and from having sex after marriage with other women.*

THE ISLAMIC CULTURAL CENTER OF NEW YORK (above), one of the country's largest mosques, combines old Islamic motifs with the modern. It was designed by the architectural firm of Skidmore, Owings, and Merrill and completed in the 1990s. Donations from around the world contributed to its construction: Pakistan and Turkey sent carpets, Indonesia presented the pulpit, and Moroccan artists did the interior artwork. (Photo courtesy of Henry Cateura.)

Omar Abu-Namous is the chief imam of the Islamic Cultural Center of New York. His background of erudition and accomplishment is appropriate to his position: he is a scholar, a former translator of Arabic at the United Nations, and a firm believer in the conservative, but far from fundamentalist, view of Islam. The interview took place in his office at the mosque and he appeared wearing a skullcap on his head and a long, black cloak. A man in his late-middle years, Imam Abu-Namous is thoroughly at ease and familiar with the community of New York, where he has lectured in universities and neighborhood mosques for over twenty years. His English is nearly perfect and he answered all the questions without hesitation. Of particular interest is the special message he voiced for New Yorkers and Americans in general about the September 11, 2001 disaster.

In his desire to share information and bring Muslims and non-Muslims closer together, the imam spoke openly on many subjects, such as marital fidelity among Muslim husbands, intermarriage with Christians and Jews, Islamic schools, one of which is being built at the Center, and the proselytizing tendencies among Muslims. The only time he showed hesitation was the moment when the author reached out to shake his hand. With a gesture of retreat, he said, "It is not the custom for Muslim men to shake a woman's hand." The author quickly withdrew hers.

As a highly respected imam in the City of New York, will you give us a personal comment on the disaster of September 11, 2001?
I would like to say right off to your readers that what happened on September 11, 2001, was indeed very devastating to the Muslim morale in this country and outside this country. Because what happened, you know, was alien, totally alien to the spirit of al-Islam. Al-Islam aims at spreading and establishing peace in every corner of the world, and making peace between humanity and God, and making humanity live up to the standards which God has prescribed or ordained for mankind, in order that His word may be the supreme on earth, He being the creator and the owner, the sustainer and provider.

So, al-Islam the religion is the spirit of God, and the Holy Koran describes the religion as a spirit. It is to spread peace and mutual love, mutual appreciation and respect, among all peoples. It says that we were created from one copy and God has made us into peoples and into tribes in order to do favors to one another. So that is God's idea: for us to do favors to one another, not to quarrel, not to be selfish. Selfishness is, you know, the poison of the earth. It is the poison of mankind.

For example, when I, for your sake, would sacrifice and humble myself to you and treat you as a respectable person, that would indeed create mutual love and mutual respect between you and me. So that is the basic concept of al-Islam. And indeed it is also the basic concept of Christianity and Judaism. But al-Islam came in order to amplify the idea, to make it clearer, to cross the t's and dot the i's. Yes, that is the *job* of Islam. In no way is it different from Christianity or Judaism. It's just a rejuvenation and revival of Christianity and Judaism, nothing more.

So I'm saying, indeed, that experience was devastating to us, that some of us, a number of members of our nation, were the cause of so much destruction, so much death, so much misery and sadness. And, in fact, it was difficult for us to apologize. It's *not* a matter of apology here. It was too big to apologize for. But indeed we depended on the understanding of mature Christians and mature Jews who would truly comprehend what happened. The murderers [terrorists] are an isolated group of persons who are very parochial, with narrow understanding. They read the text of the Holy Koran and form an understanding which is so narrow as if you would peek through the peephole of a door and think you had a view of the whole room inside. No, you would have a very small view of the room.

But at the same time, I would stress the need for mankind to emphasize the necessity for justice to be there in the world, because when justice is there, these extremists and fundamentalists would by themselves be more penalized. No one would accept them and they would have no say in the life of peoples. They would just be ignored and disregarded and disrespected. But when there is no justice in the world, these people start gaining recognition and have more say.

Like communism, for example. What made communists in the days of the Soviet Union spread so widely in prosperous countries, like Italy and France and others? *What* made it spread? It was because of the evil disseminating in the world. The communists would present themselves as people who wanted to reform, to bring good to the populace, so they were accepted. The religious extremists also present themselves in that light. They say, *Look at the evil that is taking place. We want to bring reform. We want to make things better.* And they start gaining recognition among peoples.

So the more justice and fairness we have in the world, the less ground these people would be having, and the less justice and ground they would be gaining. So we have to understand this. Justice is the antibiotic which would kill them and put an end to them. Yes. And justice indeed would bring mutual love among the followers of the religions. Why should I, for example, resent a Christian person or a Jewish person? Why? When my holy book says that my food is lawful for Christians and Jews and their food is lawful for me. And it also says that Christian women and Jewish women are lawful for me as wives. So God was preparing the ground from the very beginning of Islam, preparing the ground for peace, for mutual understanding, and for mutual cordial relationships between the followers of all the religions.

When I can, for example, get married to a Christian woman, it means two families, a Muslim family and a Christian family, can get united. Yes. And new avenues of recognition, of understanding, of relationship are opened up so that Muslims will understand Christian culture and Christians will understand Muslim culture. And they would exchange visits and exchange favors, exchange everything. This is how the religions establish peace in the world, yes, by understanding one another and being more tolerant of the differences. There must be differences because you'll find that perhaps if you have a brother, there will be differences between him and you. His likes are different from your likes, and his dislikes may be different from your dislikes.

That's why we have to become tolerant. I know, for example, that you may favor a certain dish of food. I prepare another dish of food. I should not say, *why does she love that kind of food she eats?* Dispraising it, you know. We have to be more understanding. The more tolerant we are, the happier we become, in point of fact.

There are millions of Muslims here and in Europe and there are millions of Christians in the Muslim world. In Egypt alone, there are over a million Christians. In the Arab world, there are no less than between thirty and forty million Christians—yes, that's a big segment of the population of the Arab world. *And they live happily.* They have been living there for fourteen centuries now. Nobody at all tries to interfere with their religion or faith or houses of worship. They enjoy that kind of freedom for all time. Yes. No Muslim government would tolerate interference and the Prophet of Islam, Muhammad, makes himself the enemy of any Muslim who interferes negatively with a Christian or Jew. If anyone causes any harm to a Christian or Jew, the Prophet of Islam says that he will be his enemy on the Day of Judgment. Respect and good intentions have gone to that limit. The Prophet himself would be the enemy of any Muslim who commits an act of aggression against a Christian or against a Jew. So it has been like this.

Can you tell us something about yourself?

I am originally from Palestine and came to the United States in 1979. I came under contract with the United Nations where I became a staff member, a translator and then a reviser in the Arabic translation service in the Secretariat. I worked there for fifteen years. But, at the same time, I was a person with religious leanings. In the U.S., I discovered that there was an acute shortage of Muslim activists who rendered service to the Muslim community. There were not enough speakers, lecturers, prayer leaders. The shortage was acute and I felt the need to participate. My background included Islamic studies and also Arabic-language studies at the University of London. Islam, you know, is originally an Arabic-language religion. The Holy Koran is in Arabic and the Sunna of the Prophet is in Arabic. So those who know Arabic very well have an advantage over others who don't know Arabic.

That's why I felt it was my duty to render whatever services I could. I was traveling on two tracks. One track was working for the UN in order to gain my living and the other track was servicing the Muslim community as an imam. I continue to do this now and it's over twenty-one years. On reaching sixty, I retired from the UN. Staff members retire at sixty, not at sixty-three or sixty-five as you do here in America. At sixty, at the UN, you stop in order to make room for new blood, fresh blood to step in. But if you are a translator, a linguistic employee of the United Nations, they also give you a chance to serve the UN after retirement. You can continue to go and serve the international organization. Not as a volunteer—they pay you, but they benefit from your long experience.

My position here was unplanned and occurred spontaneously. At first I was touring a number of mosques in Manhattan. One of them was the Columbia University Mosque, another, the United Nations Mosque, another downtown at Twelve Warren Street near City Hall, and a fourth mosque in mid-Manhattan. I was touring all these mosques and giving lectures at evening functions where I would be invited to enlighten the congregation as to the different aspects of Islam and other things.

How did you become the head imam at the Islamic Cultural Center of New York?

I was about to say by chance. But when we say by chance, it is *for us* by chance. But for God it's not by chance. God plans everything. Because of our ignorance, we say it happened by chance, by accident. No. It turned out to be part of a plan. A friend of mine said to me, *Why not go and say hello to the new imam at the Culture Center?* That was in 1998. I said, yes, why not? So we planned to meet just to say hello. But the new imam was so courteous, so polite, so respectful indeed that he went out to the UN to the office of the Secretariat to receive me. *He came out to receive me there.* He didn't wait for me to arrive here, at his place. He received me at the United Nations and we came here and after about fifteen minutes of exchanging salutations and greetings, he said, "I want you to be my helper, to be my assistant here."

"Why? What do you need of me?" I asked.

"The community is now divided. There is a division. On the eve of departure of the previous imam, there was some disagreement between that imam and the Board of Trustees, and the community was torn between the two. Some supported the imam and others supported the Board of Trustees."

He talked of the community's distress with the change. He wanted to reunite the members and needed someone who was familiar with the New York Muslim community and could speak to it. He asked me to do that.

I said, *Okay.*

So I came here in 1998 as an assistant imam. What I did was speak to the community, give lectures and speeches and encourage unity and bring people back to the center. Many people had left to go to other centers and other mosques. I worked to bring them back and praise be to God, my efforts were to a considerable extent successful. Some years later when the chief imam left, I was chosen to take his place.

You indicated that Muslims are allowed to marry Christians and Jews. From your experience, how do such marriages turn out?
There are problems, but there are also problems when the couple belongs to the same religion. Every day, I receive complaints from Muslim women who have Muslim husbands. They complain that they want to get a divorce. Yes, so the problems are always there. But when a problem exists between a Muslim man and a Christian wife, everybody turns his attention to it. Because now there are *two* people who belong to *different* religions, so that must be the reason. But when the two of them are Christian who have problems, no one pays attention. Actually, I think no less than sixty to seventy percent of mixed marriages are successful.

The center's new Islamic school will soon open its doors. Can you tell us something about the new school and why you feel an Islamic school is needed?
Our Islamic school will go up to the eighth grade and will teach Islamic culture and the Arabic language side by side with an American curriculum taught in English, like the public schools. The children will come from throughout the city of New York, from anywhere really. We don't say no to non-Muslims and I expect that at some point in the future non-Muslims will be joining our schoolchildren as they discover that we are, in fact, protecting children from all the evils, the social evils, that exist in our society today. We are very stern and very serious, and our teaching is against homosexuality, and premarital sexuality, and extramarital sexuality. These are out of the question. We will teach the children that we want to keep the community as clean as possible because that is the spirit of Islam. Part of that cleanliness is not to have illicit relations or extramarital or premarital relations. We have to keep our lives clean and have sex only in wedlock.

Do Muslim men actually keep themselves from having sex before marriage?
To a great extent, Muslim men—those who are religious and are practicing—keep themselves from having sex before marriage, and from having sex after marriage with other women. It may sound somewhat strange to non-Muslims because non-Muslims now have been so much involved in these practices, and they wonder how can a person stay chaste, stay virgin until he gets married.

But it is manageable, it is workable. You can do it. Just like fasting in Ramadan. Many non-Muslims wonder how can Muslims stay without food and drink from dawn until sunset, especially in summer? Well, it is doable. We find it is not impossible. It is possible, though sometimes there is hardship. But the hardship you take for the sake of God, and God will credit that into your account. So God will say, *Thank you. You did something; you experienced hardship for my sake. I thank you very much and here is your reward.* Your reward will be there.

What is the difference between Islamic culture and the national culture of a Muslim country?

Islamic culture is, mainly speaking, a religious culture, not a national culture. Sometimes national customs or traditions are incorporated into Islamic culture, as long as Islam does not object to them and they do not contradict Islam's main doctrines and principles.

So this means that not everything that existed before Muhammad, the Prophet of Islam, or in his day, was automatically destroyed or demolished or rejected. What was rejected was only what ran contrary to Islam. What was in agreement with the philosophy of Islam was kept. I will give you one example—one that Muhammad himself adopted. Before he received his mission, the Prophet was taken by his uncles—they were much older than he was—to a conference, in a pre-Islamic time, naturally, that was organized by pagans, the pagan leaders of Mecca, to help aliens coming to Mecca. Because they were aliens, they were again and again victimized by vicious, evil people who exploited and took advantage of them. They were often ill-treated. So the conference was organized to provide protection to the new arrivals who were defenseless and vulnerable. Muhammad listened very attentively to the proceedings of the conference. He was a young man, barely twenty. Thirty years or so later, when he was a Prophet, he adopted the good intention of that pagan conference, saying to his companions, *If I were invited to another conference like that, I would accept the invitation. I would go.*

The meaning is, simply, that he would cooperate with pagans if the objective was good. The spirit of Islam is very open. It's not parochial. It not only wants Muslims to cooperate among themselves, but with *all people* in the universe, if a common good is involved. There are other examples of such alliances in which the Prophet cooperated and allied himself. He joined with pagans to fight aggressors. He was in alliance with the Jews at Medina, because they were part of the population of Medina, which consisted of pagans, Muslims, and Jews. They existed together. (At that time there were no Christians in Medina and they had their own communities outside Medina.) He forged his way and concluded a treaty of defense, including Muslims, Jews, and pagans. The three were responsible for the defense of the city of Medina, each providing defense requirements and money for expenses.

Some Americans feel that Muslims proselytize too much. There is a sign outside your center urging non-Muslims to enter the mosque. Is it true that Islam wants the whole world to be Muslim?

Yes, yes. That is true. I will not deny it. That's the true reality. It's because from the point of view of the Holy Koran all messages are only one message and that one message was given to every prophet, from Abraham and Moses to Jesus and Muhammad and to all the other prophets and messengers.

The message as revealed to all the messengers, with the exception of Muhammad, was exposed to human interference. Let me be frank with you. It was exposed to human interference and so it was confused and mixed with external elements. No message with the exception of Islam is pure now, neither Christianity, nor Judaism, nor any other religion in the world, with the exception of Islam. So God, seeing that the Holy Bible was so much interfered with, God wanted to purify it, update it and send it back to the last messenger, to the last prophet, and told him that this is intended to be conveyed to all the world. Yes, this takes the place of the Holy Bible. It is the Holy Bible corrected, purified and updated. So that was what the author himself did, God. God, the author himself, did that and put it in a new form and gave it to Muhammad, the last messenger, and told him, *Give this to the world.*

As an author, if you discover that in one of your books, the printing house inserted misstatements or misquotations that spoil the meaning of your material, you would probably put out a new edition to correct the mistakes of the previous one, and to alert your readers of the misrepresentations. So that was what God did, provide a new edition. He said, *The old edition of My word has been mixed with the human word. Take this instead.*

When you refer to a Muslim man, that does not mean he is non-Christian. Muslim and Christian and Jew are the same. Yes. By the way, the words Christianity and Judaism do not appear in the Holy Bible. They don't exist, which means these two words were man-made, or man-given. Not God-given. It means they were not authorized and not approved of. The message according to the Holy Koran is named Islam. So it means that both Christianity and Judaism are Islam, the older versions of Islam, and the Koran is the newer version or the latest version of Islam. You may say Christians and Jews are Muslims under other names. Which is interesting. Yes.

So Muslims have the deep feeling that they have a trust to deliver to the people to whom it belongs. This trust belongs to all the world. For example, it's like my traveling to Pennsylvania, back and forth. I got to know the road and the dangers of that road. I hear you are traveling to Pennsylvania and I feel it's my duty to alert you to the dangers that exist on the road. There may be checkpoints or robbers, dangerous people, highwaymen, and I have to alert you to this. *Take care. Don't go this way but take another way.* If I don't warn you, I'd be betraying you. Muslims feel that if they don't bring Islam to the attention of every non-Muslim, they feel they are betraying the world. This is a psychological complex with Muslims. They think they are not doing their duty if they don't bring this message to the attention of every non-Muslim.

But they will *not* do anything if non-Muslims reject it. Their duty ends when non-Muslims reject it. They just draw the attention to it. They say, in effect,

This is a message from God. Please have a look at it and it's your choice to accept or reject it. That's it.

But rejecting this message does not mean that you have exempted yourself from the consequence. It's just like, for example, a mailman delivers a letter and you say, *No, I don't want to receive it.* If the letter included a bill, would your rejection of the letter, your refusal to receive it, would that exempt you from having to pay the bill? You still have to pay it! So this is what the Muslims are very anxious about. They need to draw your attention because we feel, in fact, that non-Muslims are our brothers and sisters and just as we wish good for ourselves, we must wish good for them. We know for sure that this message of the Koran is authentic. It comes from God and from the Prophet of Islam who for twenty-three years worked to bring the message to others, making battles, wars, exposing himself to death many times, and living as a totally poor man. As a matter of fact, when he died, he was in debt to a Jewish merchant, even though he was head of the state. He was indebted to the extent that he had mortgaged his own coat of mail.

Which also means, my dear guest, that Islam does not recognize boycott, that is, abstaining from dealing with anyone as a means of disfavor. It does not boycott anybody. The Prophet of Islam was in conflict with the Jews, more than once, maybe four times in battles with them, but he never boycotted them. His approach was, *if you are ready to make friends with me, I am ready to make friends with you. If you want peace with me, I also want peace with you.*

This is the spirit of Islam, yes, although some Muslims don't understand this as they should.

Asma Gull Hasan

A Muslim at Groton and Wellesley

American Muslim women are going to play a bigger role in interpreting Islam.

If Muhammad were alive today, he would have a Web site. He probably also would be an American. So many core values of Islam are embodied in American society.

There is no compulsion in Islam. It differs from other religions where you're told what to do. There is no pope, no central authority.

Photo courtesy of Asma Gull Hasan.

There is barely a handful of American Muslims writing about the experience of being Muslim in America. **Asma Gull Hasan**, who is in her twenties, is one of the few. She is a vibrant young voice of the new generation. Her first book, *American Muslims: the New Generation*, published in 2000, introduced a fresh way of thinking about American Islam: challenging, exuberant, creative, and unafraid of embracing modern ideas and technology. She believes that the Americanization of Islam is in process, and that it is all to the good. She speaks as a member of a young group of educated Muslims, from which very possibly will spring the leaders and spokespersons in the years to come. Her second book, *Why I Am a Muslim: An American Odyssey*, was published in March, 2004.

Asma Gull Hasan, the daughter of Pakistani immigrants, was born in Chicago and raised in Pueblo, Colorado. She is as proud of being a second-generation American Muslim as she is of being a Wellesley graduate and the recipient of a law degree from New York University Law School. She is currently employed with a law firm in San Francisco, where she resides.

When I approached her for an interview on her visit to New York, she fit me in just before her appearance on an international videoconference. She and her Muslim interlocutors in India appeared simultaneously to discuss the subject of being Muslim in America. She was gracious enough to ask me to be present in the studio. Afterward we sat in a nearby outdoor café where, over coffee and toast, this two-hour interview took place.

Before we start, can you say a few words about your name and its meaning?

Asma is Persian and Arabic, and it means "sky" in both languages. Actually, the proper spelling for it would be Asman, which means "sky," too. Asma is a feminized version. Sometimes, I'll hear songs in Arabic with lyrics about the sky, and I'll hear my name and that's kind of exciting. There is this thing in Islam about the ninety-nine names for Allah. The names indicate his qualities, and they're pretty evenly divided between qualities of mercy and qualities of power. Altogether they're called *al-asma al-husna*, which translated means the ninety-nine names or epithets of God. With *asma* in the title, and meaning "sky," it's a way of referencing something high up, higher than you, elevated. It's nice to have my name up there. [*She laughed.*] Gull means "flower" in Persian, so you can say my name means Sky Flower. I'm not really sure what Hasan means. I know that when my father emigrated here, it had two s's in it. He took one out because he thought it would be simpler. But people always want to spell the name with two s's, so I don't know if it made things simpler or not.

During the videoconference, you spoke some words in Arabic. Do you speak Arabic?

Enough to do prayers. But if I went to Saudi Arabia, I couldn't converse with anybody and would like to learn more. Do you know it's required of every Muslim to learn Arabic so they can read the Koran? It's definitely one of the things I want to do in my life.

What led you to write the book and did you have a difficult time getting it published?

My thesis at Wellesley College was on Islam in America. I started writing it as a junior and did a lot of research and finished the thesis. I graduated from college after having applied to law school and gotten into some places and not others. Confusion set in. Finally, my parents said, *You've done so much research on your thesis, why don't you write a book? You could live at home.* I hadn't lived at home since I was thirteen, and that was exciting, to be able to live at home again. So I started writing and finished the book in the spring of '97. I was twenty-three at the time.

I went to law school at New York University and would send my manuscript out at night. After coming home from school, I'd send it out, hoping somebody would take it. In the past, I had an agent when I did some writing, but nobody was interested in representing this book because no one thought it was salable. One publisher who rejected the manuscript suggested the name of another publisher, who actually took it. I think the editor liked the fresh, young voice in the manuscript. He did specify one condition and that was, *Do not change anything.* He really liked it and said it was very direct. There were few, if any, books around about Islam that were written in a nonacademic way.

When your parents suggested that you write a book, did you feel you were ready to write a book at your young age?

Yes. I always said I was going to write a book. In my family, I was known as "Asma the writer." It was one of those things. Everyone in a family has a role. But, as a child, in first grade, I never learned to read and barely knew the alphabet. I couldn't see the board and probably needed glasses. It was getting close to the end of the year and everybody else could read. The fact that we were bilingual at home may have had something to do with it, but it was before people even knew what bilingual was. My mom and the teacher met and the teacher said, "Asma's retarded. She'll have to go to a special school."

My mom said, "You just don't know how to teach her. It's not that she's retarded."

"She can finish the year here, but she'll have to go to a school for retarded kids."

I never went. What my mom did was every day after school, for an hour, we'd sit down and she taught me to read basically. She was an immigrant, but she had gone to missionary schools run by Irish Catholic nuns in Pakistan where the nuns had opened missionary schools. She knows the English language very well. And so does my father. You know, a lot of people don't realize the Muslims who come here as immigrants probably know the English language better than native speakers. They learned the Queen's English [*sic*], British English. Of course, since I learned from my mom, I was spelling things with the British spellings. I would do my homework and it would have the word color spelled with an o-u-r and my teacher would mark it wrong and my mother would say, *No wonder she thought you couldn't read. She can't spell.*

Within a month of the time my mom started to teach me, I mean, I was reading everything I could get my hands on. Pretty soon I was writing stories. My plan for the first book was to write a novel, and I've had three short stories published. These days, speaking at conferences, I tell that story about being considered retarded, and then end up by saying, *I've published a book and graduated from law school. Not so bad for a retarded person!* Everyone laughs.

Your book is drawn from your own life and from research. Where did you do your research?
I had experience doing research for my college thesis. I went to Wellesley, a woman's college which, incidentally, is very much interested in women's issues. But even there, the information I found was mostly about Islam in America, certainly not about American Muslim women. You could easily fit the books on Islam on a couple of shelves. I found news articles from *Time* and *U.S. News and World Report*, which were patronizing. They either said Muslims are terrorists, or Muslims are cute. They said Muslims are a little alienated here in America, like the Amish. The gist was, *Will they make it in America? Can this old tradition survive in heathen America?*

None of these articles appealed to me. None fit my experience, and research would have to be done from scratch. I read everything there was. Certainly since 9/11, there's been a lot more written about Islam in America. At that time, there was such a finite amount. But I read everything that was out there and in view of the paucity of information, could have written my own Ph.D. There were also some things written about Arab communities that included both the Christian Arabs and Muslim Arabs. I was able to learn some things from those and use them. When you're doing research on such a minimally covered topic, you take whatever you can get.

Happily, I knew Muslims all over the country and I had Muslim friends and I would call up people and say, *Can I come to interview you, or do you know anyone who is doing some activist work in the community that I can talk to?* I was traveling all over the country in my senior year, meeting people, interviewing them and did the same after graduating. I think now I've met just about everybody. It's funny because now that the book is written and published, more Muslims take me seriously. But then some people returned my calls, and some didn't. When people ask me which Muslim organizations are the good ones, I usually name the ones that I found responsive and helpful.

You went to Groton in Massachusetts, well known as a boys' school and now co-ed. Why did you choose to go to Groton?

From that incident about being retarded, you can understand that my family became a bit dubious about public education. Both parents had gone to boarding schools. One day my older sister came home and said, *I don't think I'm being challenged enough at school and I want to go to a boarding school.* My parents understood and decided to send us away to boarding school. We had talked about it, but it was really my sister who was assertive and took the initiative. She appears, incidentally, on the cover of my book along with me.

We hired an educational consultant and at first the idea was we'd go to school in Denver, not far from my parents. But my dad said, *Really, what's the difference whether they're one hundred miles or one thousand miles away? They'll be away in either case. Let's go to the place that is the best.* The consultant, a woman, said Groton is a really good school. It went coed in the seventies. Actually my father didn't like its being coed. The consultant said, *It's the best high school in the country, and you want the best. You'll have to let her go.* My sister got in. Neither my sister nor I went on scholarship. Dad is a doctor, a neurologist, and could afford the tuition. He's retired now. Incidentally, he was born in Delhi in India before the partition of Pakistan and after the partition, he moved to Lahore in Pakistan. My mom was born in Lahore, after the partition.

Did you like Wellesley? I've heard it's very receptive to students of different backgrounds.

I enjoyed Wellesley very much. On my student visits it was the only campus I really felt at home in. Because I am Muslim and there are certain cultural expectations and needs that I have—for instance, I don't really date, and don't drink, either—I knew that being dateless and not drinking would be a lot easier at a woman's college than at a coed college. My sister had also gone to a woman's college, to Barnard in New York, and she had a great experience. She went from being the only girl in the math department in Pueblo, Colorado, to being a top student in the Barnard science classes where the various science departments were fighting over her because they wanted her to be a major in their department. I thought that was just terrific! She's a doctor now and just finished her residency in internal medicine and is going to do a fellowship in GI medicine. Which apparently is a real growth industry because young people these days are very stressed. Irritable bowel syndrome and stuff.

Wellesley fulfilled all my expectations. It was also the first time I met so many Muslims from diverse backgrounds. There were Vietnamese Muslims—they're called *cham*. I thought, *Wow, this is so cool! Muslims who aren't South Asian!* I met Arab Muslims and other South Asian Muslims. There was one girl, a Hindu, who converted. We gathered as a community and Wellesley very much encouraged that and urged every ethnic and religious group to gather and practice their ethnicity or their religion on their own. It was great.

How did your Muslim friends react to your suddenly becoming author of this book?

Both my Muslim and non-Muslim friends were very positive. One Muslim friend said, *Thank you for telling it like it is.* I had noticed in my junior year in college that all the media either said Muslims are terrorists or Muslims are like the Amish. My friends had noticed that, too, but they never took a step to fight it because they weren't doing a thesis as I was. They hadn't sat down and looked at all the media and noted that, yes, this is actually happening. We're either being demonized or patronized. Once my work came to their attention, they were grateful. They've all been supportive.

In your book, you write of the New American Islam. One rarely hears mention of a New American Islam. Actually, you also call it New World Islam and Reform Islam. Please give us a clarification.

The New American Islam and the New World Islam refer to the same thing. Concerning Reform Islam, there's been some criticism of my book from Muslims because in one chapter I say that American Jews and Jews around the world started a secularized, more American, modern version of Judaism, so they can eat pork and their calendar is more tied to the Christian calendar and so on. I added that this is what American Muslims will need to do. Muslims reacted in opposition: *Is she advocating a Reform Islam?* They said that would be wrong because no one is allowed to reinterpret Islam. I retaliated by suggesting they just keep reading. I also said, in effect, Judaism had many more requirements, that it was a more strict religion and more in need of reform before it could become both Jewish *and American*. Islam is not in need of much reform. It is a much simpler religion. If you compare the kosher requirements in Judaism with the dietary requirements for halal in Islam, halal has far fewer requirements than kosher does. That's just one example. A lot of people took that out of context.

I said, *Do we need to have reform?* I meant it as an intellectual, abstract question. But a lot of people thought, *She's a bad Muslim, advocating reform and wanting us to eat pork.* That's not at all what I meant. In my wildest dreams I never thought the things I wrote in the book would offend anyone! One of the things I learned is that everybody is offended by something. It has been a real eye-opener for me. In some ways I regret using the term Reform Islam, but in other ways I don't, because other Muslims, besides myself, have wondered about that, too

Now by using the words "New World Islam," I mean to indicate that Muslims in America (and even in Europe) are reinterpreting Islam to fit in with their American lifestyle and have America fit in with their Islamic lifestyle. In other words, not to blindly keep doing things just because they are Islamic. For example, what do certain customs and practices really mean? Why am I doing this? Is it appropriate in the New World? The New World is changing things in Islam. Now we have Web sites that answer questions, along the lines of *Ask the Imam*. And we have matrimonial Web sites, where Muslims post their personal ads

The Internet has a group of advisors to Muslims similar to the traditional Ulama, scholars who advised believers on religious matters. Do you know of the Internet group?
I've heard there is something like that, but I've never approached them. Incidentally, if Muhammad were alive today, I think he would have a Web site. He probably also would be an American. So many core values of Islam are embodied in American society. He was a businessman and had a caravan business, which did trading. At that time, caravans were like modern technology—that's how things moved and how they were sold. He embraced whatever was available as a means of spreading the word about Islam. Certainly he would have a website, but I don't know what the address would be.

Technology is exciting, especially for Muslims in America. I grew up in a small town where there was no mosque, no one to talk with, no one to consult. If you have the Internet available to you, then you can use it to meet other Muslims and gain support from them and get questions answered. It's a great resource.

In America, which lacks Muslim scholars, believers have no one to consult. Some go directly to the Koran. Yet it's conceded that the Koran is best understood only in the original Arabic, and many translations lead to misinterpretations. What can one do for guidance?
Since many American Muslims can't read the Koran in Arabic, they *have* to use translations. Probably the most used and lasting is the Yusuf Ali translation. The Islamic center and mosque on Ninety-sixth Street in New York City has a bookstore that carries it, and it's probably available at Arab bookstores throughout the country. There is another translation that a lot of academics like, and that is the Arberry translation. This was done by an Englishman who lived in colonial times.

But even with the Ali translation, there is a problem. Yusuf Ali was a Pakistani. He was not a native speaker of Arabic and he learned it in the classroom. There are a lot of words in Arabic that have primary and secondary meanings and, if you learn Arabic in the classroom, your capability of knowing what is being used, the primary or secondary meaning, is dubious if you're not a native speaker. In many of his translations, especially in controversial areas, he went with the primary meaning, whereas the secondary meaning was more appropriate. So the translation may have come out wrong.

If you're really serious about reading the Koran, you need to read a couple of different translations in conjunction, and if you don't like the way a passage sounds, or doesn't seem right, read it in another translation and maybe it will sound better. Arabic words can mean a lot of different things. Most Muslims read the Yusuf Ali. You can buy the Yusuf Ali on Amazon.com., by the way. You can just as easily find it in a mosque. The Arberry is on Amazon. There's one by Cleary which is just selections, and that's pretty good, too. There are many. I use all of them. Different scholars have written much on the meaning of individual passages. I read what scholars have to say since they read the Koran in Arabic.

Since Muhammad received the contents of the Koran ages ago, how can it be applicable today?

The Koran recognizes that it is a living document. It is not fixed in time. It is not static. The world is always changing. The time that the Prophet lived in is certainly not the modern times of today. So interpretation or analogizing is necessary to fit changing times.

When you come across people like the Taliban, for example, and the Wahhabis who say, *Let's just go back to the times the Prophet lived in*, then it's perfectly clear what the Koran had to say about *that* period. We don't have to do any interpreting or analysis. But we have things and situations today that were never thought of in those times. Fortunately, among Islamic scholars, there is a history of using analogy. The need for Islamic scholars is thus not only to study and comment on the various translations of the Koran, but especially to interpret and analogize through their immense scholarship, on how to make the Koran applicable now. You reason by analogy. So if you look at the way the Prophet Muhammad resolved a certain dispute or question by the way he addressed it, then you analogize this to whatever the current problem is. Islamic scholars and imams do this all the time. Their thinking is, *This is how the Prophet Muhammad did it. If we analogize it to our modern situation, we should do it like this.*

We should also keep in mind that the Koran is very abstract. Even if you could read it, you might find that it's usually not specific. The Bible is a lot more specific. I've read the Bible and can say it is more direct. The Koran gives laws and principles and values but doesn't address things directly. So there are a lot of questions that may not be clearly answered by the Koran because the holy book is not going to affix itself to one answer. It knows that people and things are going to change. God knows that things are going to change. The Koran wasn't meant to be for one time. It was meant for all times.

Besides the scholars, what other sources of help are available to Muslims in understanding the Koran, the word of Allah?

There is a great source of help that derives directly from the Prophet, and that is the hadith, which are the sayings of Muhammad. They help to clarify some of the things that appear in the Koran. As an example, one of the things the

Prophet said as told in the hadith is that paradise is at your mother's feet. So that is taken to mean that you're not going to paradise if your mother is not happy with you and it is important for you to make her happy. In the Koran, it simply says, in effect, that *mothers who suffered for you in labor are very important*, and you should be nice to them. Muhammad's saying in the Hadith serves to give it some clarification. The hadith is a resource that Muslims use.

The hadith also records the Sunna of the Prophet. These are the traditions of the Prophet, the things that he did. The Sunna reveals that he was very meticulous about his appearance and hygiene. He brushed his teeth, he was very clean, and he wore perfume. These are things that were known about him. What we as Muslims take away from that is being clean is important. It doesn't say in the Koran, *you must be clean, you must brush your teeth*, but from the Sunna we know that the Prophet Muhammad brushed his teeth, and so on. Thus we have other sources that clarify things for us.

In Islam, is there any central authority that decrees that people act in a certain way?

There is no compulsion in Islam. It differs from other religions where you're told what to do. There is no pope, no central authority. There are people who have studied a lot, who have earned the right to speak about Islam and interpret it, but there's nothing in the Koran that says we have to listen to them. We can choose to listen to them, but in Islam it's very much you and God. On judgment day it's going to be you and God. It says over and over in the Koran, Allah is the final judge of us all and he's the best judge of all. Whenever another Muslim criticizes me and my book, I'll say, *Allah is the judge of us all, not you and not me*. We'll see what happens.

Do you foresee that American Muslim women are going to be in leading positions in Islam, as scholars and imams, like the men?

Definitely. I think it's already happening. I think young Muslim women are well placed in academic religion, as well as in all of American society, in all different fields, law, science, medicine, and technology. I think American Muslim women are going to play a bigger role in interpreting Islam. One of the things that's going to enable them to accomplish this is that by virtue of being American, they're free to study Islam and free to do interpretation. A lot of people wonder what is wrong with the Islamic world, that they have such problems with women. I always respond that most of the Islamic world is illiterate. Most Muslims are illiterate, male and female, and they can't read anything, much less read the Koran to see what it says and not accept what Osama bin Laden says it says. In America such a simple fact that men and women can get an education and even read a translation of the Koran (albeit not a perfect solution, translations of the Koran being what they are), they are already still miles ahead of many Muslims in Islamic countries. Poverty and illiteracy often go together, and there is so much poverty in the Islamic world and that's a real problem for Muslims and for America. We're up against that poverty. It's very easy for some Muslim bigots to tell poor, illiterate people, *The reason you're having all these problems is because of America*, since they can't read anything to see that that's not really the case. Maybe we contribute to some of the problems, but not all of them.

I think Muslim women in America are very lucky because they have the resources to be able to read, to become literate and do scholarly analysis.

Does Islam have any saints or people comparable to saints?

Islam does not have saints, in the way that, say, Catholics have saints. Prophet Muhammad is a prophet of Islam, he is *not* worshipped, and he is *not* a saint. However, there are certain Muslims, Sufi Muslims, called the mystics of Islam, who do have Sufi saints and pray to them. Many of them are descendants of the Prophet whom Sufis feel have been in touch with God and had a spiritual connection to God. So by praying to them, one is in a way praying to God because Sufi saints have an aspect of God that Sufis are able to reach and touch. So one can say there are some Muslims who do pray to saints.

Then there are certain figures like Prophet Muhammad and his companions—his son-in-law Ali who is also his cousin, his daughter Fasma, his wife Aisha—who are so important in Islam that while they're not called "saints," they are revered as people. This is especially true of Prophet Muhammad, who is thought of as the ideal person, the best person. Even contemporary accounts of him by non-Muslims say that he was extremely fair and so trustworthy that he took all your problems away from you. You felt like you didn't have a care in the world when you were around him. The Prophet and some of his companions may be equivalents of saints, in a way, but not exactly like Christian saints. The Islamic "saints," if you can call them that, are saints by being acclaimed, not canonized.

Most Americans think of Islam as a male dominated religion and antiwoman, whether it's true or not. Yet you call it a "feminist" religion. Can you comment?

I think Islam is a feminist religion because—odd as this may sound, it is true—it is the first religion we know of that has a focus on women's rights. Primary among these are a woman's rights in the areas of education and owning property. In other areas, the Koran says that the prayers of both men and women, the actions of men and women, are considered equally important in the eyes of God. Moreover, his estimation of us is in no way based on our gender or class, but on our piety, how religious each of us is.

When I was growing up, my mom talked about the rights of women in Islam all the time. It never occurred to me that being a Muslim woman put you at a disadvantage. TV would refer to poor Muslim women and newscasters would talk about *poor Muslim women*. I never knew what they were talking about. Definitely there are Muslim women all over the world who are oppressed. But they're not oppressed *because they are Muslims*. The cultures that are practiced in many Islamic countries that oppress women were practiced *before* Islam existed. Islam is only fourteen hundred years old. When antifeminist activity is found among Muslims, it often goes back to pre-Islamic times.

Why does it still exist? Because what is deeply part of a culture remains adamant and is difficult to eradicate. In American culture, take Thanksgiving. It's a big American holiday, a big American tradition. But lately questions have arisen on whether the first Thanksgiving ever really took place. There's not much proof that it did. Did Native Americans and the Pilgrims really sit down together and break bread and eat turkey? Since there's little proof, do we stop celebrating Thanksgiving? No, of course not. It's part of our culture.

Similarly, in Islamic culture (*not* religion) there is durability of cultural traditions. When the Pashtun tribe of Afghanistan, for example, the present-day Taliban, converted to Islam, all the things they did before conversion, they kept right on doing to this day. Before Islam, they oppressed women; after Islam, they oppressed women. It's part of their culture and no one has clarified the situation for them. So for their suppression of women today you cannot assume that Islam is responsible. It isn't.

From the way the Koran writes about women—and if all Muslims followed its teachings—there would be no female oppression in the Islamic world. Another example is female infanticide. In the Prophet's time, in Arabia, many people were burying their female infants alive because they felt that male infants would be more useful to them when they grew up and became more supportive. One of the things that Muhammad forbade when he first received the revelations, and started speaking and reaching out, was female infanticide. He immediately condemned it, and he's the first person in recorded history to do that. He also recognized that women have a right to a place in politics, and women were allowed to vote. This was established fourteen hundred years ago in Islam. In our own country, America, women had to struggle for years in modern times to get the right to vote. The Koran also says women should keep their maiden name. We still struggle with that here in America. I have friends who are getting married and can't decide whether to change their names. *Shall I keep my maiden name? Or should I take my husband's name?* I hear this frequently. These are some of the reasons I feel that Islam is a feminist religion.

You say in your book that you want to see Muslim colleges established with a definite religious affiliation to Islam. Few colleges that started out with a religious affiliation still have it. Would an Islamic affiliation work?

It's possible that a reason religious affiliation in colleges has fallen off is that the society at large has become more religious and students are able to explore their religion in a church or another setting. They don't need to have a school devoted to the religion to keep their faith alive. Islam has not reached that level of recognition in society. There are not too many outlets for Islamic expression and practice. An Islamic college might fill this need. Actually, there are a few colleges who have kept a religion affiliation. Brigham Young University, for one, still maintains a Mormon identity.

If Islamic colleges or universities should be established, I would have a certain percentage of non-Muslim students to keep the campus diverse and allow for those people to learn about Islam and for the Muslims to learn about other religions. Certainly I think Islam would tolerate that kind of diversity. Diversity is allowed. Muhammad had Jewish friends and Christian friends.

Do you find that being Muslim and being an American conflict in any way?

I've been American all my life and I've been Muslim all my life. I've never had a conflict between them. Any time I've felt that there was a conflict, say between American values and Islamic values, I would explore the problem. Usually I'd find there wasn't a conflict and that, in fact, they tend to agree with one another.

Being American doesn't conflict so much with Muslim values because American values are not as strong as the Islamic values. People ask me, *What are you first?* I say, *I'm both first.* There are some Muslims who say, *I don't care about being American. I'm Muslim first and that's all there is to it.* My response to them is, *You should go live in an Islamic country because we are American and we're Muslim at the same time, and those things can go very well together.* You have to have a good attitude about it.

If Muhammad were alive today, I think he would choose to be American. So many of the core values of Islam are embodied in American values and American society. One of the things I didn't get to say in the State Department talks that I do is that I hear from people around the world who say *Americans are the nicest people, they're so generous and kind.* That's what Muhammad was known for and he esteemed people like that, people who were nice, generous, kind.

And he exhorted his followers to have values that turn out to be very similar to American values. One of the Pillars of Islam is to do charity, and Ramadan requires fasting to empathize with those who are hungry and to donate to charity during that time. I think to feed the hungry and donate to charity are American values, too, not necessarily to fast, but to empathize with those who are worse off than you, and to donate. Those are important in America. There's so much between America and Islam that is shared.

When George Washington was crossing the Delaware, his followers said, *Why don't you declare yourself king?* And he said, in effect, *No, we're going to form a democracy and I'm going to be president. It's going to be a new thing. We're going to have elections.* When he was dying, Muhammad himself said, *I want you to choose a successor from amongst the surviving community. I'm not going to elect one for you. I'm not going to pick one.*

In a way Muhammad and George Washington are similar figures. They both founded something that was new and different. And they both fought for the oppressed. What Muhammad was up against was pagan tribes who didn't believe in God or believed in multiple gods and lived in a society in which no one cared about the poor or the plight of women and their needs. Muhammad said, *No. We will be accountable for our actions and we need to account to God for the things that we do. We're going to found a new society that is based on submitting to God, the will of God, and not treating people poorly.* It was very controversial to the pagans of the time. They were oppressors and Muhammad was telling the people they were oppressed, *There's value to you. You're not just a thing to be used, or mistreated.* Washington fought the British for freedom of the oppressed American colonists.

There are in Prophet Muhammad's life, and in Islam, many values that remind me of America. Liberty, freedom, democracy—these gifts that America cherishes—are also important in Islam. As an American of Islamic heritage who was born here, I'm in a good position to say.

My last question is a personal one. Would you marry a non-Muslim?
Wow! Everybody asks that. I'll have to report back. Yes, I probably would marry a non-Muslim, if I was in love with him. In Islam, incidentally, it's harder for a Muslim woman to marry a non-Muslim than for a Muslim man to marry outside his religion.

In the Koran, it says a Muslim man may marry a Christian or Jewish woman, but he must provide her with a book of her faith. He must buy her a copy if she wants it and must allow her to go and do her prayers.

If the Prophet Muhammad were alive today and revealing the revelations in the Koran, it could be that Muslim men *and women* may marry Christians and Jews. Some people say that that the translations of the Koran which said *a Muslim man* can marry a Christian or Jewish person are faulty, and should have said a *Muslim*—period—can marry a Christian or a Jew, and there would not be that gender distinction. Since translations over the years have become male-centric, giving men more rights, it's an arguable point.

My mate, whoever he may be, can come from anywhere and it's important for me to be open-minded and have an open heart. At the same time, some things are prohibited. One of the reasons that the Koran does not allow practices like dating and premarital sex is that it perceives that the man will take advantage of the relationship. Also, if the woman were to get pregnant, no one would know for sure which man was involved, but everyone would know that the woman had engaged in sex and would suffer all the negative consequences of it. To my way of thinking, the Koran doesn't allow premarital sex because it wishes to provide equality for man and woman. That's important.

Certainly I can't date with the sexual freedom that some of my non-Muslim American friends have. About which husband I choose, I'll stay open-minded and let you know.

Dr. Elias Zerhouni

Overseer of our national well-being

It's a disservice to both sides to cartoonize Islam, to emphasize just one form of dress, one concept, one position, rather than present something as it truly is in its many manifestations, in its reality which is complex and not as uniform as people might like it to be.

There is a quality of Islam that makes for happiness. I refer to family ties and relationships. They are usually of a closeness that maintains a good family structure.

I want my kids to interact with Christian friends, Jewish friends, and understand the complexity of life and society.

Photo courtesy of Office of Communications, NIH.

One of the preeminent public positions in our country, the director of the National Institutes of Health (NIH), the medical research institute that conducts and funds studies into all diseases, is held by an American Muslim physician, **Dr. Elias Zerhouni**. Since NIH's inception in the 1880s, more than eighty Nobel prizes have been awarded to NIH-supported researchers and investigators. Five of these were in-house members.

Dr. Zerhouni is the fifteenth director of NIH and the first American Muslim to be appointed to that position. Actually, it is appropriate to have a Muslim at the helm because Islam has had a long, distinguished history in medicine, science, and technology dating back to premedieval times. Islamic culture was the first to illumine Europe's Dark Ages, bringing with it a revival of learning and new Islamic advances in science, language, and medicine.

The prospect of interviewing a man of Dr. Zerhouni's position and accomplishment was daunting, especially since my background in science and technology is minimal. But the journalistic instinct, and patience, won over. It took nearly a year of pursuit before the interview took place. Happily, little knowledge of science or technology was needed on my part at the discussion. The interview is essentially about Islam and about being a Muslim in America. Especially refreshing are Dr. Zerhouni's openness of response and his lucidly described relationship to his religion.

He was born in Nedroma, Algeria, one of eight children. After earning his medical degree at the University of Algiers School of Medicine in 1975, at the age of twenty-four he came to the United States. Dr. Zerhouni completed his residency in diagnostic radiology at Johns Hopkins and was made assistant professor, then associate professor and finally full professor at John Hopkins, teaching radiology and biomedical engineering. The positions of chairman of radiology and executive vice dean of the Johns Hopkins School of Medicine followed. A principal investigator on three NIH grants, he was coinvestigator on two others. This is only a short list of his accomplishments. The others are too numerous to mention.

Dr. Zerhouni is married to a pediatrician and has three children. He became a naturalized United States citizen in 1990.

This interview was conducted in September 2002. Naturally, Dr. Zerhouni's remarks on stem-cell research reflect the situation at the time.

In a video sponsored by the United States government for overseas distribution, you said, "The tolerance and support I have received myself [in the United States] is remarkable. I don't think there is any other country in the world where different people from different countries are as accepted and welcomed as members of a society."

Since 9/11, has there been a change in the good will you describe?

There's no doubt that since then, there has been an increasing lack of understanding of what American Muslims are, and Muslims in general. I see a lot of Muslim stereotyping and what is called a "one-size-fits-all" type of analysis.

What can Americans do to correct this situation?
I think that the important thing is for Americans to demand factual information and not just accept biased, agenda-driven reporting.

Have you personally had any feedback from the video?
Personally, no; but indirectly, yes. People in the Muslim world did not believe what was shown. [*One writer called it a "Muslim-as-apple-pie" video.*] They were very skeptical about the disconnection between that video and what they perceive as official American policy. In other words, they couldn't reconcile the video's positive attitude toward immigrants with the foreign policy of the United States, as they perceive it.

The National Institutes of Health astounds the mind with the amount and quality of the research it funds. Can you describe in simple terms the kinds of research involved?
It's all medical research, both basic and applied, that looks at human health and disease in order to develop the knowledge that we need to reduce the suffering and burden of disease, both here in the United States and throughout the world.

In the emerging new field of stem-cell research, you took a leading role in helping establish the Institute for Cell Research at Johns Hopkins. Have you yourself done research in this field?
I'm not a stem-cell researcher. My efforts are more those of scientific leader and strategist. As you've indicated, I've taken some actions in that regard when I was at Johns Hopkins in establishing stem-cell research labs and making sure that the field is developed. However, I'd like to point out that stem-cell research is a very high-visibility issue and can overshadow other things in terms of reporting. It tends to take on a much larger size than the research itself warrants.

What is Islam's position on stem-cell research?
I cannot tell you what Islam's position is. There is no such thing as a single position in Islam. There is a traditional view, but that does not mean it's the universal view. You will find some very conservative trends of Islam compatible with what some people believe here—that there shouldn't be *any* experimentation with embryos. And others that are a lot more connected to the specific wordings of the Koran in terms of life starting at the fortieth day of conception, which puts a different coloration on stem-cell study. Different attitudes are all

one part of a whole picture. I don't know if there is *one position*. There is no pope in Islam in the way that there is a pope for Catholics who pronounces a single position. Throughout the Islamic world you will find varying opinions and moral scruples about different research and development. But this is true of all religions where movements are created in opposition—in Christianity and Judaism, for example. There is no one label—*anti-this* or *anti-that*—that should characterize an entire religion, including Islam. I object to anyone thinking that one size fits all when it comes to Muslims. Islam's contributions to the welfare of man are too great and encompassing. Its quality of openness is remarkable.

You've used the expression "one size fits all." What exactly do you mean by that?

What happens in the United States (I'm not really sure why—perhaps in order to simplify things) is that one opinion, one characteristic, one form of dressing among Muslims is taken up by the press and many Americans, and applied to *all* Muslims. In other words, one size fits all. One image fits every Muslim, whether it is terrorist, fascist, traditional, barbarian. But they do not represent all Muslims by any means.

If you can convey one thing from me to your readers, it is that this putting all of Islam into one bag and one understanding is a disservice to ourselves and to the Muslim world. It's a disservice to both sides to cartoonize Islam, to emphasize just one form of dress, one concept, one position, rather than present something as it truly is, in its many manifestations, in its reality, which is complex and not as uniform as people might like it to be.

Incidentally, part of the complexity of Islam may derive from its openness to all people and religions. I, for one, learned at a very young age to respect Christianity and to respect Judaism. That was probably because Islam is the third monotheistic religion, not the first, and Islam was greatly influenced by the first two. My first name is Biblical: Elias was the uncle of Abraham. When you look at the long tradition in Islam, it has really been a tradition of acceptance of other monotheistic religions and, in fact, there is no prohibition in Islam against marrying a non-Muslim. People completely ignore the openness of Islam. It is never reported or remarked upon.

The Muslim image is always terrorist, fascist, traditionalist, barbarian—with headdress. That has to change. It is the wrong thing. It absolutely hurts our country. America cannot be seen as being a country that has a caricatured understanding of such a great civilization and religion. That would be a disservice to ourselves. I hope to demonstrate to other Americans that, *Hey, wait a minute, it's not one-size-fits-all*. To sum it up thusly is a total mistake. I'm glad you're doing this book, by the way, for the simple reason it shows the variety and individuality of different Muslims.

Suppose Islamic opinion generally was against a certain kind of research that the Institutes were funding for development, how would you as head of NIH, and as a Muslim, react?

As head of NIH, one has to put private thoughts aside. NIH is a government agency. And that means that the director is an agent of our country and he or she must implement the policies of the president, the administration, and Congress. So my job is to uphold the laws as passed by Congress and implement policy. I don't think that one should inject personal or religious beliefs in conducting an official mission. I'm here to serve the entire American people, not one category or another.

Is President Bush for or against stem-cell research? His policy was worded in a way that was a bit confusing to me as a non-medical person. It said, in part, that "derivation process begins with the destruction of embryo initiated prior to 9:00 p.m. on 8/9/01." Does this mean that such processes, as the destruction of the human embryo begun before 8/9/01, are approved and those after that date are not?

I think the president has made a very clear policy decision that should leave no doubt. And that is that he does not support or condone funding by the federal government of the creation or destruction of embryos for research. But he made an exception for those that had already been destroyed prior to the time he made up his mind, on August 9, 2001, and announced his position to allow research resulting from those to proceed without violating his own principle. There is no federal funding for stem cells derived after that date. That's the policy as it stands.

With your background in medicine, radiology, and technology, you strike me as an embodiment of the types of skills and know-how Islam brought to the Western world when it was sunk in the Dark Ages. Can you comment on this?

As a doctor, I can comment on Islam's contributions to medicine. If you look historically, the Islamic countries were the ones that advanced science and technology for hundreds of years. In the Middle Ages, Islamic countries were way ahead of their times in medicine. The oldest medical manuscripts were written by Muslims beginning in the tenth and eleventh centuries. As for contributions in other sciences, in astrology, for example, there was the astrolabe that determined the altitude of the sun and other celestial bodies, and in geography, there were navigational maps that made possible the great European voyages of discovery. Throughout history there has been a different expression of Islamic societies to science and technology, and its contributions have been of tremendous importance in world history.

As I was growing up, I was deeply aware of the sciences. My father, who was a teacher, used to say, *You know, one of the great services you can bring as a Muslim is to help reestablish a leadership position of Islamic countries in science and technology with further contributions.* My father's advice seems to have been heard by other Muslims as well. To mention one, in 1999, Ahmed Zewail, an Egyptian-American Muslim, was awarded the Nobel Prize in Chemistry. *[Author's note: Dr. Zewail is presently the Linus Pauling Chair professor of chemistry and professor of physics at the California Institute of Technology. He received his Ph.D. from the University of Pennsylvania. He has many awards in the United States. From Egypt he received the Order of the Grand Collar of the Nile, the highest state honor. Egyptian postage stamps have been issued with his image on them to honor his contributions to science and humanity.]*

With the many practicing Muslim doctors in our country who came and were welcomed in the sixties during a shortage of American doctors, has there been any appreciable change of attitude on the part of the medical profession toward them since 9/11?
I don't think the attitude changed in direct professional relationships. But I see a change more in the media coverage and in the general psyche that melds all Muslims together. This seems to justify the targeting of American Muslims. That is the real issue and what bothers me is that other Americans say, *Well, that's not our problem. It's their problem.* Such an attitude isn't right for our society. We're all in this together. It's an issue that the American Muslim community deeply feels. We've always said, *All for one and one for all.*

Targeting all Muslims in this manner needs to be addressed and stopped. Books like yours and people like myself work hard to dispel that notion. And, frankly, President Bush's choice to name me as director of NIH is a testimony that seems to say, *Hey, wait a minute. Look at this American Muslim that I've chosen as head of one of our important agencies!* Our country is greater than what people portray it to be, either internally or externally. It's much greater than the stereotypical America that other nations promote as our image in their agendas. I have a strong feeling that facts and good, unbiased, comprehensive education about the reality of things, not just summarizing things in one-liners, are very important.

How large a percentage of Americans Muslims do you have working at NIH?
I really don't know. That's something we never ask. I think that is the greatness of America. We're blind to ethnic origin, national origin, sex, and religion.

One critic has pointed out, in effect, that to be a good Muslim and a good American are bipolar or contrary ways of living. He gave as an example Muslim children attending American public schools and having no place to go and perform prayer rituals. What might your

response be?
Again, another case of putting every Muslim into one bag. It is true that ortho-dox Muslims, like Orthodox Jews, have difficulty in applying their rigorous religious rules and regulations to the way Americans live. But if you look at the more adapted, moderate Muslims of a different tradition, or a more moderate Jewish person and his practices, you have no problem. So again it's a spectrum. Not all Muslims have a problem performing their prayers. Some stick to the letter of the law about ritual and others may alter the times of prayer, depend-ing on schedules. And others are less rigid in their practice. But critics make the obvious comments about how difficult it is for Muslims to pray five times a day in America.

Being Muslim, I don't see any contradiction or polarity in moving to America and bringing up my kids as Muslims. I have no problem whatsoever in believ-ing in a melting pot. If you are a very sectarian, traditionalist, orthodox person of any religion, you will be more rigid about rules than others and so may not adapt as well. But to pontificate that all Muslims are incompatible with the American way of living is basically a preamble to some form of ethnic cleans-ing. And I think we should call it what it is—another stereotype.

Have your children gone to Islamic, public or private schools?
Private schools.

How did you and Mrs. Zerhouni decide to do that rather than choose an Islamic school?
My wife and I are open-minded Muslims, interested in variety and diversity. Going to school for us is also to experience the diversity in others. To our way of thinking, putting our children into a one-size-fits-all school, or a monore-ligious school with very orthodox teaching, would limit their life experience. Diversity is the key.

We believe in an understanding, and acceptance, between peoples. We're accepting of both Christians and Jews. Why would I exclude my kids from them? It's not Muslim to say, *I'm going to exclude any contact.* It's not something that my wife and I believe in. Other people may. That's fine. They can. In Islam you have all kinds of variations on acceptance of others. I think that needs to be pointed out. I want my kids to interact with Christian friends, Jewish friends, and understand the complexity of life and society.

Are you worried that your children may in a secular American society lose their beliefs in Islam either as young adults or later?
That is a possibility. But there are many facets to belief and nonbelief. There are the atheists at one end. There are others who believe but don't practice There are others who practice very religiously. As long as my children have a sense of pride in where they come from and who they are and that they

represent a contributing part of society, that's all I'm interested in personally. And I don't want them excluded; I don't want them finger-pointed at. I want them to be part and parcel of the American dream.

In your observation, is the life of an American Muslim generally a happy one?
As far as I know, yes. I think there is a quality of Islam that makes for happiness. I refer to family ties and relationships. They are usually of a closeness that maintains good family structure. That, I think, is true across all Islam: the belief that you do not abandon your family, you do not abandon your parents, you do not abandon your brothers and sisters. That brings a certain level of happiness and solidarity across Muslim families, which I think is real. A little different from what I've observed in other parts of society. That is something you could point out. There is a closeness of relationships. I don't know if it's related to the fact that they're immigrants and a minority, or if it's an underlying tradition.

Do you and your family perform the prayer ritual each day?
Not each day. Five times a day is not a practical, urban lifestyle. It's appropriate for rural life and it was appropriate in Muhammad's time. Today you'll find a lot of adapting. Anybody who thinks you're not a Muslim because you don't pray five times a day does not know Islam. I know Islam and it allows adapting to your requirements.

Have you or Mrs. Zerhouni been to Mecca?
No.

Do you want to go?
I don't know. Again, you're going back to the typical characterization of Muslims—that all of them do this and that, like a caricature. Everybody has a time in life when he or she achieves inner peace and the trip to Mecca is one thing, one way, amongst many.

Your reasoning is valid. Then why do you think Muslims make such a thing of going to Mecca?
I think it is the only unifying element that all Muslims can share. The religion does not have a pope or clergy to unify, no single uniting Muslim authority. All Muslims share in Mecca and become one there. Whether you believe in a strict interpretation of Islam or a moderate one, you go to Mecca. It is a return to roots, to find renewed sustenance in ritual and new strength seeing millions of believers gathered as one. Islam doesn't have intermediary roots to return to and visit, like Rome or Constantinople for Christians, or like Jerusalem for the Jews. Mecca itself becomes the core of a Muslim's religious belief.

Are there any drawbacks to a religion, like Islam, that does not have a clergy to speak of?
There is a drawback. That's why, to my mind, you have a lot of these movements, these terrorist movements, these fundamentalist movements that rise for lack of clergy. They're really almost heretical in Islam, because they take upon themselves the powers of clergy. Certain people assume a temporal power and believe they represent religious truth, like a bin Laden, for example. But that is completely antithetical to Islam. The teachings of Islam have always been based on a direct relationship between you and God. Your beliefs, your morals, your values are between you and God. There's no one in between.

Aisha Abdul Kareem

An African-American doula finds her way

As a Catholic, I did not embrace the Trinity. I have always believed in the oneness of God. When I found out that belief in one God was the major tenet of Islam, I was very comfortable.

Having grown up as a colonel's daughter, I've seen the military take advantage of a situation. The opportunity presents itself: "We want to do war. This will enable us to do war, so we'll seize the opportunity."

Muslims are not supposed to eat pork. But Islam has a tradition that if the only meat available is pork, you can eat it. Islam appeals to me because it is geared toward common sense.

Photo courtesy of Henry Cateura.

Aisha Abdul Kareem, born Nan Hunter, is the first American Muslim, as well as the first African-American convert, interviewed for this book. It was by mistake. The author was looking in the Brooklyn telephone directory for someone with a similar name and chose the wrong Abdul Kareem. It was a natural, but lucky, mistake because the woman who answered had a fascinating background—her path into Islam, her life and experiences, her fearlessly expressed opinions—that makes for unusual reading.

The author's house was the setting for the interview. Aisha Abdul Kareem appeared at the door, a handsome, smiling woman wearing a long dress (to midcalf) and a hijab, a scarf swathed around her head and forehead that fell to her shoulders. She was delighted by my mistake, saying she had always prayed to Allah to find someone to tell her story to. She spoke eloquently about herself, with little urging, for one and a half hours.

In 1973, as a young adult, I was soul-searching, hoping to find a religion that suited my purpose. I was a Catholic as a child and teenager and married in the Catholic Church. But given the climate of racism against blacks, and all the other things that were going on in the sixties and seventies, I needed a change and so was looking at different religions. And I started hanging out with some Muslims, Sunni Muslims. I am a Sunni Muslim. There are many different groups of Muslims, probably over a hundred, and each takes on different aspects of the religion and uses them in different ways.

I have a little bit of everything in me: white, African American, Native American, Scottish, Sephardic Jew, and Catholic. My mother's family on her father's side were Sephardic Jews from Spain. They lived in Alabama. My grandfather did look like he was white. He could pass. Now my grandmother's father was Native American and her mother was Scottish. A Scottish woman married a Native-American Negro!

My father was an officer in the American army for all of my growing-up years. In fact, I grew up in Europe. Most of my childhood was spent in France and we lived in Hawaii and places like that. When my father retired, he was a bird colonel. He was the highest rank of colonel before you get your first star, that is, one-star general, two-star general. He's living in Washington, D.C. I still see him.

In 1973 I embraced Islam after befriending a young woman. She had me reading the Koran. I really didn't know what I was reading. And the next thing that happened I was going to a mosque on a Friday and listening to their talk about Islam, and I decided to embrace it.

I'm not sure what exactly caught me. I know I'm a ritualistic person and the discipline, for one thing, attracted me. The transition from Catholicism to Islam was not drastic because Catholicism has its ritual in masses, prayers, the rosary. Islam has very similar rituals. As a Catholic, I did not embrace the Trinity. I did not believe that God had three faces, a Father, Son, and Holy Ghost. I have always believed in the oneness of God, even as a child, even as a Catholic. I don't know where this belief came from. When I found out that belief in one God was the major tenet of Islam, I was very comfortable. There was one deity, one God, who has throughout time sent prophets to talk to people and to communicate with people for Him. That was my belief, even as a Catholic.

About sex, my perspective is that the promulgation of life should be the main focus of sexual encounters. But from what I perceive that Allah is talking about, we do have other needs and they are needs that have to be met. And you meet them within the constraints of a loving, right relationship. But it's very specific. Allah says you have to be married to have sex. It's like the Catholic Church in the sense that anything outside of that union is fornication or adultery. Similarities of beliefs like this one among all the religions are incredible.

I have been married three times. The first was in the Catholic Church and the other two were Islamic marriages. I have six children in all, two in my first marriage, three in my second and one in my third. Each ended in divorce. But my marriages and divorces are not related to my religion. I was young and made decisions in situations that weren't clear to me. Presently, I'm not married. I choose at this particular point to understand myself more fully and not be married. I have a very rich life with my children and grandchildren; they keep my life quite full-blown. Apparently, whatever I was searching for, I have finally found. I found it in Islam and found it within myself. Whatever soul-searching I needed to do, about maturing, about relationships, about what love really is, I found answers in Islam. It has really helped me find and figure out all those things.

My first two sons are Christian. I am comfortable with that because I am a former Christian and my mother, who is Catholic, helped me raise these first two sons because my lifestyle had changed. My three middle children and my last child are all Muslim. It's their choice to be Muslim and the choice of the first two to embrace Catholicism. Of my four Islamic children, the oldest is twenty-eight and the youngest is seventeen. My personal belief is that all roads lead to God. I think everybody has the right to choose his or her path in life. I encourage my children to do this.

It was when I met Malik, my second husband, that I became a Muslim. He was an Islamic brother, and it happened almost overnight. I took *shahada* (made my declaration of faith in Islam, which is the only step required in the conversion process) and got married the following Monday. I just did it and it was a very good decision. I couldn't have asked for a better husband. We didn't have any dating period, we just got married. I knew him maybe two days. I went that Monday to have a meeting with him. We sat down in the mosque and talked. By the end of the day I was married. Believe it or not, it was a very good relationship. We were the same age. We were young.

Malik was a merchant and now he works for the City of New York as an imam in the prison system. He is not an imam with a mosque but works for the City of New York as a religious leader. He goes into the prisons and works with the Muslims. Imam is the name the city uses in this type of service. Generally an imam is anyone who is in service to other Muslims about Islam. That's my understanding. An imam can run a community, or be in charge of a particular group of Muslims, just as Malik is. An imam does not carry the duties of a priest. It's being in service to a particular group, offering them spiritual guidance and information about Islam. When we got married, he had a grocery store. That day when we first talked, he said all the right things that I wanted to hear, about his attitude toward Islam especially. He is an African American like myself, and he had never been married before, but was more than willing to take on my sons and our relationship. He had never been of any particular religion before Islam. He now lives on Long Island.

When we got married, I wasn't sure of Islamic names so I asked Malik to give me a name. And he gave me the name Aisha, which means "springtime." It was the name of the youngest wife of Muhammad and his favorite wife. Kadija was his first wife and she was fifteen years older than he was, but it was an ideal marriage and he loved her very much. Incidentally, Muhammad married Kadija long before Allah started giving him the recitation of the Koran. I think most of his journey for Islam took place after her death. She was no longer in the picture when he took on the fight for Mecca and Allah gave him the recitation.

So I asked Malik to name me. Now at that time in '73 Aisha was not as popular a name as it is now thirty years later. Abdul Kareem was his last name. Abdul means "slave," and Kareem means "king," signifying "slave to the king," or "in service to God." Kareem is one of the ninety-nine names of Allah. However, if someone calls me simply Abdul, meaning "slave," I wouldn't like that. I would want to be sure that Kareem is said along with it. A non-Muslim may call me Aisha or Mrs. Abdul Kareem, but no one can call me Abdul. If someone does, I get irritated.

Now I was Aisha, and I just took Malik's last name. His former name was Kenneth Williams and now it's Malik Abdullah Kareem. We both legally changed our names.

Before I converted, my name was Nan Hunter. Nan was my grandmother's name, the Scottish Native-American lady. She was the daughter of a Scottish woman and a Native American man. They called her Nan; her real name was Mary Agnes. A very, very English-sounding name. Hunter was my father's name. My father is Scottish and Native American. His skin is light brown; he's tall, over six feet, with a very thick neck. The Scots seem to be a very tall and stately kind of people. In the U.S., given what racism has done to us, he would look like a person of color. He would be categorized with African Americans because he's a light brown person of color but, if you were to look at him, you would think he was from places overseas. He could have passed very easily as someone from the Middle East but, given the atmosphere where he lived, that wasn't possible.

I'm an RN, a registered nurse. My intention was to become a midwife but I haven't finished the required education. So I use my nursing background to work with babies, newborn babies of parents who have never had a baby. I work privately. I can also be called a midwife assistant, a postpartum assistant, a labor nurse, a doula. The word *doula* is from the Greek, meaning "in service to you," and it's a new practice. It involves going with the couple to the hospital when the woman goes into labor and staying with them in the hospital for the whole process of labor. I also help them figure out what they want to do. You see, some of the medical processes, depending on which hospital you go to, can be very oppressive and restrictive. I try to let people know that they have alternatives; they have power to be in charge of their lives at this time. I am with some clients before birth, and with some after birth during the postpartum period. Some women have difficulty making the transition to this new life and I spend time with them and help them figure that out. Medical insurance does not cover the work of a doula, so people usually pay for this privately.

My clients are not often Muslim. Most Muslims cannot afford this service, but they have more resources in their community than most people. They have friends, sisters, neighbors who come to their house and do cleaning chores. We have a community centered on the mosque and when a Muslim woman has a baby, the tradition is for the community to get together, cook and take her food, see what she needs, clean the house. You see, in Islam, after you've given birth, you're not supposed to leave the house for forty days. During that time, people take care of you, and help get you back on your feet. Most of the people that I know follow this, and during that time you're not allowed to leave the house. People bring stuff in for you. You can take a little walk, but everyday chores, like buying groceries, paying bills, are done for you. You have this time to think more of yourself. It's not meant to restrict you. It's meant to help the healing process. In this sense, Muslim women are lucky to have this because American women don't usually have this kind of attention from a community. They're usually dependent on a mother, a sister who lives far away, or a good neighbor.

Within my job as a doula, I still find time and ways to pray five times a day. First of all, every single day starts with getting up before the sun rises, at least a half hour before the sun rises. In spring and summer, it's a little earlier, about a quarter to five. I'll do a series of prayers, starting with my Sunni prayer. I'll begin with some *rakahs* and some other prayers if I choose. Rakah is a different series of prayer. I do my two series of prayers and then I do my beads. They're like prayer beads, they click together. The Hindus have them also.

They are ninety-nine beads strung together, one bead for each of the ninety-nine names of Allah. Reciting his names is meant to cleanse your heart because if you can say the ninety-nine names of Allah, if you get to say *any* number of them, this cleanses your heart and keeps you spiritually grounded, on positive ground. It keeps you thinking about God. I also read the Koran for fifteen or twenty minutes. This is my first prayer of the day.

My second prayer would be in the middle part of the day. What time is that? I follow the day by the sun. Some people tell time by a clock, but I do it by following the sun. We follow the sun more than we follow time. Usually you look up at the sun and you will know what prayer you're supposed to say. I follow the sun and say the prayer. The prayers are for your protection while you're moving about in the world and to remind you to keep God as part of your life. Now, you've done your second prayer when the sun starts to go over from the east to the west. When the days are longer, the third prayer is said just before the sun sets. The fourth prayer is said at twilight and the fifth prayer is an hour after twilight. In the wintertime your prayers are a lot closer together. In the summer, they're more extended.

If I'm at someone's house and it's time for a prayer, or if I'm traveling on the subway and there's too much distraction, I may say it when the subway stops, or make it up when I get home. You can make up the prayer later but you don't really want to put it off, knowing other things might come up. In other words, it's really important that you keep all the prayers on time, to keep the remembrance of Allah constant in your mind and in your heart. Sometimes if you get into the habit of saying your prayers later, it'll just throw you off completely.

Any sincere, practicing Catholic or Jew, or whatever, would say that religion is very much a part of his or her life. It defines who you are. You do these rituals and you do them in conjunction with living in space and time with other people. I like ritual. The prayers in ritual are constantly reminding me to stay on track. My liking for ritual may come from the fact that as a kid I was a Catholic.

I wear a headpiece. It drapes. A lot of Islamic women wear a long, straight garment, called the burka, and a headpiece. I wear the headpiece quite differently from other people. Some women drape it around their neck. You can see through my muslin headpiece. For me this is what works. My headpiece has a lightweight fabric because of health reasons. My hair type is such that it has to breathe. Certain types of material may cause problems with the scalp. Middle Eastern women do what I do: they drape something over their heads and go about their business. Some women pin it and cut off the airflow to their hair and scalp so that conditions may develop. My practice of Islam is based on what my body can take. I believe that Allah is a very loving and caring God and asks no more of you than what you can give. Which makes sense—all things have to breathe.

Some women dress with solid headpieces and pin them in the back. The Sufis can vary. A lot of the Sufi women wear the burka. They feel comfortable in it. I feel comfortable in regular clothes. People think the burka suffocates a woman, but that's not true because, beneath the burka, women don't have clothes on. That's how they're able to wear them. You don't wear them on top of clothes. You wear them on top of skin. You can be naked underneath. Depends on the person. In cold weather, you wear burkas made of heavier material.

In all religions some men have issues around sex and sexuality. That's a running theme across Judaism, Catholicism, Islam, and so on. I think women should be modest, no matter what religion they are. I'm not one for exposing my flesh. I won't wear a short-sleeved garment and I'm not one for exposing other areas. Sex sells and we see it pushed everywhere: on TV, in movies, books. We do have to be mindful of the subliminal effects of that. I wrestle with it every day, trying to stay modest because, you know, these subliminal tricks take effect, even if I'm not thinking of them. So when I leave the house, I look in the mirror to make sure I'm modestly dressed and won't attract undue attention to myself or arouse some kind of feeling. Even as a Catholic, I never wore a miniskirt. And I would never wear one now. I just don't feel comfortable with that. I've always worn long skirts way back in the sixties, midcalf.

Incidentally, I've worn a burka when visiting certain communities that use them. Out of respect for their traditions, I'd wear the burka and use the same headpiece I'm wearing now. The burka goes on first and then the headpiece draped over the front because it's supposed to cover your bosom. As for shoes, I wear any shoes I feel like wearing, high heels or flats or sandals. Some Muslim women cover their feet with socks or dark stockings. It depends on the person. Some women wear the face veil that covers your whole face. I've never worn that. It is more of a cultural tradition than an Islamic one. When you go to Mecca to make hajj, you cannot have your face covered; you have to remove the face veil. A woman can see out through the veil, but one can't see *in*. There may be openings at the eyes or a very fine netting so that everything outside is visible from the inside, but no one can see what's going on behind the veil.

It may be that wearing the veil is a tradition that arose over the years during wartime and it may be used in countries where there has been trouble with men approaching women. But it's not necessary here. Since I've been Muslim, I get the utmost respect from men. Brothers are respectful and thoughtful of me. It's because of the way I carry myself and the way I dress. I've never had a problem of that nature. I don't wear much makeup. That's only practical because, praying each day, I have to wash it off, put it on, each time. I may use an eyebrow pencil and a little lipstick sometimes, but makeup doesn't fit into my way of life. When I was a Christian, I used it but gradually phased it out.

My feeling is that if I dress a certain way when approaching God in my ritual at a mosque or at home, there's no need to dress differently in public.

What we eat and the way we cook food have nothing to do with being Muslim. Our food depends on the culture. If you have a Pakistani culture, there's a particular way of cooking. The same is true of African cultures. Islam influences the food in the way you *kill* the animal for meat and the type of meat you can or cannot eat. That's the influence of Islam. In most cultures that are Islamic in religion, they are required to pray over an animal, a lamb or cow, to calm it before killing it. The animal should not be afraid by the time you kill it. Our animals are killed upside down. After praying, you would slit its throat so that the blood doesn't sit in the animal. It's completely closed out. And then you pray again over the animal and the procedure is called halal. Jews have their laws on killing animals and call them kosher. You see the words *halal* and *kosher* in meat-market windows all over America. Halal is a tradition in all Islamic cultures. And we are not supposed to eat meat that is not killed that way. Muslims are not supposed to eat pork. But Islam has a tradition that if the only meat available for survival is pork, you can eat it. Islam appeals to me because it is geared toward common sense. It's not based in fanatical doctrine. You have flexibility to figure out your own needs in different situations.

One of the most memorable Muslims in my past is someone I met *before* embracing Islam. We were living in Fort Monmouth, New Jersey, on an army base where a lot of Jordanians and Pakistanis were being trained. Because my father was an officer, we knew officers of different backgrounds, and I met one of them, Major Latife, who was a Muslim. He was so very charming and interesting. I was nineteen or twenty at the time. He had been in America about six months, having come from Jordan or Syria, one of those places. He went to my father and asked if he could marry me. We had gone out and had lunch on occasion. I was kind of young and didn't know anything about Islam at the time. When he asked me, I was in no way ready, and I told him thank you but, no, thank you. He was such a wonderful, genuine, gentle person, and didn't have the sexism men have toward women here in the U.S. Thoughtful, well mannered. It was such a pleasure to be around him. That was my first encounter with a Muslim, male or female. Then there were younger ones I met who got caught up in some of the things that were going on in the U.S., dating, and stuff like that. But the major is someone who stands out in the back of my mind. He had a maturity to withstand, and even staying in the U.S. culture for a period time, he was still able to embrace Islam totally.

My reaction to the Trade Center disaster springs from my younger years, which were spent on military bases where my father was stationed. I've had some information others don't have about the way Americans handle things generally. My younger years in military life gave me a broad view of the way Americans handle their political, military, and governmental actions. Sometimes, when we train, we may train opposing groups. Back in the sixties we trained all these people on warfare in the Middle East. We were backing the Jews, we were training the Jordanians, doing a little bit of everything.

It was very clear to me even before the information about the Taliban came out, that the Americans had probably trained them, too, for something else in the past and since they were no longer our friends . . . I felt that something had happened to these people to make them want to do this, something very bad. Either a promise was broken, or their people were being oppressed almost beyond endurance. Most people don't come from overseas to bother Americans. I do figure something undercover was happening, something that would cause them to strike out so viciously.

I knew it was not a *Muslim* action. I knew it was isolated. Sure, they did target a multitude of people, but if they had had a chance to think of the magnitude of what *could* happen, and did, they may have viewed it differently. I don't think they had any idea it would end up with such slaughter and especially with such slaughter for other people of color. That was something they didn't think about, too. Many of the people working in these buildings were people of color. There was a good percentage of Muslims. Nobody escaped, not the Jews, Muslims, Christians, or Protestants.

I've been reading a book that Nixon wrote long before his death, and in it he mentions that in some twenty-odd years, the biggest threat against capitalism would be Islam. Okaaaay—when I read that I thought, *Islam is going to be America's next target.* I mentioned Nixon's prediction to my son and said that here twenty-odd years later it seems like a development of what Nixon said. It seems like this has been their intention all along, but they've been doing things under cover. Basically, I really do believe that this government had knowledge that that disaster was going to take place and they could have prevented it or, at least, prevented the magnitude of the disaster.

Having grown up as a colonel's daughter, I've seen the military take advantage of a situation. The opportunity presents itself. *We want to do war. This will enable us to do war, so we'll seize the opportunity.* The military is not here to serve us, as people like to think. The powers believe that people, other than themselves, are expendable. If more people realize that about our government, there is hope. Our government is supposed to be in service to us. I'm not saying that this is not one of the best places to be at this particular time in human life. America has afforded us a lot of safety and we are spoiled. But the powers that be make me very nervous because they seize opportunity. We lost three or four thousand people, but that was not enough reason to go into a country and try to devastate it. It's not enough reason to go into Peru and do the things they're doing, or into South Africa, or in Africa.

There are a lot of different things going on at one time that Americans are not paying attention to and I said to my son, *There's a possibility in the very near future that they're going to gather up all the Muslims in this country and do to them what they did to the Japanese during World War Two. Oh, yes, it's very much the agenda of the United States government that they could do that. Yes, it is.*

Muslims are the fastest growing religious group and that's what is scaring the U.S. But Muslims are fragmented. If they would come together, as the Jews give the illusion of coming together, they would stand to have more bargaining power. But they're fragmented and there are different levels of belief and different people, and the different people are doing different things.

There is a possibility that on two levels—on the level of being Muslim and on the level of being of African heritage—these specific Americans could be a target. There is a war against people of African heritage in this country, I mean, the war of racism. And Muslims of color, the ones from other countries, would be a target because America would claim that our security is threatened. We don't know the whereabouts of people who have been detained. Look, right here in Sunset Park in Brooklyn, there's a detention center with over one hundred Muslims. We can't get the names of these people. We don't know why they are there. They were picked up off the street, out of their communities, they are fathers and mothers of children, and we don't know what's going on with them at this particular time. If the government can do that on a small scale and get away with it, they would consider doing something on a large scale. It's possible. In the case of the Japanese, they took everything away from them and there were fewer of them in the U.S. than there are Muslims.

I refuse on a daily basis to worry about it. I say my prayers. I ask Allah to protect me. If rounding up of people happens here, I honestly don't know what I'm going to do. After the World Trade bombing, a lot of Muslims came out of their garb to look like everyday people because they were scared. Myself, my attitude was, *Me? I didn't bomb anybody. I'm not going to run scared.* The white people have been very nice to me. My other African-heritage people have been ticked off at me, a black Muslim, because they bought into the idea that they're being personally attacked by this group of people, the Muslims. American blacks may be associating me and other Muslims to that group—the Muslim terrorists—that came over and bombed our kin and neighbors. And they think this because the Americans say they came here and did it.

I think the terrorists were targeting capitalism. They weren't targeting individual groups of people. They were targeting the oppression of capitalism and we got caught up in the mix. And like I told other people of color, *Please don't step on me with any disrespect because I haven't done anything to you.*

And you have to remember that those people—the guys who hijacked the planes and bombed us—they were probably being oppressed on a level that you cannot imagine, for them to come to our front door and kill themselves, as well as thousands of others. What else would make them do such a thing? Suicide bombing is desperation beyond any human comprehension.

I don't want your readers to think Muslims are any different from everyday people. Our religions are so similar. The purpose of every human being is to be connected and loving with another human being and Islam really does promote that. Now you have individuals who get off the beaten path and because of their hurts and the way they've been treated, may interpret Islam in a distorted way, but that's not the standard of most Muslims. We're loving and caring human beings and we're willing to live with other human beings regardless of their religion. Sure we would love to invite the whole world to partake of Islam, but I have met over my lifetime beautiful, wonderful Hindus, Christians, Jews—people from every religion. We do embrace other people in a very loving and caring sense. And we know we live in different countries throughout this universe. I'm speaking of Muslims of all nationalities. Our religion is our unity; we believe in one God like you, and we follow the Biblical prophets from Adam on down. We just believe that religions have evolved differently, as the Jewish and the Christian and the Islamic faiths. Religions have evolved in a strange way over periods of time and handed down different things. That's our belief and we believe that we can coexist with other faiths in a good and rightful manner and bring something to the table.

Dr. Faiz Khan

**E.R. doctor and
seeker of Islamic truths**

In view of this ever-growing population of Muslims in America, the most important thing non-Muslim Americans must do is to get acquainted with what is authentically Islamic, and what is not. That means what in our way of life, our customs, our dress, our chauvinistic and male-dominated tendencies are consistent with what the Prophet said and did—and what in our way of life is not.

I challenge a conservative, immigrant imam to relate to someone from Tribeca, where my mosque is.

Some people have a misconception that immigrants follow religious practice in their native land but lose it when they emigrate. My feeling is that in a new country, among different people and religions, the native faith comes forward and Muslims do practice ritual.

Photo courtesy of Faiz Khan.

The only way to describe **Faiz Khan**, a young American Muslim doctor who tended to 9/11 victims, is that he does not allow grass to grow under his feet. An accomplished thirty-three-year-old, he is an emergency-room doctor with a dual specialty in emergency medicine and internal medicine, an assistant to the imam at two mosques, outspoken critic of his coreligionist authority figures, and world traveler seeking Islamic truths among books and institutions and sheikhs. He has visited with scholars in Morocco, Tunisia, and Turkey, among others, and lectures internationally on Islamic topics. A main concern as a Muslim believer is his search to detoxify traditions contrary to authentic Islam, to separate the wheat from the chaff. He has lived in America for thirty-three years (he came as an infant), was educated at public schools, and is thoroughly American, as well as thoroughly Muslim.

We met on a Friday (the Islamic holy day) at a mosque in Soho, New York City. He asked that I attend the service which he was to conduct as a substitute imam (he was to deliver the sermon) and that I wear a scarf on the head and a skirt that fell to just below the knees. The service completed, he led me to a French Malaysian restaurant across the street, where we lunched on mango and squid salad, turmeric salmon, a Diet Coke and iced tea. A tall, brown-skinned American of Indian-Afghani descent, he began talking, prompted by an occasional question, and did not stop until we parted one and a half hours later. His parents, both doctors, live in Muttontown, Long Island. Dr. Khan is married to an intern, also a Muslim.

Growing up in Muttontown, an upper-middle-class suburb, I was definitely different from other Muslim youths from families not so well off. My parents were both doctors and led busy professional lives. The Muslim scene in America is very diverse. What you have is an immigrant class that made good, my parents among them. They came in, a lot of educated, professional engineers and doctors who brain-drained their native land, so to speak, and really lived the American dream. There's a whole subculture of them, Indians, Pakistanis, and Arabs, too.

African Americans make up a large part of the American Muslim world, where the scene changes. They come from a very different socio-economic stratum. As a youth, I was curious and used to go to a lot of events that mixed these two groups together, including not only African Americans, but the Guyanese and other Africans from different socio-economic groups. I've always maintained my friendships with Muslims I met along the way. My family lived in various places, you see. Before moving to Muttontown, we lived in Brooklyn, right near where Brooklyn Jewish Hospital used to be. There were a lot of the newly arrived doctors from India and Pakistan living in the area, as well as some local African-American neighborhood residents who had become Muslim. They did not mix much but there was no real tension back then. It was simply "birds of a feather stick together." There's nothing wrong with that. When I was eleven or twelve we moved to New Hyde Park and after that to Muttontown, both on Long Island.

But tension does exist among Muslims in America, especially after 9/11 or, at least, I've become aware of it. There was a recent documentary which shows an American Muslim, a black woman, complaining about Arab, Middle Eastern, and Pakistani Muslims in this country demanding special attention as victims of discrimination and profiling. She said that African-American Muslims who are native have been dealing with discrimination and profiling for decades—and their plight went somewhat unrecognized or unappreciated by the immigrant class of American Muslims.

She is absolutely right. Her sentiments are totally valid. And that's a problem with people's religiosity, or affected piety. My parents' generation came here and began to realize there was a lot of cultural diffusion now that they were away from their origins. They took it in and started to say among themselves, *You know, we should reestablish our roots, we need to go to mosques and be religious.* In my opinion, it was religion as a sentiment, which goes only so far, but it was something that allowed them to go through the comforting motions. Their sentiments were good. But when it came to crossing the socio-ethnic lines and building an embracing community—a component of true Islam which recognizes no difference between one human being and another based on color or outward attributes—the embrace was less than robust.

Look, it's fine to be more comfortable within one's given cultural matrices. But at the same time, there is most definitely a deep-seated racist and classist element that exists amongst Indian and Pakistani immigrants toward others—particularly African Americans. It certainly exists, and of course it has nothing to do with piety—in fact, it is wickedness.

I think the African-American Muslim who spoke was feeling some of that. But that a priori doesn't exist in my generation because we grew up here so we're comfortable with everybody. It was more of a xenophobia on the part of the immigrants, an overriding fear of the stranger. It's a cultural ineptitude on their part, my parents' generation. At the same time, I think the African-American community needs to understand that a lot of this is just cultural. If I'm not attracted to a particular culture, I'm not going to necessarily appreciate or embrace it.

Brought up as an Indian Muslim, I never felt outside the American mainstream, and still feel deeply part of it. My family are all professional people: in addition to my parents who are doctors and myself, my wife is a doctor (she was a medical student from Pakistan and we met here), my sister is a psychiatrist, and her husband is a doctor. No, I was far more American than I was an Indian or Pakistani and my friends saw me as such. As a matter of fact, culturally speaking, I went to high school in a very Jewish neighborhood of Jericho, Long Island. I have been to more bar mitzvahs and bat mitzvahs than most Jews I know who live outside the New York metropolitan area. I can still sing all the Hebrew songs. And under the influence of African-American culture, I used to be an avid break-dancer, spinning on my head on a cardboard refrigerator box, outside on the streets with rap music in the background. My parents couldn't stand it. I was literally and culturally regarded as an American and never faced any feeling or sentiment of being anything else.

Incidentally, my sister, the psychiatrist, may sound out of place in a big family of medical doctors. But what's interesting is that the science of the soul has been a very, very long-standing established discipline within not only Islam, but also all other traditions, including Catholicism. The spiritual development of Catholic saints and monastic orders has trained the soul to become refined with an ability to taste the presence of divinity. There's a whole science built around that in Islamic doctrine and that's what the authentic Sufis fully adhere to. The science of the soul. Like my sister, I find that whole area fascinating.

But growing up Muslim, I still had to face certain routines that Islam as a religion asks. I haven't always done the salat. I've tried. Some periods of my life, less so, some periods, more so. In public schools, it was hard. Sometimes during the day, I would sneak into the auditorium when there was no one there, and I'd do it. Once a day, some days twice, and even then not all the time. But I wouldn't do it openly. Fasting during sporting events or exams was an issue.

In terms of the social challenges that faced me as a Muslim growing up here, there were the usual issues that any religious family would have to confront in a pop culture that glamorizes "sex, drugs, rock 'n' roll." We're all faced with issues like dating and girls and parties, and things like that. What we did was sneak, usually, jumping out windows at night when parents were asleep, making sure a sibling would act as a cover. My American friends who were religious, Catholics and Jews, had parents who were worried about the same things.

Sex, especially. Muslims will try not to have sex before marriage. The funny thing is that you have immigrant imams here, from countries in which moral conservatism is the norm, and where sexual licentiousness is not implicitly or explicitly provoked as it is in the Western cultural matrix. These imams stress compliance with sexual morality as if they were authorities on the subject of dealing with this culture. Don't get me wrong, their position is correct, and for the Muslim, there should not be any compromise in what is explicit in the Sharia (Islam's behavioral injunctions and law). But these imams have no idea what they are talking about, as they have almost zero experiential knowledge of growing up in this culture. So they come off holier-than-thou in their approach—and clueless to boot.

Look, I have my private life, and you have your private life. And since we're on the subject of sex, let's talk for a moment on the issue of homosexual activity, which seems to be a hot topic for religion these days. In Islam it is frowned upon and considered against the Sharia. But in the Islamic world, it is far more common than the average person would imagine.

But don't misunderstand me. The Koran definitely criticizes the people who lived in the time of Lot. The Koran is critical of their excesses and perversions, the way they expressed passion and allowed it to govern their behavior. Engaging in sex with the same gender is considered an excess, a perversion. To say that it's allowable in Islam is wrong. At the same time, Islamic doctrine is highly protective of private life, and what you do behind your doors is up to you. There's no policing, there never has been. And there's no compulsion to have to confess it to a holy man. Sexual practice or preference is not a subject of confession, advertisement, display or pride.

I know there is a group of gay Christian churches that have become members of important Christian organizations. That sort of acceptance would never happen in the Islamic world. The Islamic tradition considers it more of a privacy issue and even a lewdness issue. The Koranic verses imply, *Don't be lewd*. This covers hetero- or homosexual contexts. It's not right before God. It's not allowable in the light of Divine Guidance. But it's your business. And the criticism of Lot's people was not only the fact that they were openly lewd, or guilty of glamorizing sodomy, or perverse, but also they were rejecters of God. The attitudes of certain imams sound harshly arrogant or holier-than-thou, with a sort of "we hate them" tone. No, I don't believe it's like that. It's just that the Islamic tradition doesn't condone lewdness, in whatever form. There's no hatred or phobia of others in the equation. You want to practice what Divine Guidance considers lewd? Do it in private. That's between you and Allah…no need to advertise, march, or parade—that's a more accurate rendition of the traditional Islamic stance. One sage has rhetorically asked, *Since when did human beings start defining themselves by what occurs around their genitalia?* The crux of these issues is essentially a willingness, or unwillingness, to submit one's ego and passions to Divine Guidance.

Molestation does occur between young boys and religious teachers. As a physician, I've seen cases in Pakistan. The Catholic priests that have been found guilty do not have exclusivity in this regard. Incidentally, I've heard from sincere folks, including American Muslims, that many of the accusations regarding the Church are sensationalized and exaggerated via media frenzy. This is not to say that sex crimes did not occur, rather to say that a lot of this is snowballing hype that the Catholic Church has been victimized by.

Everyone talks about jihad, which means "struggle" or "exertion to actualize what is primarily spiritually sound." Let me tell you, my parents' most intense jihad was dealing with me as an adolescent growing up in New York. What was it like? My parents would be making sure who I was seeing, who I was hanging out with, making sure I wasn't hanging out at night, going out to parties. They kept tabs on all that. They wanted me to be with a good, wholesome crowd. Didn't have to be Muslim, just wholesome people who prioritized education—good people. Of course, girls were out of the question. Sure, I did things my parents didn't know about, as did most adolescents growing up here. I was able to persuade my sister to cover up for me when I was out late.

Talking about jihad, I'd like to clarify three other Islamic words that confuse Americans.

Islamic scholars. They're not like priests. An Islamic scholar has a degree that represents competency in a particular curriculum pertaining to religion. Scholars may be specialists, such as Koranic exegetists, hadith exegetists, jurisprudents, historicists, theologians, theosophists, philosophers, and so on. Like other fields, there are degrees of mastery and learning. [*Author's note: The hadith is a series of narratives that have to do with the sayings and doings of Muhammad. They are separate from the Koran and not part of Divine Revelation.*]

There is also the equivalent of scholars in the science of spiritual development. Sometimes these same folks happen to be scholars in the academic-exoteric sense, and are recognized as such. Other times they may not be. Similar to the tradition of sainthood in other faith traditions, spiritual masters were sometimes from highly academic backgrounds; other times, they were from a lay demographic. There was an academic background difference between Saint Augustine and Saint Francis of Assisi. Yet they were full-fledged spiritual guides in their own rights. So it's possible to be a scholar in an exoteric and academic sense, yet still be infantile with regard to spiritual development. Some of the most spiritually unrefined individuals I've ever met have been considered Islamic scholars. I've met with all types.

Ayatollahs. Ayatollah is a term used in Shia circles. There are two theological categories of Islam, Shia and Sunni. This variation has given rise to some marked differences in approach to popular piety and law, but in essence, the differences are minor and have been accentuated ever so often due to political reasons. A good portion of the world's Shia population lives in the regions of Iran and Iraq. As a title, *ayatollah* signifies one who has passed through institutions of higher religious learning, similar to those of a religious scholar, but the level of training is more than just a standard curriculum. It's like going beyond a bachelor's or master's degree, except that the sciences here are in the field of religious guidance. The term *ayatollah* literally means "sign of Divinity," and such a person is known for his mastery and erudition in religion. There are "grand ayatollahs" and titles of lesser mark. Some ayatollahs address only religious concerns, and others address areas such as politics. Islamic doctrine has always addressed both religion and politics. It is not a strict "render unto Caesar the things that are Caesar's and to God the things that are God's." In the Islamic paradigm, as in all traditional paradigms, including Judeo-Christian, all human behavior, be it collective or individual, contains within it a "vertical" or "spiritual" dimension—with its attendant implications. This does not mean, however, that Islamic doctrine imposes a parochial religious form onto government or citizens, as is commonly erroneously thought.

Imams. This is a subject I often spout off about, so please bear with me. First of all, there are different meanings to the word *imam*. There is the imam in the context of leading the prayer. That can be anyone. (I'm a member of a mosque and assist the imam when needed. You might call me an assistant imam.) In the early days of the Prophet, women were also imams since, in certain cases, the most learned in a gathering were women, and it is the most learned who should lead the ritual prayer in theory. Essentially, an imam is anyone who can lead in prayer.

Arabic is a funny language because a definition may shift according to the context. If you use the term imam in another context, a graduate of a religious school of higher learning might be referred to as an imam. Thus, imam can be used in several senses.

Speaking of higher learning, in the United States, we don't have religious schools that are qualified to produce truly erudite levels of Islamic scholarship largely because, in my opinion, there are few true scholars here. But they exist in the Islamic world. But even there I'm told the level of scholarship has taken a real hit—this is just symptomatic of the postmodern age.

Let me add some personal notes about higher learning, imams and related things. Speaking of higher learning, I've constantly searched for it in a general sense. I've been to Morocco, Tunisia, Turkey, Syria, Saudi Arabia, Pakistan, India, and England, visiting mosques, talking with scholars, seeking religious knowledge. I would just go, pick up and leave, do the whole backpacking thing, seek my fortune. Sometimes I would meet up with some very interesting individuals, sometimes they'd be scholars. My knowledge of Islam grew from my travels. I realized how diverse it was and, as an extension of this, quickly realized that "authorities," who often make rigid and dogmatic assertions, often have a poor understanding of the subject at hand.

On the subject of imams, I'd like to add that many of the older, more conservative imams in positions of power here in the States make me cringe every time they speak to someone of my generation, that is, American Muslims seeking to get knowledge. I'm thinking of one imam in particular who, I'm sure, is a great guy in his native context with his particular mold of leadership, but was quite literally laughed out of a library where he was giving a talk to a lay American audience about Islam. It's a huge problem, and I cannot underscore to you how big it is—older generations with their particular brand of leadership and attitude. They're often Arab or Indo-Pakistani and they come over and bring not only religion but the cultural baggage of their countries. Even the way they talk.

When you hear a sermon by an imam who is Arab, Indian, or Pakistani, you'll find each tends to yell into the microphone. I've given sermons where I've had Indian guys say to me, *Next time, YELL. Make our blood boil.* I'm like, No, I don't do that. I'm an American. That fire-and-brimstone stuff is way too overdone and turns the average person off. But they're trained in that dialectic. I don't mean to generalize, but that's the typical background of these imams. I challenge a conservative, immigrant imam to relate to someone from Tribeca, where my mosque is. Imam Feisal, who leads that congregation, is an American. He knows how to speak to people.

But bring someone over from abroad, you realize you have to know what precisely to ask to get knowledge from him. The average American can't learn much passively from him, I don't think. A large part is culture, accent, just natural things. But this type of imam comes here and expects the same degree of authority and influence that he got back home and he just doesn't get it. Oftentimes he drives people away. I remember, when I was growing up in Long Island, my father's generation tried to have the equivalent of a religious school on Sunday so the younger American Muslims wouldn't lose touch with the religion. And I would rather be out playing football! And the teachers came and they barely spoke English! They were funny to us. We couldn't relate to them. That was all I knew of religion and I grew up trying to assimilate myself somewhere in it. The conservative-type imam hasn't helped me beyond an elementary level.

Now that I'm grown, I realize that the Prophet, our model, Prophet Muhammad possessed (or depending on the perspective, "was given") the ability to speak to all different types of people, on different levels, and in accordance with their perspectives and understanding. Anyone sincerely seeking divinity was attracted to him as well as to the men and women who were his close disciples. By virtue of who he was and the way he was transformed, he possessed a magnetic nature as is described in various accounts, and never alienated anyone who sought authentic religion no matter what their background—the artsy folks, the academic and intellectuals, the politically inclined, the recluses, the simple, the complex, the rich, the poor, the scholastic and legal hairsplitters, the expansive liberals, etc. There are instances where imams tend to alienate folks because of the imam's cultural impositions, attitude, mannerisms; other times there are natural obstacles such as language or accent. I tell others and myself that we need to be conscious of this, and be embracing and gentle for no other reason than this is the Way of Muhammad.

Take the question of a handshake between a man and a woman. According to a strict interpretation of Islamic law, there should not be any contact between the sexes, except through marriage or immediate family. I think it's similar in the ultra-orthodox Jews or Hasidic tradition. In the Prophet's time, there was a certain way of conduct between men and women that was the proper etiquette and manner. Fine. But that was the Prophet's time and may have been the ideal. Now, we're in America, where there are certain customs. If a woman extends her hand to me, I can be a letter-of-the-law kind of guy and say, *Sorry, no*, but then create a moment that embarrasses the woman who extends her hand out of genuine sincerity or etiquette. It may even be rude to embarrass her if this takes place in front of others. Or, I can follow the spirit of humility and graciousness (the Prophet was always gracious) and respect her courtesy by shaking hands with good intentions, not to get some sort of feel or lustful high.

I've witnessed some conservative experts bend the rules when appropriate to the spirit. There are certain legal scholars who, I've been told, have actually allowed kissing in France and Morocco, to greet someone, because that's the way men and women greet each other there. Picture it: *Hello!* And then, ma'am, whah, the KISS! These scholars say that since it's the custom and as long as it's not done in an immodest fashion, it's all right. Among the "experts" in Sharia, some people don't have that accommodating perspective. If I were to shake your hand, it would be done out of courtesy and respect. But a certain type of imam might be looking at me condescendingly ... [*He laughed.*] Come on now! They've alienated a lot of the second-generation Americans because of such cultural baggage. They fail to separate what is cultural and what is authentically Islamic in accordance with both the letter and spirit of the Prophet's behavior. I'm not an expert so I make no assertions, but clearly there are different points of view. None is absolutely right or wrong.

Listen, you've opened up the floodgates. I still resent some of the religious instructors I encountered because I did not receive a complete picture of Islam from them. May I continue a bit further? They left out two important things.

Number One: They never stressed what man CAN do. Their Islam is mostly rules ... and mostly of don'ts. I've heard Americans call it a Boy Scout religion. This can't help but keep some Muslims away.

Number Two: Islam is often defined in terms of political activism, geopolitics, what's going on in Israel, what's going on in Iran, Kashmir, Kurdistan, Chechnya. Fine, that's valid, but that's *not* religion. Religion is to know Allah, to know God. It is to seek to submit one's ego to divinity—the ultimate of which is to taste the presence of divinity—and what this implies. That's religion. Everything else is a consequence of that. And that is left out, to a great extent. There may be lip service to it, but it doesn't come across in behavior. It doesn't come across in mannerisms. It is through a complete embrace of religion that one or some may truly catalyze socio-political empowerment, globally or locally. But religion should not be sought after from an ideological socio-political utility standpoint.

In all of this, I do not mean to imply that some imams are always responsible for Muslims turning away from Islam. Those who turn away are driven usually by other reasons. Some find that religion has not fulfilled them. There are probably more Muslims who do move away in the sense of not practicing or performing ritual than those that remain. There are others who grow up Muslim and have a problem. They haven't turned away because of the practice of Islam. They have turned away *from religion in general*, for whatever reasons, often because of what they perceive religion to be, and other times because the current culture makes it easy to not prioritize seeking Divinity. I say this as an observable, objective phenomenon, not as a judge of others. In my own present contexts, I am very much guilty of this as well, and of other criticisms I level.

Speaking of turning away, some people have a misconception that immigrants follow religious practice in their native land but lose it when they emigrate. My feeling is that in a new country, among different people and religions, the native faith comes forward and Muslims do practice their ritual. I'm going to try to inculcate it in my kids.

On the subject of Islamic prayer ritual, do you know where that comes from? From the Islamic perspective, the whole ritual of our movements in prayer is preserving a lot of what came even before Muhammad. In other words, the whole notion of prayer and ritual movements was pre-Koran, when Moses removed his shoes and got down on his hands and knees, when Christ got on his hands and knees and put his head down in the Garden of Gethsemane. This was all pre-Koranic. Muhammad did not introduce these movements. In fact, the Koran calls Islam the religion of Abraham, doesn't call it the religion of Muhammad, and it addresses all believers and doesn't only address the Arabs in Muhammad's time.

When Islam is discussed, one topic keeps coming up that especially disturbs non-Muslims. It is a so-called evangelical, proselytizing zeal of Muslims toward non-Muslims. I've heard people ask, *Why do some Muslims talk with such zeal and persuasiveness as if they were trying to convert you?* My answer is that I consider that a personal behavior thing. Absolutely. An Islamicist may get very enthusiastic and speak as if he were trying to convince others. But saving souls through parochial conversion is not at all part of the Koranic ethos, nor is it found in the practice of Muhammad. Yes, he was given a religious vehicle that embraced all others and was open to anyone willing. Yet other vehicles, when "driven sincerely," are just as valid in attaining God's grace, as is the way of Muhammad. I mean really, who do we think we are? It is God that guides. If we are part of the process, fine, if not, fine. Divinity is in no need of our presumptuousness.

I can further substantiate the lack of evangelicalism in Islam by paraphrasing the Koranic stance. Using today's parlance, here it is, in effect: *Look, followers of various faith traditions, here's the deal. Start following your own religion, sincerely for God's sake.* The Koran doesn't say, *Become Muslims* (in the parochial sense). There is no compulsion in matters of faith in God, or outward form of religion. It says, *Be true to your own faiths.* That's a very strong message. If there is any evangelical pursuit in Islam, some of it may be among the Muslims themselves: fundamentalists hoping to proselytize nonfundamentalists.

In spite of all this, Islam is one of America's fastest growing religions. And the question springs up, *How can we absorb such a large population of Muslims?* We will be able to, because it won't be a cultural shock. American Muslims will be very American and will just be adhering to the religion of Muhammad instead of another, or no, religion. They will be American like me, or Frank over there who is Muslim. [*Pointing to a man in blue jeans and T-shirt sitting at another table and looking like any other American.*] The one with the beard. He's American. There are a lot of them. It's not going to be a cultural shock on religious grounds. The culture shock won't be any more or less than that of other immigrant populations—Mexicans, the Chinese, Russians.

In view of this ever-growing population of Muslims in America, the most important thing non-Muslim Americans must do is to get acquainted with what is authentically Islamic, and what is not. That means what in our way of life, our customs, our dress, our chauvinistic and male-dominated tendencies are consistent with what the Prophet said and did, and what in our way of life is *not.* Our cultural, xenophobic, fear-of-the-stranger attitudes, the way our culture is very closed and antagonistic to other ways of life—are these consistent with what Muhammad teaches in the Koran? That is the test. My major emphasis resulting from 9/11 has been to convince people that what happened there has nothing to do with religion. Terrible current events, like executing policies that starve entire populations, have nothing to do with religion. It's not a Christian thing, it's not an American thing. It's a criminal thing. What I am trying to say is terrorism, or genocide, is not an Islamic thing. It's a criminal thing, no matter what the externals might appear to be.

[*Author's note: Concluding the interview, the author asked Dr. Khan whether his services as a doctor were available on September 11 and whether he was at the scene. His description of events follows.*]

I was at home enjoying some leisure and doing some reading—I don't watch TV anymore. Suddenly my pager was going off frantically. It was my wife. She was in a building in Nassau County as the towers were going down. She said, *God, do you know what's going on? The World Trade Center has been bombed and one tower has collapsed.*

My immediate reaction was to throw on my scrubs and get in the car. I was not to be on duty until four p.m. that day but went in immediately. They had closed off all the highways. I got out, took out my badge, flashed it, and said, *I'm on duty in the emergency room.* The cop car pulled aside and let me go by and not to sound like the good guy in a movie road chase, I was able to go one hundred fifty miles an hour straight down the highway. The hospital was in Queens and I pulled up to the ER entrance. The ER had been transformed into a trauma center. I started treating patients—survivors, the walking wounded, victims of smoke trauma. But after treating them, there was nothing. The others were all dead.

I met up with a friend, a doctor who is head of EMS (Emergency Medical Service) and was in charge of the whole rescue operation. I offered my services, and we made plans to meet in the morning of September 13 at the Chelsea pier. My brother-in-law who is also a doctor (and, incidentally, a convert to Islam) came with me. By the time we arrived at the pier there had been a bomb threat, so that was evacuated. I tried calling my colleague but the cell phones weren't working, of course. We were stuck. We left our car, hitched a ride with some clergy down into Ground Zero and got out. We made our way to the makeshift hospital, which at that point was Stuyvesant High School. We waited, but there wasn't much for doctors to do. There were no survivors. Literally we just sat there twiddling our thumbs.

Walking around that area on September 13 was surreal. Seeing all the papers from the offices scattered around on the road. There was such a sense of urgency in them:

"'Must be done by tomorrow!"

"Make sure you get this account straightened out by a.m." Surreal. Manhattan was transformed. Empty. Soot and ash everywhere.

In the following days, patients came in with exposure to the lungs and eyes, looking for general first aid–type care. A lot of emotional victims came in, and they were referred to counseling. My sister, the psychiatrist, actually saw some of them.

At one point I was standing with another worker at the scene. I think she was a nurse, and in a very reactionary, hysterical fashion she said, *We'd better make some country into a parking lot for this.*

Wow! You know! She was implicating people of my type, who are the Afghani in this case. Here I am, an American. I'm a Muslim, I'm part Afghani. She was able to indict, like, a whole nation for the actions of a demented few.

Apropos of 9/11 and what we've been saying, I have some notes at home taken from a lecture I attended a few years ago. I'll e-mail them to you, if you like. They're contrary to what most Americans thought of Muslims on the day of 9/11. [*Note: Following are the notes Dr. Khan sent, which he took from a lecture delivered by scholar Imran Hussein in Westchester in the fall of 1997.*]

To drive home the point that armed struggle is a last resort after all diplomacy has failed, we Muslims are told of instructions given to the battalions in the early days of Islam when war was carried out only by combatants and in places away from civilian infrastructure. Not only were noncombatants off-limits, but also so were farms, trees, and other infrastructure.

Upon engagement, the Muslims were instructed to allow the enemy the first strike and then ask for a respite. At that point, the Muslims were instructed to bring out their slain or wounded for display to the opposition and ask for the last time regarding resolution of the conflict: "Is there no other way?"

Hamid Dana

A WASP turned Muslim

We date back to the Massachusetts Bay Colony… (My mother's) mother was an Adams who was actually born in Wisconsin, but her family tree dates back to the Adams family of Massachusetts.

He [an uncle] said to me, "I wouldn't do anything like that impulsively. It's a bigger jump than say, converting from being Protestant to Catholic. You'll be perceived as having adopted a whole new culture." In many ways, he was right.

I played jazz music for ten years professionally, and then just got tired of living in saloons.

Photo courtesy of Hamid Dana.

It is surprising to find a WASP turned Muslim. **Hamid Dana** of Harper Woods, Michigan, is a converted Muslim who has an American heritage that dates back to 1640. Mr. Dana, active and dedicated in his adopted faith, does not fit Americans' image of the Middle Eastern or black stereotype. His narrative is an unusual story of one American's attraction to Islam, despite a heritage that was purely Christian.

Hamid Dana is proud of his Christian background and family and, given an opportunity, will talk about them. But he is also inquisitive. Anglo-Saxon Americans have displayed highly independent thinking in our history, and a few have been known to put aside all previous acceptances of religion when they come across a new belief that absorbs them.

Having heard that Detroit, the city and its environs, has one of the largest concentrations of Muslims in America, I contacted Imam Schweib Gerguri of the Albanian Islamic Center of Harper Woods, Michigan, for the name of a congregant who might be interested in my project. He put me in touch with Mr. Dana, a convert and a member of his religious community. Mr. Dana happily accepted the opportunity to speak of his conversion and of his feelings about Islam.

My family has been in this country for ten generations on one branch and twelve generations on another. We date back to the Massachusetts Bay Colony. We're quite sure that the first Dana came from Manchester, England (this is from circumstantial evidence). He is known to have been in the Massachusetts Bay Colony in 1640. His name was Richard Dana.

My parents were both Christian. My mother's father was a preacher in the Evangelical Church. Her mother was an Adams who was actually born in Wisconsin, but her family tree dates back to the Adams family of Massachusetts. People say to me, *With a background like that, what brought you to Islam? What led to your conversion?*

The short answer to that is prayer. At one point in my life I became curious about other religions and later began my own spiritual search. But I soon became aware that in addition to searching, I needed to practice a religion. I had noted a profound similarity in the teachings of all the great religions. I began to question some specific things in the Christian tradition I grew up in, which seemed exclusive. Without rejecting them, I simply asked God to lead me to the one I was supposed to practice. The ultimate destination of my praying was Islam.

From the moment that I consciously made my prayer to God until I finally made the shahada, the Islamic declaration of faith, it took several thoughtful years. The first person who seemed to be aware that I was considering converting to Islam was my uncle who was also a minister in the Christian Church. He said to me, God bless him, *I wouldn't do anything like that impulsively. It's a bigger jump than, say, converting from being Protestant to Catholic. In this country, you'll be perceived as having adopted a whole new culture.*

In many ways, he was right. I thought about conversion for a long time, and I also didn't want to make a move that might lead me to think, in my innermost being, that I was rejecting Christianity. I did not want to do that. I wanted it to be a positive move toward something, not a move away from something else. So I took my time and prayed about it and ultimately made shahada. That was thirty-two years ago, in 1971.

My wife did not make the declaration of faith to Islam with me. At first, she was opposed to the idea of my doing it. But, almost against her will, she slowly became interested in the religion and a couple of years later she chose to make the shahada herself.

Since converting, I've had few, if any, doubts. My prayer life has changed completely. I make the salat and go to the mosque regularly anywhere from between four to ten, eleven, or twelve times a week. I'm fortunate that I'm only about half a mile from the closest mosque. I can run over there for the noon prayer or the evening prayer. It makes it a lot easier than for someone who has to drive several miles each way. The imam is Schweib Gerguri. We have become good friends and respect each other. Actually there are two imams at the mosque. The older one is in his eighties, so he's sort of imam emeritus. He's still active in the mosque everyday for about four hours. But the younger one has assumed most of the duties.

Incidentally, I just turned sixty-eight. People ask me, *How can you get down on the floor, at your age, and extend yourself the way they do during the salat?* Actually, we don't really extend ourselves. We stay in the kneeling position. If I injure myself, which has happened, I may have to do my salat in a chair. There are aids and provisions in the mosque for people who are unable to perform all the physical movements.

There is a gentleman who comes regularly to our mosque for the noon prayers who is a double amputee. He can't kneel, of course. He sits in a chair. There is a general premise in Islam that is accepted by all the scholars: nothing that is impossible is compulsory. The Koran tells us that God does not put a burden on anyone that is greater than he can bear. If it's impossible for you to do something, it's not required. My wife is not as diligent about doing the salat as I am. Sometimes I ask her, "Do you still consider yourself a Muslim?"

"Of course," she says.

Even though the Koran tells us that God doesn't require you to do what you can't do, it still enjoins us to be steadfast in our prayer. In the hadith of the Prophet, it enumerates that prayers should be performed five times a day. It's generally considered that this is compulsory upon Muslims. It is something that you are supposed to do if you are a Muslim. However, the Koran says that there is no compulsion in religion. You are responsible for your own actions. If you're a Muslim and don't pray every day, that's up to you and it's not my job to force you to do so.

I was born in Traverse City, Michigan, but have lived very little of my life there. We moved away when I was still an infant, just over a year old. We moved back when I was in the second grade for about two and a half years and then moved to upstate New York and then to Toledo, Ohio. I lived there from fifth grade through the high school years.

I joined the Marine Corps and after being discharged, went to Central Michigan College and studied music. This foolish young man dropped out a few credits shy of graduation and moved to Detroit. We now live in Harper Woods, a suburb of Detroit, and have been here for six years.

Professionally, I consider myself a jazz musician, though I've held other-type jobs. In my younger years, the big bands were coming up but I wasn't really exposed to them because in the Fundamentalist Christian background, we didn't listen to that kind of music a whole lot. Still, my father was a trumpet player. That was before he married my mother; her father wouldn't let her marry him as long as that was what he did for a living. So he quit playing professionally and went up to the Old Mission peninsula. My grandfather had come down here to work in the factories. My father started working there as a hired hand on a farm, did it for a year or so. Then he came down to Detroit, married my mother and took her up there. And that was where I was born.

Young people ask me how I got into the jazz business. I started out as a trumpet player because that's what my dad played. He taught me to play and I went through school playing in the school band and got interested in jazz in high school. I started playing in bands in my junior year. When I went to college to study music, I switched to bass just because I thought it would be a good instrument to double on. Then, oddly enough, I started getting jobs by virtue of the fact that I was studying bass. I got jobs on campus, and got calls from nearby places like Saginaw and other spots in central Michigan. I left college and came to Detroit, thinking it was a stop on my way to New York, but wound up staying in Detroit. I played jazz music for ten years professionally, and then just got tired of living in saloons. Actually I've tried several times to get out of the business entirely, but I keep getting drawn back to it. I still play regularly.

Besides jazz, I've taught English as a second language and did some freelance acting. I never went into cherry farming like my grandfather because I've tried, as much as possible, to avoid any kind of a real job.

My family doesn't see eye-to-eye about my conversion to Islam. Sometimes we have some lively discussions about it. My brother is a devout Baptist, and my father is a convert to Catholicism. We seem to have family members in several major religions. I have to be careful because when I talk about Islam with them, really I'm only trying to clarify where Islam stands and how it's different. But I have to be careful not to let it degenerate into an argument of who's right and who's wrong. Basically, we're all of the one-God faith. That should be a big tie, but people seem to forget that. I've never been ostracized by the family, however.

The mosque in Harper's Woods here where I live is called the Albanian Islamic Center. Harper's Woods is bordered on all sides with St. Clair Shores, Grosse Pointe, and the city of Detroit. People who come to our mosque come from all those communities. Many who come to the Friday prayer are people who work in the area but don't live anywhere near here. Harper's Woods is technically in the Detroit metropolitan area, which has a very large Muslim population. It has increased tremendously in recent years. Thirty years ago, when I made the declaration of faith, I could easily have counted the Muslim population on one hand. The big influx was in the mid-seventies.

The tremendous increase has come about through immigration, conversion and from the growing number of American-born Muslims who are the children of immigrant parents. Added to this are American-born Muslims who are the children of American converts to Islam. There's an interesting anomaly among Muslims coming to the United States. Some who come here begin to practice regularly, do the salat and so on, but never practiced in their own country. A Muslim scholar who lives in California has written a book pointing out this phenomenon, citing the number of immigrants he knows of who became practicing Muslims *after* they came here. He believes that here in America, with the freedom to choose whether or not to practice it, the recently arrived Muslim looks around him and says, *Muslims here are in a non-Muslim society but they're going to the mosque every day. I've never practiced Islam. What am I missing? Let me try it.*

On the other hand, it's possible that in America some of the children and descendants of Muslim immigrants may fall away from Islam. The same sort of thing that's happening among Christian Americans. There are those who go to church only on Christmas and Easter and the rest of the year pay only lip service to their faith. Many young people today who grew up in a Christian home tend to think their elders are going to church out of habit, or because of societal pressure. They find this hypocritical and don't want to be part of it. Turning your back on the family religion is not uncommon.

I haven't gotten any adverse reaction from neighbors because I'm a Muslim. Actually, in this neighborhood, I'm not sure how many are aware that I'm Muslim. It's possible to be Muslim in America and not be known as such. My hours and habits are so different from the people who live around here and I have very little contact with them except for community functions.

Since 9/11, however, we're trying to reach out to the community and let them know that we're here, and what it is we actually believe, in contrast to what they might hear on the news. We had our first "open house" in the mosque last year after 9/11 and we're planning a second one this year. We

answer any questions the community has and we have something to eat together and express ourselves as neighbors. I think 9/11 made us realize you're not
supposed to sit on your hands until something happens. When you have a good
idea, like an open house, do it. Don't wait until it becomes necessary to do it.

After 9/11, American Muslims felt numbness. We reacted in the same ways
that Americans in general did. But I think that probably the very first thought
we had—it was part of our prayers: *Oh, God, don't let it be a Muslim who did that.*
That was a pretty universal reaction. And then we became very watchful, waiting for the backlash. And it came.

In Detroit there were incidents. There was the case of a man running a
woman down in a parking lot of a mall because she was wearing hijab. Verbal
epithets were frequently aimed at anyone noticeably Muslim. Physically, there
have been cases of people being beaten with baseball bats. Sometimes, the victims weren't even Muslim. They just appeared to be, with darker skin or
speaking with an accent, whatever. I'm sure you've heard of the incident where
six people were attacked because they were perceived to be Muslim. There was
another one back east where a boy of fourteen was beaten by two or three
white boys as his mother looked on. Fortunately, our mosque hasn't had any
noticeable vandalism that I've seen.

Frankly speaking, I don't think it was immediately obvious that Muslims were
involved in the Twin Towers catastrophe, though that was the general conclusion. There are some people in this country who make a business out of being
anti-Muslim. When the federal building in Oklahoma City was bombed, most
Americans thought it was a Muslim attack, by Muslim terrorists, until they
found out who actually did it. When the planes crashed into the World Trade
Center, people were calling it a Muslim attack almost immediately, without
really knowing. It wasn't obvious then who did the crime. And I think there
are some Muslims who still are not convinced it was an Islamic attack. There
are some reasonable doubts in the results of the investigation.

But let's suppose Muslims did do it. It was announced that some of them
were celebrating at a bar the night before. Well, if they were celebrating at a
bar the night before, they could not have been practicing Muslims. If I as a
practicing Muslim was convinced it was a good thing to lay down my life for
something, I would not be celebrating the night before by violating the pre-
cepts of my religion by drinking at a bar. If I knew I was going to die tomorrow, I wouldn't be doing things forbidden in the Koran. I think there's a lot of
reasonable doubt in what the government has told us. I don't know who did it.
Let me say that I'm sure that Osama bin Laden is not sorry it happened.
Whether he was behind it or not, I don't know. But it does seem to me that it
was a pretty ambitious project to carry off without some kind of inside help.
That's my opinion.

Out in the Midwest, because of the distance, there may be a certain detachment and a bit more objectivity about the gravity of 9/11 and where to put the blame. And so we can speculate the way Easterners who were caught in the midst of it don't do. But let me say this. Whether it's me, or Muslims living in northern Virginia, or Muslims living in New York, we all feel just as violated as every other American by what happened. But some of us are also getting it from our fellow Americans. Innocent Muslims are being put in the category of the terrorists. They may not be called actual terrorists, but they may be considered collaborators and sympathizers. It's like being caught in a vice.

I attended a conference held by the American Muslim Council near Arlington, Virginia, after 9/11. There I realized how much American Muslims were suffering the effects of the 9/11 tragedy. One woman, a social worker, was there working in grief counseling and post-trauma counseling with Muslims who lived in the Virginia area. I think New York City had similar help for Muslims suffering trauma. I met people there from all over the United States and the world.

To end on a positive note, I would like to tell you about my pilgrimage to Mecca to make the hajj. Americans rarely encounter a spiritual experience like making the hajj. I did it just once. In fact, it was the first time I crossed the Atlantic. I crossed the Pacific when I was in the service on the way to Japan and on the way back. Since then my wife and I have traveled to Japan on vacation and then we moved to Japan to live in '90 and then came back in '95.

On the pilgrimage, nothing was like what I expected, and yet I didn't know what to expect. I had heard it described several times and you build impressions, but the reality was not like what you imagined. My overriding impression was that I was not worthy to be there yet. I mean, it was awe inspiring to know that in Medina you were walking in spaces that the Prophet and his companion had walked on, and praying in the mosque that he built there and then circling the Kaaba. The Kaaba is an historic, square building that the Koran tells us was built by Abraham and his son Ishmael as the first house dedicated to the worship of one God. It is now totally encompassed by the sacred mosque there in the center of Mecca. The mosque has been built around it. At the time of the Prophet the pagans had taken over the Kaaba and filled it with idols. One of the things the Prophet did, very close to the end of his life, was to take possession of the Kaaba and rid it of the idols. It is the most sacred place in the Islamic world.

During the hajj, pilgrims are not allowed inside the Kaaba. There are so many people that the place could not contain them. Since there may be as many as two million people at the hajj, you have the feeling of seeing overwhelming sights of humanity from all over the earth. Especially inside the mosque in Mecca. I'm told that if you go there any other time of year, except for Ramadan, it's much calmer, but during the hajj and during Ramadan the place teems. I don't speak Arabic and didn't wander too far from the routes set out for me between the hotel and the mosque. But the travel agency that booked the trip—it specializes in hajj travel—put me with a group that had a Muslim scholar as a guide. That was fortunate. And I made new friends. The trip had all kinds of people from America: immigrants, children of immigrants, converts like myself, people from California, New York City. Quite a few were from the Detroit area, three or four from Boston, a group from Chicago, and there was one man from Louisiana. And I met people who were originally from Egypt, Palestine, India, all corners of the globe, now living in the United States. Our entire group was residents and/or citizens of the United States.

The hajj lasts three or four days. But I was there a week before it started and spent several days in Medina and then went to Mecca and performed the first part of the pilgrimage. There's a day off after that and you go back and perform the second part. There are two parts to the hajj, the *umrah* and the hajj proper. You can perform umrah at any time. It consists of putting on an unstitched garment, two pieces of cloth for men, one around the waist and one over the upper body, tucked and rolled so it won't fall off. It's called *ihram* and symbolizes the pilgrim state. You put that on, make the intention to perform the sacred ceremony and then you walk around the Kaaba seven times. You make salat behind the station of Abraham—he's right there near the Kaaba—and then you run back and forth between the hills seven times. These are actual hills, and are enclosed within the mosque. It is a huge mosque and will hold at one time six to seven hundred thousand people. The population of a small city, you know. The city in which I lived in Japan had a population of five hundred thousand.

The hajj is one of Islam's Five Pillars of Wisdom, beliefs and actions that are required of all Muslims. While in Mecca, I heard a sermon that said the hajj is the one Pillar of Islam we don't understand, especially the rite, which is circumambulating the Kaaba seven times. We do it because we are enjoined by God to do it. We understand the other pillars, the necessity of, and belief in, one God, the necessity of prayer, the reason for fasting, and the reason for giving alms to the poor. But we make the circumambulation of the Kaaba, for example (which is part of hajj) because Abraham did it and we run back and forth between the hills because Ishmael's mother did it, looking for water for him when he was dying of thirst as a baby. She did that until the angel of God showed her the well, called Zam-zam, which is said to have special spiritual powers and which all pilgrims may drink from. But we don't really know why we're running around the Kaaba seven times or running back and forth between the hills.

As part of the hajj, we also go to Mina, a small town about three miles from Mecca, where pilgrims perform the stoning of the devil and the sacrifice of an animal. We spend the night in Mina and then go to the plain of Arafah. Some people walk there, others take buses, but it's better to walk because the traffic jam is so intense. Everyone has to be there and you have to be there at certain times of the day. You have, for example, two million people walking or busing and all trying to get there at the same time. You're supposed to be in Arafah in time to make midday prayer, and after that we go to Muzdalifah, to do the evening prayer and the morning prayer. Then we go back to Mina and throw more stones at the pillars. The first time we go to Mina, we throw stones at the largest of the three pillars (these represent manifestations of the devil). When we go back to Mina, we throw stones at all three pillars, seven stones at each one. We cut our hair. Women are supposed to cut at least a quarter-inch from their hair and for men, the ideal is to shave the head. If you don't shave it, you should cut it close. I did shave my head.

It was, all in all, the experience of a lifetime.

Feisal Abdul Rauf

Forceful voice of reason

American Muslims now are in a better position to communicate a newer American form of Islam to their relatives abroad, and thereby influence their thinking about Islam.

America is a very easy country. You can live any way you want—you can live a Mormon lifestyle, an Amish lifestyle, or a very atheistic lifestyle. You can be anything you want in this country as long as you're not a national security threat.

Very early it was recognized that the Koran and the hadith do not speak to all issues. Many are not addressed in either. In the science of Islamic jurisprudence, there is a recognition that issues not mentioned in Holy Scriptures have to be judged by analogy, by consensus, and other sources of jurisprudence.

Photo courtesy of Feisal Abdul Rauf.

Feisal Abdul Rauf is a grand explicator of Islam, a Muslim who, through his practice and teaching, is trying to advance understanding and respect between America and the world of Islam. His great dream, and what he works on day and night, is to accelerate and shape the sociological process of an American Islam. He firmly believes that the qualities of humanism, tolerance, and equality that helped shape America will shape a new American Islam.

Imam Feisal has been imam of Masjid al-Farah, a mosque in Tribeca in New York City, since 1983 and is the founder of the American Sufi Muslim Association (ASMA), dedicated to furthering Islamic art and culture. Imam Feisal practices a mystical tradition of Islam known as Sufism. (The Sufi path seeks to discipline the mind and body in order to *directly* experience the presence of God. Unlike the Christian monastic tradition of withdrawal from the world, Sufis struggle to find God *in* the world.) He is one of Sufism's leading exponents and teaches classes in Sufism and Islam at the Center for Religious Inquiry at St. Bartholomew's Church in New York City.

A graduate of Columbia University, Imam Feisal speaks Arabic, Malay/Indonesian, and English. His lectures at synagogues, churches, and mosques, as well as on radio and television, draw large audiences. He resides in New Jersey with his family, and the following interview was conducted during a two-hour session on the telephone.

Are you a conservative or a liberal Muslim?

I do not like to pigeonhole myself. I was born in Kuwait and raised in England, Malaysia, Egypt, and the United States. I have a very varied background that has provided a wide exposure and given me a special understanding of what Islam is. Such an understanding is vital: it looks at the essential and universal definitions of the faith from the study of the Koran and the hadith. Also, having lived in different societies and noted the differences between them, I grew up exposed simultaneously to many cultural expressions of the same orthodoxy, the same theology, the same practice. This defines both my position and my direction. I do not call myself either conservative or liberal.

What are the essential differences between the three monotheistic faiths, Judaism, Christianity, and Islam?

I call them sisters in the monotheistic faiths of Abrahamic religions. As for the differences, first let's talk about Judaism and Christianity. In Judaism, you have what theologians call an *orthopraxy* (an established practice). This means that as long as you believe in the law or the laws, if you observe the Sabbath, if you have circumcision, if you observe the dietary laws, you are deemed to be a Jew. There's less insistence on what your theology might be. There's much more flexibility in what you can believe, whether it's regarding heaven, hell, and certain doctrines, which come under the heading of *orthodoxy*.

In Christianity, there is the opposite of this. There is a fundamental *ortho-doxy*, which is that as long as you believe that Jesus Christ is the Savior, you are saved, and there's much more flexibility in your practice, or on the ritual end. (This is true mostly of the Protestant religions. Catholicism is more ritualistic and the practice is less flexible.) Whatever you do in terms of prayer, dietary laws, circumcision, church attendance, there's flexibility on that. There's no common denominator that you're forced to abide by, as long as you believe in that fundamental tenet that Christ is Savior.

In Islam, there is both an orthopraxy and an orthodoxy. Orthopraxy is *correct action*. This is the Five Pillars of the Faith, the foundation of the faith. They are (1) the *shahada*, the declaration of faith; (2) the *salat*, the five daily prayers; (3) the *zakat*, giving of charity; (4) *sawm*, fasting during the month of Ramadan; and (5) *hajj*, performing the pilgrimage to Mecca. That defines the practice. As long as you do those things, you will be recognized as a Muslim and yet no one will know what your real belief about God might be.

The orthodoxy of the Islamic faith is belief in the oneness of God and the right attitude, the right understandings of God; that is, God is omnipotent, almighty; God sees and hears all; he is not deaf or dumb, or blind, or unknowing, or ignorant. Second, a belief in the angels who convey the divine commands. Third, the belief that God communicated to humanity via scripture, both oral and in written form. The belief that God communicated his guidance and messages and teachings to humanity via human intermediaries, human messengers whom we call prophets. And the last item is belief in the last day, which means that the world will come to an end; and in resurrection day, the Day of Judgment in heaven and hell, which means basically that we are accountable to God for our ethical decisions. This defines both the orthopraxis and the orthodoxy of the three monotheistic faiths, and therein lie the differences between them.

As a follower of Islam, let me add this word about the Islamic faith. You can believe in the orthodoxy and orthopraxy and at the same time have *very different* viewpoints on other things. And many of these other differences, then, come out of environment, from the culture, that is, from the pre-Islamic cultural background, the customs of the society you live in, and the political culture and climate you live in. So you can be a practicing Muslim and yet unless you are exposed to the different expressions of the different cultural environments in which Islam developed and grew and thrived, you may tend to think that only one cultural expression of the religion is Islamic, which is incorrect.

Do you agree with people who claim that there is a growing conservatism among Muslims in America?

I regard conservatism as a kind of collective psychological phenomenon that happens to people when they feel under attack. Look at America pre-9/11 and post-9/11. Pre-9/11, we had a lot of political partisanship. In other words, people were Democrats or Republican and vociferously disputing with, and attacking, each other. The right to burn the American flag was a protected right. When people feel confident, they're free to argue with each other and claim more rights.

When we were attacked after 9/11, what happened was that all America turned to the Right. For a while there was hardly any partisanship. It was considered un-American for Republicans and Democrats to point a finger at each other, and the whole country shifted to the Right. If you didn't wear a flag on your lapel or have it waving on your car or on your house, you were almost deemed to be not an American. Now what do you call that? It's a kind of natural thing that people do. Another event that happened in the few weeks after 9/11 is that people thronged to their synagogues and churches and houses of worship, and collections were up. The clergy were feeling good about it.

All this occurs when people feel under attack. And this has happened in particular moments of Islamic history. The rise of Islamic religiosity in Egypt is an example. You can trace it directly to the aftermath of the Six–Day War in 1967, when Egypt lost to Israel. A deep psychological funk resulted in the Arab world, and out of it came a heavy religiosity from which we've never recovered because people felt they were always under attack.

Do you think the average American Muslim feels that he is in a state of siege as a result of 9/11?

The American Muslim community is very diverse and I would say the sense of being under siege is felt more by certain communities than other communities. We need to go back a bit. For a long time the African-American community felt itself under siege even before they became Muslims. Witness the whole idea of the civil rights movement going back to the early '60s. When they became Muslim, they thought the prejudice they were experiencing then was a combination of the racial thing and Islam, and they felt very much under siege. That community has felt it much longer and much more strongly.

In the immigrant Muslim community, it's a function of a couple of other determinants. For those whose Immigration and Naturalization Service (INS) status was in process, things peaked and the bubble burst. They felt and still feel literally under siege. For all of those who haven't achieved a permanent residence in this country, there's a very high level of fear among them. The Muslims who have permanent residence and are more professionally successful—engineers, higher management, chairmen of companies—have a much lower feeling of being personally under siege. However, there is very much a sense of higher scrutiny that they are subject to.

Even though some Muslims living in America aren't personally involved in any of the above, they may still feel besieged because there is a natural feeling of simpatico for other Muslims who are being boxed in. When they hear of others who are suffering, it hurts them. Let's consider, for example, a Muslim woman who in her own life has never felt disempowered or disenfranchised, but has observed many other women who are. She feels the hurt deeply, almost personally.

Another interviewee, Faiz Khan, is one of your students of Sufism. He seems to be on an unending search for Islamic knowledge and meaning, often traveling abroad to consult with scholars and ayatollahs. As his teacher, do you know what he is searching for?
A good question to ask him, but I can contribute to the answer. Besides working at my mosque. I'm also a spiritual guide, a spiritual teacher of the Sufi path into the inner or spiritual dimension of faith. And in that path we learn from our predecessors, or teachers. As in any area of human endeavor, you learn a subject much more quickly if you have teachers. Faiz was seeking a spiritual guide and I agreed to take him on, even before I actually had people coming to me for official guidance. He has turned out to be a prize student. He is on a deeply felt journey to discover the vision of God, to feel that you are in the presence of God, because that's what we believe every human being actually seeks.

And then along our Sufi path, before arriving at the ultimate, there is a whole ensemble of other things that one hopefully accomplishes, such as shaping a redefined sense of identity and a harmonious relationship, not only with the Creator, but with creation. These may be all part of Faiz's search.

You have written a book called *Islam: A Sacred Law—What Every Muslim Should Know about the Shariah.* We hear the word "Shariah" mentioned frequently. What is it exactly?
Shariah is the term given to define the collectivity of laws that Muslims govern themselves by. And it is thought that these laws recognize all of the specific laws mentioned in the Koran and in the practice of the Prophet (the hadith) and do not conflict with either. Any law studied in the Koran or the hadith is definitely Shariah. The idea is that it is divinely legislated and the creator has decreed certain things for us.

But very early it was recognized that the Koran and the hadith do not speak to all issues. Many are not addressed in either. In the science of Islamic jurisprudence, there is a recognition that issues not mentioned in holy scriptures have to be judged by analogy, by consensus, and other sources of jurisprudence. As long as such judgments do not conflict with the Koran or the hadith, they are considered to be Shariah.

Are there any Muslim American groups that do good works on behalf of their fellow man, Muslim and non-Muslim?
Yes, there are such groups, and they also do good works for non-Muslims. Many of them are associated with mosques and have soup kitchens that become especially active during times like Ramadan. As the American

Muslim community continues to grow, it is developing more such communal giving.

You have said that Muslims emigrating here today are much closer to families in their homelands than immigrants of former times. What are the effects of this closeness?

Before answering that question, let me interject something that pertains. There's an article on me in the 1/24/03 issue of *The Jewish Week*, a weekly newspaper, about how I am trying to put forth a specifically American Islam, a theologically orthodox yet culturally *American* Islam that reflects the best of whatever America has to offer. That's a major theme of my talks and discussions, namely, as Islam spreads to different societies, it restates its theology in the cultural setting of the people. And our challenge today is to do just that.

Your question—about the closeness today of Muslim immigrants to their homeland families—reflects on this. In the past when people came to America, a century ago or longer, their ability to continue relationships with their families in the Old World was limited because travel was difficult, and expensive, and communications were practically nonexistent. Today we have the Internet, we have telephones, we can book a tour for six days and seven nights at post-Christmas special fares. Now I can fly actually to the other side of the world, to Malaysia, for about the same price, or less, than I could fly to the Midwest over the Christmas holidays. So, such means of maintaining communication have made recent immigrants, not only Muslims but immigrants from all parts of the world, capable of maintaining their ties with the Old World. Because of this, there is a faster and greater ability of the Old World societies to be influenced by the New World through the mediation of the immigrant communities. American Muslims now are in a better position to communicate a newer, American form of Islam to their relatives abroad, and thereby influence their thinking about Islam. This is to the good, I believe.

Another interviewee says he thinks the reason the terrorists bombed us was that they fear the cultural intrusion of America, the blending of values, and the endangerment to their way of life. Do you agree?

No. These are minor factors, very minor. Certainly, there is a natural resistance to cultural intrusion, intrusion of values at some level. But I believe that the real issue lies in an expression made famous by Tip O'Neill: *All politics is local*. Personally, I believe that the reason for the animosity of some Muslim fundamentalists or extremists against America has to do really with their inability to be part of the government process, part of the political process of their own governments. By attacking us, they are attacking their own governments. Their attacks in Saudi Arabia, for example, expressed their frustration at not being able to participate in the political process there. The reason they blame the United States is that they believe we are supporting the Saudis. They feel if the Saudi government were not being supported by us, it would have been easier for them to express their opposition to it.

In any society, whether it's Muslim or non-Muslim, that's what people want. It was what motivated the whole idea of the American Revolution and its contemporary, the French Revolution. It was about people wanting to be part of the political process and participating in the economic well-being of the country, or the wealth of the nation, and they feel they have a rightful share in that. It is my conviction that all conflicts of that nature have to do with issues of economics or politics, by which I mean that people want fair and equal representation in issues of government and in opportunities for economic well-being. The issue of different values that your subject mentioned is a factor, but it is to me not the prime factor, no more than a very small third. If a society has a political democratic regime and no corruption, if it has the principles of liberal capitalism and economic well-being, if it has democracy, there would be no worry about the issue of values.

It would all come out in the wash.

One doesn't hear much today about the Islamic institutions of higher learning in the Middle East where young men used to go for advanced study to become scholars and ayatollahs. Are these institutions still in existence?

The disinvestment of Islamic studies has contributed to confusion in the Muslim world. The classical higher institutions of Islamic learning, which were very highly regarded a century or half century ago, were ignored by their governments. The result is that the tradition of brilliant minds becoming brilliant Muslim scholars has been set aside in favor of training engineers, bankers, and other professionals. Al-Azhar University in Egypt, today, for example, does not hold the regard it had a century ago. Countries like Turkey, Iraq, and Egypt during the twentieth century sought to become more secular, so they didn't invest much in religious studies. Young professionals wanted to become military officers or engineers, and few were encouraged to take up a religious career because there seemed to be no future in it. Within a generation or two, the tradition of training cutting-edge religious scholarship had been lost. One of the things we are trying to establish in the Muslim community is an Institution of Advanced Learning where the heritage of Islam can be recaptured, anywhere in the world.

The problem is that the Muslim world needs to train future minds to think about important issues of today—for example, the separation of church and state. Such questions as, *What is an ideal Islamic society to look like?* cannot be discussed honestly in an authoritarian political climate. It can only be done in a free country and a free society. It is our hope certainly that in this country such an institute can be established. It is certainly something whose time has come.

Do you think that Muslims in America will be able to preserve their relatively religious Islamic lifestyle (prayer five times a day, attendance at mosque, fasting at Ramadan), or will it be weakened in a non-religious Western culture?
America is a very easy country. You can live any way you want—you can live a Mormon lifestyle, an Amish lifestyle, or a very atheistic lifestyle. You can be anything you want in this country as long as you're not a national security threat. My sense, though, is that in the long term, there will come out of the Muslim immigrant experience an American expression of Islam.

Can you expand on that subject, the American expression of Islam?
That is my favorite subject. I believe when you look at the history of Christianity in America, when Christians first came, for example, within a couple of generations the religion assumed a different character from the Christianity of the Old World. Actually, even in the Old World you had differences between German Lutherans and Swedish Lutherans, so much so that when they came here, they wouldn't even speak to each other. The same thing with Judaism. The Jews came here and they established their immigrant synagogues and you had Polish synagogues and German Jewish synagogues and Hungarian synagogues. And God forbid, if you came from a family of German Jews and you wanted to marry a Polish Jewish girl—that was considered like marrying downward in society. But after a generation or two, a culturally American Judaism emerged, and more than just cultural. I mean, look at what's happened to Judaism in America. There is Reform Judaism and Reconstructive Judaism. These are all American phenomena and when you look at, say, the different Baptist churches of America, these transformations are a uniquely American phenomenon.

So it is my conviction that the same thing is bound to happen to the Islamic experience. How it will take shape is something history will determine; but we can, by looking at the history of our Christian and Jewish predecessors, foretell some broad outlines. The idea of an American Islam excites me because I believe it is an American Islam that will provide the solution on a couple of major issues. The issues, let's say, of the separation of church and state in Islam will come from American Islam or the American Islamic experience. And if and when that comes about, I'd like it to be known that American Islam was its parent and nourisher. The notion of democratic pluralism, the notion of liberalism, capitalism, mediation between the Muslim world and America, will be dealt with in the American Islamic experience. American Islam is the solution. It's like Islam with an American flag attached.

The many different religious experiences in America, and the impact of America upon religion, are something that I've been reading up on and studying. For a while I thought Muslims were going through a separate religious experience peculiar to Islam in America. But then I realized it's *not* part of the Islamic experience; it's the *immigrant* religious experience. Let's trace a commonality of experience: Witness what Protestants went through, how Protestantism changed and reformed itself, the forming of different sects and denominations, many of which took root in the immigrant experience. Consider the history of America Catholicism in America. It was the American branch that led to the reformation of Vatican II. Many people don't realize what a profound influence America had on Vatican II. American Catholicism became the tail that wagged the Vatican. Today American Catholicism is probably the most influential arm of the Catholic Church.

Thus, by looking at the American Protestant experience, the American Catholic experience, you begin to see patterns that are common with the Muslim experience. You'll note that America has had a tremendous, transformative influence on Christianity and Judaism. The same, I believe, will be true of Islam in America. If there aren't obvious similarities, if there isn't a median component, then, in effect, take a microscope and use a different level of focus. You get new perspectives somehow that really put things into place.

Can America be considered the hope of the Islamic world?
Everybody looks to America, and therefore American Islam has to lead. We have to lead. Because the rest of the Muslim world is in a miserable funk.

Is it the only hope for Islam?
Yes, but also for America. If our Department of Homeland Security was born out of 9/11, it was born out of the flash point that led our American leadership to believe that such destruction was the true face of Islam. If the Department of Homeland Security is to be successful, its most powerful ally would be an American Islam that represents the real Islam of moderation, acceptance, and love.

It could be America's most powerful tool.

Aumrita Choudhury

Bridging Islamic school with Kennedy High

I like being with different kinds of people instead of only Muslims. I feel comfortable with children of many different religions—Catholics, Jews, Protestants.

Sometimes, when she [mother] doesn't cook, we'll go to McDonald's or Taco Bell. My brother can drive and he takes us.

Since 9/11 things seemed to change. I get the impression from everywhere that people think all Muslims are bad. But we haven't changed.

Photo courtesy of the Ahmad family.

Fourteen-year-old **Aumrita Choudhury**, shown on the previous page with her mother, Sharmin Ahmad (whose interview appears elsewhere in this book), has made the jump, at this writing, from Islamic school to a public school, John F. Kennedy High School in Silver Spring, Maryland. It is not an easy thing to do for a student reared in a school like the Muslim Community School in Potomac, Maryland, which she attended for over ten years. It had religious ambience, where girls wore green uniforms and head scarves, prayers were performed at noon and midafternoon, and the boys and girls sat in separate areas of the classroom. That school is one-tenth the size of Kennedy. But an even more momentous change for Aumrita is her sudden catapulting into pop culture prevalent throughout American high schools, where girls wear blue jeans, date, and are not averse to using racy language. Nonetheless, Kennedy is also a place where she is tasting the delicious small freedoms of American culture. Most of her friends at Muslim Community decided to stay put; very few chose to make the switch. Of those who did, some returned to the old school.

In her narration, Ami (most of her Kennedy schoolmates call her Ami because they can't pronounce her name) describes her journey and the consequences thereof. They are changing her life, adding variety no less than personal strife and challenge. Overall, the change is molding her into a tested, involved American girl. On her part, she is introducing to "insular" young Americans a new kind of living and spiritual practice.

I am Aumrita Choudhury. My mother tells me my name means "life-giving, heavenly nectar." Most of my friends call me Rita. At school, those who can't pronounce my name call me Ami. In French, that means "friend."

I am fourteen years old and am in my first year at John F. Kennedy High School. It's a public high school. Up until now I've been going to an Islamic school. I like it at Kennedy. You see more people there. And different types—not only American Muslims. At the Islamic school, everybody was Muslim. At Kennedy, most of the students are Christian. There is one Buddhist, and some Jews. There are a lot more things to do at Kennedy, especially extracurricular activities. The biggest class I have is thirty but most of them are small, fifteen or so. I've made new friends, both boys and girls. There are about two thousand students at Kennedy. In the Islamic school there were two hundred, from nursery to eleventh grade.

Every day we did part of the salat, the *zuhr* at midday and the *asr* in the afternoon. We performed them, in Arabic, in the masjid (the mosque), which is in the school. Before starting the prayers, everybody would go to the bathroom where we did the *wudu*, which is the washing of the hands, arms, face, and feet to make ourselves clean. We had one more class after the prayers and then we went home and did the last two prayers—the *maghrib* at sunset and the *isha* at night. The early-morning prayer is called the *fajr*. Now that I'm at Kennedy, I don't say any prayers at school. I get home about two in the afternoon and start the prayers then. If you don't have a chance to do the salat when you're supposed to, you can say the prayers later in the day when you're not so busy.

We also had a special Islamic studies class and that was about two or three times a week. They taught it at levels suitable to the grades. Arabic class was begun in the first grade and upward, and we eventually learned how to read it. I went through six or seven years of Arabic. I may write and read it, but can't really understand it. They start teaching you words and stuff in about the sixth or seventh grade. In the earlier grades, they teach you the letters, and how to put them together, how to read them. I liked it because when I learned how to read, I could read the Koran. In English you learn the words right away and can speak them, but in Arabic to speak at all you have to be very patient. In print you read from the right side to the left, then you go back to the right side, and read to the left, all the way down the page. My older brother can't understand spoken Arabic, but he also can read and write it. My stepdad speaks Arabic. He's an Egyptian.

At the school I learned about Islam and how to be a practicing Muslim. Now that I'm in a public high school, I don't plan to continue Islamic studies. There is a Saturday class for students like myself, but I'm not going to it. In Islamic schools, the boys and girls are in one class together, but they separate the room into two sections, one for boys and one for girls. So you don't sit directly next to the boys. That's the way it is from kindergarten right through high school. The only time they separate us completely in different rooms are in the Islamic education class and physical ed.

At first I didn't think I would be able to adapt to Kennedy. So many students, and the school itself was so big! So many classrooms, so many hallways. It was confusing at first. I've been here since August 23—almost two months. I've gotten more used to it and feel better. So far I've met about four Muslim American students. There are more. I couldn't tell whether they were Muslim but after we started talking, they told me. I said, *Oh, I am, too*. You can't tell by looks, really.

At Kennedy, my classes are the usual freshman classes. As my language choice, I'm taking Japanese. A foreign language is required. When I was very small, my brother and me used to watch those Japanese cartoons on television. I just got interested in the language because they actually speak Japanese in them and there were subtitles. It just seemed like an interesting language. A lot of people think Chinese and Japanese are alike, but they are very different.

At home my mother and stepfather always speak English. They never talk in Arabic. My mother is from Bangladesh and she speaks Bengali.

We go to a mosque usually during celebrations like Ramadan when you fast for a month. During Ramadan you abstain from food and water all day and you eat your main meal in the evening, usually in a mosque. You also go to the mosque at this time to pray. We try to go two or three times a week during Ramadan.

At Kennedy, I usually wear jeans and a T-shirt, not too short. I don't wear a head scarf. I dress like everyone else. For a while, I was thinking about wearing a head scarf, but then decided it would be too hard. It would be weird for other people to see my wearing it one day and taking it off the next day.

At the Islamic school, I wore the head scarf every day. The uniform for the girls was a dress that came down to the knee or right above the knee. They changed the uniform a few times. The one I used to wear was a green uniform with black cuffs and black pants. Families bought their own pants. The school gave us the uniform. The pants had to be black. We were allowed to wear sneakers, any color. The boys had to wear a green shirt and black pants. Green is the color of Islam.

When I grow up, I think I might start wearing the head scarf. I don't mind people knowing immediately that I'm an American Muslim. It's just I don't know yet if I will be able to manage wearing it all the time, in the spring, in the summer. It's not always comfortable.

At the Islamic school, they served lunch every day. They served a lot of different things, like spaghetti, tacos, hamburgers, something different each day. Sometimes an Iranian dish like rice and beans. I liked it. And I like the salmon curry my mother cooks. She makes it with tomato and lima beans. Sometimes, when she doesn't cook, we'll go to McDonald's or Taco Bell. My brother can drive, and he takes us.

I like being with different types of people instead of only Muslims. I feel comfortable with children of many different religions—Catholics, Jews, Protestants. You learn about their religion, and they learn about yours. I would say that I am religious. I think about God and I pray a lot. My mother is religious. My grandmother who is visiting us prays and does the salat every day. She lives in Bangladesh. She is visiting us and seeing an eye doctor.

From my class at the Islamic school, all the boys, except one, went on to a public high school. Of the girls, only four out of eleven or twelve left and seem happy with the change. But generally, the girls like the Islamic school more. Even some of the ones who go on to a public high school leave and come back. The four girls in my class who left seem comfortable in the new school. But one of my friends who is in tenth grade left public high school this year to go back to the Islamic school. My brother, by the way, now goes to the University of Maryland.

When Muslim students leave public high school and go back to a Muslim school, I think it's because of the new environment. A friend of mine asked a Muslim girl why she came back and she said, *Oh, the school. Almost everyone is white and you begin to feel different. It isn't easy to be there.*

At Kennedy I've joined the field hockey team but right after that, the sniper shooting started and the games were all canceled. Other than that, I take karate and horseback riding outside the school. At my old school, they didn't have that many sports for girls and couldn't get a female coach. But we did have a karate team. The karate coach is the same one for boys and girls. They were trying to form a volleyball team but no one knows what happened to that. The boys had all kinds of sports and had a coach just for themselves.

My mom doesn't want us to watch anything that's bad on TV or in the movies. Too much sex or shooting is out. I watch cartoons. But a lot of my friends, other Muslim girls, watch shows like *Friends*. They're allowed to. We go to movies. We recently saw *The Tuxedo* with Jackie Chan but I liked *Shanghai Knights* with Jackie Chan better. We've seen *Minority Report* with Tom Cruise and *The Bourne Identity*. Action movies are okay.

On 9/11, when that terrible attack happened at the World Trade Center, I was still at Islamic school. They brought us down to watch the news on the TV. At first, I thought the plane had accidentally flown into the building. We didn't know what was happening. They closed the school early. Since 9/11 things seemed to change. I get the impression from everywhere that people think all Muslims are bad. But we haven't changed. We had an assembly at school. They told us to be careful of any strangers on the grounds. They told us to keep making a good impression outside.

Later on, there were two snipers who were killing people from their car in the Maryland, Washington, D.C. and Virginia areas. I wasn't that frightened and I still went out. My feeling about these things is that if I get shot, it's God's will. If God wants to take you, He'll take you. But a lot of kids are scared, and their parents, too. The kids who used to walk to school, their parents are now driving them. My mom doesn't want us to go out when it's not necessary. When she went out to buy gas, she used to take us with her, but not now.

Alma Jadallah

Is conflict resolution a new way to bring peace to a badgered world?

I am often asked, "If this field had been more advanced, could it have helped prevent 9/11?"

After 9/11, people started to realize that the average person should become more interested and understanding of what's going on in the world and not leave everything up to the academics and politicians.

I like being in America. I was educated in Western schools in Cairo and am therefore bilingual and well-versed in English ... America allows me to perform at my fullest potential.

Photo courtesy of Alma Jadallah.

The large number of American Muslim women like **Alma Jadallah** who attend colleges and universities and receive advanced degrees in different disciplines is surprising in view of the fact that these women are considered downtrodden. Some emigrated from other countries where they attended school and in this country continued their education for advanced degrees. They are among our brightest and most successful graduates and their accomplishments in professional life are impressive since English is not their native tongue. They are entering the medical, business, legal, management and computer fields and are even spearheading paths in new disciplines. Three of these women are profiled in this book. Two are foreign born and one was born here. They are Asma Hasan, an American-born author and lawyer; Sharmin Ahmad, a Bangladeshi who attended George Washington University; and Alma Jadallah, who is presently studying for her doctorate in conflict resolution at George Mason University. Alma Jadallah's narrative follows.

Since September 11, the field of conflict resolution is especially relevant to our times. The fateful day in the year 2001 had one very positive result: it has given this fledgling discipline a tremendous spur. The central aim of conflict resolution is to revolutionize the relationships between nations, between communities and between opposing points of views. A still-developing discipline, it promises bright hopes for mankind's future.

Ms. Jadallah, an American Muslim woman born in Saudi Arabia, narrates a fascinating account of the history and development of this field, as well as her own involvement and personal journey in it. Ms. Jadallah, whose full name is Alma Abdul-Hadi Jadallah, is a graduate of George Mason University in Fairfax, Virginia, where she is now studying for her doctorate. She is also, simultaneously, a senior organizational consultant at a Fortune 500 company and a wife and mother of two children. All of this serves to indicate the strength and determination of American Muslim women in their enactment of the American dream.

Not many people know of my profession. It is of relatively recent origin and has come into more prominence since 9/11. It is called *conflict resolution*, and you can call me a *conflict practitioner*.

What is conflict resolution all about? It sounds like a very desirable thing, but what exactly is it? Can it be a possible solution to some of the world's great conflicts? Accepting the assumption that conflict is an integral part of life—whether it is war or certain groups dominating other groups—this field is very much interested in finding and understanding alternative ways of dealing with it. Scholars, particularly from the international-relations field, realized that all our responses to conflict of whatever source were not giving us adequate solutions. So they became interested in studying conflict as a science on the community, international and global level. The objective was to introduce a paradigm shift that allows a more constructive, elaborative resolution of conflict, particularly as it relates to deep-rooted issues that deal with ethnicity and identity.

As time went on, more and more people got interested and a program began developing and drawing in from many different disciplines. It borrowed from sociology, specifically, how people behave in a community. It started to borrow from psychology and to study interpersonal conflict, that is, how two people might interact. It started to study environmental conflict, conflicts over water resources around the world and over indigenous lands. And thus the field began addressing different conflicts on all levels, interpersonal, group, communal, national, international, and global.

We looked at how individuals deal with conflict both on the intrapersonal and interpersonal levels, hoping to understand what constitutes right or wrong for them and how to better understand their reaction to conflict situations that they find themselves in.

The field became interested in understanding how culture contributes to a people's value systems and how it influences their choices when their value system is being threatened. We also looked at how it would inform future resolution of issues and what constitutes a resolution that is acceptable. Take, for example, the abortion conflict in the United States. It is one that continues to polarize communities and has led in many instances to violent reactions from individuals and groups. Any meaningful resolution will have to incorporate and be considerate of the value systems of the individuals and cultures involved.

The field has become involved in many different arenas. For example, on the international level, it took the Northern Ireland conflict and the Arab-Israeli conflict and started studying the sources of each and how the parties are addressing it and what role other actors contributed to it. In the Arab-Israeli conflict, many conflict resolution practitioners have facilitated problem-solving models in workshops with formal and informal actors with the objective of breaking down psychological barriers that hinder cooperation on any sustainable solutions and that help address intergroup conflict. Other models include educational workshops and dialogue projects that create a safe environment for interaction.

The conflict-resolution program at George Mason University was initiated by a group of concerned scholars and citizens. John Burton, an Australian diplomat, was one of the leading founders of the program and introduced basic human-needs theory as a foundational theory for the field. In it he argues that there are basic human needs that will be pursued by individuals at any cost and unless fulfilled, the individuals will do anything to satisfy them. For example, the needs for identity and security are often pursued by certain groups and, unless they are satisfied, they are pursued violently.

John Burton capitalized on his diplomatic experiences to help introduce the idea of third parties. In Burton's methodology, third parties can be impartial facilitators who can, through a controlled communication process, help foster an open and supportive environment between disputing parties. They can help them analyze the conflict, examine their perceptions of one another, and assist them in working through an innovative approach to deal with the conflict.

In 1981, the late Brian Wedge, along with Burton and other colleagues, continued to help develop ICAR (Institute for Conflict Analysis and Resolution) and train professional practitioners in conflict management. The program now is known internationally for its Masters and Ph.D. departments. ICAR continues to work on many protracted conflicts.

And so the conflict resolution field started to gain interest and it was very strongly associated with what is termed "peace studies." One of the giants in peace studies is a Norwegian named Johan Galtung who has written many publications on the subject.

Peace study is understanding different models of reconciliation and ways with which people can reach inner peace and external peace with the environment. Galtung writes extensively about the role of religion in the way individuals understand violence and non-violent approaches. He discusses the Abrahamic religions and how they compare with Buddhism. Galtung's work helps us understand nonviolent approaches to conflict and helps inform future actions that could implement these approaches.

Among the questions Galtung is trying to answer is, *How can nations and people resolve deep protracted conflicts through nonviolent actions, such as forming a human chain to offset war in war-torn areas?* Galtung and Burton were very strong contributors to the field. And after them, many other people who now comprise the faculty at George Mason have made valid contributions. The university has a complete curriculum in conflict resolution. Students can study for a master's degree. In the nineteen-eighties, George Mason was one of the first institutes to offer a doctorate.

For the future, my hope is that the study of conflict resolution will inform us on how best to address deep-rooted issues that continue to polarize us and how to assist in reducing violent responses to these issues and thus enhance our ability to work collaboratively and constructively with one another. It seems that we keep failing to think about different ways to deal with issues related to poverty. In spite of all the existing programs to eradicate hunger and avoid having a disenfranchised community, we still witness high levels of conflict and institutional inability to respond to it.

We need to rethink ways and come up with approaches to deal with harmful adversity between people. For example, in the United States, litigation drives most of our responses to issues. If anything, it contributes to an increase in adversity and ruptured relationships. Today, we see more and more interest in one form of dispute resolution, called "mediation." This allows the parties in the conflict, through the assistance of a skilled and trained mediator, to come up with the most sustainable solutions that can address the grievances of both sides. Mediation now is offered in the courts to divorcing couples, in small-claims court and in business to help resolve conflicts.

I am currently president of the board of one of the largest mediation centers in northern Virginia. Northern Virginia Mediation Services offers mediation services to the community with the objective of assisting communities and parties in the peaceful resolution of conflicts.

People historically have mediated situations. We study mediation models across cultures with the objective of identifying those that are meaningful for people from different parts of the world. Therefore, mediation—not necessarily the way we practice it in the West—has been practiced over time. In North America it has become institutionalized and we find that many individuals from very diverse professional backgrounds are interested in learning about it. The field is so young and a lot of people are interested. Some call themselves conflict resolvers and come from many disciplines. Some work in social services, in the law, in international relations, in nongovernmental (not-for-profit) organizations, or NGOs. (These are organizations that allow an opportunity for other representatives from the communities to have a say in decision-making and allow more participatory, representative views in the decisions that happen.)

Incidentally, it is very critical for us practitioners in conflict resolution to understand the role of non-governmental actors. They are often present in not-for-profit or for-profit organizations. John McDonald and Louise Diamond coined the term "multitrack diplomacy." It is an approach utilizing different levels of activities from professionals to help support peace-building and peace-making in a society. On one level, you have the political, like President Bush, presidents of countries, diplomats, kings, queens, the official hierarchy within a society. This level might be called Track One, the official track. Another track might be influential leaders in the community. Religious leaders might be another track. The way we'd like to think about it is that these are levels and tracks that we practitioners can partner with. We believe that society has so many different layers and the question becomes, *How can they all come together and contribute to better ways of justice and fairness to help support peace-making and peace-building in their communities?* They would be resources that you could pull on and train and work with to help introduce change in a community. They become a critical mass to help support the required change.

I am often asked, *If this field had been more advanced, could it have helped prevent 9/11?* This is the question I've chosen for my dissertation: the perceived role of conflict resolvers in a critical event like September 11, 2001. People interested in conflict resolution have been saying, *Are we equipped enough to deal with such a critical event and if so, were we able to address a critical event like 9/11?*

Every time something happens, we witness top-down responses to the issues, mostly power-based, often reinforcing the dominance of one particular group or ideology over the other. Without a deep understanding of the root causes that lead or have led to extreme violent behavior, there is no real resolution to the issues. Robert Fisk, a prominent British journalist, who spoke at George Mason recently, addressed the theme of *Why they did it, not Who did it.* [Referring to 9/11.] So we're always arguing that if we understand the deep-rooted sources of conflict, then we can help facilitate an environment in which all the stakeholders help formulate solutions that are meaningful and sustainable.

A core component of the field of conflict resolution is to *think preventively*. It was John Burton who coined the idea "preventive thinking." And Galtung takes an analogy from the medical field that says we need to look into the health of society and think preventively the same way preventive measures are taken to avoid sickness. If we were to foster a conflict-resolution education that helps individuals understand how to better build inclusive processes that would include *all* stakeholders, it may very well serve as a preventive way to help address conflicts that occur because of exclusionary behavior or uninformed action. The desired goal is to be proactive, mapping out any potential sources of conflict as, for example, the lack of representation of certain groups in a community. To empower communities, you teach, educate, and create an environment for people where there is healthy dialogue and preventive thinking to help foster collaboration and integration and diffuse any potential sticking points that may lead to escalation. You think of alternative ways to deal with conflict.

Does that make sense?

Let's bring it back to your topic. Take the Islamic community in North America as an example. One of the things that continues to surface all the time is the lack of representation of the Islamic community on an institutional level, whether it's in the government or in the area of natural profit. So, if there were grievances, i.e., things that the community felt were important to them but never expressed, then at some point, the trigger may be an escalation, something may happen in the community that would escalate into a public conflict, something in the public arena.

If you were to think preventively, every time there is something important in the community that may affect members of that community, the first question you'd have to ask is, *In this roundtable of people who are making decisions— let's assume it's a roundtable—does it have someone from the Islamic community to talk on their behalf? Are these people true representatives of the community? Do they represent the community on gender levels? Do they represent women and children?*

You start thinking preventively and you facilitate within that community dialogue the handling of whatever problems need to be addressed. And that would be a preventive way for engaging in civil discourse with a community that is part of the larger society. And you do the same with other groups. You can take it to ethnic groups and across educational levels. Thus, we encourage a lot of the preventive work that needs to be done.

It's important to clarify an important point in my explanation of conflict resolution. At the core of it is the idea of a third party, that is, practitioners, people who are specially trained in facilitation and problem-solving and dialogue processes. The third party must be professionally qualified to do this. It should not be done by mediators who do not have the background and expertise that are required.

I am one of these practitioners of the conflict-resolution field. We're a professional group that has developed over time in North America. That is our role. We think we have a ticket to facilitate more constructive dialogue when things don't go well. Again, take 9/11. We might we have prevented it, but we don't know that. But we know we could have brought communities, I refer to polarized communities, together—we like to think that this could happen—to talk about the issues, to talk about the sources of the issues, to bring together more collaborative sources.

What, specifically, could I and my group have done to prevent the disaster of 9/11? What could we have done as a nation to prevent it? A lot of stuff, of course, and I don't have the full answer. Maybe gain more understanding of the Islamic world? More understanding of the grievances they had against the United States? Have engaged them in a more preventive way, rather than in a reactive way? There were pockets of discontent. Instead of having people imprisoned or put away in cells, we could have gone and done more education, look at really what was the source of this anger, of this discontent, actually rage, because the act was so inhumane. It was horrible. These are the things we didn't do, the questions that remain unanswered. These are things I'm going to be asking and discussing in my dissertation. That's why my dissertation interests me so much because we have these grand ideas and theories that should explain behavior.

Very recently, my colleagues and I used some of our own guidelines to create a community dialogue after the tragic event. We wanted to see what we were actually able to do before 9/11, or could have done. We gathered in our homes a network of people that we knew. We wanted to dialogue and see how we could support one another in our communities. To describe the gathering briefly: We had a couple of sessions and we were lucky to have an African-American member with her community. The objective was to engage in a dialogue around racism and prejudice and for members of both communities to exchange experiences and insights on how best to address it. We convened at her home and we created a safe forum in an environment where people could speak their minds without being threatening to one another. We also did public speaking when we were asked, for that seemed to be of some value to the community.

In many ways, I think that after 9/11 people started to realize that the average person should become more interested and understanding of what's going on in the world and not leave everything up to the academics and politicians. The Middle East shouldn't be just a case study. This is reality. This is real. It impacts on our children. For me personally, 9/11 was threatening on many levels. First, as a mother who fears for her children, and as a wife who fears for her husband. It impacted on my work, on my religion. I'm a Palestinian by descent. There were so many levels of identity that triggered my emotions. And also my allegiance to this country as an immigrant by choice.

I continue to ask questions that drive my dissertation topic. In all of this, could I, as a conflict expert, or aiming to be an expert, offer anything? Did my field equip me with any tools to deal with such a critical event? And how do I know that I made a difference? How would I know that there was something that we were able to offer?

How we ask the question is very important. Asking in the right way could bring more fruitful results. This is a very important point that many of my colleagues who are doing other research are interested in for both teaching and instruction purposes. How do we *frame* the question? You just don't ask who did it! You ask *why* they did it. What is it within our institution that fosters that kind of anger or rage? Why is there such a polarized debate? It isn't even a debate. *You're either with us, or against us.* Why aren't we asking, *how are we all in this together?* Why aren't we using a more appreciative approach in our questioning? We call an appreciative inquiry a question that is put in a gentler, more accommodating mode, like *When we lived well together, what was happening then? How did Alma, a Muslim from the Middle East, and her family behave as good neighbors in their American community? How did they bridge the gap between their cultural background and the new culture that they adopted?*

To repeat, you ask the question in an appreciative mode, not mentioning something that is unflattering but a positive aspect. Not *Why is Alma, an immigrant from the Middle East, so different from her American friends?* but rather, *How do Alma and her American friends have so much in common that they are able to work well together?* The framing is so important and by that I mean how you pose the question, even how you design your thinking about it.

Now that I've told you all about my work (and my passion), let me tell your readers a little about me personally. I was born in 1959 in Saudi Arabia. My father was a businessman there. He is of Palestinian descent. In 1961 he decided to move the family—my mother, brother and me—to Cairo where there were more educational opportunities. We stayed in Egypt for twelve years. My father decided to go back to Saudi Arabia for business reasons, but the family stayed on. Saudi Arabia was still young in developing good education opportunities. In Cairo, my mother went to the American University (AUC) and we benefited a lot from that. I trace my American education, at least informally, to her involvement at AUC.

We also lived in Kuwait, where I went to the American school, and then in Amman, Jordan, where I went to high school and did undergraduate work in English and philosophy. I worked for one year at the ministry of information in Amman and one year at the English broadcasting service where I presented an hour of classical music.

I met my husband Sami (who grew up in Gary, Indiana, by the way) in Amman. He was a general counsel for a company in Saudi Arabia at the time. After marrying, we lived in Saudi Arabia for two and a half years and then we moved to the West, to Geneva, Switzerland. We're parents of three children. Jamil, our first-born child, was named after his grandfather. Our tradition is that the oldest son names his first son after his father. We have twin girls. One is called Laila, a very old Arab word that means "beautiful evenings." Eric Clapton has a famous song with that name. The other twin is Diala. I don't know what that means. My husband picked it.

We moved permanently to America in 1989. Sami was working overseas, but I came with the family to have residency here. My children were born Americans because Sami was American. (He was not born here but had lived here for over forty years). But the children were not naturalized. Frankly, the move was more for getting my citizenship and fulfilling the requirements. We settled here and decided that the United States was better for professional development for me. I went back to school in 1992 and got my master's at George Mason University. I worked for one year with the university and decided to pursue my doctorate.

We settled in Fairfax, Virginia, because it was near my family: my sisters-in-law lived there. Sami was traveling a lot and I needed to be around family. Why Fairfax? The husband of one of Sami's sisters worked for the federal government and that's how the family got there. Another sister followed and then we followed. There are a lot of Muslims in Fairfax. One reason, of course, is that it is close to the federal government and academic institutions. I think the number of Muslims in the area is about one hundred thousand to one hundred and fifty thousand. George Mason University has a Muslim chaplain, as well as chaplains from other denominations. There is much diversity in the Washington metropolitan area.

I like being in America. I grew up in Western schools in Cairo and am therefore bilingual and well versed in English. For me, reading is not a problem. I don't think in Arabic. America allows me to perform at my fullest potential. I stayed home for a couple of years for my children and was able immediately to go back to school. I was also able to work on many, many levels in my community in a very short time. Where could you do this? In less than ten years I am active in so many organizations and feel an integral part of the community. I initially came here because my children are American citizens. But now, I am here by choice.

Chaplain Dawud Agbere

A Muslim chaplain ministers to our military

Military chaplains are not supposed to proselytize … However, chaplains are free to explain their particular faith to those interested. Some are driven by curiosity, while others want to learn about the beliefs and practices of Islam. Others come to ask questions about the misconceptions being peddled, to find out for themselves the true teachings. Still others come solely as seekers, looking for alternative religious paths.

When I enlisted in the U.S. Navy in 1996, there were only two Muslim chaplains on active duty serving in the army and navy. Today we have 12: seven in the army, three in the navy, and two in the air force.

Photo courtesy of Dawud Agbere.

This interview is especially timely in view of the fact that in September 2003, a Muslim chaplain who was assigned to serve the spiritual needs of Muslim prisoners at Guantanamo Bay in Cuba, was arrested under suspicion of espionage, improperly assisting prisoners, and possible other breaches of military duties. The story was widely covered in the media. After being confined for three months on suspicion of espionage activities, he was freed. However, the authorities continued to investigate other possible violations of the military code. The story may become another instance of our need to keep an open mind.

If Americans are curious about what, generally, a Muslim army chaplain does, they will find much to learn on these pages. **Chaplain Dawud Agbere** not only serves the Muslim military, but soldiers of every denomination, and is involved in every aspect of army religious life. By setting forth the duties of army chaplains, be they Christian, Jewish, or Muslim, he specifies the spiritual help and guidance they supply. Reading his interview may strengthen confidence in army chaplains who are Muslims, and thus serve to disarm Islamaphobia wherever it exists.

When he was interviewed, Chaplain Agbere was posted on temporary assignment at Walter Reed Army Medical Center in Washington, D.C. He was then transferred on full assignment to Fort Bliss in El Paso, Texas. Soon after that, he was sent to Iraq on a temporary assignment and at this writing (as of mid-2004) is still serving there.

Will you talk briefly about your background?

I was born and raised in Ghana, a former British colony, on the west coast of Africa. The third of five children, I was raised by two practicing Muslim parents. I am married and my wife shares my African and religious background. My academic pursuit has spanned three different fields (education, political science, and religious studies) in three different countries (Ghana, Sudan, and the United States). My college education began in Sudan where, between 1987 and 1990, I pursued a course leading to a diploma in education and Islamic studies at the International African University (formerly Islamic African Center). In 1994 I graduated from the University of Ghana with a combined major in political science and Arabic.

When did you arrive in America and how did you decide to become a chaplain/imam?

I came to the United States in the nineties and the navy was the first branch of service I joined as an enlisted sailor. But after a year of service, I requested to be discharged since I had decided to become an army chaplain. Four years later I obtained a master's degree in religious practice from the Graduate School of Islamic and Social Sciences in Virginia.

I opted for army chaplaincy because I consider ministry, first and foremost, as an act of faith. Secondly, it is a response to the dire need for qualified Muslims to serve as chaplains in the military and I thought I could make a difference.

As a chaplain at Fort Bliss, what exactly are your duties toward Muslim American soldiers?

As the only Muslim chaplain on the installation, I'm responsible for the religious and spiritual needs of the Muslim community. I plan, coordinate, and conduct Islamic religious services, as well as provide area coverage for surrounding military installations. Also, I serve as a resource on Islamic issues for other chaplains and military leaders.

Do you work with non-Muslim servicemen and advise on any matters other than Islamic?

Yes. My duties and responsibilities encompass all religions at Fort Bliss. I am special staff officer and advisor to the commander and the staff on matters pertaining to religion and spirituality, morale and morality as affected by religion. In these capacities, I am responsible for the unit's religious program and, therefore, issues regarding religion, morale, and morality are my prerogatives. I plan and execute the unit's religious program in line with the commander's guidance and intent to provide for the spiritual and moral development of soldiers and their families. This includes prayer breakfasts, religious studies, and spiritual-fitness classes.

I provide chaplain support to soldiers and their families and facilitate free exercise of religion and spirituality of all personnel regardless of religious, cultural, or national background. Among my duties are counseling, pastoral care, training to boost morale, stress management, conflict resolution, briefing soldiers as to their religious rights, and providing pastoral visitations to sick soldiers and their families.

What is the difference between a chaplain and an imam?

Traditionally, the imam is the one who leads Muslims in prayer and conducts other religious ceremonies. As the religious leader within the military Muslim community, the Muslim chaplain is the equivalent of the imam. He leads his community in prayers, delivers the sermon (*khutbah*) during the Friday midafternoon prayer service (*jum'a*), in addition to other services outside the expertise of the traditional imam. Chaplains are members of the clergy, but Islam has no clergy. However, as far as my understanding is concerned, the difference is either functional or semantics. For instance, the title chaplain may denote an affiliation with public institutions, such as the military, prisons and hospitals. Also, unlike the imam in the local mosque, the chaplain ministers to people within and outside his faith tradition.

Another difference is that the chaplain has to meet certain educational requirements and must be endorsed by a recognized Islamic organization to serve with these institutions. This is not necessarily the case with imams. It's important to note, however, that Muslim chaplaincy is the American Muslim community's response to the religious/spiritual needs of Muslims within the socio-political sphere.

You mentioned that there is a dire need for army chaplains in the military. Can you address this need?

When I first enlisted in the U.S. Navy in 1996, there were only two Muslim chaplains on active duty serving in the army and navy respectively. Today we have a total of twelve: seven in the army, three in the navy, and two in the air force. I remember in basic training how I had to struggle against many odds to meet my religious obligations. My company commanders knew nothing about Islam and therefore were not helpful to me as far as religious accommodation was concerned. There were some civilians who volunteered on Sundays to give instructions on Islam to basic trainees. But because they were not in the military, they couldn't convey my concerns and struggles to the appropriate quarters. I realized from that experience that we need Muslim chaplains in uniform to properly cater for the religious needs of Muslims, as well as to educate and advise military leaders on Islamic issues.

What educational requirements does a Muslim chaplain have to meet?

In the military, he must have a master's degree in a relevant field. I know the federal prison system also has the same requirement. These requirements place them on a certain academic pedestal. However, the imam in the local mosque (I'm speaking strictly within the American context) may have less equivalent or even more academic training than the chaplain, for example, a Ph.D. In fact, some of these imams are accomplished scholars in their fields.

Are you fluent in Arabic? I've heard that it takes many years to achieve fluency.

I'm not sure how you define fluency. I can humbly say that I can communicate fairly well in Arabic, that is, read, write, speak, and do serious academic research.

Has Arabic been helpful to you personally and in your work as army chaplain?

Yes, personally and professionally. Among other things, Arabic has made it possible for me to access Islamic materials for my work from their original sources, without having to grapple with translational gymnastics. I've also gained some respect among many Muslims I've come into contact with because of my Arabic background. Believe it or not, as far as some American Muslims are concerned, Arabic is a measure of competency for imam/chaplains.

Is Arabic in any way similar to your native language, Ghanaian?
The answer to that is an emphatic no.

What do Muslim chaplains wear at their service?
Muslims don't have an ecclesiastical dress which they are mandated to use. Mostly their particular cultural background dictates what is acceptable for their status or otherwise. For instance, while in the U.S., a lot of imams wear suits and ties for their service, but the same may not be appropriate in a typical northern Nigerian mosque. The white outfit I am wearing in the picture you have is not something specific for chaplains or imams. It is only my preference. The dress or gown is actually a cultural costume of the Arab Gulf states. It has different names in Arabic, but the popular name is *abaya*, which is translated as "cape" or simply "gown." The cap is popularly called kufi.

Have you had non-Muslim soldiers convert to Islam?
Military chaplains are not supposed to proselytize. We are not here to make converts out of soldiers. Our raison d'être is to facilitate for the free exercise of their faith or lack of it.

However, chaplains are free to explain their particular faith tradition to those interested. Some are driven by curiosity, while others want to learn about the beliefs and practices of Islam. Others come to ask questions about some of the misconceptions being peddled around, to find out for themselves the true teachings. Still others come solely as seekers, looking for alternative religious paths. This last category includes soldiers who either have no religion at all or are dissatisfied with the traditions in which they were raised. I've seen non-Muslims soldiers in all of these categories accept Islam.

Are there any Muslim women in the military?
Yes, there are. Some were raised Muslims. Others embraced Islam in the service.

Is Islam as practiced here different from Islam as practiced in Ghana?
I think the major difference is knowledge. The average Muslim in America is more likely to be more knowledgeable about the beliefs and practices of Islam than his or her Ghanaian brother or sister. That is understandable considering the differences in literacy rates and educational opportunities between the two societies. I believe both are doing their best to meet their obligations toward their Creator.

How did you, as a Muslim, cope with the tragedy of 9/11?
I was stationed at Fort Sill, Oklahoma, when 9/11 struck. It was a difficult time for the Muslim community. I lost a cousin in the attack. However, we were able to process it among ourselves and moved ahead with our lives. It was a busy

time as well. I was sought after for interviews, lectures, as well as for responses to newspaper articles. When I reflect on 9/11, I see it as a test of faith.

Is Agbere an adopted Islamic name, or is it a family name?

Agbere is a tribal family name. Dawud is the name I was given at birth. It is the Muslim name for David. However, I would like to clarify an important point. There seems to be a tendency for people to confuse Arabic names for Islamic names. It's a fact that traditional Muslim names are Arabic. However, an Arabic name may not necessarily be Islamic. Likewise, an Islamic name does not necessarily have to be Arabic. It's the meaning of a name, not language, that determines its Islamic character or otherwise. For instance, tradition tells us that Prophet Muhammad made some of his companions change their names when they first embraced Islam because their original names had bad meaning, and thereby conflicted with the teachings of Islam.

How many generations has your family been Muslim?

Four generations. My great-grandparents were the first to embrace Islam.

Do your siblings still practice the religion of Islam?

Yes, they do.

How many children do you have and do you plan to send them to public or Islamic school?

I have three children: a daughter, Bilqiis, who is eight; my son, Ejaya, who is one; and my baby son, Tilahta, who was born in 2003.

This issue of which type of school we will choose for them is something my wife and I have been discussing lately. The fact is, we may not have the luxury of sending our kids to an Islamic school, even if we would like to, because one may not be available and would require tuition. In any case, we would love to send our kids to a public school. It is economically prudent. I'm a product of the Ghanaian public school system. However, like other parents (Muslim, Christian, Jewish) we have concerns with some of the values kids pick up from the public school system.

By no means am I suggesting that the Islamic schools are perfect, and for that matter, the private school system in general. They do have their problems, too. As far as we are concerned, education is more than learning to read and write. It's a process of total transformation of the human person, intellectually, socially, spiritually. We place a high premium on issues like respect, discipline, modesty. These are nonnegotiable, and I expect schools to impart these values to my three kids. I hope I can send my kids to whichever school meets this expectation. We are also considering partially raising them in Africa to afford them the opportunity to appreciate their ancestral roots.

Zaki Hanafy

Immigrant cabbie, former lawyer, with a love for the U.S.

" *As an Egyptian lawyer practicing in Alexandria, I read about the American system and the law … I realized there is something of much value in the U.S. and it led me to leave my nation, leave my people, leave my career, and come here to live and stay. How I would live didn't matter.*

Since 9/11 I'm happy to say that no customer or passenger has ever insulted me or made unflattering remarks by associating my religion with the terrorists.

I'm not concerned about bringing them [children] up in American culture … American culture is not much different from that of any other country. "

Photo courtesy of Henry Cateura.

Zaki Hanafy has been a cabdriver in Brooklyn, New York, for over ten years. He is a Muslim, born in Egypt. Before emigrating to New York in 1985, he was a trial lawyer and comes from a family of professionals.

Mr. Hanafy came here specifically because he is enamored of human rights, and the United States is the only country he knows of that grants them to everyone living in it. He is here in tribute to that great gift that America provides. Despite the fact that language and finances have kept him from pursuing the law in the United States, he does not act like a disillusioned immigrant. He is happy to be here and both his children are American-born. His narration reveals an exceptional idealism and love for this country.

I'm an immigrant Muslim who came here from Egypt eighteen years ago, and have a few things to say—drawn from my own experience—about American immigrants. As far as I can see, there are three kinds of people coming to the U.S. Some come because they respect the American Constitution and the rights it grants all human beings. Others come to live here because jobs are available. And some come for advanced education in the sciences and technology. I belong to the first group.

When you come over to be a citizen, like myself, because you respect the American Constitution and what it provides for people, this means you know the value of America, what's good in America, and how it is different from other places. For myself, as an Egyptian lawyer practicing in Alexandria, I read about the American system and the law. I not only read the U.S. Constitution, but also the constitutions of Egypt, European nations, the third-world nations and I could see the differences. So, I realized there is something of much value in the U.S. and it led me to leave my nation, leave my people, leave my career, and come to live here and to stay. *How* I would live didn't matter.

Now I want to make a comment on religion, which is the subject of your book. I come from a nation that has *two* very popular religions. The first is Islam and the other is Christianity. Now, I am a Muslim in [largely] Christian America. That doesn't bother me at all. We have a lot of Christian people in Egypt who live peacefully side by side with Egyptians. When I grew up, in school, the student beside me was a Christian. We lived together. I shared all his celebrations with him, Christmas and other occasions. When he got married, I went to the church. We don't have much discrimination or hatred for different religions. But this doesn't mean that there was no extremism on each side. We have Muslim extremism and fundamentalism. In Egypt we suffered a lot from this. Sadat was killed. The reason he was killed was because he was a man of peace. He made peace with Israel and this didn't make the extremists happy and they did what they did with him.

I also want to say that people no longer come to the United States to exercise their religion, as the early Americans did. Today people come looking for jobs, education and, especially, for freedom—*liberty*.

Liberty is a word that covers many things. Liberty is not meant only to exercise your vote or your religion. Liberty is human rights and the United States Constitution guarantees liberty for all people. This is very important. Now everywhere in the world, there are laws called human rights. But the laws are not necessarily enforced. The question should be: Is the constitution of this nation respected by its leaders, is it working, is it enforced? In America the Constitution works. It is respected, it is enforced, and it provides *liberty*. I'm here since 1985. I don't find anything that bothers me, especially in the field I know, which is the law. I drive a taxi limousine now, but originally I was a lawyer. I see how the law is enforced here. The United States Constitution, the human rights laws, are real. They're not only in the books.

As for the disaster of September 11, this is the way I, as an American Muslim, see it. Look at the people who did it. Number One: they are *not* American citizens. They came to this nation for some ulterior purpose. They didn't come to be an American, like myself, or even to work here. If we look more deeply, some came as students, but they were not serious students and if they studied, it was not to be a doctor or engineer. Incidentally, those who do study and become doctors or engineers, they're of great benefit, and if they stay here, as a good number do, they're going to be of benefit to the people here. If they go back to their country, they will benefit the people there.

The men who caused the World Trade Center disaster are not normal people. They are sick in the head. They are Muslim but do not understand Islam correctly. And even people who *teach* Islam do not always understand Islam correctly. Certainly, all Muslims believe the Koran is God's word, coming through the Prophet Muhammad. But remember, the Koran speaks in Arabic symbols and words, and many Muslims cannot read Arabic. Actually, the Koran makes a point of identifying who exactly knows the meaning of these words, and who is able to interpret these symbols and words. It says *God knows, the Prophet knows, and people who are scholars of the Koran know*. Not everybody can understand the Koran in the same way that he reads the newspaper and understands what is meant. So when you have a Muslim saying, *The Koran says this, the Koran says that, we don't do this, we don't do that*, stand back, he may be all wrong. By simply reading the Koran is not the way to understand it.

Now, how does the average Muslim know his Islamic religion, if not directly from the Koran? The average Muslim is Muslim because he is told, and thereby learns, that you have to believe in God, that Muhammad is a prophet, and this is how to pray, this is how to fast, and how to do this, how to do that. But the Koran has a lot more things than that. The Koran's breadth is enormous and talks about everything in human life. It says everything can touch human life. Understanding all that is revealed in the Koran is not an easy job.

In the Middle East, North Africa, and other parts of the Muslim world, there are scholars who devote their lives to the study of the Koran and all its complexity. They also serve to answer questions from Muslim believers. Incidentally, imams are not always scholars. They are people who know the rules. They can show you how to practice your religion, how to get ready for prayer, how to pray, how to give *zacat* (a certain percentage of your money for the poor). But they cannot interpret the Koran for anyone.

Muslims who cannot read or write Arabic need help from scholars in understanding the Koran. Most translated versions of the Koran in any language are often faulty and erroneous. However, scholars are not easily available, but they write books on many Koranic subjects. If a Muslim cannot get to a scholar personally, he can check to see which scholar has written on the subject that interests him and consult the work. Because of the killings on 9/11, many people here looked for books to explain what the Koran says about killing. Does it allow killing?

There is *no* support in the Koran or in the hadith *for* what happened on 9/11. What happened is a criminal act and in the Koran, the punishment for a criminal act is death. Islamic law is very adamant about personal safety. The safety of all human beings is an important part of Islamic thinking. When a man stops a car to rob it, when he mugs someone on the street with a gun at his head, whether the victim lives or dies, the act itself is punishable by death. What is most criminal about these acts is that they create *fear* in the victim, and creating fear in the victim, even without killing him, equals death for the criminal.

Even today, some non-Muslims have the mistaken notion that Muslims believe in killing based on text from the Koran. This is completely wrong. I'm against what happened. Islam is against what happened. You may say I say this because I live here, I'm an American, I like America, my kids are born here and grow up here and so I'm biased pro-America. No, as a believer in Islam, I condemn what happened because there's no support for it from either Islam or the hadith. What happened is a criminal act and, I repeat, in the Koran, the punishment for a criminal act is death.

Now I will talk about my job in Brooklyn Heights. I work for a car and limousine service as a driver. That's different from the medallion-type taxi service where you go out on the street and hail a cab. You call for our service in advance and we come to pick you up, and take you where you want. I've been with my company, called Promenade Car Service, since 1991.

When I first came here in 1985, I looked for other things. I was a practicing lawyer in Egypt and there's no doubt that what I do now seems very far from my background and experience.

I came here with a bachelor's degree in law. But my background was of no value here mainly because of the language barrier. Another reason is the nature of the work itself. Soon after arriving, I went to a law school to see what I had to do and how many credits I needed for an American law degree. The admissions counselor said something that made sense. Number one: this is going to cost you a lot of money and number two: after you finish, you will find that the field you could work in would be very limited. And it would be very hard for you to take the bar exam to get the license to practice. And being foreign born, you would find it almost impossible to be a criminal defense lawyer. You'll probably work in some area like immigration law. Or in real-estate law. It won't be trial work.

I used to be a trial lawyer! What he said didn't sound like something I would like. It was more like shuffling papers. But I had to work. I didn't have any skill as an electrician or carpenter. The only thing I could do, know how to do, was drive my car. So I looked for work driving a car. This is how I got into the taxi-driver business.

At the same time I tried working in grocery stores. But the owners said to me, *You don't look like a very handy man.* They would look at me up and down, and say, not too happily, *Okay, give me your phone number. I'll call you.* [*Zaki is over six feet and slightly bent in the shoulders.*] One of them said, *The way you look or something, it doesn't seem right to tell you,* "Put the stuff here, or put it down there." I did two or three jobs in stores. I even went to a pharmacist looking for work.

There are a lot of Muslims from Pakistan, Egypt, Arabia, and Bangladesh in livery cab work. The majority of drivers are immigrants, mostly from Muslim nations. You'll find very few Americans in this business any more. If you call for a cab, you'll find a Muslim. It looks like all the Muslims are driving cabs. You see, most immigrants would like to settle in a Muslim community and find jobs in it commensurate with what they did before coming. But that's rarely possible. So they follow in the footsteps of those who came before—in my case, cab driving. But that doesn't mean they don't do other kinds of work. If you go into a doctor's office with a name like Khan or something similar, he is probably Muslim. But you don't pay attention to that. You go there to get well and you trust his judgment.

New York City has a concentration of taxi business that is different from other American cities. If you look at Manhattan, people who get around don't have a car, or don't use it if they do have one. Why? Because there's no spot to park the car anywhere. If you wanted to put it in a parking garage, it would cost like fifteen or twenty dollars. Sometimes it's ten dollars for the first half hour. So New Yorkers can't use a car to go to work, because the expense of parking doesn't pay. And they have to worry about insurance, accidents, repairs. It's cheaper for people who live in Manhattan to use a cab. So cabs are a needed business.

I'm happy to say that no customer or passenger has ever insulted me or made unflattering remarks by associating my religion with the terrorists. Never! This may happen outside New York, in the country at large. It may also be that I haven't had to face such a situation because for the past ten years, I've been working in the area of Brooklyn Heights. This area has a more sophisticated group of people who believe in "Live and let live." I know many of them, we talk and we've become friendly. Sometimes, when they call for a car, they make a request for me. I had a customer a few houses down from here on Willow Street. It was a family brownstone. He was a CEO for a company in New Jersey, and every weekday, for over two years, I'd pick him up and take him to Jersey. Then he moved out there.

I don't get back to Egypt much. My mother and father passed away. My brother and sister come to visit me. One of them is a doctor and the other was an official in the Egyptian CIA. I have three children, a boy and two girls. They did not go to Islamic schools. My son is nineteen, has just finished high school and is going to Brooklyn College next year. His first two years will be general studies, and the next two probably management or business. He hasn't decided yet. My girls are fourteen and ten.

I'm not concerned about bringing them up in an American culture. I know the kids look at movies and TV shows with lots of violence and drugs. American culture is not much different from that of any other country. Why am I not concerned? If there's stuff on American television parents don't like, they can stop it. Even cable gives you ways to control what your children see on the channels. You can lock out anything you don't want the kids to see.

Children the world over are subject to the same temptations. We're all human beings. I don't see any differences in the way people behave, no matter where they're from. When I was sixteen, I acted in a certain way, and I see my son acting in the same way now that he's sixteen. It's not just TV that's shaping him. The thing there is—under freedom—more opportunity to see things, to hear things. There's no control from the government for some stuff. But even if they did control certain things, you can be sure that won't wipe them out. There are too many ways of getting around a situation. And if something is controlled in public, how can that be controlled when done privately?

When all is said and done, parents must take the responsibility for their kids, and teach them everything, including religion. If you don't take them to church—you rationalize that your friends don't do it and it's not part of the culture—American culture is not to be blamed. Lack of responsibility on the part of parents is. If we don't do our duty, we are to blame. Anyway, there's nothing in American culture that tells you *not* to teach your kids. It's not the duty of our culture to tell your children how to behave, how to be friendly with your neighbors, how to keep your children from throwing candy wrappers in the street, or sticking gum on park benches. That's up to you.

I do the salat, all five prayers, every day. But I'm a taxi driver and I can't pull up with a passenger behind me and say the *salat az-zuhr* at midday. So it's perfectly okay to postpone the prayers till I finish work. You're making a relationship with God, and God certainly doesn't want you to pray to him and get fired. That's not his way. Islam has very humane rules and I wish I had time to explain some of them to you.

I want to point out that if you are Muslim and live in a neighborhood with people of other religions, you are a role model and should do everything properly. If you do something bad, people in the neighborhood might say, *Oh, look at what's happening! Islam is bad*. You represent Islam in that community and so you must be a very good person. Otherwise, you are not a Muslim. We have to be careful how to act in a non-Muslim community.

Someday I'd like to go to Mecca and do hajj. Someday, when I can afford it, both with money and time, and with peace of mind.

Shirin Devrim

A Turkish delight

Very few people know that the Ottoman Empire [founded by the Turks] was a meritocracy. You attained high positions through merit and valor. There was no such thing as a pure family background to help you get ahead.

Women under Ataturk were excused from wearing the veil. He never forbade women from wearing it … He did pass a law forbidding men to wear the fez, the hat Turkish men wore, and they started wearing fedoras.

The worst thing that happened to Islam is that we did not have a Reformation. In many Islamic countries, the law is still Sharia and there is no division between state and religion.

In her narrative, **Shirin Devrim**, a Turkish Muslim actress, writer and socialite, brings to life a lost world of Muslim kings, princes and princesses. As the stepdaughter of Prince Zeid al-Hussein, brother of King Faisal I of Iraq and a relative of the present king of Jordan, she—together with her brother and mother, the prince's wife—became members of the Iraqi royal inner circle. (Prince Zeid's family were direct descendants of Prophet Muhammad.)

For a period of her childhood, she led a fairy-tale life, meeting members of royalty, political figures, artists, writers, and the heads of state of both the Middle East and Europe. Her mother's family, the Shakirs, was a very old family that is known in Turkish history as having produced scholars, administrators, statesmen, soldiers, a general and founders of madrassas (Islamic schools). Their accomplishments extend from the Ottoman Empire to the present day. Later generations of the family, including her own, were artistic and became writers, painters, etchers, musicians, ceramists, and actors.

Ms. Devrim's two books of memoir, *A Turkish Tapestry: the Shakirs of Istanbul* and *Shirin*, give evidence of this extraordinary heritage, set forth in a forthright manner with little embellishment. In this interview, she not only evokes a glorious time gone by, but also glimpses of the new Turkey in which she grew up. It was a Turkey westernized by Kemal Ataturk, who brought in modern ways and European-style dress.

A vibrant example of the contemporary, educated Muslim woman with a free lifestyle, untied to religious ritual, she is, at the same time, deeply and emotionally attached to Islam. She was born in Ataturk's time and calls herself a secular Muslim. Some conservative believers do not regard her as Muslim at all. She retaliates by saying, *Being secular does not mean that I'm not Muslim. Secular in Turkey indicates that state and religion are separate.* Also a determined activist, she has been seen parading in protest on Middle Eastern and other issues in front of national embassies and the United Nations.

Despite her ties to Turkey and Islam, Ms. Devrim is a citizen of the United States and has spent a major portion of her life here. She is a graduate of the Yale Drama School, has performed on our stages in plays from Shakespeare to Tennessee Williams, and has taught drama at several American universities. She is married to an American, Robert Trainer, and lives in New York City. Ms. Devrim consented to be interviewed in the Trainer apartment on

Pictured above are Ms. Devrim's mother and stepfather, His Royal Highness, Prince Zeid. He was the brother of King Hussein of Iraq.

Beekman Place, where the walls are lined with pictures and memorabilia relating to past centuries, as well as paintings by her mother and by her brother, both well-known painters, ceramics by her cousin, and lithographs by her aunt. In our tête-à-tête over tea, Ms. Devrim often took a question and flew with it, occasionally leaving the original subject behind. No matter. The tea was delicious and the sweets were Turkish delights.

How far back can you trace your family?

We have traced it to the tenth century. The family came from central Asia, like many of the Turkomans. The Turks came from the walls of China and kept going and going and going and forming bigger clans. There was a Turkish kingdom in central Asia at one point. In the tenth century the family came to the Anatolian peninsula.

The Ottoman Empire started in 1228. Two centuries later they captured Constantinople and went from the Caspian Sea to Vienna. Nobody realizes that the Ottoman Empire lasted six centuries. That's just about the longest of the empires. To my mind, it was the most tolerant of all empires. They occupied countries but all they took from them was taxes. They did not impose their religion, or language, or their ways, and they usually used governors chosen from the local people. They were not colonizers; they were military occupiers.

Very few people know that the Ottoman Empire was a meritocracy. You attained high positions through merit and valor. There was no such thing as a pure family background to help you get ahead. Here, you always ask, *Where are you from? What is your ethnic background?* I never did that in Turkey because everybody has mixtures of background. But after having lived here, I myself get into this drill and, on meeting Turks, I ask, *Oh, and what is your family background?* They look at me and say, *What a question!*

Take my background. Both my grandmothers were from Crete. Now they could have been Greeks that converted to Islam, or they could have been Turks that went to Crete. We don't know. Among my Muslim friends I have one who is an Albanian, another is Bulgarian, another Yugoslav, another Circassian, another Hungarian, another Kurdish. They're all mixed, like the Americans.

What amuses me very much about America is that America boasts of being a "melting pot." I call it a "pecking order." I went to universities here, I was an actress, I was a professor, I am a writer here. But when I married my husband and went to the big American Middle West to live among the capitalists, so to speak, I was shocked to see the structure of the society and what a pecking order it was. The WASPs were right up there. They didn't even include Catholics. There were no people of French background, or Italian, and they sometimes used terms that sounded funny. *Polacks?* I said, *Who are the Polacks?* And they said, *They're the Poles.* I was amazed at the attitude. Because in

Turkey, we were surrounded with Armenians, Greeks, Jews, all ethnicities, all part of our lives, all equally accepted. I had three governesses: one was Jewish, one was Armenian and one was Greek. We had cooks: one was Turkish, one was Greek. We had jewelers who were Armenian. We had lawyers; they were Jewish. We had bankers; they were Armenian. We had landlords; they were Greek. And this was our society. And here I come from Turkish Society—with a capital S—but have never known what prejudice is.

I think Islam is a very tolerant religion. In summers we lived on an island in my grandfather's house. On one side there was a Catholic church, on the other a Muslim mosque and above us an Orthodox monastery. The bells used to toll, and the muezzin would chant *Allahu 'akbar* (God is great). Once a Catholic priest asked my grandfather, who was a general, whether the church procession could go through our garden because our house was between two streets and there was the church on one side and the procession would have to go all the way around. *Sure*, my grandfather said, *come through our garden*. For that procession, incidentally, an uncle dressed up as John the Baptist. We also celebrated Christmas, because we had foreign governesses who were Christian.

As you grew up, did your family practice the daily prayer ritual?

My grandmother did. She used to pray five times a day. She was very, very religious. And every evening after her chores, she used to put a white scarf around her head and sit in her pristine room. It was like a chapel. I remember the room always smelled of white jasmine. And every evening, as the sun rays penetrated this wonderful chamber, she read the Koran. *Every* evening, this was her relaxation.

For me, grandmother was my vision of Islam. She was goodness, kindness, generosity. Once a week she used to go downtown to take a ferry to a place where they helped the poor. It was run by holy Muslims, called *wali*. They are holy persons who are not quite saints but similar to them. There are no saints in Islam. We pray to the wali, ask for help, go to their tombs, light candles. We ask them to help us.

As a matter of fact, my maid who is Turkish and a Muslim told me that yesterday there was a story about walis featured on TV. It seems there was a wali who had reached great heights of goodness and after he died, his son reached ever greater heights. When the son died, they brought him to the gravesite to be buried next to his father. It appears the earth and the immense gravestone prepared for him rose by themselves, without being lifted, as a tribute of love and appreciation for his good works. According to the story, the earth and stone remained in that position, half raised. And to this day pilgrims go and pray there.

As a modern Muslim woman, how do you pray?

I've been in mosques, but I don't go there to pray and unlike my grandmother, I do not perform the salat.

I pray with my hands open, palms up. I don't put my hands together. Every time a plane takes off, I will open my hands—I'm sure the passengers think, *What is she doing?*—and I will pray. And every time the plane comes down, I will pray again, thanking the Lord that we arrived safely. I pray in the street when I'm upset about something. *Oh, please, Lord, help me.* I pray in a church, in a synagogue. I don't believe in anybody between me and God, and that is very Islamic. I don't want anybody [being] between us, just God and me. I make my own decision. I don't like anybody in between. Why do I have to have a man who is going to read to me all the stuff in the Koran? I am talking to God. I'm having a wonderful time talking to God.

And the thing is, I am blessed because I have a feeling that He likes me. I just love God. I love Allah. We have a nice little conversation and when there are difficulties, I'll say to Him, *You're pulling my leg. You're testing me, aren't you? But you're going to get me out of this.* And He does, He's been very kind to me.

Your ancestors started madrassas and ran them. Can you describe a madrassa?

Madrassas are religious schools that teach the Koran and the Shariah. The Shariah is God's law as established in the Koran and hadith. Later on my ancestors who established madrassas then became scholars and writers.

Incidentally, one of these scholars was a mystic. He stayed in his room practically all of his life and prayed. He lived in the eighteenth century. In the early nineteenth century, my great-grandfather decided there were too many scholars in the family and determined to do something about it. Because he was afraid of his wife, who would certainly stop him, he kidnapped his son and put him in a vegetable carriage and covered the boy with vegetables. He took him to a military school. The boy became a colonel and had two sons. One of them became a five-star general and the other a grand vizier of the Ottoman Empire.

Speaking of ancestors, I had another ancestor named Jevat who became a grand vizier under Abdullah Hamid, the cruel and terrible sultan known to cut off the heads of people under him. Jevat served under him for four years and still kept his head. Abdullah Hamid had a magnificent palace, which is now a boys' school.

Who or what was the biggest Islamic influence in your life?

Perhaps the biggest Islamic influence in our family was my stepfather, a Hashemite prince, Emir Zeid of Iraq, who was a direct descendant of Prophet Muhammad. The Hashemites were the dynasty that ruled Mecca from 1343 to 1924. They claimed descent from Muhammad through the line that went back to his great-grandfather, Hashim b. 'Abd Manaf, who gave his name to Muhammad's clan. The Hashemites have provided the kings of Iraq and Jordan.

My stepfather, the prince, was the forty-third son or generation of the Prophet and is descended from Muhammad's daughter. King Hussein was a Hashemite and therefore a direct descendant of the Prophet. The Sharifi, also members of the Prophet's family, are much larger in numbers, but the Hashemites are *direct* descendants of Muhammad's daughter.

Prince Zeid, my stepfather, was very kind, good, genuine and unassuming. But he did not display his religion in customary ways. The real, wonderful Muslims I've known are unassuming people. For them, it's God, and faith. And they are accepting everything as God's will.

You refer to the Supreme Being with the Anglo-Saxon word, God, not Allah. Why is that?
Because we're talking English, that's why. If we were talking Turkish, I would say Allah.

What languages do you speak?
I speak Turkish, German, French, and English. But English is my real language. I was educated in English and went to Barnard College and Yale University. I had an English governess and learned English and Turkish simultaneously.

You've had two mixed marriages. Can you comment on Islam's acceptance of marriage to a non-Muslim?
What is interesting is that my family as Turkish Muslims married people of different nationalities and religions. Two of my husbands were Americans, of Protestant background. My mother married an Arab prince; my aunt married a Hungarian Jew. My brother married a Polish Catholic; my other brother married a Swedish Lutheran. One uncle married a French lady. The other one married an Italian. What I'm saying is that the image of Islam is intolerance. Actually, my experience of Islam is tolerance.

Before Kemal Ataturk brought Western ways to Turkey in the nineteen-twenties, did women ever have a chance to enter the professions or the arts?
There were women of eminence. We had famous poets—upper-class women in literature who used to write poetry—all before Ataturk. But with Ataturk, women really took off and today you'll find educated, professional women everywhere. The first time my husband Bob came to Turkey with me, I took him to a party at a friend's house. She was a Ph.D. from Mount Holyoke in Massachusetts, and every woman in that room spoke English and each one of them had a career. My husband couldn't believe it. He had known the Spanish aristocracy and they didn't even speak English, let alone have careers. And here he is in Turkey, a backward Muslim country supposedly, and he meets all these

brilliant women. My best friend is a journalist, another runs a theater, another is a doctor. Honestly, I don't have any friends that do not have careers. Once I took my husband to a bank. Among the bank personnel, there was only one man, and he was the doorman. You wouldn't believe you were in Turkey! From the president of the bank down, they were all women. This was some years ago.

Has the freedom given to Turkish women been generally beneficial for society?

Women under Ataturk were excused from wearing the veil, and that was largely beneficial. What is interesting is that he never forbade women from wearing it. He was too smart to do that. Incidentally, my mother took off her veil before Ataturk came along. He did pass a law forbidding men to wear the fez, the Turkish hat, and the men started wearing fedoras.

But right now, there is a down side to women's freedom in Turkey. There are two extremes of dress. Some are going very religious and covering themselves up the way we never did, the way our parents never did. Or they are undressing themselves in such a manner that even I am shocked. I go to Istanbul and see so many women have got their stomachs showing, with their belly buttons on display because that's the fashion. I scorned one of them. Once at the hotel, I saw a woman—she had helped me because my grandniece was choking and she gave us some water. I said to her, *Thank you, madam.* She was lying by the pool with her big breasts like this. [*She drew a circle in the air.*] All exposed.

"What are you?" I asked, thinking she would say French or Italian.

"I'm Turkish."

The moment she said, "I'm Turkish," I said, "How DARE you lie there exposing yourself like that? Aren't you ashamed?" I said. "You're a Muslim! Our mothers were veiled! What are you doing?" She picked up her things and ran away. The situation has gone both ways. Once in the late fifties, when I kissed my Turkish husband in a taxi, the driver turned and said, *This is not a whorehouse.* He didn't approve of our kissing in the back seat.

Now they're kissing in the parks, holding hands, even while swimming they're rubbing against each other. I mean, it just drives me crazy. The religious people have sprung up and they are going to win the elections. One hears they'll get twenty-five percent of the vote. They're coming back with a vengeance. The thing is that I, as a modern woman, almost feel I want to be with them because the way women are behaving today is shocking. The pendulum swings both ways. It's like the growing pains of democracy.

What do you see as Islam's biggest problem?

The worst thing that happened to Islam is that we did not have a Reformation. In many Islamic countries, the law is still Sharia and there is no division between state and religion.

Where were you on 9/11?

I was in bed, watching the news and we saw the first building with the smoke coming out and everybody saying, *There's a fire!* Then I saw the plane coming and said to my husband, *That plane is going so low! I think the plane is going to hit the building. Why is it flying so low?* And then we saw the second crash. The whole thing was unbelievable, unbelievable, and then when I found out that there was a bunch of Muslims doing this, the fanatic bastards, I was just absolutely furious. I was furious that man could do this to man, whatever they may be, Christian or Jewish, man doing things to man. *What man has done to man, no animal has done to an animal.* This is true throughout history, when you look at the horrors: in Bosnia—three thousand people killed and thrown in a ditch—then Rwanda….And now they're doing it with planes, another atrocity of man against man. I was embarrassed that the killers happened to be Muslims. If you ask me, I'd say there has been more killing in the name of religion than for any other reason. Really, it's a miserable world.

There's no question of that.

Incidentally, do you know the real meaning of the word *jihad?* It means to improve yourself. In Muslim armies they used the word *jihad* with the soldiers. *You are going to fight, but if you die you are going to heaven. You are fighting to promote your religion and if you die for this cause, you will improve yourself and go to heaven.* Dying in battle was their jihad. The 9/11 terrorists probably thought of 9/11 as their jihad.

As an activist, did you offer to help in any way?

No, because we were on our way to Turkey to attend a retrospective of my brother's artwork. Everybody in Turkey was shocked. Horrified. I mean *really* shocked and horrified.

Let's consider some positive things. What appeals to you most about Islam?

Its classlessness. The lack of class. How can I explain it? I will sit with a fisherman, and he will call me "sister." This is another tradition we have. We always call one another "sister," "aunt," "grandmother," "mother." Now they're calling me aunt. They haven't called me "mother" or "grandmother" yet. The taxi driver calls me *abla*, which means "older sister" and shows respect.

I can sit there with the fisherman and we'd chat and have a cup of tea, or something, and he would never feel inferior. No. It's like this Muslim woman, my housekeeper, who served us coffee. She's a peasant, a farmer's daughter. She has a dignity about her. I will say, *Sit down, talk. Let's talk about something*, and she'll sit and we talk. You can be as nice as you want, but people do not become familiar. I love to communicate with them because their dignity and their humanity touch me. Everyone is so kind and cordial. Once I was complimenting a porter, thanking him for his courtesy, and he said, *Well, sister, after all, we have a long tradition.* They take it upon themselves to make you happy. That's what it is. When a waiter serves you a cup of coffee, he takes it upon himself to make you happy with that coffee.

I think it comes from Islam, the religion. It communicates a dignity about man. Vulgarity does not exist in social intercourse. Before the Prophet came, it was terrible. People were barbarians, full of violence and hate. This current violence has nothing to do with Islam. It is a tribal, pre-Islamic culture that still exists.

Have you ever worn Islamic clothing?

We went to Baghdad when I was sixteen because my stepfather, who raised me, was the great-uncle of the king, and became regent while the king was traveling. My mother and I had to wear such contraption. I have photographs of us in these black clothes. Oh, it was terrible. We looked like witches. We wore the big black abaya, which goes all the way down to your ankles, and the thick veil comes down like this. [*She made a gesture from her head to her neck.*] You have to learn how to flip the veil, which we had to do when we talked or went shopping in the bazaar. It's an art to flip. When you discuss price and give money, you open it, and then cover again.

We used to go to the movies, the royal family and I. They liked my company because I was so lively. They wouldn't go to the movies without me. It was an open-air theater and the boxes were open. Everybody knew the royal family had arrived just by the sight of us. The family were all tiny, and I was tall like this [*She gestured.*] and stood out. We looked like a bunch of black crows in a box. We used to sit, all covered in black, and then we used to open the veil and watch the movies, and at intermission close it. We ate ice cream at intermission and I used to hold the veil up, eat ice cream, and then cover again.

At that period—this was 1942—Iraqis were still veiled, particularly the royal family. I used to go riding and I remember getting in our car with the chauffeur driving. We had the arms of the Hashemite crown painted on the doors of the car. We drove to the desert and an officer of the king would come, and I would throw off all my black wraps and go riding. The Bedouins of the desert thought I was a foreigner when they saw me in short sleeves and breeches.

Oddly, Bedouin women, the women of the country, didn't cover their faces. I read somewhere that, back in the seventh century, it was only the aristocracy that used to wear veils. The lower classes, and especially the whores, didn't wear them. Sometimes the whores pretended they weren't whores and wore veils. If they were caught, they were flogged.

As a theater person educated in America, how were you accepted in the Turkish theater?

In the 1960s when I was working in Istanbul, there were forty or forty-five theaters and six were city theaters, subsidized by the municipality. I was the first woman director of these city theaters. The directors had always been men. The first show I did was *Taming of the Shrew*, which happened to have eighteen men in the cast. This was the big challenge of my life because their attitude was, *Well, who is this female who studied in America and is telling me what to do? To hell with her!* I had to fight, and it was the battle of the sexes. And the play was also. So that battle came on stage, and it was so lively that the audience stopped the show with applause eleven times on opening night.

Incidentally, in gratitude, I went and sacrificed a lamb. We do that in the way of appreciation and gratitude to Allah. That's part of our religion. I bought a live lamb and put him in the trunk of the taxi and took him way up to a cemetery where the wali are buried. I took the lamb to an attendant at the mosque, and the animal was sacrificed and given to the poor. It was a gesture of gratitude. I was so grateful to Allah for giving me the courage to take on this challenge of directing eighteen Muslim men the first time in Turkish history! And to have the show stopped eleven times by applause! I didn't know how to thank the Lord and did so by giving to the poor. We always give alms. That's called zacat.

Is giving alms, or zacat, a natural Muslim reaction to good fortune?

From my experience, yes. It is natural for me. Once I almost had an automobile accident. So I immediately gave some alms to the poor. We also give a certain percentage of our income. We have to. Muslims also build things in thanksgiving. Have you been to Istanbul? There is a clock tower in an area that my uncle actually built. A friend's father built the mosque. Another friend's father built the fountain where you wash before you go and pray. People built and gave things. We provide for the poor always.

In the Muslim household, we have another way of giving or providing. When I was a child, people took in orphans and brought them up as their children. In our house there were two orphans. My grandmother brought them up. They were neither servants nor family children. They were in between. They helped as servants but when they were grown, you marry them off and give them a trousseau. My grandmother married both orphans off and gave them each a trousseau. My aunt had a male orphan and when he was grown, she bought him a taxi, thus making sure he could provide for himself. Until the end of his life, he used to call my aunt "mother." He was there at her deathbed. She took care of him. She had two of her own children, who didn't mind him calling her "mother." One son became an ambassador, and his brother was a taxi driver. But they were brothers. This was a wonderful tradition.

I have a Muslim friend, Turkish, who is a director, a Yale graduate, not married, no children. His family are all dead. His mother brought up one of these orphans, a boy. My friend now has Alzheimer's disease and is being taken care of by that boy. He calls my friend "my brother." My friend has always befriended him, bought him a house and a car. Now he takes care of my friend. You see, the orphan is so grateful that he *has* to pay back. Every household had one, the rich and not so rich. Everybody I know has had one.

Has your husband, a Protestant, adapted well to living in two religious cultures?
I'm religious and he's not. He's a white, Anglo-Saxon, Protestant Episcopalian but he goes to church just occasionally. Religion doesn't seem to mean much to him. I've never heard him mention the word God, or prayer. He says the word God only when he curses the computer——dammit! Bob's a New Yorker, by God, born on Sixty-second Street. He went to Exeter and Harvard and then Harvard Law. One of those really civilized ones. Can you imagine me married to a redneck? I'd kill him the next day. [*Calling to her husband.*] Darling, can you come here? Madam was asking me how you're coping with this Muslim woman.

[*To Mr. Trainer, who joined us.*] When you go to Istanbul, do you enjoy the ambiance, the culture and being with Turks?
I've always enjoyed everything in Turkey. I love Shirin's family and friends and thoroughly enjoy being with them.

[*To Ms. Devrim*] In your long life together, have you talked much about Islam?
Actually, it isn't Islam we talk about. It's the Turks and the Americans and world politics. Religion-wise, we never argue at all.

Yuseph Sleem

The children gain a foothold

For a boy growing up in Palestine as I did, life is very similar to growing up in Bay Ridge, because in Bay Ridge, there is such a large Arab population.

People who speak and write Arabic are needed in many areas—the FBI, businesses, the oil industry. If I become a doctor, which I plan to do, and have patients who are Arabic immigrants and don't speak English, it will be helpful to communicate with them in their own language.

Think of the Oklahoma City bombing. That was a terrorist attack, but people don't say it was a Christian act of terrorism because Timothy McVeigh was Christian. And I don't think we should call 9/11 an Islamic act of terrorism because the perpetrators were Islamic.

Photo courtesy of the Sleem family.

Fort Hamilton High School, which **Yuseph Sleem** attends in Brooklyn, New York, has two distinctions. One is that it has more American Muslim students than any other high school in New York City (as of this writing) and, secondly, the Arabic language is offered for study along with such traditional foreign languages as French and Spanish. The interview with Yuseph took place in a small conference room next to the principal's office. Yuseph was a senior at the time. With credentials in hand, I had requested a meeting with a male student. The principal, Jo Ann Chester, turned the request over to Robert Laurenzano, counselor of student affairs, and asked him to find a willing Muslim student. The search proved oddly difficult. "If you want a girl Muslim, I could get you a dozen. But the boys are diffident and suspicious and think being interviewed isn't very manly." But he did finally find a teenager, a serious and unsmiling young man, who was not embarrassed. The school insisted on getting his mother's consent and asked that Mr. Laurenzano be present. These are the kinds of precautions that Fort Hamilton usually takes to protect the safety and well-being of all its students.

Yuseph Sleem is a seventeen-year-old Palestinian-American Muslim. His mother's family came from Palestine in the 1920s and, on this side, he is a fourth-generation American. His father was born in Palestine and migrated here after the 1967 war when Israel took over the West Bank. He came here as an Israeli citizen (most Palestinians are born citizens of Israel) and eventually became an American citizen.

I was struck by Yuseph's confident and matter-of-fact manner. Despite loyalty to the United States, where he was born, he did not hesitate to speak with sympathy and feeling for Jerusalem and its population of 2 million homeless people.

He is a tall, good-looking teenager and a member of the Fort Hamilton swimming team. A straight-A student with an average above ninety, he had just won membership in the National Honor Academy and a full scholarship to St. John's University in Queens, New York.

My father was seventeen—my present age—when he came over here. He came with a younger brother who was fifteen. Just the two of them. My father started working for the Arabs who were already established here. While he worked, his younger brother, my uncle, went to school and graduated from high school. Eventually they opened a business together.

I have three brothers and a sister. Two brothers are older, and my sister and the other brother are younger. The two older ones both graduated from Fort Hamilton. The oldest one is in medical school and the other is at Brooklyn College studying computer science. The med student is at Mount Sinai University. My sister goes to McKinley Junior High. The neighborhood we live in, which is Bay Ridge in Brooklyn, used to be mostly a Scandinavian-Irish neighborhood, but now it's very mixed. There's a large Chinese population coming in and a lot of Arabs. The Russian population is exploding also.

My father has a share of a cooperative supermarket. It's a corporation with many owners. He has worked in supermarkets all his life here. My mother doesn't work. She has five children to raise. When I graduate from Fort Hamilton, I plan to attend Saint John's University in the borough of Queens. It borders on Brooklyn. I've already been accepted and I will major in premed and then go on to medical school.

At home we speak both English and Arabic. My father speaks mostly Arabic to us. But my mother—she was born here—usually speaks to us in English. But she understands and speaks Arabic as well. I lived in Jerusalem for ten years of my life, and there I learned Hebrew, since they speak both Arabic and Hebrew in Jerusalem. The reason we went there was that my mother wanted her children to see where we came from, the land of our ancestors, and to experience the different culture. I lived here until I was five and then we moved—my mother, brothers, and sister—to Jerusalem. My father went back and forth because of his business.

The experience of living there was great. I started school at five years old and so everything seemed natural. My brothers were older and had been going to school in Brooklyn, so the transition was difficult for them. I fit in much better and was able to pick up the Arabic language quickly, and assimilated easily into the society.

But when it came time for us to leave Jerusalem, I wasn't sorry about leaving. I was fifteen and wanted to come back to the United States because I think of myself as primarily an American. I was born here. And then, of course, with all the tensions and troubles happening over there, I wouldn't have wanted to stay.

Today, speaking and understanding Arabic is a big plus. It's in demand. People who speak and write Arabic are needed in many areas—the FBI, businesses, the oil industry. If I become a doctor, which I plan to do, and have patients who are Arabic immigrants and don't speak English, it will be helpful to communicate with them in their own language. And if I ever wanted to work in the Gulf region, where a lot of American projects are going on, it would be a good thing to know Arabic.

For a boy growing up in Palestine as I did, life is very similar to growing up in Bay Ridge, because in Bay Ridge, there is such a large Arab population. So starting to live in Brooklyn again, after a ten-year hiatus, wasn't that hard. No one raised an eyebrow at my arrival, because with such a large immigrant population people are used to new faces coming in, and you don't feel strange or out of place. I don't know how it would be in other parts of the United States, but New Yorkers are used to new faces.

Fort Hamilton is the high school in my area and everyone living here goes to the school. I started here as a junior and even if I wanted to go to another high school, like Brooklyn Tech or Stuyvesant, I couldn't, because you need to take entrance exams and I didn't have that opportunity.

[*At this point, Robert Laurenzano, the counselor of student affairs, who was sitting with us, added a few comments. "This is a zoned high school. You can only attend this high school if you live in the limits of this zone. We are not a specialized school. We do not have any op-ed (educational-opportunity programs) except for one, the computer-science program which has only fifty seats. Admission to it requires an exam.*

"Fort Hamilton has the highest or second highest proportion of Arab students of any high school in New York City. The numbers fluctuate. I know for certain that last year we were the second highest and I heard that this year we are the highest. These numbers simply indicate there are now more Arabs in the Bay Ridge–Sunset Park community of Brooklyn. The population of Arabs in the school reflects the area, but it does not mean that Arabs from the entire city are admitted.

"Arabic is offered as an elective course. We don't have too many classes in Arabic except in terms of an elective subject. It's not a very popular elective as one might think, mainly because the students who might benefit from it already speak the language. We also offer a variety of classes of English as a second language in our ESL programs, which can be taken in place of our usual English language courses. The ESL programs are extensive in terms of serving non-English-speaking students of various linguistic and cultural backgrounds. So if an Arabic-speaking student comes to our school not speaking English, there are many levels of ESL classes available where he can learn English and move on. For students who take Arabic as an elective language (in place of French or Spanish, for example), we have classes that can take the student up to the Regents level, which would be level six."]

The quality of education in Jerusalem depends on the school. I went to a private school over there and the education was excellent. They taught us four languages, which were mandatory: English, Arabic, Hebrew, and French. In science, many of the topics we're studying here now I already studied in my school in Jerusalem.

And, not surprisingly, in Jerusalem we study the Koran in school. It's taught as a regular subject. Just as you memorize poetry here for an English class, you memorize the Koran over there. Some people memorize the Koran from cover to cover.

I do the salat every day. I don't have time to say the noon prayer at school, but there is time to say it after school. I've never asked the school for a special spot to pray, but I don't believe there is one at Fort Hamilton.

[*Explaining the school's official stand, Mr. Laurenzano said, "To my knowledge, no one among the students has asked for this. Under the American concept of separation of church and state, public schools do not usually allow students to leave the classroom setting for prayer obligations. I'm not one hundred percent familiar with what the requirement is, but I can state that if there is a reasonable accommodation that can be made, upon request it would be made. That is to say, if we can provide a central location for students to meet at a preset time, upon request it would be arranged. But since we are the largest public high school in the city and extremely overcrowded—we have over one hundred ninety-eight percent utilization—space is at a premium. However, if the request is reasonable, if there is a corridor or other area that can be used for a few moments, and if we can provide it, we will. We need to remember that Muslim prayer is not a still, silent moment. It's kneeling, folding arms, a whole process. And space and time are needed.*

"With our numbers, it does sound strange that we haven't had the request. It may be that because the teens, the high-school years, are a tentative period in the lives of children, students are preoccupied with other issues. If I may speak frankly, the population in our school seems to be a blend of those who want to assimilate and fit in and those who are very strong in their cultural and religious beliefs. Today I'm learning just now how much Yuseph is involved in his culture. I know something of his abilities academically—having looked at the computer and the teacher recommendations—but I'm just now learning how involved he is in Islamic culture."]

Even if I can't say the noon prayers because of class obligations, I can postpone them and pray two of the prayers together. I do that if I have to. I do the salat every day and do it not because my parents want me to, but because I want to do it. Because I've studied my religion extensively over there and I've always attended mosque regularly. Even here, I attend mosque regularly. By that, I mean every Friday, our holy day.

I will do hajj but it's not my immediate aim. Hajj is required only once in a lifetime and people don't want to go when they are not financially able to. They want to go later in life when they have fewer family burdens and can enjoy the experience fully. But if I could afford it, I would go anytime.

I was fifteen at the time of the terrorist attack on 9/11. It was a terrible tragedy to American Muslims. In Jerusalem and all over the Middle East, there were candlelight vigils. It was a setback for the whole world.

But my reaction, which was full of love for the victims, and sympathy for their families, was a bit different from that of other Americans. I think to myself that my reaction wasn't as shocked as it was for other Americans because having lived in the Middle East for ten years, I'm used to such violence and bombings. I didn't actually witness a bombing but I heard about suicide bombings on a daily basis, almost.

I know the misery that exists over there. Right now there are about ten million refugees living around Israel that were expelled from their lands in '48 and '67. I think that's the number. They have nowhere to go and are just waiting to return to their homes. Everything that happens over there between the

Israelis and Palestinians happens over the territory. That's the main objective. The refugees are waiting to return to their homes.

On a local level here in Brooklyn, there was much shock and disbelief in press reports that a certain imam in a Brooklyn mosque had collected large sums of money at his mosque to aid Islamic terrorists. Non-Muslims were amazed that a spiritual leader of a religion could do such a thing. But again I wasn't that amazed or shocked. I don't think criminal acts are unique to Islam. For example, how can Catholic priests commit acts of sexual abuse on children?

I don't think American Muslims are basically any different from other Americans. Religion is just something between you and God. It's a faith that you believe in. It should not make you distinctly different from anyone else in a society. But since the 9/11 attacks, Muslims are singled out in the media. You get a feeling that terrorism is now connected to Islam, in a way, because it was portrayed that way after the September 11 attacks. Think of the Oklahoma City bombing. That was a terrorist attack, but people don't say it was a Christian act of terrorism because Timothy McVeigh was Christian. And I don't think we should call 9/11 an Islamic act of terrorism because the perpetrators were Islamic.

Mubarak Abdul Jabbar

Muslim among the law enforcers

I don't think Islam has anything to do with making you a good officer or a better officer. It makes you a better person.

[American Muslims] were assimilating into the mainstream, or so they thought. And now to find that coworkers dislike or hate you because of your religion, when this country is supposed to be a country tolerant of all religions, is a terrible thing.

Me being a man, my blending in is much greater than a woman's blending. I figure it's because the religion says that men can adjust in a non-Muslim society and dress appropriately because they must make a living and maintain a woman and family ... But we're speaking of two different economies because now we live in a society that requires two paychecks per household. And the Muslim wives wearing a head scarf at work can create problems.

Photo courtesy of Mubarak Abdul Jabbar.

Officer **Mubarak Abdul Jabbar** has been a transit policeman for over fourteen years in the New York City Police Department. Raised in the Bronx, he is the first black officer, and the first Muslim (by choice, not birth), to be elevated to the executive board of the Patrolmen's Benevolent Association (PBA). The police union has long been rent with hostilities between PBA members on the one hand and the Black and Latino members on the other. As an indication of the importance of the promotion, the *New York Times* published two separate profiles on him barely a month apart.

On learning that he was a practicing Muslim, I called the PBA for an interview, spoke with his partner, and left a message. Some time later, he responded cordially and set up an appointment. We met in his small office in downtown Manhattan, with a window that displayed a full view of the city. A tall, personable man with a short beard and thin mustache, he was apologetic about being three minutes late. He was dressed in a gray business suit and as he sat, I noticed, with a start, that he was wearing a leg holster with a short-barreled, 38-caliber pistol strapped to his ankle.

Some journalists find him uncommunicative on certain issues. In this instance, speaking as a Muslim among the law enforcers, he talked—with no holds barred.

I'm often asked about my name. Let me explain. I picked it with a friend who helped educate me in Islam. I chose Mubarak, which means "blessed," but it can also mean "congratulations," so it depends on the context. My friend chose the last two names. Abdul is often used as a prefix to another noun. It means "servant," or "slave." Jabbar translates as "strong or compelling force to do good." So my name means, "Blessed servant compelling others to do good." It was rather prophetic since some time later, after adopting it, I became a policeman.

I'm called "AJ" by my coworkers. It doesn't much matter to me. AJ became a thing. It started in the eighties when I came on this job. There were very few Muslims around then. I knew two, and there weren't many more. At that time you pretty much knew everyone. Of the two I knew, one had a Muslim name and the other did not. Being called AJ was a way of transcending the hostility and apprehension and allowing the everyday functions of being a police officer to proceed more easily. It made my coworkers more comfortable.

It's just like when you have immigrants come to this country. They make modifications to their name, or some clerk hands out a new name because he can't spell the old one. The new name usually fits into the culture. Being called AJ is similar; it's just a modification. It has no bearing on *who* I am. It has no bearing on the religion. Everyone who calls me AJ knows that I'm a Muslim and, for the most part, shows me respect for me being a Muslim.

My mother was a Baptist who worked in a restaurant. My father was not religious and was a hat-factory employee. When I converted to Islam, he worried about it. He felt it would be one more strike against me. But that didn't hold me back and I converted as a teenager. Remember, I'm a kid of the sixties and seventies, and at that time we were very inquisitive. Not just the black kids, but all the kids. We were into political action and things of that nature, from the hippie movement on down to the black liberation movement. Elijah Muhammad was the first introduction I had to Islam, even though it was a perverted introduction. For the most part, we knew of no other Muslims. The Nation of Islam was all we knew. For the majority of African-American Muslims of my time, that was our introduction. Malcolm X, Louis Farrakhan, Muhammad Ali were the big names. Before that in our urban environment, you very rarely heard of a Muslim. I'm not saying there weren't Muslims around because there were. But they weren't as prevalent, they weren't as visible, they tended to be secretive and quiet.

But after my introduction to the Nation of Islam, I began to read. One day I met up with a girl I knew to walk her home. She was visiting her best friend. The girl, incidentally, later became my wife. I was training in martial arts—all my friends used to train in martial arts—and so I made a good bodyguard. Her best friend had at the time converted to Islam. I met her and her husband and he started telling me about the more correct Islam and its followers, as opposed to what we were learning at the Nation. At first I was resistant and said, *You don't know what you're talking about. They're camel drivers, you know.*

But as you sit and listen and talk, you realize that what you had from the Nation of Islam was a perverted type of Islam. This was the real Islam that opened my mind to reading and realizing that what the Nation of Islam was teaching was incorrect. Pure and simple.

My friends didn't think much, one way or the other, about my conversion to Islam. You have to remember that for the majority at that time, religious beliefs were very shallow, to say the least. They didn't really believe, one way or the other. But, oddly enough, at that time, to take a step into Islam was a bold and manly thing because you were saying that you were going to forsake all the things that you were doing as a teenager, like running the streets, chasing girls, drinking beer, and all that kind of stuff. So when you converted to Islam, you were respected. With a little resentment sometimes. Like your best buddy wanting to know why you can't hang out with him no more. But for the most part there was a great deal of respect. They realized you were embarked upon a life of discipline that they were too weak to follow. A lot of friends would tell you that. They liked what Islam taught but their rebuttal was, *Listen, buddy, I gotta have my beer, I gotta have my ham.* In fact, they'd sometimes tell me, *Oh, you're too young for that, man. You're too young. Live a little.*

My wife and I were childhood sweethearts and she also was a motivating force in my coming to the religion. She was aware of it before I was through her girlfriend. So she became aware of the true teachings of Islam before me, and she motivated me. Because, you know, when you like someone as a kid, you get a crush on her and want her to be your girl. And you do things that you might not have done. But because you're trying to impress her, you read up on things and so you have a conversation.

Mind you, the religion has a strong moral code and the things she allowed me to do, like kissing and hugging before Islam, she didn't allow any more after Islam until we were married. She used to say to me, *Now you can't do that.* And I want to find out why I couldn't. I wanted to identify with things that she was identifying with. That was also a motivating force. When we became Muslims, she took shahada a couple of days before I did. We did it together, and to this day we're still together.

My wife wears the head scarf and long skirt and pants with a long tunic. If you wear pants, you should wear a long tunic for modesty. My children were all brought up Muslim. My oldest daughter has graduated from college. All my kids went to public school; even my littlest one is there now. At school, as Muslims, they've had some small problems from the religious standpoint, as much as for being different, like wearing head scarves. My girls all wore them. The boys weren't really that different because they didn't have to wear the kufi, or skull cap. Sometimes they wear the kufi and sometimes they don't. The boys aren't really identifiable as Muslims.

Even me. Me being a man, my blending in is much greater than a woman's blending. I figure it's because the religion says that men can adjust in a non-Muslim society and dress appropriately because they must make a living and maintain a woman and family. This can be done more readily if they're not immediately identifiable as Muslim by their dress. That's so in theory, but we're speaking of two different economies because now we live in a society that requires two paychecks per household. And the Muslim wives' wearing her head scarf at work can create problems.

In ideal situations Muslim women stay home and the man goes out and makes the money and takes care of them in the proper manner. This allows the women to dress appropriately as Muslim women. But my wife works and my daughter works. My wife dresses as a Muslim woman in an office. She doesn't work for a Muslim organization. Unfortunately, we don't have too many Muslim organizations that can employ all the Muslims in New York. That's one of the problems that we have economically: we are not where we could or should be. There's still a lot of bias and racism in the workplace. We cannot ignore that, and in some post-9/11 situations, bias was strengthened by another kind of bias made up of fear and suspicion. American Muslims have lost their jobs, not because of something they have done at work but because of so-called patriotic feelings, and they as Muslims are being pushed to the side. We need to develop an economy so we can employ our own. But that's a goal that takes a long time coming.

I do my salat every day. It's not an option. The perception is that it's tedious but when you really add up the time doing the requirements, not the extras, it only takes about fifteen minutes, five times a day. The wudu, or washing of your face and limbs, isn't done five times. There are certain rules: if the wudu has not been violated by passing wind or going to the bathroom, it stays with you all day and you don't need to repeat the washing with each salat.

I've developed my own routine. Most people in my office know me and what I'm about, especially my secretary. If she sees that the blinds on my office windows are drawn and the door is closed, she doesn't come in and doesn't let anyone else come in either. She knows I'm doing my salat. Even when I was on patrol—for fourteen years—my partners accepted the routine. It was only for a few minutes. At first when I was a brand-new officer, it was very difficult. I might miss it, couldn't make it on time because you have foot posts—a difficult situation. But as I became more senior in my job, I would go by the mosque—I patrolled an area where there were quite a few masjids or mosques—make my salat and come out.

My partners liked it when it was Ramadan time, the month of fasting. They'd say, *Oh, Abdul, man, you must be starving*, and pretend to commiserate with me. But when it was time to break the fasting, they changed their tune. I'd go do my salat, the fasting would be over for the day, and the mosque would hand me a heaping plate of fresh Mideastern food *and* plates for my buddies. Then they'd lick their lips and slap me on the back. They liked Ramadan and didn't mind working with me at all.

I don't think Islam has anything to do with making you a good officer or a better officer. It makes you a better *person*. And in terms of being a better person, you try to exhibit this good side of your personality in everything you do. So maybe to some extent it impacts on your policing style. Policing is a rough business. Sometimes you can be compassionate, and sometimes compassionate you just cannot be. You have to do the task at hand. I don't know how Islam affects this. Obviously, you're not going to do wrong things, just as a lot of my fellow officers don't. They have their belief system, whether it's Catholicism or Judaism, or whatever. They have their belief system and I'm quite sure that motivates them to do the right thing. If you have a choice of doing something correct, or something incorrect, you choose to do the right thing.

Around the office, I have the reputation of possessing a certain level of peacefulness. Some may think it comes from my religion. To be quite candid, I really don't know. As a youngster, like most kids, I was hotheaded, had a temper, still have a temper. If it's true that I have that quality of peacefulness, I don't know how much Islam contributed to it, or whether it's just personal demeanor. But Islam may be a contributing factor. Like most people, when you know that you're here in life as a passenger, that eventually you're going to get to your destination, then why let the trip get you all bent out of shape? Because in reality you cannot control it. You have to deal with what is put in front of you, not let it consume you, and move on.

I don't think that my being Muslim had anything to do with my appointment to the board. Some might think it a step to deflect public criticism of the treatment of Muslims since 9/11. Look, I've been in this union business a long time. And my name has been batted around for years. Prior to the merger of the Transit Police and the New York Police Department in April 1995, I was supposed to be put on the board of the Transit Police. That had nothing to do with being Muslim. In this business you work hard, you develop an ethic, you develop a following, and that would get you elected.

More to the point is the thinking that my being *African American* had something to do with the appointment. That's probably more of a factor. Some people might say, *The times being what they are, he received the job because he's African American*. Again, look at the résumé. It's one of the most extensive résumés of union activity here. I've held every position in the union, from alternate delegate to chairman of the board of directors. So I figure I've earned it.

But, you know, race is always a factor. In our culture, sadly, when an African American receives anything, it's always, *Did he get it because he's black, or did he get it on merit?* We always receive something because *we're black, because we're this or that*. But I like to believe that I received it on merit. I've been in transit over eighteen years, doing this union business. I don't want to be naive, but I like to believe that.

I can't put my hand on any particular incident where I can say bias was exhibited toward me, definitive bias because of my religious beliefs. However, I know it was. I know from things that occurred. One occurrence was in the academy, while we were training in the range to learn weaponry. The range instructor, who was a born-again Christian, a Hispanic fellow, can't remember his name, came up to me and said they were going to fail me.

"Fail me?" I asked. "For what?"

"They think you're with the BLA (Black Liberation Army) or some other subversive group because of your name." At the time law enforcement had a problem with subversive groups that were getting members into the Police Department.

"This is what you're going to do," he said, talking to me. "I can see you're not anything like that. Make sure you get on my group." They had lines in the academy that the men could join.

He continued, "Make sure you get into my group. If you fail, I'll fail you.

But if you're not failing, I'm not going to fail you."

He added, "When you come back to the academy, if I'm still here (you usually go back in another three or four months to complete that part of the training) make sure you get with me again."

Little things like that, but I was really shocked. At the bias and inferiority that were implied on the part of authorities. You're coming into a culture. This is the only culture I know, American culture. This is my country, this is where I'm born, raised, finally achieved a milestone coming into the Police Department. It shocked me. It's just like when I was a kid and I first went down south and learned there was a black church and a white church. It was shocking because you only knew one church as a kid. Coming up as a Baptist, there was just one church. Being a northerner I never came up against the concept of upfront … you see it on TV and you may have read about it in literature but you never were confronted with it. So when I was a kid and I was going to play with my cousins, and they said, *Oh, no, that's the white church and this is the black church*—it's a similar type situation, you know.

Today there are many more Muslims in the Police Department than when I started. It's to the point where we're trying to establish a Muslim law-enforcement organization. There's one national law-enforcement Muslim association that just started. It really doesn't have that much participation. But it's the beginning.

What you have now, fortunately or unfortunately, however you might perceive it, is a lot of foreigners who come into the department. The influx of immigration and easing of the immigration laws bring in a lot of Muslim foreigners. Most of the Muslims on the job now are foreigners because they take advantage of municipal employment. I can't speak on what their motivations are, but I can say their experience in being accepted is easier than it was for African Americans. For myself, coming up in this culture and being African American, from that experience I can say it was difficult dealing with the police. We have a different history with the police than what foreign Muslims might have because with them, you can't tell whether they're Caucasian or what.

The difficulty Black American Muslims have with the police rises out of the fact that, in our Black and Latino communities, the police *police* harder. Maybe it's because our crime rate is what it is. So what happens is that a lot of time a youngster coming up has to navigate very strongly so that he doesn't get any minor infractions or violations that would prevent him from coming onto the police force.

Now, when you're coming from another country or if you're living in a different neighborhood and living a little more *upscale*, you don't have the confrontation with the police, as the kids in the African-American communities have. Unfortunately, the statistics are what they are. An African-American kid gets the short end of the stick when it comes to the police enforcing the law.

The wink and the smack on the behind just don't come to him as readily as it does to a kid living in upscale Park Slope in Brooklyn. A lot of times you get the kid who is doing the same thing a black kid is doing, but they grab the African American kid, take him to the precinct, put him through the system. Whereas the other kid who may have a mother or father who has a business, or the father is a doctor from Pakistan, gets a spank and that's it. Subsequently, when these kids become eighteen, nineteen, twenty, and want to take a police job, the African-American kid has these infractions on the record that keep him from getting the job, whereas the foreign kid who behaved like the black kid doesn't have them.

I honestly feel that the distrust and suspicions that some Americans have toward our Muslim community since 9/11 will dissipate. Look at the history of our country. In World War Two we had the same feelings toward the Japanese Americans and the Italian and German Americans. After Pearl Harbor was bombed, we were taking the Japanese and putting them in concentration camps. That's the reality of our country. Our country goes into a shell and anything that's not "White Anglo-Saxon Protestant" is really not American. That's the view of our countrymen. No one is truly an American unless you're white and Anglo. And if you're not Protestant … But that's dissipating because of the numbers of Americans of other backgrounds. The post-9/11 hysteria is not unique in our history.

We perpetuate this all-equal democracy, and when you see discrimination coming out, it really shocks you. You see it even in Islam here in America. When a white guy takes shahada at the mosque, the others act like fools. They're so glad that a white guy became a Muslim. [*Author's note: for an account of a white man becoming Muslim, see the profile of Hamid Dana, a white Anglo-Saxon American, who converted to Islam.*] A Black guy takes shahada, and the feeling is, well, okay … [*He laughed.*] That, sadly, is global racism. We got global racism. It's unfortunate, but that's the way life is.

The only way we can truly break down distrust—and I can go back to the African American experience in this country—is when you begin to integrate and you expose your culture to another culture, when you begin really to open your heart to see what others are like. In the U.S., we live a segregated life as we grow up until we are maybe eighteen or go to college or when you get your first job. Most people in our culture do not interact with another culture until you go to school, until you go to college or get a job as an adult, when you come downtown and work with an Italian guy or a Polish guy. We perpetuate a myth of pluralism in this democracy but in reality we live segregated lives until we are adults. Sadly, the only thing you know about a culture is what you see in the media. You think you know about blacks from what you see on TV until you interact with them. You think you know about Muslims from what you see on TV. Right now the TV image of Muslims is that they're bloodthirsty, backward, and only interested in jihad and killing everybody. We don't control the media and the media is not responsible in a lot of respects. The media also portrays the image of the Muslim now as being bloodthirsty, but when you look at Muslim history, it's contrary to all this. The media makes much with the word *jihad*.

The jihad concept you hear so much about, you only do to protect your religious beliefs. Like any religion. The Crusaders felt their religion was threatened, so they fought. But here, the media creates the images and we live in a country where we have a lot of media. It perpetuates racism, it perpetuates the racism within the African-American experience, and the racism of the Italians against the Irish, and the different religious groups against one another, the Baptists and the Klan against the Catholics, and so on. The media creates, and they turn you on and they turn you off. They make you hate, they make you love. Adults share the responsibility because we thrust our children before the TV or send them to the movies.

It's at a point now where children, even grownups, don't read any more. Years ago, before you had black-and-white TV in your house, you used to listen to the radio as a family. And you would read the newspaper to find out what's happening. I came up with that generation and when we first got our TV, you would look at the black-and-white TV, but you would also like to read the paper so you can talk with your dad or your mom or whatever. Or go to the library—a good way to escape your poverty.

What Muslims have to understand is that we all have to persevere and be patient. And this too shall pass, *if* you're patient and persevere. It is shocking how since 9/11, TV and other members of the media have turned against American Muslims. Most of the Muslims in this country (with the exception of the crazed few religious fanatics) have nothing but positive thoughts for the U.S. They were assimilating into the mainstream, or so they thought. And now to find that coworkers dislike or hate you because of your religion, when this country is supposed to be a country tolerant of all religions, is a terrible thing. But the African Americans weren't shocked because they know America. Based on their own experience, they view America a little differently.

In spite of our changeable behavior, Americans seem unaware of the resentment and hatred toward America that it creates. They have their own view of America, the view that all the world loves us. Sadly, it isn't so. I have coworkers here who just went on a trip to Italy. They were shocked at the venom and enmity the Italians in Italy have toward Americans. I like to travel and when you travel you hear the people of other countries talk about America because it is so prominent in international politics. You realize a lot of the urban people of different countries *don't* like America. But you don't know this because the media makes it seem that everybody loves you. Internationally, you're loved and everybody wants to be an American. But when you break the boundaries and go abroad—I'm not talking about going to a tourist country in the Caribbean—you realize that America is not viewed with love, and that's a culture shock to a lot of people.

One of the things that would help to enlarge our vision is to have our kids travel. The kids should go on international trips to see what other worlds look like. Unfortunately, our kids don't travel. They're fed through the media, what the world is like. And when you begin your first trip (mine was to Egypt), you are shocked at the poverty outside the big cities, the extreme poverty. Americans need a world view of things. It's taken for granted that we have a middle class here. When you go overseas, you see the rich or the poor and no middle class. It's that simple.

Speaking of travel, as a true Muslim, I've done hajj and been to Mecca. And speaking of getting to see other people and nations, you do this when you do hajj. You are one of over a million and a half people who are crowded into one open-top mosque, walking around the grounds in a compressed area, marching, all dressed in one white costume to show the universality of all men, the equality of all men before God or Allah, wearing the same white cloak. It's a very physical experience, but awesome. And as you grow older, you appreciate it more.

My wife and I want to do hajj together. But now that I've got this position, we can't make plans. One thing at a time.

Omid Safi

Academic, reformer, world citizen

" *Islamic studies have been the neglected child of the academy. Fortunately, the picture is changing.*

We've come to realize, sadly, in this past century that if we don't attach value and recognize the worth of lives of all peoples, it becomes much easier to kill them.

When our son and daughter were born, my wife, who was raised as a Catholic, and I thought it would be important for them to have a foundation and decided that we would teach them about both religious traditions and raise them as Muslim. "

Photo courtesy of Omid Safi.

Among the few scholars of Islam in our country, **Omid Safi** is one of the most vocal, communicative, and available. He responded enthusiastically to the invitation to be part of this book, which he felt would help fill the terrible chasm between Muslims and their fellow Americans. He not only provided an interview, but has also written the introductory essay on American Muslims. His erudition is immense: all three of his degrees—bachelor, master, and doctorate—are in Islamic study. In addition to teaching at Colgate, he has published *Progressive Muslims: On Justice, Gender and Pluralism*, hundreds of articles, book reviews, conference papers and has four more books on Islam under contract. He is also interested in rethinking the ways that the academic study of religion is conceptualized within an academic framework and, along with two colleagues at Colgate, is working in this area.

Born in Jacksonville, Florida, to Iranian parents, he spent a portion of his childhood living and being educated in Iran, and finished his advanced education in the U.S. He is truly a product of both cultures, the American and the Iranian. The combination has served to produce a sensitive, clear-eyed hybrid of two highly different, hugely separate worlds.

The subject closest to his heart is a new form of independent, contemporary Muslim faith called Progressive Islam, which he discusses on these pages. "In America," he says, "in spite of the prejudices ... Muslims have the freedom, the social space to undertake a humane, pluralistic and inclusive understanding of Islam in ways very difficult to do in their home countries. It is a whole new thinking on Islam ... a *progressive* understanding of Islam."

Perhaps the most striking element of this interview is the unqualified stand that Professor Safi puts forth on the partial responsibility of America itself for the terrible disaster that befell us on 9/11/01. It is a view rarely mentioned by the press or on television but one that is held by thoughtful (albeit silent) Americans throughout our nation. Anyone with a humane, universal sense for justice will understand and empathize with it.

Is it correct for me to call you an American Islamic scholar?
It is correct. With a term like that I wonder which of those three words gets the most emphasis. It's certainly the case that I'm an American by birth, born in this country, having lived here for more than half of my life. I'm married to an American, have three children born here. At the same time, I also have connection and roots in other parts of the world that are very dear to me. So I wouldn't want those to be lost in calling myself American.

What, then, would be a better way of describing your position?
I would start out at the most general. I'd call myself what I am, which is a human being who both happens to be, and chooses to be, Muslim. And I am someone who is privileged, and also burdened, by being American, who has a

lot of the blessings and freedoms and opportunities that come along with being American.

But also I am very consciously and deliberately someone who struggles with the question, "What does it mean to be born into a civilization that is politically, economically, militarily the most powerful in the world today?" Because of that, I'd much rather start off by calling myself admittedly a human being who feels the greatest solidarity with other people all over the world, rather than starting off by calling myself an American something something.

Where did you spend your formative years?
In Iran. In the early '70s—and this may come as a surprise to some readers—my family made the choice to go back to Iran, where they are originally from, basically because they thought that Iran was a more family-friendly, safer place to live. Which in many ways it was and even continues to be, despite all the turmoil taking place there. I grew up in Iran from the time I was one till I was fifteen years old. So really the formative years of my childhood were spent there. And then in the summertime we would usually come back to the States or go to Europe or somewhere else. In a sense, my parents wanted us to be able to move back and forth between the two cultures with some level of ease. We were very fortunate that we had the financial means to be able to do this.

Is your father a businessman?
He's a physician, a pediatrician actually. He has a great love for children and that drives much of his work.

You received your Ph.D. in religion with "a concentration in Islamic studies." What does that phrase mean? Did you first study all faiths and then Islam?
That's the way that our program was set up. You generally start off by studying what people used to call comparative religion, so you would study a number of different religious traditions. My own training exposed me to the study certainly of Islam but also the Christian tradition, Judaism, a little bit of Hinduism, Buddhism, things of that sort. Then once you have had a few years of that kind of general exposure, you would then begin to focus on one particular project, one particular tradition, and even there the hope was that you would continue to bring tools. So for my particular study I ended up using some contemporary philosophy that had developed in late twentieth century Europe, people like Michel Foucault, a postmodern French philosopher. He revolutionized our understandings of the body, sexuality, state power and surveillance, and so on. I tried to apply such modern insights to Muslim societies that lived a thousand years ago. That's a good example in some ways of what these programs are designed to do.

The other reason that sometimes we resort to these convoluted phrases, like "a degree in religious studies with a concentration in Islamic studies," is that the term that previously people like myself used to describe ourselves is Islamicists, that is, people who specialize in the study of Islam. More recently, unfortunately, some people in this country, like Jerry Falwell, have started to use the term Islamicist to mean Muslim terrorist. So not entirely from our own choosing, we have found other terms to use, like "a specialist in religious studies with a concentration on Islamic studies."

When you received your Ph.D., were other Americans also receiving degrees in Islamic studies?
Islamic studies really has been the neglected child of the academy. To get a sense of this, take a look at what the departments of religion in most American universities have tended to look like. Fortunately, the picture is changing. But five or ten years ago, even today, if a department had six or seven people, generally what you found is that four or five of them would focus on things that emerge out of the Christian or the post-Christian part of the world and one person would do Jewish studies. It's been only in the last ten years or so, I think, that people have taken very seriously the fact that Muslims make up more than one-quarter of the world's population and that every university should have its own specialist to talk about Islam as a religious tradition—not primarily as it relates to contemporary conflicts and political issues in the Middle East—but Islam as religion, the same way that we talk about Christianity as religion and Judaism as religion. That picture *is* changing but, admittedly, we're still a long, long way away from where we need to be in this country in terms of the graduate-level study of Islam. The number of places that one can go to study Islam as a religious tradition is very small.

Duke University, where you got your full higher education, was one of the first schools to grant doctorates in Islamic studies. What other schools grant doctorates in this field?
The other two are the University of North Carolina (one of my advisers was there) and North Carolina State University. These three are very prominent in Islamic studies. I would say that in the last ten years or so, they've turned out as many graduates in Islamic studies as other departments in other fields.

Is there any reason that they are concentrated in one part of the country?
In the case of Duke, the reason that there is a flowering of the Islamic studies program is that there have been a multiple number of scholars in the region. In the time that I was there, three or four people were on staff whose main interest was the study of Islam as religion.

The field is young and still forming. Other places with Islamic programs usually have only one person who teaches the entire field of Islamic studies. If you have only one person, it's really not enough to have a whole program. Consider the critical mass of Muslims in the world and you realize how small and problematic Islamic religious study is here in America. Look at even the most respected places. Stanford University does not have a full-time religion person devoted to Islam. Harvard Divinity School, which is perhaps as reputable as any institution, does not have a full-time person devoted to Islam. The University of Chicago's Divinity School has only recently hired such a person. From what I am told, all three are taking steps to remedy that situation. That is a positive development in some ways. But we're just massively behind the amount of study available in the Christian and Jewish traditions and even behind the studies available of Hinduism and Buddhism.

There are people on campuses who know something in a general way about Islam, but their main involvement is in other departments, such as Middle Eastern studies or history. Their primary approach is not to Islam as religion. It may be true that our emphasis in Muslim studies has been on an historical or political approach, and on the study of contemporary conflict. For a moment, let's talk about it in an American context. Anybody who studies the 2000 election between Bush and Gore is not necessarily somebody that you turn to for a discussion of Christian theology. Right? In the case of Islam you have people who study, let's say, contemporary political science, and they're also having to explain to people the nuance aspect of Islam as religion.

Were the teachers of Islamic studies, who flowered in numbers at Duke University, of Middle Eastern origin or were they American?
No. All Americans. Some were Muslim, some were non-Muslim. But I would say that even the ones that were non-Muslim definitely had a very humanistic approach to the study of Islam. It certainly was not a polemical engagement.

Is there an Islamic college or university here in the United States?
There is an undergraduate institution, but the few attempts we've made in that direction have not been successful. Not because religious colleges are unknown here. Certainly there is a large number of Catholic institutions, such as Georgetown and Notre Dame. Some of our finest colleges started as Protestant schools. Even Colgate, where I teach, started out as a religious school. Brandeis University has had a long and ongoing involvement with the Jewish religion. We simply do not yet have a comparable situation with Islamic schools. There is now an ongoing attempt to start something like a religious institution, but it basically takes $100 million. If you happen to know somebody who has $100 million, let me know.

You spent your childhood in Iran. When you returned and entered our educational system at age fifteen, were you upset by the attitude of some Americans toward Muslims?

It has not been the best. When we came in the mid '80s, you had a not-so-pleasant situation, but in some ways it was still much better than it is now. I think today it is absolutely the low point, or at least, in the time that I've spent in this country. The main reason is that, in the mid '80s, basically what was going on was the hijackings, the airline hijackings that would take place from time to time. As a result of that, there was an ongoing series of negative associations.

Were the hijackers mainly Muslim?

Of Muslim Arab background, to a large extent. But the occurrences were infrequent and in some ways distant enough from the experience of most Americans. While we saw it on TV, it wasn't happening in New York or Chicago or LA. In many cases (not all), they had a peaceful resolution. It was a matter of negotiating some kind of thing. All of that obviously changed with 9/11. And what I feel is the lowest point of mass-level hatred—I don't know of any other word for it—is the prejudice and hatred that resulted against *all* Muslims. I don't recall such hatred at any other point in my own life. When I turn on the TV, almost on a daily level, there is such a barrage of negative images of Muslims, without a corrective of other Muslims who are working to bring humanity together, and that sort of thing.

I live in New York, watch the news programs but do not get a sense that there is a contempt toward Muslims in them. What specifically are the images you refer to?

Of course, you're not going to see a situation where somebody comes on TV and says explicitly, *All Muslims are evil*, except for the Jerry Falwells, of course. But we're not talking about the Jerry Falwells.

I have two things to say about it. For those of us, especially those who live in the Northeast or live in places in the country that have a good bit of racial and ethnic diversity, many of us, I think, I hope, look with quite a bit of disdain at that kind of a commentary from people like Jerry Falwell, and we don't really find it to be representative of the kind of America we want to be living in or perceive ourselves as living in. I fully recognize that. At the same time, given the fact that I am someone who spends a good bit of every year traveling to the South to visit my family and my wife's family, I think we have to be open and up-front about the fact that the kinds of statements that people like Jerry Falwell and Pat Robertson and Reverend Graham make with that negative perspective really are representative of a much larger percentage of Americans than we would ever be comfortable admitting to ourselves. Again, I don't take them to be representative of all of Christianity in any way, shape, or form. But I think that they do represent a significant voice within the self-identifying Evangelical Christian communities. Within those communities there is a kind of rampant, and I would say racist, hatred for Muslims. If you take a look at the fact that a quarter of the people in this country self-identify themselves as born-again Christians, you begin to realize that this is not exactly a marginal kind of perspective.

The second thing that I would say—and again I would agree with you that this kind of hatred is not explicit on the part of the news shows—is by making an analogy. Imagine a situation where every single time you see a murderer or crack dealer on a TV crime series, every single time that person is African American, Puerto Rican, or Mexican. At some point the cumulative weight of those depictions—not any one single individual story line—but the cumulative weight would produce objections: *Wait a minute, you know, I live in New York City where thousands of Puerto Ricans live and work in ordinary jobs and it's just absurd that every single time I see a Puerto Rican on TV, he's depicted as being a drug dealer.* And people would rebel against that and ask the networks to have their shows more balanced and a fairer representation of what a drug dealer looks like.

What I'm saying is that when you take a look at the way the American Muslim population by and large is depicted, you get similar distortion. People like my parents don't show up in TV series. You don't get a picture of the mainstream American Muslim community. We're six million plus strong and yet I would say over ninety percent of the images associated with Arabs and Muslims in the media is tied to situations of violence and conflict. Thus, over time, there is an unconscious association of Muslims and Arabs and violence. And that's what I find problematic. It's not that I think, for example, Peter Jennings or Tom Brokaw themselves are at fault. In fact, I think they're delightful journalists. But it's more the fact that we now have a twenty-four-hour round-the-clock media and they tend to follow the mantra of, *If it bleeds, it leads.*

So that mantra became a focus, a prefixed focus, on situations of conflict. For understandable reasons, there's a great level of conflict that takes place in and around the Muslims today, but when those comprise the predominant activity that we see in our media, that's where my problem is. I've asked my friends, *Can you name any mainstream American TV show that has a regularly occurring positive Muslim character?* The answer is no. How absurd, when you realize that there is the same number of American Muslims as there are American Jews. Think about the number of TV shows that have regularly occurring Jewish characters who are not automatically slandered. Or consider other ethnicities of similar size. The fact is that there isn't a single Muslim who shows up as a father, as a mother, a community member and not as a terrorist or a politician. That's where I think the problem lies.

Ethnic Americans get a bad deal from the entertainment media, especially Italian Americans who have been tainted with the Mafia association. The fact that the majority of Italians are respectable, with children growing up to be political, corporate, and academic leaders doesn't impress the media.

I remember when *The Sopranos* began, there was a whole set of conversations coming out of the Italian-American community, saying, *Wait a minute, we've gone down this road.* Imagine if that was the exclusive and predominant image associated with Italian Americans! It is not. That's what American Muslims want to see. New images of what we're really like. Kind of what you're doing with this book. You're taking a cross section of the American Muslim population so that you have teachers and doctors and engineers and scholars and policeman and taxi drivers, people from all walks of life. And that's in a sense all that we're asking for, to be represented fairly to offset what we're exposed to visually.

In view of everything, what do you think is the future of Islam in America?

I'm someone who wakes up every morning and makes a deliberate choice to remain hopeful about the future. The way that I like to look at it is that in terms of the ongoing presence of Muslims in America, both parties involved have to keep changing. It's not just Muslims and their understanding of Islam, but also that America itself has to continue to change to reflect the wholesome presence of these new friends who inhabit its shores now.

Things are happening. I'll start first with what is happening in the Muslim community, We all know there is now a large population of Muslims in America. One of the most exciting changes—and this is a tribute to the kinds of freedoms and opportunities that are present in this society—is that in spite of all the prejudices, this sizable population of Muslims has the freedom, the social space in which they can undertake a humane, pluralistic, and inclusive understanding of Islam in a way that would be very difficult to do in many of their home countries. I do think that is a tribute to this country, and I refer to the emergence of a whole new thinking on Islam that many people call a progressive understanding of Islam.

While many of us, myself included, have roots in Muslim countries, it's easier now to have this kind of conversation and more than that, an opportunity to attempt to establish communities in this country with the rights and freedoms that we are guaranteed. If that continues, I think that that would be the most positive outcome that I can foresee for the future of Muslims in America: Muslim American communities with a progressive understanding of Islam that could then serve as a role model for Muslims all over the world. And to some small extent, this is already happening. Muslim countries, ranging as far as Malaysia to Egypt to South Africa, are inviting this new kind of Muslim based in the U.S. to their home countries to give lectures, do workshops, and share their vision with Muslims abroad. Sometimes these American Muslims are invited back to their own countries to give lectures, do workshops, and share their vision of a progressive Islam.

It is a vision that has been allowed to be nurtured and developed slowly over time in this country. And again I think that this is directly because of things like freedom of speech, the right of people to practice their religion, things of that sort which this country does afford. And those are very positive developments. So that in a sense, if you want to think of it, we're not just looking at Islam coming from the outside to this country. You're seeing a reprocessing and reinterpretation of Islam in this country which is being recycled through the rest of the world.

Michael Wolfe, a writer on Islam, characterizes you as a progressive Islamicist. What are the differences between a progressive Islamicist and a traditional one?

For this purpose, let's call it progressive Muslim as opposed to Islamicist. It is a very simple and a basic idea, and I don't think it needs to be shrouded in elaborate terminology. Many people agree with the basic idea of Islam and that is simply the notion that each and every human life anywhere in this world, male or female, Muslim or non-Muslim, rich or poor, has precisely and exactly the same intrinsic worth. I want to say that this particular perspective—that each human life has the exact same worth—is also a secular humanist kind of perspective.

But while it's harmonious with secular humanism, it's different because there's a *religious* perspective. The religious part is directly built on Koranic and Biblical understanding. We look back at the passages within the Koran and the Book of Genesis in the Bible—that talk about God breathing his own spirit into humanity. We take those passages very seriously. We say that it wasn't just Adam that had the breath of God in him; it is, in fact, each and every one of us. And if each and every one of us—Iraqi, American, Afghani, Palestinian, Israeli, Indian, Chinese, Japanese, South African—if each of us has this breath of God breathed into him, then each and everyone of us is entitled to a God-given sense of dignity and human worth. And then our task would be to acknowledge that and to remove any obstacle that dehumanizes people and devalues the worth and value that life gives them.

Jewish perspectives and Christian perspectives are very resonant with this kind of view. All of us in the Muslim community, the Jewish community, the Christian community, the Hindu community, we're all working together on this shared acknowledging of the worth of all humanity.

But we're also struggling against other people in our own religious communities that—some call them traditionalists, others call them fundamentalists—say, *No, not everyone has exactly the same value.* What's more, they believe that truth is something bound up to their own community. Thus Muslims of this sort think, *Only we have been granted the full realization of truth and everybody else is misled.* Evangelical Christians take very literally the notion that, *None shall come to the Father unless through Christ.* Or those members from the Jewish community who look at only the Jews as being the *Chosen people of God*, and *No one else has equal access to a relationship with God*. And, in a sense, we're challenging all of those. We're challenging anyone who would set up that kind of exclusivist understanding of who is entitled to access to truth and think that some lives are more valuable than others.

We've come to realize, sadly, in this past century that if we don't attach value and recognize the worth of lives of all peoples, it becomes much easier to kill them, or to remain silent when they are being killed. And I think we have seen this—you know, very few people are aware that in the last generation or so, in a place like Congo in Africa, three and one half million people have been slaughtered. And why don't we recognize this and act? I would say it's because we don't attach, at the end of the day, the same level of worth for African lives.

From the perspective of somebody like myself, that kind of attitude is profoundly racist, and we tend to dismiss it by either not talking about it or if we talk about it, we say, *Well, these people have been killing one another forever and there's nothing we can do*. I think that's unacceptable. Their parents love them every bit as much as I love my daughter or my son, and they're entitled to living a life of peace and justice where food is not something that they have to beg for, but something that can be earned. The progressive view, as opposed to the fundamentalist view, believes that *all* human life is equally worthy.

Will progress that has been made here toward a more progressive kind of Islam create a situation where America might acquire an important position in the world of Islam?

I do think it's a possibility and it's something that Muslim reformers have been talking about and predicting for a few generations now. But I want to be clear about this: It can take root not just in America, but in many places of periphery. Thoughtful Muslims everywhere realize that places like Saudi Arabia offer nothing in terms of this kind of a progressive, inclusivistic understanding of Islam. Where they do find it is in places along the periphery of the Muslim world. Look at a country like Malaysia, which really is trying to establish itself as one of the leading voices of progressive Islam worldwide. Look at South Africa, where Muslims, albeit in a minority situation, have provided an incredibly inspiring model of a progressive community. And I would add to that list America, where even as a relatively small, marginalized population, American Muslims can take part in that global progressive understanding of Islam. But this is not a given and this is something that would have to be earned through a lot of struggle.

I'm going to get down to something not often talked about. As far as you know, what is the extent of ultrafundamentalist Wahhabi belief in the United States?

It's very hard to put a number on it for a simple reason. Most people who in fact follow Wahhabi teachings and the Wahhabi interpretation of Islam may have never heard of the word Wahhabism. In fact, if you ask them, *Are you Wahhabi?* they're likely to say, *No, I'm just a Muslim.* You have to take a very close look at where they are getting their understanding of Islam. In the same way that very few people in this country are likely to say, *I'm a fundamentalist Christian.* They might say, *I'm a born-again Christian,* or *I'm an evangelical Christian.* But many people do not use the word *fundamentalist* to describe themselves. That's one of the challenges we have to cope with. But I think what we can do is to recognize that Wahhabism, a movement in Islamic thought, started out in the eighteenth century in what is today Saudi Arabia. Essentially, it's an extreme form of Islamic exclusivism. Not only does it state that Jews and Christians and others have no access to truth, it goes even further and says that most *Muslims* do not have access. In a sense, the only interpretation of Islam that Wahhabism accepts is its own.

This is something that goes contrary to the previous twelve hundred years of Islamic thought, where even Muslim scholars would have profound disagreements about an issue. They avoided acting as absolute authorities. They would preface their work with statements such as, *From where I'm situated, this is how I see something but I can see that from where you are, it looks drastically different.* That's really much more the way Muslims historically have tended to look at situations. The kind of dogmatic behavior that you get from the Wahhabis is very unusual, if not unprecedented, in the history of Islam.

Why has it become so prominent? It's basically very simple: *oil.* Before 1930 when oil production really kicked off in Saudi Arabia, Wahhabis by and large remained a very marginal group in the Muslim world, very marginal. It's really through the production of oil that they started getting their hands on billions and billions of dollars. The Wahhabis started out as a group of what in this country we would call clerics, a religious-minded almost-clergy class (even though that term is not used in Islam).

The way the Wahhabis established themselves in power was by forming an alliance with the ruling dynasty of Arabia, which was a family called the Saud family. This is where we get the name Saudi Arabia. To imagine it, think of a clan made up of people like Jerry Falwell and Pat Robertson who align themselves with the ruling dynasty of the Bushes and decide together to rule America. In a sense (frightening thought) but, in a sense, that's what you have taking place in Saudi Arabia. It's a linkage of the fundamentalist group of interpreters of Islam with a ruling dynasty. They interpret Islam in a certain way and after they got their hands on oil, they became able to export their vision of Islam, some would say, bastardization of Islam, all over the world. When we think of missionaries, we tend to think of Christians who go to Africa or to China to convert people. What the Wahhabis have actually tried to do is to send missionaries *to convert other Muslims.* They send missionaries to Africa, to Malaysia, and to the United States. This is, in a sense, what those of us who self-identify ourselves as progressives end up having to fight. Some Muslims who never have heard of the word Wahhabism may be influenced by it. Their understanding of Islam comes from the mosques, the Islamic centers, and the Muslim Students Association that have been shaped by people and literature provided to them by the Wahhabis.

Then Wahhabism is an evil force in America as well?
As a matter of principle I avoid using the word evil. I don't use that word whether one is talking about America or Islam because it too easily leads to demonization. I would say that Wahhabis and others influenced by them are supporters of exclusivism and they are an obstacle toward unity and bringing people together.

Have they made their influence felt in some American mosques?
Yes.

How deep was its influence on the tragic events of the World Trade Center?
The group that by now most Americans are familiar with, al-Queda, who destroyed the World Trade Center, can only be understood if you understand Wahhabism. Al-Queda wouldn't exist without Wahhabi ideology. It is more than just Wahhabi ideology. It is more than just Wahhabism. Most Wahhabis are simply obnoxious fundamentalists, but they are not, by and large, physically violent. Al-Queda takes the next step and says that you have to combine Wahhabi ideology with the actual killing of what they call the Crusader-Zionist alliance, which is basically, *Kill Christians and Jews.*

It's hard for me to overemphasize this for our audience, but this is an unprecedented statement in the history of Islam. Even when you have had theological differences with Christians and Jews, Muslims never randomly killed them. In that sense, it's hard to see it as anything but a bastardization of centuries of Islamic thought.

To bring the questioning back to a more personal note, is your wife a Muslim?
She is not formally a Muslim.

Did she convert?
No. She did not. Under traditional Islamic law, at least Koranically, it is clear that Muslim men can marry non-Muslim women. The prophet Muhammad himself had a wife who was Christian. I'm not referring to Khaddifa. It was a woman by the name of Mariam, or Mary. So the precedent goes back a long time.

Can a Muslim woman marry a non-Muslim man?
That's where some controversy comes in. There are today many Muslim feminists such as myself asking the question, *If it is permitted for men to marry a non-Muslim, what is to keep women from doing it?* There are all kinds of justification that people have given which they feel explain the prohibition set centuries ago of a Muslim woman marrying a non-Muslim. But I don't think it explains the case any more.

Is your wife Christian?
She was raised Catholic.

If you prefer not to talk about this, just tell me.
Up to a certain point. We haven't gotten to that point yet.

Please tell me when we do. Does she still practice Catholicism?
If that's defined by going to a church every Sunday and receiving Communion, then I would say no. If it's defined in an ethical way, of having very strong faith in God and leading a life of love and service to humanity, then I would say absolutely yes.

Have both of you had to accommodate yourselves to each other from a religious and ethical point of view? If so, how have you worked it out?
On the days that I have a sense of humor, I would say that accommodation takes place on those days that end in a y.

Can you amplify a bit?
Accommodation takes place on Thursday, Friday, Saturday, Sunday, Monday, Tuesday, Wednesday, all days that end in a y. Accommodation takes place every day. I think most marriages probably do, but especially marriages where people come from different religious, racial, and cultural backgrounds. There is a kind of everyday accommodating and compromise that goes on, and our marriage is certainly no exception.

In what religious tradition are you and your wife raising your children?
We felt it would be important for them to have a foundation, so we thought that we would teach them about both religious traditions and raise them as Muslim.

She agreed to that? Her understanding is extraordinary. How old are your children?
We have a ten-year-old, a two-and-a-half-year-old and a six-month-old.

Would you like them to attend school here or in the Middle East?
Given what our family is and what it looks like, we are people who live in this country, partly for reasons of employment and partly for reasons of choice. Primarily we are going to be spending the bulk of our life in the U.S. However, one thing that does matter greatly to me is that my children be knowledgeable and comfortable moving back and forth between the two cultures in the same way that I've been able to do. One of the great benefits that my parents extended to me was the fluidity of moving back and forth and being able to be at home and at ease in different places. It's partly for that reason that I identify myself as a human being to you.

Providing my children with a chance to feel at home in different places and countries is ultimately the largest gift that I can give them. It's not to downplay their Muslim-ness or their American-ness but I don't want them to think of themselves as American before *human*, or as Muslim before *human*. To gain that kind of understanding, I don't think you can do it by spending all of your life in one place surrounded by people that look always like you, and I think you need to be in conversation with other people and to travel if at all possible. Last summer my wife and I had a chance to take our children and about fifteen university students to Turkey, which is a wonderful modern Muslim country with a profoundly pluralistic past of Muslims, Jews, and Christians living side by side.

Turkey was an amazing period of growth and discovery for all of us, but especially for my children. There instead of seeing the criminal stereotype of Muslims depicted on American TV, they could see people on the street, real people, attractive people, the waiter who brought us Turkish tea in a tearoom, the waitress in a favorite restaurant who would perform small kindnesses for her American Muslims. In one restaurant, they would bring us a plate of the biggest, ripest strawberries you had ever seen in your life and place them in front of my daughter. Every single time we went there, they'd place beautiful strawberries before her. Because my daughter is, praise God, extraordinarily beautiful, they must have taken a liking to her and every time they could, they would present her with beautiful strawberries. That little act registered more for my wife about the humanity and warmth of Muslims than a thousand hours of lectures about Muslim stereotypes on American TV. It's something that's real; it's something that you see, an experience that becomes a part of who you are. The next time that somebody says, *Well, Muslims are this and that*, you know that that's not true because you have seen it, you have tasted it, you have experienced it. That's the kind of experience I want to be able to give my children.

Can you give us your educated take on the question that is asked endlessly: What happened on 9/11, who did it, and why?
The question is always appropriate, given the fact that 9/11 is the most significant act of violence to take place on American soil, and I would add, since the

genocide of the native peoples of this country. We tend to forget sometimes we've had other times in our history when nearly three thousand people have been wiped out on a single day. Because 9/11 happened in the modern portion of our history, because it happened in front of our eyes, and because it happened after most of us arrived in this country, it's a day that shapes American history, so I think it's an important question to ask.

Here's how I understand the events of that day. Let's start out by acknowledging responsibility and by talking about the fact that, no matter what the political or religious motivations of the people who undertook this action were (and one can and should have a critical conversation about that, as well), the actions of 9/11 represented the brutal murder of twenty-eight hundred civilians who were not just American citizens but citizens of some forty different countries. Of those twenty-eight hundred people who were killed from many nations (the final number is not really known), it is certain that over two hundred of them were of Muslim background. So this represents not just the killing of Americans but the killing of human beings from all over the world, and included in this number are Muslims.

Do you think that the terrorists themselves knew they were killing Muslims as well?

I don't think they cared or that it crossed their minds. I think the actions of 9/11 obviously are not random targets of violence, but a methodically planned out course of action in view of their *choices* of destruction and it's important to point them out. Let's think about where they hit.

They hit the World Trade Center, which is perhaps the symbol of American commercial and economic might. They hit the Pentagon, which is clearly the symbol of American military might. The plane that fell down in Pennsylvania was planned to hit the White House, and that was the symbol of American government. So this was a deliberately chosen attack at the very symbols of American economic, military, and civic might. There's a profound level of hatred expressed against American institutions, and this has to be pointed out.

The attackers not only came from a Muslim background, but the way that they justified the attack was specifically based on a select reading of Islam. I'm not one of the people who would say that these people are not Muslim. I radically and profoundly disagree with the interpretation of Islam that they have. But I do not deny, I cannot deny, that what they did, they perceived and they justified of themselves.

As a comparison, think of a group like the KKK, which most of us in this country find utterly unacceptable, distasteful, and full of hatred. When one listens to them, they justify their hatred by citing select passages from the Bible. Even though I may think, and you may agree, that they don't represent the ideals of Christianity, it's important to realize how they perceive of themselves, on their own. This is exactly how I look at the al-Queda members of 9/11. Even though I find the actions of these people hateful, I have to acknowledge that they're justifying themselves based on their reading of Islam.

What are the ethics of war in Islamic law?

The specific action that al-Queda members undertook, despite their purported allegiance to Islam, is, to the last element of detail, rejected under Islamic law. Let me explain. In Islamic law, even in a time of warfare, which al-Queda members see themselves as being in (at war with America), there's a way in which one has to fight. There's an ethics of war, and those legal teachings state that one cannot kill civilians. You can only kill soldiers on a battlefield but you cannot kill civilians, you cannot kill women, you cannot kill children, you cannot kill the elderly or the sick. You can only kill an adult male who's facing you in the battlefield. Now, from the perspective of someone like myself, who's a pacifist, even that could be avoided. In any case, our Islamic law has been defied. Those are the only people you are allowed to kill and when you look at the casualties of 9/11, it is clear that they absolutely violate the principles of Islamic law itself. Not only was 9/11 a violation of a code of conduct that we Americans believe in, but also from the perspective of Islamic law, the action violated the rules.

Should America itself take on any responsibility for what happened on 9/11?

Yes. It is not just Muslims who have to take responsibility for this action and face the extremism in the Muslim community, but as Americans we also have a responsibility. And here's where, I think, our responsibility comes into play. One has to realize that al-Queda members, when they talk about why they undertake this action, will point to things like the history of the U.S. supporting dictatorial regimes in the Muslim world, which is the case. And they talk about—and again this is something that makes many of us uncomfortable but I think it has to be talked about openly and compassionately in a national dialogue—they talk about the history of five decades of support for Israel in the face of ongoing persecution of Palestinians. To pretend that these two actions do not enrage and hurt and bring so much suffering to people in the Muslim world is to simply deny the reality. What we need is a national dialogue among Americans.

I have to disagree with, and challenge, and resist the course of action that the terrorists have undertaken and I must continue to do that as a person who is committed to moral teachings. At the same time, I also have to be committed to changing the course of action that we as Americans have been taking in the rest of the world. So that when people think of us, they don't think of us as supporters to evil regimes and the supporters of Israel. They should be thinking of us as people who go around feeding those who are starving and establishing schools and hospitals, and things of that sort. One of our challenges is removing the sources of terrorist justification.

How can America change?

Her job isn't complete. She has to continue to evolve. I'm in accordance with Martin Luther King when he perceived of America as the great unfinished experiment. I think we are. We are an incredibly noble experiment in human history, but we're half-baked. And we have a long way to go. When I take a look at the erosion of civil liberties, when I take a look at the PATRIOT bill—the so-called PATRIOT bill that gave Ashcroft and the Justice Department the ability to take away so many civil liberties—and the second one that's on the way, these are elements that Americans like me would have to resist. It's precisely in times of fear, like right now, that it is most tempting to give up those elements of civil liberties that make us a great nation.

If America is worth saving, it's worth saving not because it is a regime without liberties but precisely because we are a democratic free society. If we give up our freedom, then there is nothing worth saving. That's the challenge.

In concluding, is there one last thing you'd like to say?

Yes. Let me talk briefly on two terms that we use all the time, nationalism and patriotism. Especially since 9/11, there's a marked rise in American nationalism, where we see ourselves as superior to the rest of the world. It's something that people like me are obliged to resist because we simply see ourselves as human beings whose lives have no more worth but no less worth than anybody else's on the planet. We've seen, especially in the time leading up to the Iraq war, some of the ugly side of nationalism when you think of the tensions with the French and things of that sort. That's the dark side of nationalism.

Where I would feel more comfortable is greater use of the word *patriotic*, not in the sense of waving the flag and stopping the process of thinking, but rather *patriotism* in the sense that we talked about with Dr. King. I refer to thinking of America as the great unfinished experiment and the sense that we have to hold this country accountable for our highest ideals and standards. We recognize that we have an imperfect history with Native American peoples, with African Americans, women, Asian Americans, now with Muslims, but at the same time we must urge ourselves along to the highest level of morality and justice that we're capable of as a culture. And that's what I would see as being the good *patriot*.

Sharmin Ahmad

A father's assassination in the Indian subcontinent

There are a lot of good secular values in American culture that are similar to Islamic values, beautiful values in the society around us, such as honesty, compassion and hard work. As for some of the bad values, the secular-minded themselves might do well to expel.

When I look in another person's eye, I see a reflection of myself. Seeing myself there, I take this to mean that this person is a reflection of me. We are part of each other.

People don't realize that the Muslim community came to this country for peace and a good life. It was a great opportunity. Now that is sort of shattered. We are blamed for someone else's crime.

Photo courtesy of Sharmin Ahmad.

Among the foreign-born Muslim women who furthered their education after arriving in America and then went on to lead impressive professional lives, there is **Sharmin Ahmad** (on previous page with her daughter), born in Bangladesh, east of India. In true American fashion, she has combined both her activism and work life outside the home with managing a family of husband and three children. A separate interview with her fourteen-year-old daughter, Aumrita, appears elsewhere in this book.

Sharmin Ahmad's interests and pursuits sometimes overlap, but the currents remain constant. Her primary interest is the education of her children, which especially engages her at this writing because her daughter enrolled for the first time in a non-Islamic school. Ms. Ahmad has a background as an elementary schoolteacher and is now an interfaith consultant and lecturer, social and environmental activist, and feminist for the empowerment of women worldwide.

She writes poetry and is also the author of a book for children, parents, and educators that appeared in November 2003 in a bilingual English and Bengali edition, which is available in the United States via e-mail: reepia@hotmail.com. True to the author's hopes and beliefs, it is the story of a soul's journey to this earth, soon to be born as a little girl, who has to find the right mother to guide her and her generation toward peace, nonviolence, and a united humanity.

Sharmin Ahmad's personal story, as revealed on these pages, speaks for itself. She is the daughter of the founding prime minister, leader and statesman, Tajuddin Ahmad of Bangladesh, who in 1975 was slain by the military coup d'état. Her mother, Syeda Zohra Tajuddin, rebuilt her husband's party after he was murdered and became a critical figure both for Bangladesh and for women. She is a descendant of the Prophet's family.

Are you happy with the way things are going for your daughter Aumrita at John F. Kennedy High School?

I'm happy with the way teachers are caring about the students and Aumrita seems to have blended in very well. She's a festive kind of kid. She loves being with people, and she loves socializing.

But I also feel there's so much peer pressure on unnecessary things. That concerns me. For example, when we were her age, even in our regular public schools, we had uniforms. This isn't only in our country of Bangladesh, but in the majority of countries, public schools have uniforms. There is less competition with wearing what, and so on. With everybody similarly dressed, academics was the main concern. However, even though she wore a uniform at the Muslim Community School in Potomac, Maryland, she hasn't worn a head scarf in the street. She wears modest American clothing. But when we have the festival of Eid al-Fitr, the special occasion that ends the month of

Ramadan, she dresses up in Bangladeshi dresses.

I have no concern with the way she dresses, and she gets good grades. What concerns me is the overall effect that this emphasis on dress and on pop culture and pop music puts on things. There's not much interest on what is going on in the world. I would like her generation to be a bit more concerned about the world, what is happening around us, and not so much concentrated on what's going on in pop music or shallow sitcoms.

Pop music, pop culture, are fine but they should be balanced with some understanding of what's going on in the society, where we are, particularly today. I personally feel you need to be a very vocal, conscientious member. Even in the school system, the violence, the language—people use harsh words which they pick up from the movies and TV. When I talk to teachers about this, they tell me that the parents are doing two jobs, in the home and outside the home. They don't have much time.

I'm afraid we may lose the critical thinkers of our next generation.

Do you and your husband both work?
Yes, we do.

How do you manage working and all your other activities, like bringing up a family?
I started to work full time after my kids came to a certain age. I worked as an elementary-grade teacher, and we would go to the same schools and come back the same time. Although I have good academic credentials, I got low pay, but still felt that with such a schedule, my children wouldn't miss me and there would be somebody in the house to look after them. It's a schedule that allows you to build a foundation of home support. It did work. With Aumrita, I did not have any major concerns. When parents aren't home, there's no one to talk with. Kids bring home a lot of confusion. They need guidance.

Do you have other children?
I have a son named Taj Choudhury, who is almost five years older than she is. He's a student at the University of Maryland. He loves government and politics and is debating a choice between business and government and politics. Next year he will take one course in Islamic studies and likes to explore languages and cultures. He's also a black belt in martial arts, and plays piano and composes music. Like Aumrita, he attended the Muslim school until the eighth grade.

Both Taj and Aumrita are children by my first husband. My present husband, Amr Abdalla, an Egyptian Arab, has a son, Joseph Abdalla, by a previous marriage, and he also lives with us. These three children make up our family. Joseph is also a black belt in martial arts.

What languages does Taj study?

So far, he has taken Spanish, Yiddish and already knows Bengali. I taught him that. We're not of Arab descent, we're Bengali. He can read and write Arabic. He reads the Koran in Arabic and received first prize in recitation—that's readings from the Koran. It has a special technique and is performed in a very rhythmic and melodious way.

[*Author's note: The Muslim Community School that Taj and Aumrita attended offers a unique approach in teaching science to students, connecting Koranic revelations with our modern scientific understanding. Taj, who was in the sixth grade at the time, participated in a regional science fair and the theme of his project on astronomy described the Koranic concept, with chapter and verse, that foretold of scientific discoveries, such as the big bang. For this contribution, he received the certificate of merit from the National Space Club "in recognition of superior understanding ... and a demonstrated ability to apply this knowledge."*]

Since your husband is Egyptian Arab, do you find that in the practice of your Islam as a Bangladeshi and his as an Egyptian Arab, there are occasional differences of opinion or customs in the home?

Fundamentally, no. Culturally, there are some differences. Islamic culture differs in different countries. For example, the largest Muslim nation, Indonesia, speaks a different language and dresses differently from Muslims in Arab nations. (The Arabs, by the way, are about twenty percent of the total Muslim population across the globe.)

Islam is a monotheistic religion with multifarious interpretations and expressions. It's fundamentally the same in all countries when it comes to the belief in the unity of God, and the practice of prayer, charity, compassion, justice, and so on. Then, how it expresses itself is according to culture. An example of this is during Ramadan when all day you are without food or water and then at sunset you break the fast. Ramadan lasts for twenty-nine or thirty days depending on the lunar cycle.

Now, how cultural expectation comes to play within the religion at Ramadan is that after breaking our fast with dates (a practice among Muslims universally following the tradition of prophet Muhammad), we Muslims from the Indian Subcontinent prefer to eat hot/spicy and deep-fried food such as lentil fritters, eggplant fritters and *chola bhaji* (a fried, dark brown legume) as appetizers before the main meal. In Bangladesh, *piaju* (lentil fritter) is very popular as a Ramadan appetizer. Piaju is made of orange-colored lentils (known as *masoor daal*). The lentils are soaked in water for a few hours. Then they are coarsely blended with a little water, together with finely chopped onion, cilantro, green chilies, a dash of turmeric powder, ground cumin, ground red pepper, and salt. These ingredients are mixed to a paste, then divided into small balls, and deep-fried gently in hot oil until they are golden brown. They're so tasty! In fact, to us, the Ramadan meal without piaju is incomplete. Some say, *Piaju means Ramadan is here.*

When we were married, my husband, the Egyptian Arab, said, *What is this deep-fried spicy thing? Where is the soup?* I was astonished. I soon learned that Egyptians generally don't eat hot, spicy foods. They use the least amount of spice. Garlic is their main spice which they use with tomato in most dishes, similar to Italian food (one side of Egypt is on the Mediterranean). After breaking the fast with dates, they begin their meal with chicken or lamb-based soup. So, when my husband asked me, Where is the soup? I said, What? Soup for Ramadan? What we do now is compromise: I make soup, I also make piaju, and he got to love the piaju, and we love the soup.

As your children grow up and become more and more a part of the secular world of America, how will you try to keep them focused on Islam?

Kids are like birdlings in the nest. Once they start to fly, mothers and parents have the least kind of involvement. As they grow, I will continue to guide them, but it would be a different way of guiding. I recall my own experience of growing up in Bangladesh. The home environment was open. It was not strict and the Islamic values that were there were not pressed on us in a harsh or rigid way. But our own religious seed was implanted. What happened, in my own case, was that I explored and explored, continued to read and in later years I got more involved in interfaith activities, in finding the commonalities between religions. I'm indebted to my parents who had sown that seed. I had my confusions, I had my rebellion as any teenager, and went through periods of distress. But I'm sure that the seed, once it's planted well, will grow into a beautiful human being. And I'm sure that my kids, no matter what, will find the right course and direction.

You used the word secular to describe America. I don't think Muslims should think in terms of *secular* (meaning American) versus *Islamic*. There are a lot of good secular values in American culture that are similar to Islamic culture, beautiful values in the society around us, such as honesty, compassion, and hard work. As for some of the bad values the secular-minded themselves might do well to expel. It's not either/or.

How old were you when you came here? Can you tell us about your education?

I was twenty-four when I came here. I received my bachelor's level degree in Bangladesh in liberal arts. When I came here I took a master's in women's studies at George Washington University and I also concentrated on early-childhood education on a graduate level.

Why do you call yourself an activist? What kind of causes are you involved in?

Whenever I feel there is a social plight that needs to be explored and talked about, I take it up and organize people or I join an organization to show solidarity and support. There are many issues that draw me, including interfaith groups, feminist and pro-women humanitarian issues, and environmental problems that I feel very deeply about. I'm very much involved in what will happen in the future if we don't love and protect the environment that is nurturing us.

In interfaith issues, where does your activity lie?

I am very active in interfaith issues and have worked as a consultant and received so many invitations from various universities and institutions to talk about commonality and bridge-building across the religious boundaries. Interfaith communication is ongoing with me and I was delighted when the Soroptimist International in USA gave me their Woman of Distinction award in 1996 for outstanding contributions in the field of international good will and understanding.

Related to interfaith, I also believe with each fiber of my being that every society and civilization, including the Christian, Islamic, Judaic, Hindu, Buddhist, Native American, and others, has something good to offer. There is no *clash* of civilizations, as Huntington stated in his article "The Clash of Civilizations" [first published in *Foreign Affairs Journal*, New York, 1993], but an *exchange* of civilizations. As Islam opened the door for the European Renaissance, it also became enriched by Greek and Indian philosophy and science. And there are certain universal values that we all share, such as honesty, kindness, charity, good work ethics, humility, and so on. I encourage my children to relate to the larger American society through these values, and resist vices such as drugs, alcohol, premarital sex, music and movies promoting sex and violence.

I ask them to understand that Islam is not the only religion that resists those vices, but all spiritual and religious traditions do. I try to introduce into their own lives the beauties and gifts of different civilizations, like piano music in classical western music, as well as the songs of Rabindranath Tagore from our own Bengali culture and Sufi music from Islamic mystical tradition. Hopefully, by planting these seeds in them, they will blossom into a flowering tree giving fragrance to humanity. In any case, I will have tried my best.

Incidentally, it was through my interfaith activities that I found my husband. We are forever grateful to the Bethel United Church of Christ in Arlington, Virginia, for bringing us together. That church invited me to speak on women in Islam and invited him to speak on the Arab world. At that time I didn't know him well. I met him just twice, briefly, at human-rights conventions. He said, *Why don't we sit together and prepare our speeches, what we plan to say and all that?* In the process we exchanged our hearts. Nine days before the presentation and within five months from our first meeting, we were married. The church celebrated our first wedding anniversary with a grand party.

My husband, incidentally, is named Amr (no vowel in the second syllable because in Arabic it is pronounced differently). He did his Ph.D. in conflict resolution from George Mason University and currently he's a professor of the Peace Operations Policy Program at George Mason. He has developed dynamic training programs in conflict resolution for the grassroots Muslim community. He is very much involved in the interfaith dialogue.

We have been like buddies in our interfaith journeys and I feel very grateful that had it not been for the church initiative I wouldn't be married to an Egyptian Arab. You see, I come from a Bengali culture, from Bangladesh, and culturally we are very different. The religion may be the same, but the expression, the dress, even food habits are not. I had no problem with this, but at the same time I was not thinking about moving in that direction. Now that we have been married for almost five years, I can say from experience that cultural differences provide an excellent opportunity for enrichment if one thinks about it, and love and faith become the true connection of our hearts. The Koran makes an excellent point about spousal relationships: *And among His signs is this, that He created for you mates from among yourselves, that you may live in tranquility with them, and He has put love and mercy between you* (Koran 30:21).

Can you talk more about interfaith? I think it's the only hope for the future, particularly in view of the racist attitudes that fundamentalism of a religion promotes.

I can only answer your question about interfaith more fully by circuitously describing what has happened to me in the past. This will also explain my work for the empowerment of women. I have to delve into some of my background. But it is partly political, so please bear with me. I come from a highly political family.

Bangladesh was part of Pakistan at that time and was known as East Pakistan. My father, Tajuddin Ahmad, was the general secretary and he was one of the main thinkers and visionaries of Awami League, a large-scale political party—*awami* means "people's." So what happened when Pakistan came into being in 1947, was that East Pakistan, under a decision based on religion, became part of Pakistan despite being twelve hundred miles apart and culturally different. [*Author's Note: Geographically, India lay between the East Pakistan and West Pakistan provinces. Both sections were separated about twelve hundred miles with India lying in between.*] But soon East Pakistan realized that the British were being replaced as colonial masters by Pakistani military rulers who succeeded in turning East Pakistan, or Bangladesh, our part of the country, into a colony. This meant that East Pakistan's resources were exploited for refurbishing their section of the country, which is West Pakistan.

Despite the fact that we constituted about fifty-six percent of the population of entire Pakistan, we had the least representation. We were also discriminated against economically and politically. My father was a deeply spiritual man and he got very disgruntled by how religion was abused and misused by the Pakistani military rulers. In their hands, Islam became a symbol of repression. They used it in a sectarian way to disseminate the idea that Muslims of other races and cultures and people who did not belong to the Islamic faith, belonged to a subhuman species.

My father came from a very devout Muslim family and he took up the cause of the exploited groups. In December 1970, there was a general election for the first time in which my father's party won a landslide victory over the economic democratic program the opposition was espousing. People rejoiced that finally Islam could be properly used, in a country whose people—Buddhists, Christians, Hindus, Muslims, the tribal people, all together—would comprise a country where justice would prevail, without economic exploitation. People would be able to determine their own future through democratic means.

The next course would have been that the West Pakistani military leaders as promised would be handing over power to the elected party. (I cannot separate myself from my political background—it's deeply connected.) The Pakistani military group did not hand over power. Instead, in 1971 on the twenty-fifth of March, they started a mass genocide in which more than a million people were killed and countless numbers of women and girls were raped. Within nine months, this huge genocide occurred. Unfortunately, the Pakistan dictators were helped by the Kissinger and Nixon administration, full fledged.

The Bengali people, and myself as a child, were seeing the very imperialistic nature of the United States government. Good-hearted people, like Bob Dylan, George Harrison, and Ravi Shankar, who had always cared for people's movements, sang songs in our behalf. Even Senator Kennedy supported us by coming to the war fronts and visiting the refugee camps. These were the people who defended us.

So I became a refugee at the age of eleven because of the genocide against the Bengali population. My father, as the founding prime minister and a wartime leader of the liberation war, had to flee. After he formed the government in Bangladesh, he was pushed back and had to take shelter in India. He founded an exile government there. So our lives were in danger, our names were on the death list. We crossed the border to India at the end of May.

Distraught at all that was happening, I told my mother that I wanted to do something for our country. I missed it and life as a refugee was not good. She said, *Why don't you start to pray to God for the freedom fighters and pray for your father that he become successful in liberating?* I knew how to pray, but wanted to have more formal understanding. So I bought the prayer book, *How to Pray in the Islamic Way.* Then I wanted to see how people pray in *other* religions, so I got a book on Buddha who, like Muhammad, found wisdom of equality through meditation. So perhaps meditation can also help me, I thought. I also looked into Hindu mythology, which showed the power of prayer. In a sense, spirituality for me became synonymous with freedom.

Then my father and three colleagues were brutally killed in prison by a military coup. The same group also killed the father of the nation, Sheikh Mujibur Rahman, and members of his family in his residence. The CIA was aware of the coup, and encouraged it—I'm not speaking out of my own experience. It was also documented. My father was murdered in 1975 when I was fifteen and living in Bangladesh.

When my father and top leaders of my father's party were killed, the party was shaken up. The military rule began, and my mother, who was about forty at the time, a widow with four children (the oldest being fifteen and the youngest five) took up the whole dismantled party and got involved reshaping and rebuilding the party my father left behind. In spite of threats of the military government, she went door to door, village to village, rebuilding the party. And I don't think she ever missed any prayer, she is so devout and spiritual. She also believed absolutely that, in nation-building, women should have equal say as men. And people have revered her since then. She became a critical leader in the most crisis-ridden period of our nation, Incidentally, she is a descendant of the Prophet's family, and her name is Syeda Zohra Tajuddin. The last name, which is after my father, means "crown of religion." Muslim women are not required to change their last names after marriage, but my mother did change hers out of love for my father.

What do you personally bring to the issue of interfaith?

In my speaking engagements, when urging the acceptance of all peoples of different cultures and religions, I like to point out that when I looked in another person's eye, I see a reflection of myself. Seeing myself there, I take this to mean that this person is a reflection of *me*; we are part of each other. Unless we start our mission with that perspective, we'll always fail. We'll become prejudgmental unless we see in the other person a reflection of ourselves. Otherwise, we will breed a self-righteous kind of mind-set that's not good.

Who exactly are your audiences, and what is their reaction?

Non-Muslim Americans usually, but also Muslim audiences, especially in mosques. Although the majority of local mosques I attend are progressive, some have been very orthodox and when I started to speak, they didn't like my point of view. These people are funded and guided by believers in an ultra-orthodox Saudi doctrine called Wahhabism. I'm not referring only to financial help that Wahhabis give to mosques, but also to instilling the Wahhabi way of thinking.

May I digress for a moment to the Wahhabis? Wahhabi doctrine has been able to spread so far because Wahhabis have the petro dollar money. I know this sounds like a horrible thing to say, but I find it is so. Such mosques are the offshoot of a Wahhabi philosophy in which women and non-Muslims are considered subhuman as species. They don't say it, but that's how you can read it in their actions. In their country, people of other faiths are not allowed to perform their religious rites in public. If they do, they will be severely punished. And, as a woman, I find it difficult and a great challenge to speak out, but I do speak nonetheless, and I get a lot of support. For those who don't agree, I say: *Sorry, I know I can't change the whole world, but these are my feelings and I want to share them with you.* Incidentally, as for the World Trade disaster, I have no problem thinking the attackers were influenced by the Wahhabi doctrine. Out of nineteen attackers, fifteen were Saudi citizens.

In my own experience I can cite an example of this Wahhabi-type thinking. In one mosque where my husband and I went to speak, my husband was given the podium and I was asked to sit in the back with the other women and speak from there. I felt that that was an insult to my religion. If I had known beforehand about this, I would not have accepted. My husband didn't like it very much either, and we agreed that next time we would definitely ask what the setup would be.

But on the whole, aside from Wahhabis, I've received overwhelming support from other groups. When I talked before a Maryknoll audience, a Catholic group, they asked for my views about women, which I gave, and there was a huge burst in the audience, clapping, standing up, men and women both. Everybody was enthusiastic. I've spoken before Jews at Rosh Hashanah, Methodists, and others.

Do you find the diversity of faiths a help or a hindrance among people?

A help actually. I often quote this verse from the Koran, which says, *O mankind, we created you from a single pair of a male and female and made you into nations and tribes so that you may know one another. Verily, the most honored of you in the sight of God is the most righteous of you* (Koran 49:13). So I feel the Koran is saying there is diversity, and through diversity you know one another. And this knowing occurs when there is no hatred of one group toward another. Knowing each other at a deeper level can help dispel hatreds, so it works both ways. Diversity is created by God, and that's why we have different languages, different cultures, different thinking.

Early Muslims understood this and that's why Islamic civilization came into being. Muslims went and studied Greek and translated the *Republic* of Plato into Arabic. And today the version of Plato's *Republic* that we find in English was originally translated from Arabic to English, not directly from Greek to English. The Arabs became the pioneers in gathering up much of the world's wisdom and knowledge and translating because they understood the Koran's plea that you go and learn from one another. That's how we became enriched. The Muslims went to India and studied Indian mathematics and they universalized the Indian invention of zero. This knowledge was held by only the upper caste, but the Muslims came and made it universal. Their idea was that knowledge must be shared; it must not be garnered for yourself. You garner and then you share knowledge for the common good.

What drew you to feminist issues?

Growing up in my family environment I always had the feeling that women are absolutely equal to men. We may have a complementary role like giving birth to kids and breast-feeding, which men can't do (I feel sorry for them). Giving birth and breast-feeding are no detriment, no inhibition to progress for women. They are wonderful gifts. When I came to the U.S., I went to school, enrolled full-time and met many feminists and women leaders. And I was forming my own ideas about who I was, how far I would go, what I would accept and not accept. I did not accept ultra feminist interpretations. At the same time I reflected how Gloria Steinem herself is becoming so spiritual, from her very rebellious past. She came to the realization that inner change is not secondary to societal change. Indeed, when we look inward we realize that our greatest struggle is against our own inflated egos that have transformed patriarchy into a tool of oppression and turned God, who is neither male nor female, into a merciless male dictator. Our greatest struggle, then, is to dive deep into ourselves to rediscover God through our love and humility, so that peaceful societal transformation is possible.

Then after I graduated I started to work full time and, while working, I was meeting people. I was always going to conferences and meetings of different organizations and I helped found an organization to help Bangladeshi women. There were groups here of Bangladeshi women who asked me to join them. We decided this was the time for us to do a lot of charity work and help our sisters at home. So we became an extension of the Bangladeshi support network.

Please address your pro-women humanitarian involvement.

I became a cofounder of an Islamic think tank near Washington, D.C. in 1993 and it's called Minaret of Freedom Institute. The institute has a very progressive attitude toward women and we do a lot of research on human rights and women's empowerment. Currently, I am a director and the secretary of the organization. Our public is both Muslim and non-Muslim. On behalf of the institute, I attended the Beijing women's conference, where my colleagues and I offered three or four workshops showing how the new thinking of Muslim women is emerging, with the help of the Koran and the tradition set by the Prophet.

Please address the World Trade Center disaster. Do you think Muslims are mistreated now because of the blame Americans tend to place on them?

At that time, my daughter was attending the Muslim Community School. Just after the 9/11 attack, I heard the announcement that the schools were being closed and everything shut down. My first reaction was, *Oh God, am I living in the third world?* I had already seen a genocide, destruction, and terrorism. I said to myself, *I can't believe this is happening here.* It was disbelief and bewilderment. My heart went out to my daughter, thinking, *My God, people will blame us.* I went to the school to pick her up and, as I drove out of the school, three or four cars were passing and people booed and made all kinds of dirty comments. My daughter was wearing a scarf and I was wearing a scarf because I was going to the school. I don't usually wear a scarf outside. I try to dress modestly but don't wear a scarf. I became very concerned. When I got back home, a friend of mine called and we agreed to do something.

Actually, 9/11 hurts us very deeply. People don't realize that the Muslim community came to this country for peace and a good life. It was a great opportunity. Now that is sort of shattered. We are being blamed for someone else's crime. At the same time, people don't know that we lost many Muslims in the World Trade Center. Bangladeshi, Pakistani, and Arabs were working there. Some were professionals or officers working in high-scale jobs in corporations, others worked in lesser jobs. A newly married Bangladeshi couple was killed. She was on one of the top floors of the World Trade Center and had a good computer job and was killed along with her husband who was also working in the building. Some were struggling to make some money to send home and bring family here. They all came to this country hoping for a good future.

On September 16, we organized a women's rally, my friend, who is a lawyer, and myself. We held it in a Rockville courthouse-square park on the sixteenth of September. When I was calling my Muslim neighbors to come to the rally, many were very concerned about coming out because many wear a head scarf and were worried about how people would react to them. I applaud their courage because many did come—with scarves, to show that, yes, we are Muslim women and wear scarves, but we don't represent that heinous mindset that caused the disaster. On that day we were able to gather one hundred people or more. It was about half men and half women. We got local speakers and it was covered on Fox TV and in local newspapers. We as Muslims and as women showed our solidarity. We are sisters of those killed in the World Trade Center.

Generally, how do you think America has responded to the disaster of 9/11?

I feel that America has responded in a negative way and is going down a negative road. I am referring to the almost complete lack of soul-searching dialogue among the American people and the American media. Did America have any part in bringing this about? is a question you almost never hear. There is a deep silence.

Mary King, a top official in the Carter administration and now a professor of peace and conflict studies at the University for Peace of the United Nations, Costa Rica, has written on this subject. In an article entitled "Why Do They Hate Us? America in the Eyes of the World," she says, in summary, that after 9/11, there should have been more soul-searching, more discussion on such questions as, "Do the new policies for waging a war on terror offer effective means to win that war?" "Are such policies new, or do they continue the same policies that precipitated the present situation?" "Aren't current U.S. policies calculated to increase hostilities against the U.S.?" Further, she said that what gets beamed by the giant media conglomerates to Americans over their breakfast cereal is professed unity, and almost no dissent!

Other voices of consciousness, such as professor Noam Chomsky, historian Karen Armstrong, historian Howard Zinn, veteran British journalist Robert Fisk, Indian writer Arundhati Roy have raised similar questions and concerns on how a dialogue did not take place.

The response seemed to be, in effect, *Let's beat them up! Let's beat the hell out of them!* It came out of a revenge mode that is not healthy. This way, terrorism will not stop. In order to curb terrorism, one has to dig deep to find the causes of conflict and address it with insight, and just diplomacy. It does not mean that the perpetrators, who terrorize innocent people, should go unpunished. They must be punished. But that's just a short-term solution. In the long run, our U.S. government must address the whole issue of maintaining a double standard, in supporting occupation, and allying for oil and domination with the ruthless monarchs and dictators who carry out atrocities against innocent people. The U.S. government must alter its imperialistic mind-set and embrace justice and compassion to deal with the whole issue. By following this route, the U.S. will act appropriately as the only superpower with the ability to bring a wave of peace throughout the world.

Yearning for peace, and this longing for transformation, must first begin in our hearts.

Safaa Zarzour

A principal protects his brood in an angry town

❝ *The boys dress very much like boys dress in the average prep school: a white shirt, black or navy blue dress pants, and a tie … The girls wear a long navy blue dress and a scarf on the head, light blue for small girls and white for older girls. The scarf covers the head and wraps around the neck.*

When it comes to fighting, drugs, guns, gangs, things that fall more in the sphere of morality, we hardly ever have to worry about the students.

For a realistic number of Islamic schools in America, I would feel comfortable estimating from two hundred to two hundred fifty. These are sustainable. If you look at them one year, the next year they are still standing. ❞

SAFAA ZARZOUR *is pictured here speaking with a student. (Photos courtesy of Safaa Zarzour.)*

In Bridgeview, Illinois, on the evening of September 11 after the World Trade Center tragedy occurred, the news brought protesters, mainly local white residents, into the streets. They began walking toward the local mosque and the Universal School, the Islamic school next door. The paraders showed menace, and the police came and took control. For several weeks after that, police patrolled the area of the mosque and Universal School, and succeeded in keeping fights and verbal attacks to a minimum.

A day or so after September 11, **Safaa Zarzour**, the principal of Universal School, received a letter full of profanity and threatening remarks aimed at him, his family, and the school. He found himself taking his wife and daughters to live on the second floor of their house for fear of someone throwing rocks through the windows on the ground floor. At school he patrolled the halls and schoolrooms, advising the students on emergency measures. But at no time, he said, did he feel despair because "that's part of life." Today, life at the school and in his home has returned to normal.

Mr. Zarzour is in his late thirties and came from Syria sixteen years ago (at the time of this writing). He studied for a bachelor's degree in mathematics at Arkansas State University. After completing his teacher certification at Louisiana State University, he received a master's degree in school administration from the University of Illinois. Currently, after school hours, he is pursuing a law degree at DePaul University Law School. He is married to an American woman of German descent. They have four daughters, all American born.

As principal of Universal School, he has made it an underlying theme of his educational program that it is possible to be—at the same time—a Muslim and a good, solid American. He teaches both dignity and tolerance and sees no conflict in praising Allah and saluting the United States flag. To his way of thinking, the most important aspect in achieving this is getting along as another American minority. At best, American minorities live and work together, and for American Muslims, it is a very different issue from the ones Muslims face in countries with a Muslim majority.

Despite the fact that the school has returned to relative normalcy, he still feels compelled—before his students leave on day trips—to repeat his favorite pep talk: *Do us proud. I'm sure everything will be fine, but as we've always told you, if you misbehave people will blame the whole community. They will say, look at those Arabs, look at those Muslims. If somebody says something bad to you, just say PEACE and walk away.*

Since 9/11, with the wave of anti-Islamic feelings that has swept the country, it is more necessary than ever to give the students this pep talk. The interview below took place on an early morning in January 2003 on the telephone between Bridgeview, Illinois, and Brooklyn, New York.

What does an Islamic religious school provide that the public school does not?

I believe that religious schools in general, whether Islamic, Jewish, Catholic, Lutheran, whatever the religion or motivation, have the desire to see their cultural and religious heritages transmitted to future generations. In order to do that, it is not necessary to have everybody educated in a religious environment or religious instruction. You do need, though, a few or a critical number who will then provide some kind of example of how to continue to live on with Islam, or any religion, and its traditions. Finding a way to practice Islam in a largely non-Islamic culture will be through the children  who are provided with a religious environment, as well as a regular American education. They will somehow have worked through the kinks and problems. Basically, they are the important players in finding solutions on how you can keep your religion and, at the same time, how to be an active and productive member of the society in which they live. I think the schools play a very important role in this.

Do I understand you correctly? Do you mean that a child who goes to a Hebrew or Lutheran school can give others of the same belief, but who do not have that schooling, ideas for a standard to live by?

Exactly. When our Islamic kids grow up and go to college, I know what they experience. Other Muslim students who have had no instruction in the history or practice of Islam come up to them and say things like, *You went to an Islamic school. Can you explain? I heard this about Muhammad. Is it true?* The student who went to an Islamic school will give him accurate information. But he'll also be able to guide on other issues, large and small.

I've heard of a case of an Islamic college student having to make funeral plans for a parent who died. He wasn't taught any religion and didn't know what the proper etiquette is for going to the mosque, setting up a funeral, or even how to conduct himself at the graveyard. The Muslim way is distinct and different, and the average Muslim going to public school doesn't know any of that. Parents are often too busy earning a living to stop and transmit burial customs to their children. From what I've seen, I'm convinced of the value of what a child gets in an Islamic school, for he can act as a funnel of knowledge to others. This may be a minor feature of Islamic education, but it does fit into the larger picture.

SAFAA ZARZOUR (above) supervising a party at the Muslim Universal School in Bridgeview, Illinois, where he is the principal.

Can you give us a quick count of how many Islamic schools there are in the U.S. and what grade levels they offer?

I've heard there are about three hundred seventy-five to four hundred schools. About a hundred of these are not sustainable, in that one can't be sure whether they are schools or attempts at a school. There are some that are very small, with thirty-five or forty students, but many of these are alive this year, but gone next year. For a realistic number of well-functioning Islamic schools in America, I would feel comfortable estimating from two hundred to two hundred fifty. These are sustainable. If you look at them one year, the next year they are still standing. In our area of Bridgeview, we have six or seven other Islamic schools. There is, I believe, an Islamic school in just about every state with the exception, perhaps, of Utah and North Dakota. Some states have upward of fifteen or twenty schools.

The majority of them go up to the eighth grade. Only about thirty or forty of them have a high school, although many are now enlarging into high schools. In the next five or ten years, I estimate that over half of them will include high school. My school is from prekindergarten to the twelfth grade, including high school, of course.

What is the dress code at Universal School?

The boys dress very much like boys dress in the average prep school: white shirt, black or navy blue dress pants and a tie. The tie is navy blue, and it's always long pants. Anything that comes to the knee would not be objectionable, but the uniform does not include that. The family buys the outfit.

The girls dress in a long, navy-blue dress. . They wear a scarf on the head, light blue for small girls and white for older girls. The scarf covers the head and wraps around the neck.

What percentage of your curriculum is devoted to Muslim civilization and the Arabic language?

To begin with, we have eight periods in a day. One is for lunch; one goes to Arabic, and one to Islamic studies. The remaining five are for the regular American curriculum, exactly as you would have it in any other school, private or public. This program applies to all our grade levels.

What is the discipline like at Universal School? I have a sense that it is much more disciplined than the average public school.

There are many types of discipline, and the answer depends on which type we're talking about. When it comes to talking in the classroom, we have a peculiar problem. Often the teachers are personal friends of the parents of the kid, or the kid sees them in the mosque and in the community all the time and feels very comfortable with them. So it becomes easy for the kid in class to sit around comfortably kidding and talking in the teacher's presence. This kind of familiarity brings on a too-comfortable, easygoing attitude in the schoolroom. I think this causes a discipline problem that public schools don't have. We have to keep reminding the students that although the teacher may be a friend of the family, in the school he or she is the teacher.

When it comes to fighting, drugs, guns, gangs, things that fall more in the sphere of morality, we hardly ever have to worry about the students. They are not on our radar screen very much. When we worry about them, it's always in the context of a child at school having after-school friends who may talk to him about such things. In this case, if the child mentions them at our school, we follow up by contacting his parents and making sure they are aware of the situation. But we don't have those problems *within* the school. Again, they're not on our radar screen. We do not have to worry about the safety of the kids, the kids getting into fights, beating up on each other, that sort of thing.

Apropos, when I was studying for my master's at the University of Illinois, I came across some interesting statistics on school discipline. In a class on character development, the teacher brought up a list of the top ten discipline problems in the schools in the fifties and nineties. In the fifties, problems were things like chewing gum in class, restlessness, talking. In the nineties, it was sexual assault, drugs, gangs. I commented to the teacher that we in Islamic schools are still dealing with the fifties problems.

We continue to have a discipline situation where the worst thing is a kid who insists on chewing gum after the fifth or sixth time he's asked not to. The very top nuisance, that one that drives our teachers crazy—one that public schools with their T-shirts never have—is the boys struggling to get out of their ties. Or tying their ties in a funny way, or having them fall loose, or not having them on at all, that kind of thing.

From your school, what percentage of graduates goes on to college?
Ninety-five to one hundred percent. But not all go away from home. Some parents can't afford to send them away or simply don't want them to be that far away. Sometimes both parents or students may feel they need two or three more years of family life. Some may go to the local community college. We've had students who get twenty-eight or thirty on the ACT and end up going to the local community college.

What types of four-year colleges do your graduates go to?
The colleges our students are accepted at are becoming more and more impressive. Five years ago, we had our first student accepted by what we consider a prestigious university. In this area we consider the University of Chicago and Northwestern very prestigious. In recent years, either our valedictorian and/or salutatorian has been admitted to one or the other. And last year we reached a point where we had five out of twenty-one graduates, about

twenty-three percent of our students, admitted or enrolled at the University of Chicago or Northwestern.

I am thrilled to have my students apply to Yale or Cornell or Harvard, but many times their parents tell them to forget about living out of state. So they end up applying at the University of Chicago or Northwestern. In 1997 I had such a student. He actually achieved fifteen seventy out of sixteen hundred on the SAT and he got admitted to Cornell in computer engineering. So I do know we have students who are capable of being admitted. In my eight years as principal, there have been from five to seven students who applied to Ivy League-type universities outside of Chicago. I'm very happy with the quality of the students academically. Our goal is to have a hundred percent admission to four-year colleges.

Do you have any non-Muslim students? An imam told me he would not be surprised if within the foreseeable future, parents of non-Muslim children may want to send their children to Muslim schools because of the discipline and atmosphere of morality that Islamic schools have. Do you see any possibility of this?

I do. Islamic schools that are located in urban areas tend to have non-Muslim children in their schools. An urban African-American population with some means and volume also tends to send their children to Muslim schools, even though they may not always be Muslim. Islamic schools in suburbia do not draw many non-Muslims.

I think eventually what the imam said may take place. And I believe it is no different from the experience of other religious schools. Religious schools tend to draw thoughtful parents. You would be shocked to hear that prior to the advent of Islamic schools, of the surprising number of Muslim kids in Catholic schools. Muslim parents looked around and said, *I do not want my child to go to a public school and be subject to all the problems that exist there. The Catholic schools subscribe to the same moral code that I do. They are my best alternative.*

Even today, in Chicago, I hear of parents who send their children to Catholic schools. They feel that Islamic schools are too young and inexperienced. Catholic schools have been around for a hundred-odd years. And if they may want their children to have strong academic backing, they still, despite the emergence of Islamic schools, send them to Catholic schools. Incidentally, concerning the African-American community, it occurs to me that, in time, they may be sending their children to Islamic schools in greater numbers, as they realize more and more that a good percentage of their forebears were brought here as slaves from Africa with names like Malik or Ahmed, or whatever. When they find, for example, that the fifth or sixth grandfather was named Malik or Ahmed, or whatever, such knowledge—and acceptance—may further lead them to an Islamic education for their children.

From my observation, I can say that African-American Muslims—even those who were totally deviant from Islam in the form of the movement of the Nation of Islam—are known by non-Muslim blacks as a group that are for discipline, self-respect, hard work, not depending on others, and not letting others take advantage of you. Because they have shown these qualities, I am not surprised to see them drawn to our more regimented schools. When an Islamic school opens in an urban area, an area where there is a significant African-American population, I've seen enough of them come to that school to enroll their children.

Of course, in suburbia throughout America, that's not the case. Until Islam is accepted as a mainstream religion, white America will avoid Islamic schools and not put its children there. Why? Because they're not sure of those Muslims, what they do, who they worship, what they advocate. Until they are secure about these things, there is no other value that will prevail. The fact that those Muslim kids are not going to smoke or be exposed to drugs, or whatever, is not going to be enough draw.

I'm hoping and praying that—I know it will take a while to accept in suburban America—that Muslim schools will be considered just like Catholic schools, like Jewish schools, like Lutheran schools. I pray for the day when parents in the neighborhood who have enough Muslim neighbors and their children play on the same block, will feel comfortable enough to say, *Let me check out this Muslim school nearby. Instead of my child being driven or bused to school, let me go and explore it.* I'm hopeful that this will happen. But it may take from twenty to fifty years, depending on what lies ahead.

Rumors are circulating that Saudi Arabia is funding certain Islamic schools where fundamentalist thinking is emphasized and financing bright students to attend them. Do these rumors have basis?
Of course, I've heard them. My response is for anyone to look around and study the graduates of Islamic schools and where they are today, who they are, what kinds of lives they lead. They're everywhere in American universities. You will find them in law schools, medical schools, engineering schools, schools of sociology, and they are your average American.

Having said that, in the Muslim community in the U.S., there is a tradition of fund-raising within the community to build schools and mosques. Incidentally, mosques and schools are not separate. Generally in Muslim countries, up to about a hundred years ago, every school had a mosque, every mosque had a school. They are so intertwined that most Muslim donors do not make a distinction between them. You give to a mosque and at the same time you give to a school, and they are the most popular institutions in Islam for receiving financial aid from donors of all types. Then there are people with the task of collecting money from donors. These fund-raisers collect from outside the U.S., and sometimes right here in the U.S.

Most Muslim countries are too poor to give donations and, naturally the

Gulf countries—the only rich countries—contribute at times. For example, they have contributed to build the King Fahd Mosque in Los Angeles. In fact, King Fahd himself may have contributed. I know of the Islamic Development Bank that tries to support different projects all over the world. They also support mosques and schools. All in all, you will find a good number of schools or mosques that have received donations here and there.

But I will say that absolutely, categorically, I am not aware, at any time, of anything that is done quid pro quo, where anyone who has any control may declare, *We do this for the sake of that, or we do this to prepare for that. Nothing like that.* In fact, our Islamic schools in general tend to be liberal. I've heard myself of people overseas who might have considered me for a donation, but thought I was too liberal and would say I don't even qualify for a religious donation, even though by American standards, the school may be considered very conservative.

My school, Universal School, is completely independent. Our board of directors is responsible for fund-raising and has final word on everything.

Do graduates of Muslim schools and other American Muslims feel apart when they first venture into American society as young adults?

Young practicing American Muslims often feel on the defensive in trying to explain their practices. If they feel odd, it's not because they want to be separate but because the person across from them is not understanding what they are doing. The other reads into what the Muslim is doing as something strange and outré. It is a source of discomfort. It makes him feel odd, but he's not doing it deliberately to be odd. I tell my students that it is a situation of circumstance. If you have never seen a Christian make a sign of the cross and then see someone doing it, it would throw you off. What's he doing? What's it about? But you would quickly get used to it because it's part of the dominant culture and you don't read much into it. The opposite is true for Muslims. Others are not used to it. A few realize that this is what a Muslim does. This is what a Muslim believes is the thing to do to please God: a man needs to put his forehead on the ground; a woman needs to wear a scarf. *And there's nothing beyond it.* This situation of awkwardness can only continue as long as it is not a common sight for the average American.

I tell my kids: *You are the pioneers in this area. And it depends on you whether future generations of Muslims are going to have to continue to be in a position of having to explain themselves constantly. So persevere in these practices. Believe that you are being rewarded by God for persevering and that, because of your perseverance, the rest of America will get used to these rituals and practices and start to understand what a Muslim does and feel comfortable about accepting it. And only then will you not have to feel on the defensive.*

I think the majority of American Muslims feel comfortable about practicing ritual in public and it gives them a social strength. But there's a group that basically feels that there's too much pressure and abandons Islamic practices in public. These Muslims may do it on their own, in their home or behind closed doors. But let me tell you, if there is anyone I would feel afraid for, it's the person who is forced to have a split personality. I am never uncomfortable with anyone going through stress about practicing the religion or having to face the criticism and looks from others. These I find to be far healthier than those who become two different people. They are one person in the office and another person at home. What this creates in them, the contradictions, is far more disturbing to me.

Your family brings American and Islamic cultures together. Your wife is an American Baptist, you are a Muslim from Syria. You have five daughters. From such different religious and cultural backgrounds, how did you decide to marry each other, and how is the marriage working out?

Actually, our marriage comprises the main source of my hope for the future. I believe that my marriage constitutes a microcosm of what can happen on a larger scale in relation to the fusing of two cultures, a fusing without inherent contradiction. But it also represents a larger understanding that we have as Muslims, and *that* I would like to share with you.

Islam considers itself an actual extension of Judaism and Christianity. It considers Christianity as a natural extension of Judaism, and that Islam itself is an actual extension of Christianity. As a result, Islam does not view the conflict between the three religions as caused by the religions themselves. If you look at the essence of what Muhammad has preached by looking at the Koran itself, the text itself, you'll see he preaches very much what Jesus preached, which was very much what the Old Testament prophets preached.

The differences between these three great religions are not inherent. They are ideological and theological differences created by their followers and not in the heart of the religions themselves. Islam believes that if there is a possibility of agreeing to disagree on those differences, the rest of the agenda can be identical. And on moral grounds, a devout Jew, a devout Muslim, a devout Christian would have a very similar agenda. They would very much oppose similar things. The religious conflict in the three religions stems from ideology.

Because of all this, Islam allows Muslim men to marry not only Muslim women, but Christian women, and Jewish women. But a Muslim cannot marry a person who does not believe in God. And he cannot marry a person who worships stones.

To get back to my marriage: When I met my wife, she was a Christian. When we started talking and realized that ours could be a personal relationship beyond just talking about religion, we began discussing the kind of life we could have for ourselves, and in what kinds of ways we might raise children. We agreed on most things. There is very little difference between us on what we want our children to do and not do, what kinds of values we want to instill. We want them to be hardworking, upright. We want them not to lie, not to get into things like drugs and alcohol that will destroy them. We don't want them to cheat. We want them to be people of their word.

From the beginning, even before my wife became a Muslim, we sat down to talk about how we would raise a family if we got married. As for the marriage itself, her main concern was, *Would you force me to become a Muslim?* She had the impression that I would have to do that and that's what she was afraid of. Her family members warned her about this. I brought her the Koran and told her, *As a Muslim, I cannot force you. In the Koran, God tells me that I can't do that. When Muslims do that, they are violating their own religion.*

We talked about other issues. What helped me probably was that she was raised in a religious environment. Her family did not drink alcohol; her family did not look favorably upon dating or having a premarital relationship. There was very little to disagree on. And we decided to get married, with the understanding that she could remain the rest of her life as a Christian and I would remain the rest of my life as a Muslim. And we would build our lives together on that foundation.

It so happened that after one year, she began reading more intently about Islam and began asking the tough questions. Once they were answered for her, at some point, she said, *I want to become a Muslim.*

But I would have been very content if she had stuck with what she had. It wouldn't have bothered me, *not* the way I was raised, *not* the way I understand Islam. Now I cannot say the same for other Muslims, but I can say that, within Islam, I have the textual and historical backing for what I believe. The others live with the current culture and I don't know how much any Arab or Muslim can rely on the current Arab or Muslim culture, given how turbulent and how incoherent and how contradictory and sometimes repressive it is.

Your marriage, your profession as educator, and your philosophy all lead to the conclusion that you are dedicating all your energies to proving it is possible to be both Muslim and American. Is that true?
Yes. The world's future may lie in that very concept becoming a reality. In the past, Muslims lived in their own nations, and Christians in theirs in Europe and America. A Christian finding himself in an Islamic country was not a factor in public life. He had little importance. In reverse, the same was true of Muslims living in Christian countries. Each was a nobody. Neither culture looked each other in the eye and said, *I am going to find a way where we will both practice what we believe at the same time, and do it in a form and way that will not step on your toes.* America was created to fill this great human need and achieved the goal.

What do you have to say about 9/11?

I have a gut feeling that that act of mass murder at the World Trade Center by dreadful Islamic terrorists was their way of destroying the reality of having a credible and already existing Muslim presence in a Western society like the United States which treasures democracy, and where both cultures have been living in harmony. I am part of this society. I am an integral part of it, and can practice my religion here and am loyal to this society because this is where fairness and justice exist. The terrorists did not want Muslims and Americans to live together in the future in a good relationship. To them, we are heretics; American Muslims are heretics to those people.

And that is what pains me most. Because we Muslims in America want to be part of the American system and believe that living under the Constitution does not contradict our religion. This enrages terrorists who say, *You're not a Muslim anymore.* That is why in bombing the World Trade Center, they couldn't care less if there was a Muslim inside because to them, by virtue of that Muslim choosing to live in America, he is no longer worthy of living.

Sadly, Muslims in America feel that we are now on the attack from both ends. My fellow Americans look at us and say, *You are the fifth column, you represent those people, and so you are on the outside. I don't trust you. I don't like you. I'm going to look at your institutions. I'm going to make your life miserable.* We respond and say, *How can you say that? Like other religions, Islam can grow in the West and have its place. We can find a way where we can both live together.*

But it's not possible to say this and the fact that you are saying it puts you outside the fold. I wish every American would understand. Deep inside every law-abiding American Muslim, there is the hurt that he is *nowhere*, he is being questioned *everywhere*.

Is it really possible for American Muslims and non-Muslims to live amicably together?

I believe it is. Look at it on a grand scale. It is the one thing that can save the future of the world. If we have a credible community of Muslims who are American, who recognize and are proud of their religion as they are of being American, if we can live as neighbors and learn how to proceed for the future, then we may eventually provide the model for the entire Muslim population everywhere on how to achieve peace. If this doesn't happen, the clash of civilizations as exhibited on 9/11, which is advocated by extremists on both sides of the divide, may happen again.

Lobna Ismail Kronemer

"I'll answer any questions about American Muslims."

We Muslims are your friendly neighbors, your teachers, your doctors, your lawyers. We are your gas-station attendants, your 7-Eleven convenience-store employees. We're your nurses. We're your professors, your students. We're your taxi-cab drivers, your grocers and pastry makers…. We're your policemen, your writers, your emerging comics, your emerging politicians. We're your friends. Look about. You'll see us everywhere.

Carol, my best friend in high school [in Florida] was an Evangelical Christian. We shared the love of God, we shared the desire to do good in this world, and to be good. We shared the same values. We reached a place of mutual respect for one another … The Evangelicals would have their prayer meetings in the band room before school started and they would bring their Bible. I joined them and would bring my Koran. We both read from our holy books.

LOBNA ISMAIL KRONEMER with her two young sons and husband Alexander Kronemer, a documentary filmmaker. (Photo courtesy of Lobna Ismail Kronemer.)

Thirteen years ago, **Lobna Kronemer** founded a company called
Connecting Cultures, which foreshadowed the pressing need for
post–September 11, 2001 cross-cultural communication between Muslims
and non-Muslim Americans. At its start, the company's focus was on people
abroad. After September 11, it focused entirely on Americans. Programming
her efforts through the years to become a first-rate trainer in cross-cultural
communication, she has nursed her company lovingly along to its present
high standing on the American scene. She herself is the main teacher and
lecturer. Her training sessions include both Muslims, to whom she describes
American ways and methods, and non-Muslims who learn about Islam and
the way Muslims live and act. Acceptance of religious diversity is an important part of the program. Thus clued in, each party becomes more culturally
competent to associate and mingle with the other.

Among her clients who see the need to educate their staff in these matters
are top conglomerates like federal and state agencies, AETNA, Walt Disney
World, the army and the navy, Campbell's Soup, the Justice Department, the
Foreign Service Institute, Marriott International, and Merck, to name a few.
She also provides diversity training for schools, policemen, and federal
employees. Her innovative training seminars, given throughout the country,
are very popular, for she brings warmth and heartfelt devotion to her work,
often sharing her real life experiences with prejudice, stereotypes and misinformation.

Lobna Kronemer is the author of *Doing Business in the Middle East and
North Africa* and *Finding Diversity: A Directory of Recruiting Resources*. She
has appeared on the national media and on major international news programs.

What do you call yourself professionally?

I am a cross-cultural communication trainer and president of Connecting
Cultures, a company which started with the mission of helping people outside
the United States understand how culture impacts the way that we communicate and the way people interact with other cultures and religions. After 9/11
the corporation shifted its aim and focused entirely on the understanding of
Islam *here* in the United States, on understanding American Muslims and Arab
Americans, and in providing cultural competency to American corporations,
government agencies, and other institutions in their dealings with Muslim
customs and ways.

Our goal in providing guidelines for cultural competency is to heighten
awareness, increase knowledge as to ways we can communicate and work
across faiths and cultures. The goal works to minimize tensions and sensitize
people like the police, managers, educators, and leaders who want to create
and maintain an inclusive, bias-free, harassment-free community, be it school,

workplace, or neighborhood.

After the attacks of 9/11, my first call was from the Justice Department, specifically from the Community Relations Service (CRS). It has been a long-standing customer in terms of training law-enforcement officers, human-rights commissioners, educators, and other personnel. We focus mainly on law enforcement because there has been an increase in hate crimes, discrimination, and physical and verbal abuse on Muslims and, sadly, on others who look Muslim or Arab.

In my training presentations, I emphasize that Muslims are multicultural. They come in all colors, physical features, and ethnic backgrounds, and the same is true of Arab Americans. I did a training in New York last week and there was an officer who came up to me and started speaking Arabic. He was a redhead with freckles. Who ever heard of a redheaded, freckle-faced Muslim? My main mission is to open peoples' hearts and minds to Muslims beyond the image of the dark-haired, brown-skinned stereotype. When you open hearts, you can shift the way people think, and that's going to change the way they behave and act toward Arab and Muslim Americans.

What's the difference between Arab Americans and Muslims?

Not all Arab Americans are Muslim. Some are Christian. But because of their ethnic origin, they're getting a lot of flak. I talk to both the Christian and Muslim Arabs. I recently produced a video, and some scenes were taken in an Arab Christian church here in Washington, D.C., showing people taking communion, singing hymns in Arabic, and priests giving sermons.

In your training sessions with the Justice Department, do you mention the Muslims who have been detained since 9/11 without proof of wrongdoing?

I don't get involved on a case-by-case basis. What I do is provide basic understanding about Muslim culture and faith, and also suggest practical tools to consider in noncrisis, nonemergency situations.

For example, one of the main questions we have is from policemen who want to know how to show respect to Islam in handling certain crimes. In California recently, an officer asked what should the police do when they find that a Muslim prayer rug has been deliberately soiled and defaced? They want to be sensitive to an important article of faith and not offend anyone. I had done research and was able to respond: *After the police investigation, the rug should be wrapped and thrown out.*

I was once asked about a copy of the Koran that had been defiled. I consulted an imam who said that once the Koran has been desecrated in any way, it should be shredded or burned following an investigation.

Where were you born?

I was born in Lafayette, Indiana, an American born and bred. My parents came here on scholarship to study at Purdue University. We are originally from Egypt and they're still living in the States. Actually, we left the Midwest when I was a year and a half, and my parents moved to Florida to continue their studies at the University of Florida. I grew up in a small town in central Florida in a strong Christian Evangelical community. We were the only Muslim–Arab–North African–American family in town.

How were you treated by your non-Muslim neighbors?

It was a very positive experience. That's what gives me such hope. My family were people with good intentions who didn't have a community of their own to cling to, so they became involved with the PTA and local community events. The larger community did not isolate us and were very accepting. I did not feel discrimination as such. For me the issue was not about my national origin or my religion. It was the color of skin, which was brown. I came into the schools when desegregation was taking place. In those days you were black or you were white. And so I remember in elementary school that the question to me was, "What are you?"

My answer: "What do you mean?"

"Are you black or white?"

My answer: "Neither, I'm Egyptian. We don't identify based on race."

That caused some tension. Carol, my best friend in high school, was an Evangelical Christian. We shared the love of God; we shared the desire to do good in this world, and to be good. We shared the same values. We reached a place of mutual respect for one another. I remember the Evangelicals would have their prayer meetings in the band room before school started, and they would bring their Bible. I joined them and would bring my Koran. We would both read from our holy books. It was very respectful.

Some Evangelical preachers have made negative remarks about Islam, causing great distress. Can you comment?

Yes. Unfortunately after 9/11, much has changed. And after 9/11 everything has changed between my best friend in high school and myself. It is one of the most painful aspects of post-9/11 for me. We live in the D.C. area and, after 9/11, I heard from many old friends asking if I was okay and they conveyed concern that I might be subjected to the rash of backlash incidents toward Arab and Muslim Americans. But I never heard from Carol. Months later I got an e-mail that was very unlike her. It basically said she can't stand by or tolerate or accept the faith that persecutes her people. I realized she was referring to my faith. I knew that in evangelical churches today strong anti-Muslim statements are made. But when she speaks of "those people" (Muslims) with disdain, I can only say, *Have you forgotten "those people" are your friends whom you knew and admired? Those people are my grandmother, my parents, my brothers, my sons?*

A couple of years ago when we had our twentieth high-school reunion, Carol came from Oklahoma with her daughter and stayed in our home. How could she lump us with religious extremists in this way? I remind myself that she went to Oral Roberts University and used to be an Oral Roberts singer. I have so many pictures and memories of us together from high school and our twentieth reunion. My last exchange with her was just a few weeks ago. To be honest, there wasn't much sincerity in the message and the sense of respect we had for each other was missing. This has been hard. I must focus on the many Christians and Jews who are open to building tolerance and mutual respect.

What's interesting about the Evangelicals is this. Their interpretation is really one that doesn't believe in a pluralistic nation. In order to get to heaven, they think that you must accept—they would say this even to other Christians—Jesus Christ and be born again in their church. Even Catholics are condemned to hell along with other denominations. Evangelicals believe that unless you accept *their* way, through *their* church, you will never get to heaven.

Can you give us a brief summary of your work with a client?

We deal with a corporation's Muslim and non-Muslim employees. Mostly I've worked with ExxonMobil and their dealers. The emphasis is mostly on how to work effectively and efficiently with their Arab-American employees here in the United States. We do it by working with the managers who oversee the dealerships, and I talk with them about some of the considerations to be made with Arab Americans and Muslims. I address communication and work styles, sensitivities, gender issues, nonverbal conflict, and so forth.

My impression is that many gas-station attendants and owners are Muslim. Is that correct?

Yes, there is a high percentage of Arab Americans in these dealerships.

How does your husband fit into your work?

He was, for some time, my co-trainer. At ExxonMobil we trained together. But he also partnered to co-produce and circulate the film on the Prophet called "Muhammad: Legacy of a Prophet," a PBS documentary, which he did with Michael Wolfe, the writer on Islamic subjects.

My husband is an American Muslim but he is a white guy from Pennsylvania and his name is Alexander. Actually, he is far more knowledgeable and far more well read and capable of talking about the faith than I am. He is the scholar of the mind and I'm the scholar of the heart. He provides answers to questions like, *What does the Koran say about Christians and Jews?* or *What does it say about women's rights?* or *What is jihad?* He can provide sources in the Koran and the hadith.

What do you speak about before American Muslims?

When I speak before American Muslims, I focus my efforts in building confidence in themselves and convincing them that *in themselves* they are part of American culture. I focus on their real-life experiences and deal with the stereotypes and the barriers and attitudes that stereotypes create against them in the minds of non-Muslim Americans. Muslim stereotypes are based on either lack of information or on misinformation. When other Americans see us, they think, *Oh Muslims? They're from over there.* How many times are our children being told, *Go back home.* But this is the only home we've ever known! People tend to think that American and Muslim don't go together. There is no clash! Being an American and being a Muslim are in no way opposite, or clashing. That's who I am! That's all I'm known to be.

How do you handle that subject of Muslim stereotypes in your program?

I have a definite plan for this. On stage, I use every tool available: the hijab, the flowing robe, placards, slides, a blazing light, silence, interaction. I put on a performance and literally get the audience to join in. I start off the training without speaking. I wear a hijab on my head and a flowing dress, and I put up a slide, overhead in blazing light, and ask the audience, *What are some of the stereotypes of women dressed like me?* They say words like: *uneducated foreigner … don't speak English … anti-American … can't work … can't drive … oppressed … not my friend … terrorist … un-American … fanatic.*

And then I speak, my speech is American without accent, and they hear me, as you hear me, and I say, *And yet I'm none of these things. I am a southerner. I am an American. I am a soccer mom. I'm a businesswoman. I'm a college graduate. I'm a former Miss Softball America Pitcher. I'm a recipient of the DAR's Revolution Service Award.*

That's how I start and I'm right out there with them. The point is for them to stop and think about their stereotypes because stereotypes are the biggest barriers facing us—stereotypes that paint images that we're not American, we don't speak English, all those negative things. Such things influence the way we think and behave and lead us to make decisions that can have an adverse and painful discriminatory impact.

What are other tools you use in your work?

Whatever works. At a recent workshop, a police officer was in tears. I had installed a slide above the audience, with a line at the bottom saying, *We, the people …* that appears in the Constitution securing the blessings of liberty to all Americans. Above that was a list of various ethnic groups that make up our nation with a line crossing out each. The word "Irish" had been crossed out, "Italians," "Catholics," "Jewish," "Sikhs," "Muslims," "Arabs" were all crossed out. Since 9/11, certain new laws curtail the liberty guaranteed by the Constitution. At this point, I say, *Do the rights guaranteed by the Constitution apply only to a selected few and not the whole panorama of Americans? September 11 created a crucial question: Are we going to stand collectively, or in fragmented groups? Are we, "We the people" or "Some of the people"?*

The police officer was very moved as the words hit and made him realize how the Arab Americans and Muslim Americans must feel to have their patriotism suddenly questioned. That's been really hard for us and it makes me worry about my children because that's not the America I grew up in. That America was positive. People thought we were cool: *Your family is from Egypt? How interesting! You can't eat pork? Why?* The kids liked to tease and ordered pepperoni pizza. My children are faced with challenges. They ask me, *Mommy, why is it they're always showing the Muslim as a bad guy on TV?* I keep hoping the film my husband made and the training I do will help them.

What myth about Islam do you find most objectionable?

The myth that women are oppressed and have no rights—that's the biggie. When looking at Islam, people have to separate the doctrine from the cultural baggage. In Islam, a woman has the right to choose a marriage partner. She has the right to a divorce. She had the right to own property long before American women had that right. She has the right to keep her maiden name. She has the right to work and to be educated.

The Taliban form of Islam, where many antiwoman myths spring from, is as foreign to me as it is to any other American. I don't recognize my religion in the Taliban version, which demands that women dress in a certain way and dictates the rules of feminine modesty. In true Islam, there is no compulsion. No one can be made to do anything.

There is no question that there is a great deal of strife, politically, economically, socially concerning women's rights and other issues in much of the Muslim world. I'm not going to argue that. Any country in poverty faces the same ailments as many Muslim countries: lack of democracy, lack of individual freedom and rights, plutocratic dictatorships and repressive regimes, and so that's where it's coming from. But what happens is people look at them and say, *Oh, they're Muslims, that's Islam, that's the way it is.*

Is there any justification for American anti-Muslim attitudes?

No, because *all* Muslims are being blamed for the actions of a demented few fundamentalists. When Timothy McVeigh blew up the government buildings in Oklahoma—he was also a kind of fundamentalist who felt that America was not standing by the true interpretation of the Constitution—Muslims and other people didn't blame all white male America for his actions and thus criminalize the innocent. They recognized that McVeigh was demented. Why can't America act more rationally and not put the shadow of blame on all

Muslims for the crazy actions of terrorists?

How can the average American get to know American Muslims?

Unfortunately, a whole generation of Americans who do not know Muslims and are ignorant about Islam have had their introduction to the faith through the most volatile, ugliest, most extreme of tragedies. Our youths are under its influence. And that hurts. And that's why we continue to try to reach every single American, young to old, white to black, Hispanic to Asian, Jew to Christian, and let them know who American Muslims are. We have to. Because that was a big calamity, and Americans must see the peaceful, tolerant, American face of Muslims.

With this in mind, let me further explain myself and bring our American Muslims to the attention of your readers:

I am an American woman, a nice American, if I may add. I'm educated. I'm out there cheering my boys on for soccer games and I volunteer for the arts-and-crafts night. I'm one of millions of Muslims who feel and act exactly as I do.

We Muslims are your friendly neighbors, your teachers, your doctors, your lawyers. We are your gas-station attendants, your 7-Eleven convenience-store employees. We're your nurses. We're your professors, your students. We're your taxi-cab drivers, your grocers and pastry makers. We're your restaurant owners and waiters and the cooks who serve you stuffed grape leaves, taramasalata, lamb kebabs, tabouli, baklava. We're your policemen, your writers, your emerging comics, your emerging politicians. We're your friends. Look about. You'll see us everywhere.

Why haven't the Muslims spoken up against 9/11?

Since that fateful day, Muslims everywhere in the U.S. have been asked this constantly recurring question: *Why are they so silent? Why haven't we heard from them in the press?* But we responded! All our organizations condemned it. Every Muslim country condemned the attack, except for one, Iraq. We have put out statements and bulletins and sent them to television and radio, written to the newspapers. But we simply haven't received enough coverage.

The media people themselves come up with the answer: *If it bleeds, it leads.* And if it doesn't bleed, there's little or no coverage. Wars, massacres, mass murder, atrocities take the leads. Statements against acts of terror by American Muslims get little, if any, space. Their contributions are ignored. But we as Muslims should be heard and we've got to do better. We're partly to blame. Our organizations weren't equipped for the onslaught of needs. We did not have institutions in place that were needed. We are young but we're learning, and 9/11 taught us a lot.

For those of you who insist we haven't responded, this is a response: *We accepted the invitation to be in this book. Please read and make our acquaintance.*

What keeps me hopeful is that despite the lack of coverage on press and TV, we're still being asked to come and speak. I speak to teachers, to principals, and I was just asked to address a fourth-grade class. I'm going to Florida next week to speak to human resource managers from all over the country about Muslims in the workplace. On the following day I will speak to police officers in Miami. Happily, we *are* being asked, *How do we get to know the Muslim community better?* and *How can we be more sensitive to serve and protect it?* Such questions make me most proud as an American.

Are there other trainers like you?
Currently, after a morning initiative with the Justice Department, training police officers, I have a program for future trainers where Arabs and Muslims from local communities are taught on how to deliver our training in their own communities. So it's basically spreading our models, revealing the tools of how to be an effective presenter.

How are newly arrived Muslim immigrants faring in this environment and what is being done for a comfortable adjustment?
I don't work in the area of newly arrived immigrants—my focus is on the American-born Arabs and Muslims who speak English as well as most Americans. For arriving immigrants, there are now masjids that are trying to educate them and make them aware of their rights and about getting involved in the community. The recently arrived are having difficult times, especially now with mandatory registration. It's very hard. But local leaders are also trying to educate and inform them. Also, we need to partner with our local law enforcement officers and our schools and teachers to help the immigrants adjust to the new culture and understand the role and responsibilities of the police and to American ways generally.

Our schools and the police mystify them. In their home country, a Muslim mother never goes to the school unless there's a big problem with her child. And suddenly here she's told, *Come and volunteer. Let's hear from you.* Back home the police are perceived as brutal and fearsome and more like protectors of the government and not the people. But the immigrants are told it's different here: *Officers police your community and they're here to protect you.* This takes some adjustment in their thinking.

Is there any remark you'd like to end with?
When I see an Arab or Muslim, what he or she brings to mind are thoughts of great food, hospitality, graciousness toward others, beautiful gold jewelry, music and dance and warmth amongst the people. How can this group be feared, or considered our enemy? How can that be? There must be some mistake.

Dr. Abdul Jamil Khan

Establishing Islam in upper-class Long Island

I never came here for what people call money and earnings because if I had returned to India, with my advanced American medical education, I would have been well off.

We differ only as individuals … Muslims, like Christians and Jews, believe in one God and they believe in the Old Testament prophets, Moses, Abraham, David, Solomon.

In this country, the Islamic religion is following American trends. We now have a Muslim chaplain in the prison system, a Muslim chaplain in the army, a Muslim chaplain in the hospitals.

You call them imams or chaplains, either one. These people have to have some education. Somebody has to speak for them and certify they know the job. So there are schools and an educational institution for this kind of imam.

Photo courtesy of Linda Cateura.

Dr. Abdul Jamil Khan, who is presently associate chairman of the department of pediatrics at Brooklyn Hospital in Brooklyn, New York and former chairman of pediatrics at Brooklyn Jewish/Interfaith Medical Center, is a shining example of the flock of doctors from India and Pakistan who came here in the sixties and seventies to expand the ranks of a decreasing number of American medics. A good number of these immigrant doctors were Muslim, with their own prayer needs and special holidays, but what they offered were ready-to-use skills in doctoring and a knowledge and fluency in English. Dr. Khan's record of achievement in the field of pediatrics, both as practitioner and professor, and in leading medical societies of America, is impressive. Despite his devotion to medicine, he has a special attachment to Islam, the religion he was born into and has practiced all his life. He is one of the founding fathers of the Islamic Center of Long Island in Westbury, New York, a foremost community center-and-mosque in the Eastern United States.

The following narrative, based on a long interview that took place on a Sunday afternoon in his suburban home in Muttontown, Long Island, is witness to this devotion.

I was born in India, in a city called Allahabad. This is a city of high-profile politicians like Jawaharlal Nehru and his daughter, who came from there. It's about two or three hundred miles southeast of Delhi. I go and visit India every year and have the opportunity to speak my native language. But certainly I do feel like an American and am very much at home in New York, which has become like New Delhi to me. Here in New York there are at least half a million people from the subcontinent of India and Pakistan—Hindus and Muslims and Christians—who make up part of the mosaic of this city. You have dozens and dozens of Indian restaurants and shops and everything else. It's a global village in action, and I feel at home.

Back in the sixties there was a wave of doctors coming to the United States from India, Pakistan, and third-world countries. Their primary objective was to get further education and then go back to their countries as highly respected doctors with advanced American degrees in medical specialties. When I came, I already had completed my degree in pediatrics in India. I came for subspecialties in pediatrics, like mycology and kidney disease, which were not available in India. Even now, they're not available.

Incidentally, the majority of the doctors who came from Pakistan would be Muslim. You would also find some Hindus among them. Now the majority of the doctors who came from India, my country, would be Hindu, and a minority of them was Muslim. So you could say I was in the minority. Bangladesh is also a Muslim country, and the majority of doctors who came from there were Muslim. These doctors from different countries were culturally different from one another.

But after my training there were some changes in the immigration laws, and because there was a lack of American doctors, foreign doctors were allowed to apply for immigration. Meanwhile my children were growing up and it seemed wise to spend a couple of more years here before going back. So I did apply, got the green card, and then we stayed on, and on, and on.

I should explain that I never came here for what people call money and earnings because if I had returned to India, with my advanced medical education, I would have been well off. All my contemporaries who came here and returned are very well off. They became chairmen of departments in medical schools and have since retired. My main objective was to get advanced training, and I also could have returned without a problem. But I kept on staying and then I drifted into becoming a U.S. citizen. My wife is also a doctor; we went through training together in India. We both came here for further training. My son, Faiz, was three months old when we came and my daughter was born here. They grew up here and were happy, and we stayed on.

For Americans who were nonplused by the sudden unexpected appearances of Indian and other foreign doctors in American medical offices, let me put in a word on the economics behind it. I'm referring to the United States importation of foreign doctors from the subcontinent of India, Bangladesh, and Pakistan. As a medical educationist, I can tell you what the economics are from the American perspective. America graduates about fifteen thousand doctors from medical schools every year. But there are twenty thousand jobs available every year (this figure includes four thousand who retire annually), so there is an ongoing shortage of about four thousand doctors. Our American system does not want to open new medical schools. It is cheaper to import doctors than to make doctors. So the four thousand doctors have to come from over-seas—Europe, Asia, Africa. And, of course, young Americans go out of the country to study medicine. There is a very good medical school in Grenada in the West Indies, for example, from which my daughter graduated four years ago and then finished her residency in New York, where she now practices. The balance has to be maintained, and so four thousand more doctors need to be hired annually.

At this time, the number (out of four thousand) of doctors coming from India and Pakistan has decreased significantly. What needs to be done is to regulate the system so that each country can send doctors to America, if they so wish. India and Pakistan supplied a lot of doctors for one reason: the education in both India and Pakistan is through the English language. So we had no difficulty in going into American residency training because we were all taught in English in our own schools. To repeat, our education was in English and we spoke in English and there was no problem. America gives doctors who wish to emigrate an exam to pass, which, incidentally, is the same exam that medical students here take. If you pass, you're allowed to come.

Things have changed and have become more cumbersome for incoming doctors. When I came in the mid-sixties, America was desperately in need of foreign doctors and would send airfare for free. The examination board did not charge for their fee until you were established. They would say, *Take the exam but don't pay, since doctors can't afford the fee in dollars. When you start working, then pay.* They would also send you part of your pay in advance. These benefits no longer hold.

That's my professional background, and now I come to Islam. I am a Muslim, but I have a different definition of being Muslim. You are interested in people who follow the religion of Muhammad, which is a very narrow definition of being Muslim.

To go back a bit. Islam is a relatively new religion started in the sixth century—Judaism and Christianity both predate it. So it is about fifteen hundred years old and if you consider that we have four generations in a hundred years, it began sixty generations ago. Before that, everybody, including people who are now Muslim, was a non-Muslim. Now to my definition of being Muslim: If you read the Koran, which is the holy book, it says that everybody is a Muslim *who submits his will to God, or is at peace with God.* The word "Muslim" is Arabic and means "one who is at peace with submission to God." It comes from the Semitic root *s-l-m*, which means "peace." A Muslim is a person who follows peace. *Shalom aleichem* is a Hebrew phrase meaning "peace be with you, peace be upon you." "Islam" is derived from the same root, *peace.*

So you are a Muslim, a Jew is a Muslim, a Muslim is a Muslim in the sense of the meaning of the word itself: a Muslim is a person who follows peace. The parochial difference between you and me is you're following certain outward forms of Islam attributed to the way of Jesus. Those outward forms or injunctions are a bit different in the Islam of Muhammad and I'm following those codes. The essence is the same. The goal is the same. The Koran embraces this diversity as a matter of fact.

That's the difference. We differ only as individuals. Otherwise, the belief in one God actually is the only real denomination. Muslims, like Christians and Jews, believe in one God and they believe in the Old Testament prophets, Moses, Abraham, David, Solomon. The Koran mentions these prophets and accepts them and exhorts us to believe in them. Our holy book says, *I have sent many prophets since the time of Adam.* Those prophets were sent to all people, all over, and the Koran says, in effect, *Muhammad, you are the last of these messengers.*

Some prophets are mentioned in the Koran, but the vast majority is not. They existed before Muhammad. Among these, one can surmise that Zarathustra was a prophet. And the words and advice of Buddha reflect prophetic qualities. And God is telling Muhammad, *You are the last of the prophets*. Now, you can say the Koran is very flexible as it embraces the prophets and great leaders of religions before Islam and in calling all believers in one God, *Muslims*.

It's interesting to note that there are Jews and Christians who are Arabs by race and speak Arabic. It is their language. They use Arabic terminologies in their religion, be it Jewish or Christian. They don't use the word God, they use the word Allah. They eat the same food as Muslims; they speak the same language, and use the same terminology. In other words, in Christianity you have diversity. And it happens that an Arab Christian is much closer to an Arab Muslim in his social interactions and social traditions than with a Catholic Christian, say, from Italy. A Catholic from Italy has a different culture, background and language than an Arab Christian, his coreligionist.

When I started to practice here in America, as a pediatrician in an American hospital, I never felt that I was being discriminated against because I was of a different color, an Indian—and a Muslim at that, never. I've worked for the last twenty-seven years in a Jewish hospital and not the patients, not my colleagues, not my friends or students ever gave me that impression.

And even since 9/11, no, absolutely not. My coworkers, physicians, Jews, non-Jews, Christians, Americans have given me no problems along that line. Certainly, we've had discussions on the how and the why of 9/11. But we recognize that it had nothing to do with Muslims and Islam. It is an act of deranged criminals who do not follow the scripture the way it should be followed. They make their own interpretation. The same way that you have the Christian right and other extremists in Christianity who make their own special interpretation of scripture. And terrorist groups like the Ku Klux Klan. Fringe groups have always dogged established religious systems in every country. The world has become smaller and this type of criminal today has an extended reach. It is shocking. They come and do dreadful things. Shooting at airports, for example. It's frightening.

Initially, when I came here in '65, there were few mosques, two in Brooklyn and one in Manhattan. But it is not necessary for you to go to a mosque to pray, which is another way of saying, *performing your salat*. You can perform the prayer in your office, your room, your home. And as a busy doctor who has little spare time during the day, I pray when I can. Each prayer takes only three or four minutes. It is your own personal salat. But on Fridays the salat has to be a congregational prayer. A congregation is defined by a minimum of three people. In other words, if you can get together three people in a small room on Fridays, you fulfill your salat. The Friday service includes a sermon.

As time advanced, as Muslims multiplied, most of the hospitals started setting aside a room as a mosque. In my hospital, a Jewish hospital, I told the administration we needed a room for the purpose and the administration was very happy to set one aside. On Fridays, the doctors, the technicians, the nurses, those who are Muslim, would gather, twenty people, thirty people, and one of the group would lead the prayer as an imam.

An imam can be anybody. I am an imam, anyone who knows how to perform the prayers can lead the salat. There is no special education needed. In the Catholic and Jewish religions, you have schools, seminaries, and colleges. There is nothing like this mandated in Islam. But there are people who can take on religious work in education. In Muslim countries they are appointed to the position. For example, in many mosques in Saudi Arabia, Egypt, Turkey, the imams are appointed, even in India. They get a salary. To get such an appointment, you need some basic education. The government provides the salary, but the appointment is made in consultation with Muslims of status and the government. So there are religious institutions geared to this. But they are not mandated.

In this country, the Islamic religion is following American trends. We now have a Muslim chaplain in the prison system, a Muslim chaplain in the army, a Muslim chaplain in the hospitals. You call them imam or chaplain, either one. These people have to have some education. Somebody has to speak for them and certify that they know the job. So there are schools and an educational institution for this kind of imam. But, generally, to be an imam, a special education is not mandatory. A carpenter can be an imam, if he knows how to pray and if there are people who back him. He can lead a congregation in his own workshop.

Both of my children, son and daughter, went to public schools. They attended Jericho High School nearby. My wife and I feel that the education necessary to become a good Muslim lies right in the home and we did not send them to a full-time Islamic school. Practicing one's religion is part of living. Daily living is living as a Christian, or Jew, or Muslim. You pray, utter the name of God repeatedly, pray as the family teaches you to pray. We taught our children the salat, our prayer ritual. We ourselves taught them the Koran. My mother taught me the Koran as a child. When my children were small, my mother came to live with us and she taught the Koran to my children. The Koran came through the Prophet Muhammad in Arabic, and the rituals of salat are in Arabic.

One of the differences between Islam and Christianity is that our prayer language is different, the language that praying is spoken in. Our liturgical language is Arabic; the Catholic Church mandated theirs to be Latin, though today Latin is not used so much. Jesus never knew Latin, Jesus knew Aramaic. He spoke in Aramaic, and Aramaic is nothing but Arabic. Basically, Arabic is an extension of Aramaic. There is no language today that serves as the Christian prayer mode. One can pray in any Christian religion and use his own language; there is no one liturgical language for all Christians, as Arabic is used by Muslims. My mother taught the prayers to the children in Arabic and thus enabled them to recite the prayers in our liturgical language.

There are some Muslims who recite the entire Koran in Arabic. I finished it as a child. My son and daughter finished it, too, before they were twelve, under my mother's guidance. I helped, too. The teaching from parents is very necessary because children follow whatever their parents teach them. I transmitted what my mother taught me to my children. But they went to the public school system.

Today they practice Islam.

My daughter is married to an Italian-Polish gentleman. [*He pointed to a picture on an end table.*] You see that? It's my daughter with her husband. Both of them are doctors. He became a Muslim. Actually he became interested in Islam, not through her, but through some Muslim doctors at the hospital he works in. He hung around with them and got very involved, and became Muslim. Then he married my daughter. But he was introduced to Islam through this group of doctors.

Most marriages in this country evolve when the boy meets girl, or girl meets boy (families rarely prearrange them). If it happens to be a Muslim and non-Muslim, they may marry anyway. It happens all the time. Islam permits a male Muslim to marry among people who follow the religion of Jesus or Moses. And such marriages work well. It's because much of the cultural mode is similar, like stories of heaven and hell and judgment. Ten years ago, if asked whether I preferred to have a child of mine marry a born Muslim and not a convert, my answer would have been *yes*. Now my answer is *no*, because we keep learning every day and now I realize that Lennie, my daughter's converted husband, is probably a better Muslim than most other Muslims.

I was one of the founders of the Islamic Center of Long Island in Westbury, Long Island. This is how it happened. After deciding that we would stay in this country, my wife and I became citizens and soon moved the family to Muttontown on Long Island. A group of about ten or fifteen other Muslim American doctors living in the same area, and myself, got together and talked about the need for a place to pray, to do things, both for social and community activities. For this, we started utilizing local churches, synagogues, and schools. We rented them for Sundays and we would congregate, have fun, connect socially; and we began hiring instructors to teach Islamic education. The churches were very generous in letting us come in and use their premises. A church here on Jericho Turnpike, a Quaker church, was especially good to us. They opened up their school and we used it often.

After a while, the group of doctors started collecting money, did fund-raising, dug deep into their own pockets and in about three or four years we collected enough to buy some property in Westbury and build a whole center, including a mosque. For this center we did not seek or accept any donation from any country, nothing from Saudi Arabia, nothing from Kuwait, nothing from Pakistan. We wanted to build the system here that would be an example for American Muslims.

There are many sects in Islam. There are the Shiites, the Sunnis, there are people like the Taliban, there are those from the Saudi Arabian pie and the Egyptian pie. We said, *This place will be just Muslim.* Anybody, everybody is welcome here and we don't accept anyone's advice. For example, if the Saudi king wants us to do anything, we would not agree to it. We are under no one's control. We are independent and we collected our own money. Roughly, we have spent about two to three million dollars. The center started in 1983. In ten years time it was up, and now for ten years it has been there. It's a beautiful place, and every Friday we have the congregational prayers.

The center has also become a site for educating non-Muslims in our customs and prayer methods. The Police Department might call us and say, *we have a number of policemen who would like to watch how the Muslims pray.* We say, *Fine, you are welcome. Come tomorrow.* They come and sit behind the congregation and watch the salat being performed. Jews and Catholics call to say they want to come and watch the prayers. The center has also become the site of interfaith activities, and it's really active. Non-Muslim doctors from different areas come here, because they are getting many patients who are Muslim and they want to understand the Muslim religion. They come to this place to see and watch and discuss things.

Friday is our holy day, and on Fridays, the main congregation shows up for prayer. We probably have about five hundred–plus people arrive on that day. Since Fridays are not a general holiday, most Muslims go to a mosque that is nearest their place of work. So Muslims come here who don't live in the area but work in the neighborhood in the shopping centers, offices, and other places. We don't have special collections, but there are boxes so they can chip something in. We do not have an imam. We have a person who takes care of things, and at the same time, he leads the prayer.

In our mosque at the Center, there are many converts who were Jews or Catholic. You probably know that in this country Islam is the fastest growing religion. After 9/11 the *New York Times* reported that the growth of Islam has gone up. Incredible! People are now reading more about Islam, they're discovering Islam, and it appeals to them because it gives one the option of being very free in your religion. It is between you and God. There is absolutely nobody who can put the holy water on you and bless you. You are blessed by God.

I want to give you a document, which is framed. It is the last sermon of the Prophet. It is the speech he made before he died that was recorded and made available to be framed. I have it and will give it to you. In it, he says everything. He says being an Arab, being black, being white doesn't mean a thing to God. What God likes is piety. Being pious, you are closer to Him and being non-pious you may be away from Him. It is not your color, it is not your language or profession that keeps you away from God. That is what it says. We live in a racist world. In the Prophet's time it was very racist. Every society was racist. Even today society is racist, in spite of all the religions. In spite of all the hammering on you and me and everybody else, we still feel more comfortable with our own race. Unfortunately. But Islam is one religion that opposes racism and works against it.

I have never found any difficulty at all being a Muslim in America. Because I realized that in this country people are on their own, and make their own mark, and one's religion has little bearing. In the workplace, you are a worker and you are either a bad worker or a good worker. Outside, you are a good man or a not-so-good man. You are judged by performance. Religion has absolutely nothing to do with it. Nothing. And that is what I find in America different from any other country. Compared to England or anywhere else on earth, America is absolutely different. It's a nonreligious country. Whether the president has a religion or not does not pertain (unless his religion interferes with his conduct of government). Religion is your own business, your private business. It is never in the workplace. But that does not affect your interaction with others or your interpersonal relationships.

As a contrast to America, think of England. The queen is a figurehead and the queen has to be an Anglican Protestant person. And there is an official church, the Anglican Church, with the Archbishop of Canterbury, so it is still technically like a Roman church, a Roman country, a Christian country. The subjects of the queen are not necessarily all Christian, but she is the Christian head. She is called the Christian monarch. France is different. There is no queen; religion no longer has much clout. France is like America.

I have been to Mecca twice, once for hajj, which was the year before last. I did not get very emotional doing hajj. It depends on your own motivation. If you want to become emotional, you can certainly become emotional. But I see religion as more practical—more as a mold to reform oneself as a human being. And these rituals, like performing the salat, going to hajj, fasting, are rituals that reform you and improve you as a human being. But by going to hajj, I also realized that the Muslim community is so diverse and so big—you have white men, you have fully black men, you have yellow men, you have short people, tall people. It is amazing. That hits you, and it hits you from two perspectives. You realize that human beings are one family. And that Islam is the only religion that salutes this and brings this into practice, into one place. There is no other religion of this kind. What it says, it practices. And anyone can sit anywhere. There is no hierarchy that says, *I have to sit in front*. There is no separation of chairs and benches for bishops, priests, and laity. When you go into a mosque, wherever you find a place, you sit. Nobody says, *Move. Mister Important Person is coming*.

Whether you are a Pakistani or Indian Muslim, an Arabic Muslim, a Muslim from France, or from the U.S., hajj makes you realize that in front of God, there is no difference. Everybody is the same, rich and poor, black and white, brown, yellow. That dawns on you during hajj, that hits you. It hits hard.

Al-Haaj Ghazi Y. Khankan

Bringing Muslims and non-Muslims together

... back in the fifties, at a local Rotary Club where I was speaking to members and their wives, one lady raised her hand and said, "Excuse me, I know where the Middle West is, but where is the Middle East?"

Muslims Day: USA was established in 1984 ... The idea was that the third Friday of December would be set aside as a time to educate Muslim children, their classmates, and their teachers about the many, many Muslim contributions to civilization.

In the early eighties, under the late Cardinal John O'Connor and the late Dr. Muhammad T. Mehdi, we formed a group called the "Islamic-Roman Catholic Dialogue"...Another interfaith group is called American Muslims and Jews in Dialogue and still another called the Jewish-Christian-Islamic Commission of the National Conference of Community and Justice.

Photo courtesy of Linda Cateura.

Al-Haaj Ghazi Y. Khankan has devoted a lifetime to explaining Islam to Americans and correcting the impression that Islam is a fearful, warlike religion. He has answered thousands of questions dealing with the religion, the civilization, and its way of life. He calls himself an educator who specializes in the field of Muslim and non-Muslim American relations, but his pupils are not necessarily in the classroom. They are community leaders, Catholics, Protestants, Jews, ordinary Americans, schoolchildren, teachers, college students, radio listeners, TV watchers, and anyone else who is interested. One of the more vocal and available Muslim-American personalities on the current scene, he is a favorite of our media.

In his interview, Mr. Khankan sometimes chose Arabic pronunciation, forms, and phrases not used by others in the book. A few of these have been retained, such as al-Haaj before his name, which is explained more fully in his interview. To avoid confusion, the author has generally made the Islamic terms he employs consistent with those in the rest of the book.

Mr. Khankan's background is extensive. He has been executive director of the Council on American Islamic Relations (CAIR) in the New York office, which responds to the press and TV on all matters pertaining to Islam. He is director of Interfaith Affairs and Communications at the Islamic Center of Long Island, Westbury, New York, and has cofounded many interfaith groups. As director of *The Voice of al-Islaam Broadcasting* in New York for twenty-five years, he met and interviewed Muslim and Arab leaders during his travels throughout the Middle East and the U.S.

Mr. Khankan studied at Aleppo College in Syria and at the American University of Beirut, Lebanon. His education was completed in this country at the University of Southern California in the fields of business administration and international relations. A U.S. citizen, he has lived here for nearly fifty years. His wife, who was one of his students in a class in Arabic that he taught, is American Ukrainian. They have two children, both born and raised in the U.S.

Your name sounds unusual, even for an Arabic name. Can you explain it?

Al-Haaj is an honorific title given to those who perform their pilgrimage to al-Ka'bah Mosque in Mecca. The pilgrimage is called al-hajj, and the person who performs it is called al-haaj (with two a's), the pilgrim. Al-hajj is one of the five pillars of Islam.

Most Arabic names have a meaning, and Ghazi means a "conqueror." The middle initial stands for my father's name, which is Yahya (pronounced "yah-yaa"). That is the name of John the Baptist in Arabic, who is considered one of the prophets in the Koran.

Khankan is of Turkish origin and goes back to the days of Genghis Khan, who united the Mongol tribes and later conquered parts of the Muslim world.

His grandson, Kublai Khan, converted and became a defender of al-Islaam. So the name Khan actually means "chief," or "leader," or "king." The word *kan* in Turkish means "blood," so the translation of Khankan is something like saying, "royal blood"!

Speaking of meanings, when someone says Al-Islaam, the word refers to the religion. Al-Islaam actually means the submission to the will of Allaah or God and to live at peace with all of Allaah's or God's creation. It is derived from two verbs, "to submit" and "to be peaceful."

When did you come to the U.S., and why?
In 1954, I came from Syria, where I was born, to complete my studies. My plan was to go back to Syria after finishing my studies but things changed back home. My parents moved from Syria to Egypt and the situation was not quite as I expected, and so I continued living here and became a naturalized citizen eventually.

What languages do you speak?
My mother tongue is Arabic, of course, and I speak French, which I learned in Syria during the French occupation. Then I learned English at Aleppo College, an American school in Syria, and while I was in California studying at USC, I learned to speak Spanish.

You have resided for many years on Long Island. What is the Muslim population on Long Island?
There are over seventy thousand American Muslims living on Long Island, in Suffolk and Nassau counties. In the New York metropolitan area, there are about one million.

Please describe your duties in the Muslim organizations you've worked for.
To begin with, at USC I was elected vice president and then president of the Arab Students Association on campus. Then I moved to New York City and became the national director of the Organization of Arab Students in the USA and Canada. This was 1960 and we served the needs of one hundred seven chapters all across the colleges and universities of the USA and Canada. Afterward, in 1965, I cofounded the Action Committee on American-Arab Relations, to improve relations and understanding between both sides. In the eighties, I cofounded the National Council on Islamic Affairs. This was a group of Muslim scholars and activists who saw the necessity of educating the American public about their American Muslim neighbors. Americans literally knew nothing about al-Islaam and about Muslim and Arab-Americans. The wall of ignorance has been immense. To give you an idea: back in the fifties, at a local Rotary Club where I was asked to speak to members and their wives, one lady raised her hand and said,

Excuse me. I know where the Middle West is, but where is the Middle East? This is a factual statement.

The organization I am working with since 2000 is CAIR-NY, the New York office of the Council on American-Islamic Relations. CAIR is a national advocacy and civil-rights organization based in Washington, D.C., and has chapters throughout the country. Its very important mission is to defend the civil rights of Muslims and other Americans and to explain al-Islaam to the powerful organs of communication, the media, and also to Americans generally. We also seek to explain America to the Muslims. It is an ongoing effort to create understanding and acceptance of each toward the other and to clarify opinions and clear away doubts.

Aside from my organization work, in my job as director of the Voice of al-Islaam Broadcasting in New York for more than twenty-five years, I traveled extensively, meeting and interviewing many Muslim and Arab leaders both in the U.S. and throughout the Middle East.

[*The following are some of the remarks that Mr. Khankan has made in speeches and appearances throughout the country, addressing both American Muslims and non-Muslims. His abiding aim is to explicate and unite, to change and amend for the better.*]

Equal footing for Islam:
I urge ABC to produce a TV version of *Religion on the Line*, a program that would include a Muslim host on equal footing with the three other religious groups now represented on radio. Currently on the radio show, there are a rabbi, a minister and a priest—there is no Muslim.

Advising a Muslim student on how to dispel the notion that Islam promotes terrorism:
Just simply be the ambassador of the Muslims in your surroundings. Invite your classmates to the nearest Islamic center. Encourage them to read translations of the Koran, the holy book of al-Islaam. In it, they will find that al-Islaam teaches peace and is one hundred percent opposed to terrorism. Terrorism has no religion. When Timothy McVeigh bombed the Oklahoma federal building, nobody said it was "Christian terrorism." When Dr. Baruch Goldstein took an automatic rifle and mowed down Muslims worshipping in Hebron's Abraham mosque, nobody said, "This is Jewish terrorism." Judaism does not teach terrorism, nor does Christianity, nor does al-Islaam.

Educating others about Islam:
Since 9/11 it is a challenge and an opportunity to work harder in educating Americans about Islam. Ninety-nine point ninety-nine percent of Muslims had nothing to do with that dreadful and un-Islamic act. It is unfortunate that

some Americans started behaving in an uncivilized manner by attacking Muslims, harassing them, burning their mosques, beating Muslims who happened to be working in their neighborhood—in other words, taking the law into their own hands. We should not go back to the days of lynching mobs. It is wrong to blame seven million American Muslims and three million American Arabs for the deeds of a few terrorists, whom we strongly condemn. Guilt by association is illegal and uncivilized.

On reexamining our foreign policy:

We need to reexamine our foreign policy in the world, especially in the sensitive area of the Palestine question. We know from statistics, for example, that since 1949, we have given the Israeli governments one hundred thirty-four billion dollars and helped them take over the homes of the Palestinian people, and made them refugees. The U.S.-made F-16s and helicopters that shoot rockets and tanks, donated by our government, are being used by the Israelis to kill more Palestinians. And so the one point two billion Muslims and the Palestinians think that we are in cahoots with the Israelis against the Palestinian Muslims and Christians.

There is discrimination in our foreign policy. In comparison to what we gave Israel, we have given less to all the people of sub-Saharan Africa, all the people in Latin America and the Caribbean—combined. Why this economic discrimination?

This also makes people in those countries dislike us. We have to be even-handed and fair in reporting the news and commenting on it through the American media. Unfortunately, many people in the media are biased when we deal with Muslim-majority countries.

On getting Muslims to educate their neighbors about themselves:

As Muslims in America, we should do more to educate ourselves. We should do more outreach programs. The Islamic Center of Long Island and other mosques, for example, every week invite school children, college students, medical doctors, police officers, and teachers to their Islamic Center to explain things and answer their questions about al-Islaam.

I urge all mosques to do the same or better. Americans are thirsty to know more about al-Islaam. Muslims should take the message of the mosque outside its walls. At the Long Island Islamic Center, we answer all invitations for speakers; we go out to churches, synagogues, civic organizations, schools, colleges to explain the true Islamic way of life because this is one venue still free from bias and control, compared to some media outlets.

On sensitivity training for police academies:

We do sensitivity training for the police academies of Suffolk County and Nassau County and others. Muslims have a very wealthy heritage that should be explained and shared with all those who want to know.

On being your own ambassador of goodwill:
Do not stay within the four walls of the mosque. Be proactive, take care of your neighbors, be the best ambassador of al-Islaam in America through your own personal behavior.

On creating interfaith groups:
I urge all Muslim leaders to create programs of ongoing dialogue with other religious and civil-rights groups. The Islamic Center of Long Island has initiated dialogues such as American Muslims and Jews in Dialogue, Multi-Faith Forum, and others.

You are very active with interfaith groups. Just what is an interfaith group?
Interfaith groups bring together people of different faiths, like Christians, Jews, Muslims and others who interact and explain their faiths to others and learn about the faith of others. This has been going on since the days before 9/11. In the early eighties, under the leadership of the late Cardinal John O'Connor and Dr. Muhammad T. Mehdi of New York, we formed a group called the Islamic–Roman Catholic Dialogue. The National Council on Islamic Affairs and the Roman Catholic diocese of New York joined ranks and produced it. We started a monthly dialogue, which still meets to date. The cardinal was personally interested in the dialogue. Actually, the pope at that time put out a statement concerning the relations of his church with other communities and had mentioned al-Islam as a very important religion in the world. Indeed, we have more than one point two billion Muslims in the world, so it is important to get to know something about them.

There is another interfaith group called American Muslims and Jews in Dialogue and still another called the Jewish-Christian-Islamic Commission of the National Conference of Community and Justice. The two groups include people of several faiths, and I am a member of both. The Long Island Multi-Faith Forum, to which I also belong, is an interfaith group that includes not only Muslims, Christians, and Jews but also Baja's, Brahma Kumar's, Buddhists, Hindus, Jains, Native Americans, Sikhs, Unitarian Universalists, and others. This forum presents periodic community dialogues that build bridges of understanding across religious, racial, and cultural boundaries. These events have ranged from a theological "Meeting of the Minds," with Cardinal Arinze and Muslim and Sikh respondents, to an interfaith dialogue on interfaith marriage.

After the terrorist attacks, the Multi-faith Forum was a key group in defusing backlash against Long Island's extensive Muslim community, estimated to be more than seventy thousand. The forum repeatedly arranged for Muslims to speak and presented educational programs to diverse audiences throughout the region so that Long Island residents could gain a better understanding of our Islamic neighbors and their traditions. Shortly after 9/11 the forum, in coordination with the Catholic Diocese of Rockville Center, held an interfaith prayer service at St. Agnes Cathedral in Rockville Center, attended by over one thousand that included all eleven world religious traditions currently belonging to the Forum.

Recently, in October '03, Telecare, the TV production of the Diocese of Rockville Center, in cooperation with the Islamic Center of Long Island, began airing a TV series called *Our Muslim Neighbors* as part of the dialogue. In the nineties, I was part of a weekly TV program called *Father Tom and Religious Leaders* for about three years, also as part of the dialogue.

CAIR sends releases pertaining to Muslims to political figures and the media. What prompts you to send out a release?

Our weekly CAIR-NY releases often are based on our petitions. I send out a weekly petition and release, as the case may be. We are very sensitive to anything pertaining to Islam and our feelers are always on the alert. For example, we knew that on the anniversary of 9/11, there were going to be a lot of attacks against innocent Muslims. So we wrote to the president urging him to speak out and make sure that the religion of al-Islam is not accused because the terrorists, it was claimed, were Muslims. We explained that al-Islaam is opposed to terrorism and we condemned it. We called upon the president to address the nation and condemn anti-Muslim hate speech and hate crimes that took place immediately after the 9/11 tragedy and to make the address before the anniversary. I wrote to the president in September '02 and, in fact, he came out in November '02 and said that some of the negative comments that have been uttered about al-Islaam do not reflect the sentiment of the government or the sentiments of most Americans. He went on to say that al-Islaam as practiced by the vast majority of Muslims is a peaceful religion, a religion that respects others, and that by far the vast majority of American citizens respect the Islamic people and the Muslim faith. He declared that ours is a country based upon tolerance and we are not going to let the war on terror and terrorists cause us to change our values. So we thanked him for that. The Muslim community was extremely gratified at the outcome of the CAIR letter.

Other releases and petitions that CAIR-NY has sent out have had similar success. A law was passed which allowed Muslims to be arrested on the grounds of "secret evidence" and they were not given a chance to defend themselves. Then a bill was introduced in Congress called "Secret Evidence Repeal Act." CAIR-NY wrote letters to some of our congresspersons, specifically Carolyn McCarthy from Nassau County, Long Island, urging her to support that bill. And she did, writing us also a very sympathetic letter. We

petitioned Congressman Gary Ackerman and others, urging them to condemn all anti-Arab and anti-Islamic expressions and activities. He wrote back,
condemning such acts. This type of activity that I do through CAIR-NY and
the Islamic Center of Long Island can bring satisfactory results.

What have been the biggest problems for American Muslims since 9/11?

The misunderstanding of Islam and the tendency by some members of the
media to associate our Islamic way of life with terrorism. In fact, the word terrorism is often paired with the word Islamic, like the phrase "Islamic terrorism." Anyone who takes serious time to read the holy book, the Koran, will
find out that al-Islaam is opposed to violence and terrorism. Fighting is
allowed only in self-defense. Anyone who reads the Koran will realize this.
You see, terrorism has no religion. Terrorism is not Jewish, Christian, or
Islamic. Terrorism is perpetrated by individuals, not by religion.

How did the symbol of the crescent and star come to represent Muslims here in the U.S.?

The symbol of the crescent and star has been used by Muslims throughout
history as a symbol of the Muslim people, but not of the religion of Islam. For
example, it appears on flags of some Muslim majority countries and the flag of
the Red Crescent Society, which is similar to the Red Cross. In the eighties
this secular symbol of the crescent and star was used in conjunction with
Muslims Day: USA in New York, New Jersey, and Washington, D.C.

Let me tell you how Muslims Day: USA was established in 1984. About
nineteen years ago some Muslim parents, whose children were in public
school, came to the National Council on Islamic Affairs, to complain. They
asked, in effect, *What can our children do during the December holiday decoration
season? All the classes are decorated with Christmas trees and Hanukkah menorahs,
and there is nothing for them.* So we came up with the idea of Muslims Day:
USA. The idea was that the third Friday of December would be set aside as a
time to educate Muslim children, their classmates, and their teachers about
the many, many Muslim contributions to civilization. The textbooks of social
studies are shallow in their teaching about Islamic history and civilization, and
so every December we focus on these contributions.

We made an agreement with the Board of Education of the City of New
York that, whenever a decoration is put up in classrooms with the Christmas
tree and the menorah, the crescent and star would also have a place in the decoration. There are also flags with the crescent and star. In fact, we have progressed to having the crescent and star placed in front of municipal buildings
in the borough of Brooklyn, the borough of Queens, the borough of the
Bronx, then inside the Empire State building, in front of the World Trade
Center before the disaster, in Penn Station, Grand Central Station, Chase

Bank, Citibank, the New York Public Library and at the Fifty-ninth Street and Fifth Avenue corner of Central Park. And then in Washington, D.C. itself, in the Ellipse Park near the White House, where the national Christmas tree and the national menorah are placed, a national crescent and star are also placed. On Long Island, the crescent and star are placed in front of the old courthouse in Mineola and at C. W. Post's Long Island University.

I hope that through CAIR-NY, this idea will be adopted throughout the nation. America is known for its diversity and its multiculturalism. I think this is a healthy way of celebrating and recognizing our American Muslim neighbors.

What kind of relationship should we strive for between Muslims and Americans? What can we do to effect such a relationship?

Muslims and Americans? Firstly, we should avoid using the terms Muslims and Americans. It would be better if we avoid stressing the distinction between them because seven million Muslims are Americans. American Muslim citizens represent all races, ethnicities, and colors in the USA and the world! You would be more accurate to say between Muslims, Christians, Jews, and others.

Beyond this, there has to be an understanding. There has to be a continuous dialogue. There has to be a dialogue between civilizations, not a clash among civilizations. We should be talking *to* one another, not *at* one another. There's a wall of ignorance that has to be chipped down. The Muslims are Americans, as Jews are Americans, as Christians are Americans. We are part and parcel of the American diversity. There has to be tolerance and acceptance through education and civilized interaction to effect such a relationship among *all* Americans.

In view of the fact that Islam is growing rapidly, please address the fear that many people have that their fellow American Muslims may one day outnumber all other Americans.

I strongly believe that we are *all* Americans. We came on different ships, but now we're all in the same boat. Whether an American is a Jew or a Christian or a Muslim or whatever shouldn't make any difference. America is our home and we have to learn how to row that boat to a port of safety, and live together in harmony. All of us Americans are immigrants, some are first generation and others several generations. Our hosts are the indigenous inhabitants, the American Indians, the original Americans. We are all created by God Almighty from Adam and Eve. We are, therefore, brothers and sisters in humanity.

Prophet Muhammad, peace be upon him, emphasized: *There is no superiority of a white person over a black person, or of a black person over a white person, except in righteousness.*

So let us all, as Americans and as human beings, compete in doing righteous deeds. Let us all, as Americans, work together for the moral rearmament of America and the world, as one nation and one humanity under one God.

By the way, the Arabic word for God Is Allah. In French it is Dieu, in Spanish it is Dios, in Italian it is Dio. In the Koran, God or Allah is not a man or a woman. Allah has ninety-nine attributes, and some of them are the Creator, the Compassionate, the Merciful, the Just, the Only One, the First, the Last, the Judge, the Loving, and so on.

Muslims believe that there is only one God or Allah, that Muhammad is the Last Messenger of Allah, that Abraham is the friend of Allah, that Moses was spoken to directly by Allah, that Jesus, son of the Virgin Mary "by the will of Allah," is from the Spirit of Allah, that Allah's religion, revealed to all the Prophets through the Angel Gabriel, is ONE religion, that is, submission to the will of Allah, and to live at peace with all of God's creation; that the original teachings and revelations given to Moses in the Torah and to David in the Psalms, and to Jesus in the Gospel are all codified without any human changes or revisions in the Koran.

Muslims also believe that our destiny is known to God; that there will be a day of judgment; that our deeds and intentions in this life will determine our future life either in Paradise or in Hellfire; and that there is life after death. So you can see that al-Islaam is similar in many aspects to the monotheistic teachings of Prophet Abraham, Moses, and Jesus (peace be upon them). And that al-Islaam is *not* a foreign religion; otherwise Judaism and Christianity would also be considered foreign because Prophets Moses and Jesus, peace be upon them, received Allah's revelations also in the same area of the Middle East, where Prophet Muhammad, peace be upon him, received Allah's final and complete revelations. Therefore, in reality America is based on the Judeo-Christian-Islamic tenets, not just on Judeo-Christian tenets.

Yes, we came on different ships, but we are really in the same boat!

Amira Al-Sarraf

Hijab and all, she lives the good life in Pasadena

Basically, I dress Western, but I do wear long sleeves and looser clothing. I wear pants but with a shirt that covers my backside. On going out, I wear the hijab, following the Koranic principle: when you go out, dress modestly and cover yourself.

It's not unusual to be Muslim and American, and have a very normal kind of life.

We used to take our children to Disneyland in Los Angeles. As it often happened, I trailed behind my husband to deal with one of the children. But my husband does not want me to be seen lagging behind him. People might think we're the stereotypes of wife relegated by her man to walk behind him.

AMIRA AL-SARRAF pictured with her family. From the left, Safiya, ten; Amira; Ali, fifteen; Amin, eighteen; Sermid, husband and father; and Adam, seventeen. (Photo courtesy of Amira Al-Sarraf.)

In this narrative, **Amira al-Sarraf**, an upper-class American Muslim wife and mother, describes her education, her family, her teaching, how her family copes with the stereotypical thinking of people and the kind of life her family leads. Readers will find much of interest here in the similarities, and dissimilarities, among American families.

Los Angeles and its suburbs have a very large group of American Muslims, including the upper-class professional Muslims, as well as the lower echelons of minimal economic means. It is as a member of the upper professional class that Amira al-Sarraf speaks. She is typical of many college-educated Muslim women: married, with children, working part time. Born of a mixed marriage (Catholic and Muslim), she graduated from the University of California–Berkeley and is married to an American Muslim lawyer. Her father was a medical doctor and a founding member of the Islamic Center of Southern California. A modest and deeply thoughtful person, she specifies during the course of her interview what kind of clothes she wears, what her family eats, how many of them perform the daily five-prayer ritual, and all the other disciplines that go to make up Muslim American living. Of special interest is how she combines Islam (sprinkled with bits of Catholicism, in her case) with the American way of life.

Amira is an Arab name. It's my real name and it's not Islamic or adopted. It has two meanings, "princess" and "leader." I like the latter. Al-Sarraf, my married name, also is not Islamic. It's an Iraqi surname and means "banker." My maiden name is Elfarra, a Palestinian name. My father was Palestinian. As a matter of fact, I've not legally changed my name. Many Muslim women maintain their birth names as part of their identity. They do not really follow Western tradition in taking on the husband's surname. Usually, children take the father's name. Elizabeth is my middle name, which is a traditional Catholic name. At my birth, my mother was Catholic, and I guess that's how they negotiated our names. My siblings have Arabic first names and English middle names. My mother is half German and part French and British, and she's a third- or fourth-generation American, born and raised in Missouri. Elizabeth is her middle name.

My father was born in Palestine and came here in his late teens to go to Trinity University in Texas. He entered the undergraduate program there and then transferred to UCLA Medical School. He was a physician here in Los Angeles for about thirty years and passed away two years ago. He was a Muslim, a practicing Muslim. And for the most part my siblings and I are also practicing Muslims. As in any family experience, there are differences among us in how we practice and how we interpret our faith and how much it means in our lives. If you asked my siblings if they are Muslim, I think they would say they are, but the practice of Islam differs among us.

After her marriage, my mother was not well received in terms of continuing to be a Catholic in the Church, since she married outside the Church. She raised us with a belief in God and good moral values and as we grew older, she nursed her thoughts about her own religious situation. When I was in college, she made a decision to convert to Islam, and she is now a practicing Muslim.

Couples of mixed marriages face the question of how they are going to raise their children. In the very beginning, I have memories of going to church a few times. At the time, the Muslim community in Los Angeles was quite small and not organized. My father took the lead in getting together with other families and they became the founders of the Islamic Center of Southern California, which is a notable organization in the Muslim community not only in Los Angeles but nationally. He did that because he realized there was a void—there was no place for his children to go to learn about their religion. He took on the challenge and helped found the center. It started very small and then grew and I would say that I got most of my understanding about Islam through regular visits to Sunday programs and activities at the Islamic Center. But college was the most formative time in making the choice of pursuing my faith.

Los Angeles has a big Muslim community, and Muslims are spread out among the suburban areas. Pasadena, where I live, is part of that picture. It's about ten minutes from downtown Los Angeles. It used to be a quiet town, but it has become a bit more cosmopolitan. Islamic schools are popping up all over the place. There are about ten or twelve in the Los Angeles area. Orange County, south of us, has several because it has a dense population of Muslims, like in Anaheim, for example, which lies southeast of Los Angeles. But these areas are not like Little Tokyos, with people concentrated together. They are more spread out. Angelenos live mainly in the suburbs.

Most of the residents in our immediate area are professional people, physicians, dentists. They're in the high-end group and live in nice homes. But there is nothing blatant or ostentatious about them. Our houses are not set off in enclaves. Muslims in the lower economic scales can be found in downtown LA near the Islamic Center. It's hardly a high-income area. Families are struggling. They have modest apartments and live close to public transportation. I would say that the middle- and lower-class Muslims are rather mixed in. There are parts of Pasadena with lower-income housing, and you'll find Muslims there.

After high school, I wanted to go away to school because of a need to establish myself as an individual. In a family of five children, it was hard to stand out on my own and be strong in commitments and not feel I'm just going with the flow. I felt that attending UC–Berkeley would be right for me. What was great was that Berkeley was a very eclectic community. And there were so many different things going on. That's a great attribute and I loved it. At the time, I had already made a conscious decision to make Islam more part of my life.

For one thing my praying was not regular. When anyone else prayed, I prayed, too, but did not include it in the schedule. I was not saying the five required daily prayers by my own volition and didn't plan for them. I felt ignorant: if someone asked me about my faith, what would I say? I didn't feel prepared, and wanted to learn more. So I started reading the Koran regularly (as well as other books), and took classes to form an understanding and identity as a Muslim.

The Berkeley Muslim community was very interesting. There were people who had just left Iran (this was the early eighties after the revolution). There were groupings of young people, many college-educated abroad, who were trying to forge their way in the States. There were people who were very strict about the separation of men and women and then there were the more liberal. All different types, and for me it was a challenge, navigating to figure out where my version of Islam might fit in. It was fascinating.

At college my intention was to go into social service. But I married early and left school. Later I went back to Berkeley and went into classes in Middle Eastern studies with an emphasis on Islamic civilization. This was more out of interest than as a profession. I also took Arabic for two years and was considering double-majoring but never actually studied much in the social-service area. In my early twenties, I focused my attention on the family. As they got older, I became more interested in the area of education and began working and teaching at an Islamic school.

My four children range in age from ten to eighteen. Naturally I would prefer they marry Muslims but am not sure there will be a choice in the matter. If they decide that they've found a non-Muslim they really care about, I won't spend a lot of time working on them *not* to do it. But often during their childhood, whenever the subject came up, we would talk about how important it is to try to marry someone of your own faith. Our talks related to their own lives and their being able to pass on the knowledge and the traditions of Islam to *their* children. And this is so much harder when you're married to someone who is not Islamic. At the same time, interreligious marriage often brings other difficulties. At this young age, children's mind-set is probably toward marrying someone like themselves, if they think about it at all.

As an Islamic family, we're not strict about following certain rules. About eating halal meats, for example. We do buy our meat from a halal market, which means that the animal has been killed mercifully, without prolonged suffering. In restaurants, we would never eat pork, but we can't naturally concern ourselves on whether the meat was killed by a butcher saying the name of God over it. There's a verse in the Koran that basically allows you to eat the meat and the food of the "people of the book." That phrase applies to Christians and Jews who lived by the Old and New Testaments. Living in a predominantly Christian/Jewish society, we are allowed to eat their meat.

There's another point of view that says if you are not able to kill the meat, saying "in the name of God" as you kill it, you can say "in the name of God" before you eat it. What you're doing, really, is reminding yourself that this animal did not die in vain, that it died to support you nutritionally.

I do the salat every day. But I'm not sure about my children. They have a consciousness about God. There's *them* and there's *Him*. They're still young and forming.

I do not attend the mosque frequently. The reason perhaps is that we maintain a lot of activity and contact with the Muslim community through the school. That's where all my efforts are, and the weekends I use to do things with my family. Incidentally, my husband also does the salat every day.

Actually, I think our family's practice of Islam is about average for most American Muslims. It's not unusual to be Muslim *and* American, and have a very normal kind of life. But you're not going to find many Muslims at bars; you're not going to find them at places where women are degraded, such as topless bars. I think the Muslims we know, who are like us and have a similar lifestyle, are the mainstream, conservative-type religious Muslims. Women choose to dress more modestly in the community. How Muslim women dress is probably the most distinctive feature that non-Muslims pay attention to.

Basically, I dress Western, but I do wear long sleeves and looser clothing. I wear pants but with a shirt that covers my backside. On going out, I wear the hijab, following the Koranic the principle: when you go out, dress modestly and cover yourself. At work, most women keep the scarves on. You have parents coming in and out, and it's just more appropriate to have it on and actually more comfortable. The only time women take it off would be at someone's home where the guests are women, or at a relative's house where there is only family. I pin the scarf and tie the loose part of it behind my neck. If it's the right material, I do pretty well in most kinds of weather. I'm happy during winter because I'm much warmer than everybody else.

The burka refers to a long dress that comes over your face. The abaya is like the burka but it doesn't necessarily cover your face. It's a big piece of cloth, which is held at your chin to keep from falling. You'll find the abaya in Saudi Arabia and those areas. Do I know women who cover like that? Most of the women that I'm around do not cover their face. Most of them don't cover their hair, but they do dress modestly. Some women wear the *jilbab*. A jilbab is like a long dress or coat. They're often in beige or blue and worn over a short-sleeved dress. They'll wear a regular scarf that doesn't cover the face, but it looks a bit more Middle Eastern.

Remember, there are Muslim women who pay no attention to Muslim-style dressing and look like Western women. Just as in most religions, you have various degrees of practice and belief. I met a man in the doctor's office the other day. He was Jewish. And he talked about how Jewish he was and all this. And he said, *But make no mistake. I'm an atheist.* I'm sure that there are Muslims, too, who are atheists. But to me, if you're going to call yourself a Jew, a Christian, or a Muslim, you should adhere to their basic tenet, which is belief in one God.

I think that Muslims, wherever they're living, have to decide for themselves and determine what their adherence and practice of Islamic faith will be. They should decide what influences they're going to include in their lives. This is a wonderful thing about Islam: a Muslim decides for himself on the practice of his religion. It is between him and Allah. A Muslim growing up in Saudi Arabia picks up practices that are particularly Saudi, a girl living here in the United States picks up practices that are particularly American. I don't see a whole lot of difference—*they're both Muslims.* For example, a Muslim American, having studied the religion and ascertained that there is nothing in Islam that says men and women have to be completely separate in a gathering, decides to mingle and interact. If you actually study the ways of the Prophet, you'll see that he used to have interaction with women and talk to them. On the other hand, there are strict Muslims who long ago made the decision that men and women must sit separately.

Beyond this, beyond what the Koran says or does not say, Muslims act according to the national cultures they're brought up in. A person growing up Saudi, let's say, follows the culture that surrounds him. He's not necessarily making conscious decisions to do certain things. He's following what everybody is doing. By the same token, you have girls here who are influenced by American culture and when they go to a store to buy something to wear, they're not necessarily thinking about their faith and what it says about modesty. They're going to wear what looks good and are not concerned with questions like, *Should it be long sleeves? Should it be loose? Does it go below the knees?*

Thus you're going to find a good number of Muslims who are adopting basic Western dressing which, although non-Muslim, usually covers the body as required. If you asked them their religion, without hesitation, they would say, *I'm Muslim.*

Because of this power of local and popular cultures in dress and other areas, it may happen that Muslim immigrants who come here will find that Islam and its practices will gradually lose their hold on American-born descendants. It's a danger. There are many at-risk Muslims absorbed in lifestyles and habits that are contrary to Islam. Besides dress, there are questions concerning sex before marriage, dating and so on. One statistic claims that sixty percent of American girls have sex by the time they're high-school seniors. This is a different kind of world.

One cannot talk about American Muslims today without the subject of the Islamic treatment of women rearing its ugly head. Most of the world blames

Islam, the religion itself, for the maltreatment. But the fact is, Islam is *not* to blame, but the culture and nations where Islam exists. Such treatment is rooted in a nation's fiber and no amount of study of the Koran, which condemns such treatment, will persuade people otherwise. It is in the culture and was there long before Islam entered the picture. For example, when a father in an Islamic country makes the decision on what man his daughter marries and can force her to marry that person, it's culturally accepted because that's what fathers do in that country. Islamically, when you go to the sources, it's very clear that a woman *cannot* be forced to marry any specific person. It's her choice whom she marries. But things are mixed up and Islam gets the blame. The intertwining of culture and religion makes the practice of Islam more difficult.

What is wonderful about America is that here Muslims have the opportunity to delve into their faith. They can go to the sources, the Koran and the hadith, which are separate from culture. There you find the unvarnished answers. There you will find that the Koran esteems women and gives them their rightful place in human society.

Fortunately, there are many American Muslim women who are trying to fight the widespread belief that Islam is to blame for female maltreatment. They donate their time and energies to establishing groups to help other Americans understand Islamic tradition. They disseminate accurate information about women in Islam and dispel the stereotypes. My sister is very active in this kind of activity. Her name is Laila al-Marayati and she is a physician by profession. She was president of one such group, the Muslim Women's League, and is now their official spokesperson. She is wholly dedicated to correcting the Islamic image and served as a U.S. delegate to the UN Commission on Women held a few years ago in Beijing. Hillary Clinton appointed her to a commission on religious minorities along with Jews and Christians. On this, she served for about three years.

The league's members give talks, prepare position papers, and hold conferences on female circumcision. They provide information that it is *not* an Islamic practice and *not* sanctioned by Islam, that it is a *cultural* practice. In Pasadena, the league has a summer program for young Muslim girls and maintains a sports camp for them. They are also involved in issues that relate to Muslim women in other parts of the world. When Muslim women were raped in Bosnia, members of the league joined a coalition here in the Pasadena area and went with them to help counsel the rape victims and try to help them to lead a normal life. But the league is mainly focused on events here in the United States, especially education.

For Muslim women, the biggest effort should be toward education. They should be educated about their rights as Muslim women, so that they can advocate on behalf of themselves in America, not only within their own families but within the society at large. But most importantly, it is *within themselves, within a Muslim community*, that they need to know what their rights are.

I think definitely there's a dignity in our womanhood that God intended us to have and, fortunately, there are many mechanisms in our society here in America that can potentially safeguard a woman's dignity and her religion. But, at the same time, I feel there are many influences today that lead women *not* to respect themselves and not live up to their dignity as women. The way our media highlights and makes jokes about female sex attributes is a prime example of this.

Muslim men are much maligned as *husbands* here in America because they are considered perpetrators of this maltreatment. But despite what you hear, there is a common thread that runs through all their upbringing in the Islamic religion, and that is, *respect for women.*

This common thread applies to all parts of the world. It is one of the highest principles in Islam. Westerners, not knowing, sometimes might be quick to accuse. And this has made my own family more careful when we appear in public. My husband is very much aware of this. We used to take our children to Disneyland in Los Angeles. As it often happened, I trailed behind my husband to deal with one of the children. But my husband does not want me to be seen lagging behind him. People might think we're the stereotypes of wife relegated by her man to walk behind him.

Come, come up next to me! he would whisper, quietly but insistently. These dramatic notions that people have here color the way Muslim men and women interact.

Muslim men do respect women, some more than others perhaps. In my days at Berkeley, I found that Iranian men were much more respectful than some of the Arab men we hung around with. They made sure the women ate first, they helped serve the food, and helped cook the food. They were much more open about those things. Not all Muslim men are the same. There's so much diversity among the Muslim community among different people. When a man is educated, and if his outlook is really derived from the Islamic principles, he will know what his faith expects from him. He is more likely to follow the tradition and principle in Islam that promotes respect for women. I think that women and men both need to remain educated about that. Most of what you'll find in terms of the mistreatment of women, you're going to find among the uneducated people. They are human beings, but not the finest human beings. There are issues of domestic abuse in Muslim families, but that doesn't mean that the religion sanctions or condones it.

I think Muslim women are happy in American society and enjoy taking part in their community events and activities without any encumbrance. There is something wonderful about the freedom to practice your religion here. And the way we go about doing what we need to do without having to answer to anyone. We can drive. We can dress the way we like. We can educate ourselves to our full capacity. There are no restrictions on us, as you find in some other countries. A similar independence for Muslim women is found in Malaysia and Indonesia. There is such a vast difference between Muslim women in Malaysia and Muslim women in Saudi Arabia. Saudi Arabia isn't the end-all and be-all of Islam, as some people like to project.

Now there are some Muslim women who are not comfortable with the way women in general are treated in this country. Cultural influences in the media make them feel uncomfortable. I've known a few women who have gone back to live in Arab or Muslim countries where that was less pronounced. But even in those countries there are influences you can't control.

In the wake of 9/11, my personal experience has not at all been worsened by any backlash against Muslims. In terms of how we're being dealt with, I personally haven't had much that is negative. In fact, the society we're surrounded by here in Pasadena and the neighborhood is filled with people who reached out and wanted to be sure we weren't becoming victims of backlash. They seemed to want to show that they were examples of Americans with the true American spirit of help and friendship. They exemplified the American spirit in a time of need. We had gatherings with neighbors. Here at the Islamic school I work in, churches and other schools reached out to us.

Oddly, this terrible tragedy has helped to bring out the Muslim community. It has brought out the best in our neighbors and in us. It thrust us more into public life and I think that's important. We were shy and just doing our thing and went along in our lives. We made little effort to reach out to our neighbors. 9/11 encouraged us to be more giving, more open to reaching out to people who are in our immediate world.

But the experience has also been negative for American Muslims because of the kinds of laws that are now in place. Many decisions can be made without constitutional rights being a concern, because it's a time of war. There's the fear that the legislation going through, the rules that are being carried out, tend to restrict the rights of the Muslim population in this country. We all know of numbers of people who have been detained for little reason. There's more of a free range now to create a climate of restriction.

I teach in an Islamic school in Pasadena called New Horizons School. It was established to give Islamic children everyday life experience and an education in all the established subjects, *including* their religious education. It completely takes the place of a public school in that it provides a core curriculum, such as math, science, English, history, but it also provides a religious education in Islam. In our Koran class, important themes and values of the Koran are taught. We have an Islamic studies class which basically provides the children with an understanding of the practices and beliefs of their faith, historical information about the life of the Prophet, stories from the Koran about the various prophets in the Koran. The class also includes a look at Islam today and how young people are expressing their faith. Arabic language training is also given. It starts at preschool, where it is more verbal. As we go into kindergarten and first grade, it becomes more written. The average Islamic school goes up to about sixth or eighth grade. Some schools around the country now have high school programs. Our graduates go to public schools or private schools. Each family pays for its own tuition. Unfortunately, although we pay taxes, we don't get to reap any benefits from that. We pay for the full tuition, like other American families who send their children to private or religious schools. Tuition is high: it's from five to seven hundred dollars a month.

Sadly, we're finding that our Islamic school is more accessible to parents who are either very well off, or who aren't well off at all because these families are usually eligible for aid. Under these circumstances, the middle-class families in our schools and other private schools are struggling and losing out. Generally speaking, families have two or more children, and if Mom doesn't work, and there's only Dad's salary, it can be a terrible drain. To raise money, we do fund-raising, sell cookbooks, have benefit dinners and there is some aid for these families from the school budget.

All my children have attended Islamic school. Two have graduated. Overall, I think they've enjoyed our school. It's interesting that my two older boys, who have gone on to public high school and to college, like to go back to visit their friends from the Islamic school. They've formed lasting friendships. When they were in public high school, our boys would tell us about their classes and how they had to talk about their religion, and remembered the things that were taught at the Islamic school. This helped to form and strengthen their identity as Muslims and they now feel comfortable with who they are. It had a lot of benefits.

My older son has just started at George Washington University in Washington, D.C. A lot of the emphasis is on prestigious colleges, as it is for most college-age Americans. At the same time, my son narrowed it down to a few choices. He did look to see whether a college had a Muslim community, what their activities are, whether there's an MSA (Muslim Students Association). He got on the wait-list at Johns Hopkins and we considered it seriously. His area of interest is international affairs and political science. We looked at all the courses and professors at Johns Hopkins and they had not a single foreign-sounding name on their faculty, not from Africa, not any. It was very Anglo, if I may describe it that way. We felt that perhaps the university was not as diverse in terms of getting different kinds of perspectives on world issues. If you're teaching international affairs, it might be a good idea to have some diversity within your faculty. He found that at George Washington, there was.

I think there's a benefit for Muslim children to be taught their faith and establish an understanding of it. That's important, especially at a young age when it can become part of their makeup. But there's also a benefit in being among others of all religions and also in contributing to the diversity and cultural exchange of schools themselves. At a college like the American Islamic College, it is, I believe, focused on a more in-depth Islamic studies program. Anyone who seeks a good grounding in Koranic knowledge, the hadith or sayings of the Prophet and Islamic law, won't usually find these areas taught in depth at most places except at an Islamic college. It is also true that the schools and colleges around the United States are providing, more and more, a deeper, more serious study of Islam than in past years.

Walid Ahmed

Practicing Islam in a cold climate

Muslims believe in heaven and hell … From the hadith, the description of heaven is very happy. If you and me were to dream of something of unbelievable beauty, that would be Heaven. It's nothing like the human eye has ever seen, the sounds like nothing human ears can hear.

Non-Muslims get the impression that Islam is a much more lenient religion toward sinners. That is true, absolutely. Then what makes Muslims bad? When they do something bad to human beings, when they start killing Jews or Christians. The people who destroyed the World Trade Center were definitely bad Muslims.

Let me emphasize that all Muslims do not wear the same attire. They are influenced in the way they dress by their own culture and traditions, both men and women. … What happens is that after they have been here for a while, they adopt the local dress. In Anchorage, they'll wear blue jeans. And then you can't tell a Muslim American from other Americans.

When Islam in America is mentioned, we think mostly of the mainland states, and it comes as a surprise that there are American Muslims living in Hawaii and Alaska. In Hawaii, there are about three thousand Muslims and from all indications in the local papers and the Internet, they are surprisingly well organized. The Muslim Association of Hawaii, for example, has a strong voice in local affairs. The Muslim presence is felt but, unfortunately, in more recent times it has been somewhat resented. After September 11, hundreds of leaflets containing threats and disparaging remarks toward Muslims have been found near the mosque of the Muslim Association in Honolulu.

The picture is different in Alaska. There are about eight hundred to one thousand Muslims scattered all over the state. Some are active, and some are not. The religion is largely unorganized and scrambling for position. In Anchorage, for example, groups and associations with high-sounding names have one-man operations and scant members. They appear for a while on the Internet and then disappear. The IslamInAlaska.com Web site has ceased to exist. Their purpose had been the promotion of Islam in Alaska, especially aimed at the new generation. The young people weren't interested. More stable, older Muslims who live in Anchorage still attend one of the two mosques available. Though small in numbers, they pursue their faith.

How does one find an imam in Anchorage, Alaska, to interview? The answer is via the Internet, in a circuitous way. Hoping to reach the hinterlands and Muslims outside our usual boundaries, I tapped in the words "Muslims in Alaska" on my keyboard. Loquacious, lengthy text about mosques and Muslims in our forty-ninth state came up. On scrutiny, however (all this information being further explored on the Internet and telephone), the facts and figures seemed to be interrelated. One led to another and then back to the first, names got confused, some didn't seem to exist, and people weren't talking. Finally someone, an ex-Catholic now a convert to Islam who had lived in Brooklyn, came to the rescue. With the mention of Brooklyn bonding us, he talked and provided an earful on the local Muslim scene. There were only a few imams in Anchorage, he said, and he would certainly suggest Imam **Walid Ahmed** because he was the most sincerely involved. With a little further research, Imam Walid Ahmed seemed a natural for the purpose and several calls brought us together—on the telephone.

Walid Ahmed's mosque is called the Islamic Community Center in Anchorage. Here he leads both men and women (the women usually sitting at the back) in prayer every Friday. The physical conditions of his mosque are limited, but the congregation remains faithful to the imam. He is a person deeply and emotionally involved with the religion, and he is one of the few imams who have survived so far in the area. Self-taught, he has read and reread the Koran hundreds of times, and feels qualified to lead in prayer. Along the lines of a true prayer leader whose devotion outshines erudition, he is very attentive to the needs of his small umma, or community, and brings to his calling boundless love and enthusiasm.

The interview is brief. Imam Walid was a little hesitant at first when asked about personal things, but as soon as questions on Islam itself came up, his voice and words took wing.

Where were you born?

I was born in Alexandria, Egypt. Before coming to Alaska, I lived in Brooklyn for eight years.

How long have you been an imam?

I've been an imam for about eight or nine years. Let me explain. An imam is not always someone who graduates from college or has advanced schooling in Islam. But often he is someone with a lot of background and information about the religion, like myself. We have a small community here and many are Muslim. Someone was needed to conduct prayers. I know a lot about the Koran, the hadith, about the Prophet, and I began to lead the Muslims. It is like a volunteer job for me. I'm doing it but not taking any salary or anything like that.

What is the size of your congregation?

I would say around fifty to eighty. There are a lot more Muslims in Anchorage, but they don't come to a mosque. Mine is not the only mosque in Anchorage. We have two.

Are you a U.S. citizen?

Yes, ma'am.

Why did you leave Brooklyn and come to Anchorage?

My brother was living here and he told me a lot about Alaska. He suggested I come and visit and see how I liked it. So I did. It's a less busy life. It's not crowded. You've got more elbowroom. It's a different environment, different atmosphere.

When did the Muslims first begin to come to Alaska?

I've heard the first Muslims began to arrive in 1956.

How do Muslims make their living in Alaska?

The usual jobs: working in small businesses and restaurants, teaching in school, like any other community. Some are cabdrivers.

Do you have a family here?

I'm married and have two boys. They come to the mosque occasionally, but they're still too young.

How do your sons dress?

The boys dress like other American boys. My wife dresses more like an American, too. She doesn't cover herself from top to toe, as some Muslim women do. But she covers herself good enough to be a Muslim. She doesn't flash it.

What accounts for the way a Muslim dresses in Alaska?

First of all, let me emphasize that all Muslims do not wear the same attire. They are influenced in the way they dress by their own culture and traditions, both men and women. They don't all adopt the traditional Muslim image of robes and such, but dress like everyone else in their homeland. When they first emigrate, they continue to wear the same type of clothing that others in their native country do. For example, on arrival, Pakistani Muslims dress like Pakistani Muslims. What happens is that after they've been here for a while, they soon adopt the local way of dressing. In Anchorage, they'll wear blue jeans. And then you can't tell a Muslim American from other Americans.

Do your children go to a Muslim school?

They go to a public school. There are no Islamic schools in Anchorage.

[*Author's note: It was at this point, with the next question, that Imam Ahmed seemed to let go. Up to now, he seemed uncomfortable answering personal or general questions and yet because of his courtesy, he had responded as seriously as possible. Now, as we broached the subject of Islam itself, it was as if he had thrown off a heavy mantle to give free rein to a favorite topic. He spoke with great energy.*]

Have you made hajj? Why do Muslims everywhere respond so enthusiastically about making hajj? One source calls it a universal journey for meaning, transcendence, and peace.

I haven't yet made hajj. You ask what is so wonderful about it? I don't think that the Western press and all the media reflect what really goes on in hajj. They don't reflect the reality, ignore it, with barely a mention. Every year, it is the biggest gathering of human beings from all over the earth in *one* place. I'm saying the *biggest* gathering, let's say about four to five million, no one knows how many. All these people make hajj for one thing, one thing only: *they go to worship*. Not for trade, or for making money, or for doing business. They go to worship. They all dress the same in a plain, white robe. They don't talk about where you come from, or the color of your skin, or whether you're Indonesian or African. You know what I mean?

And once you're there, you feel at peace with yourself. You forget about the material stuff here in this life. You become involved in doing something to please God and also to please yourself. Over there, there is no sexual thing, even if you have your wife. Over there, everybody is the same. You are all sharing in the same tradition, the same culture. You see Americans. You want to see Europeans? You see Europeans. Africans, Egyptians. You see them. It is probably the biggest convention ever held in one place.

And they talk to one another. They know how to communicate with one another. Everybody seems to fit in. I know an American guy here in Anchorage. That guy did hajj and he's an American! He's a wonderful man and has a family, with wife and kids. I asked how he liked the hajj. *The only time I had peace with myself was when I was there*, he said.

If you could have looked at his expression, his face and hear how he described it! It was a holy and wonderful experience for him. This is what it's like. It's a different level of being and most people never experience it.

Do Muslims believe in heaven and hell? I don't see much written about this.

Absolutely, Muslims believe in heaven and hell. The way the Koran speaks about hell doesn't say how big or how small it is. *But it is going to be bad.* How bad? Really bad. The way the Koran describes it puts the fear in your heart. On the other hand, from the hadith the description of heaven is very happy. If you and me were to dream about something of unbelievable beauty, that would be heaven. But reality cannot describe it. It's nothing like the human eye has ever seen, the sounds like nothing human ears can hear.

You've asked about my life in Alaska. Forget about me personally. Forget about Muslims as individuals. The important thing is that Muslims pray and worship God. In the mosque, I lead the prayer but do what everyone else does. That's it, that's my job (except when a member of the community seeks advice). So if you want me to talk about Islam as a religion, I can do that. I can explain a little and *how* the Muslim people believe. Let me ask the questions.

What is Islam? The word "Islam" is an Arabic word. The meaning is "submission." "Muslim" means "he submits his face and himself to God, to the creator."

What is Allah? Allah is the same as when you say God.

What do Muslims believe? They believe in one God, there is only one God. The one who created the whole universe, the one who put the soul in our body, the one who gave us life, and the one who will take this life back.

Do they believe in just one holy book, the Koran? No, they believe in other holy books and the Jewish prophets. As a Muslim, you have to believe in the Bible, in the Torah, in Moses, you have to believe Noah, you have to believe Abraham and you have to believe Jesus, as we believe Muhammad. You have to believe all the holy books because they came from God and prophets were the messengers with the message that will lead humans to the way to God. That's what the Muslims believe. I say it again: they believe in the Bible, they believe in the Torah, they believe in the Koran. They believe in every holy book brought from God through the messengers.

Do they believe in one prophet more than another? Muslims see no difference between the prophets. They don't say this prophet is better than that prophet. If a Muslim says that, he is breaking the law of Islam and he is not a good Muslim. It's not man's job, yours or anybody else's, to say, *This prophet is better than that one*, or *That message is better than this one*. They all came for the benefit of man. This is how Muslims believe. If you read the Koran, you might be surprised to discover that the Book mentions Aissa, or Jesus (Aissa is Arabic for Jesus), more than Muhammad. Moses is mentioned more than Muhammad. Yet Muhammad is a prophet, like the others.

What makes a Muslim bad? Non-Muslims get the impression that Islam is a much more lenient religion toward sinners. That is true, absolutely. Then what makes Muslims bad? When they do something bad to other human beings and bring them harm. If Muslims start killing Jews or Christians, do we call them good Muslims? No, they're bad Muslims. The people who destroyed the World Trade Center were definitely bad Muslims.

What else does an imam do, besides leading the prayer? An imam advises. If he sees a man ignoring his prayers and not doing the salat, all he can do is advise him, give him the wisdom, and then the man is responsible for his own doings. Imams are not like Catholic priests who impose penance. All we do is advise. No penance. But we do have rules and regulations and laws. If a man does something outrageous, he would be punished. But who will punish him? A priest? No. An imam? No. Then who? There is the government. When a Muslim murders another, then the government takes over and he may be put to death. Allah demands punishment, but He doesn't punish a man for not praying. He punishes him when the man does something that he should not be doing, like harming other people who don't share the same beliefs.

Michael Wolfe

Heir to three monotheistic faiths

Socializing with Muslims is easy for me because they don't need booze to have a good time. I don't drink and never have ... Most of my Christian and Jewish friends don't seem to know how to celebrate anything without a glass in their hands.

I notice a new openness on the part of American Muslims toward others. Since 9/11, mosques and Islamic centers across the country have engaged in more exchanges with people and institutions of other faiths than over the entire preceding decade.

Islam provides for me an amazing intellectual and spiritual toolkit. By intellectual, I mean that there is nothing mysterious or not understandable about it. It is simple and direct.

MICHAEL WOLFE in Riyadh, capital of Saudi Arabia, in 1996. (Photo courtesy of Dorinda Ennis.)

This is the story of **Michael Wolfe**'s conversion to Islam with special emphasis on the whys and wherefores. He was introduced to the religion in North Africa where, after finishing college, he lived and traveled for three years in the 1970s. During this time, the friendly and very satisfying encounters with local Muslims served to spark an enduring interest that later came to fruition when, in his forties, he made the declaration of faith that signaled his conversion.

What makes Michael Wolfe's decision of particular interest is that he was Christian on his mother's side and Jewish on his father's. He had in his background two monotheistic religions, neither of which seemed to satisfy him until he came across the third monotheistic faith—Islam—that, for him, completed a cycle. He has been formed and deeply influenced by all three of them and finds them equally important to his formation as a thinking and spiritual human being.

Michael Wolfe is enamored of words. He is a poet with several published books of poetry. He founded and ran a small-press publishing company in northern California. He is the author of one book of fiction and other prose works including: *The Hajj: An American's Pilgrimage to Mecca; One Thousand Roads to Mecca: Ten Centuries of Travelers Writing about the Muslim Pilgrimage; In Morocco*; and his latest, *Taking Back Islam, American Muslims Reclaim their Path.*

He also produces television documentaries, and lives in Santa Cruz, California.

How did you discover Islam?

Like most Americans, I managed to graduate from college without learning anything at all about Islam. I went to Wesleyan University in Connecticut and majored in Greek and Latin and poetry. Writing had always drawn me, and when I finished school, thinking that teaching and writing were good company, I taught for a year. But I soon realized the only thing those two activities had in common was a pencil. I stopped teaching and went to work as a journalist. Shortly after, I went to North Africa and learned about Islam from people who were very hospitable to me on a daily basis.

I wasn't drawn to Islam by its vibrant culture, its sophisticated law, or its very practical metaphysics. Nor did a book, a group or a teacher attract me. I came to respect Islam as I experienced it, in day-to-day interactions with urban and rural Muslims in the Maghreb—an enormous plot of North and West Africa that links the modern nations of Morocco, Tunisia, Senegal, Ghana, Nigeria, and Niger. After finishing college, I lived and traveled there by bus, train, and truck.

I became pleasantly familiar with Islam, by living among its African practitioners. The way the religion connected and served people in their daily lives, without handicapping them, impressed me. Although in other parts of the world some groups of Muslims were already using religion to cut themselves off from others, this was certainly not the case in West Africa in those days. Muslims lived and worked with their neighbors, who were chiefly Christians and animists. Sometimes, in matters of hygiene or trade, Islam even seemed to improve things for non-Muslims. Beyond the ease of their social relations, I greatly esteemed the lightness with which everyday African Muslims carried their faith. I liked *where* they carried it, too—not on their sleeves, but in their hearts and heads.

But I did not become a Muslim then. In fact, I did not become a Muslim for another fifteen years even though I had a very positive experience with Muslims. What happened was that later, in my early forties, I began to feel that a dimension in my life just wasn't there and began to look into spiritual things. Doing that, I automatically found myself turning toward Islam because it seemed such a *direct* approach. I liked the fact that it did not require anything in the way of an institution, or a priest, or a rabbi. It's just you and God and your practice. So it's not daunting and didn't require, for me, a great change in life.

And it still hasn't. I basically do all the same things I ever did. I've just added Islam, and I haven't spurned my Christian and Jewish background. I don't feel that I have jettisoned them. Were I entirely an atheist, I still would not jettison my Christian background and my Jewish one, too. Because the images of those worlds, those associations, all that cultural weight are embedded in me and all of us who have been subject to them in one way or another. Such religious traditions are part of our being, the way we think and act. So I've never decided at any point to abandon one thing in order to be something else. I still feel much more like I'm adding on. And I'm not a culture seeker. I am an American. I don't ever intend to be anything else. What I was born to, I'm quite happy with.

For me coming to Islam, becoming a Muslim, was very much a matter of learning a few prayers and taking on an attitude of patience. More patience in myself was something I really wanted. In Islam, it's the concept of God willing something. Something—for better or worse—happens because God wills it, not because you made it happen, or because you screwed up and didn't make it happen. Recognizing that it's God who wills things to happen is an element in human life that makes a big difference. But it's very possible to overlook and think you're running the show and creating everything around you. But I don't look at things like that now. Having embraced Islam, as Muslims say, I have a different view of the world.

When you became Muslim, were your blood relatives surprised or upset?

I'm sure. But you should know I was forty-three or forty-four years old. My mother and father had both passed away. I think my father would have been puzzled. We all got along very well and I was raised to experiment. I grew up in a small Midwestern town of about ten thousand people, which had many different churches and religions. We slept over at one another's houses on the weekends, so I went to all the churches in town. We were always encouraged to look at the other side of the street. Most of my friends were Christian, but I also learned some Hebrew and went to a synagogue of Reform Judaism on Sundays. So I had something like a multifaith upbringing. It never seemed odd to me. In reflecting on this, I'm sure that my friends were shocked or taken aback. But when I did convert, it wasn't something like, oh, well, now I'll take up a new religion. I needed this. I was a mess. I was trying to save my soul.

What percentage of your friends is Muslim?
About half.

Are you more comfortable with them?
Socializing with Muslims is easy for me because they don't need booze to have a good time. I don't drink and never have. I find socializing with non-Muslims more of a test. Most of my Christian and Jewish friends don't seem to know how to celebrate anything without a glass in their hands. That's a little bit of an issue for me. It doesn't have anything to do with religion, but with levels of social comfort. I'm not a great partier anyway. But my friends are my friends.

You are half-Jewish, half-Christian, and now all-Muslim. You're made up of the three great monotheistic religions. Has your heritage made your path into Islam easier?
Yes. For one thing, having some familiarity with the Old and New Testaments from birth, and from the cultural inlay of that literature and all its associations, made me realize that Islam is part of the same monotheistic tradition. And I don't see any need to privilege one over the other. If you only know about one religion, then the tendency is to associate the other religions with something lesser. My notion is that these religions partake of the same ethical themes.

You know Muslims—not all, but some—have a hard time right now separating Israel and Jews, just as a lot of Jews have trouble separating Islam from Palestine. Probably because I have all these religions in my makeup, I don't have any trouble doing either. The religions come together for me and make sense.

What is it about Islam that especially appeals to you?
It provides for me an amazing intellectual and spiritual toolkit. By intellectual, I mean that there is nothing mysterious or not understandable about it. It is simple and direct. For me it's more effective than Christianity. I don't really benefit from mystery. The mystery of the Crucifixion and the Resurrection as centerpieces of religion don't have much power for me. They must and obviously do for other people, but that kind of element is not my style.

Something without mystery works for me. That's part of the appeal of Islam. Actually, Judaism gave me more than Christianity. Judaism has amazing irony, sense of humor, cultural base and a real, incredibly literary culture, unbelievably so. My love of books which is a huge part of my life comes from that, I'm sure. Some things in Judaism are given comparatively short shrift, including the concept of the afterlife, which is not well developed at all.

Why do you think Jews pay little attention to the afterlife?
It's just a different emphasis on things. Their emphasis is on what it is to be morally and ethically developed and all of this takes place *in the present*. Let's not worry about what's going to happen to us. That will depend on what we're doing right now. Of course, this is true, but there's a very powerful emphasis on that and a kind of de-emphasis on the other. At least, that's my experience of it.

You are the author of several books and the one that intrigues me most is *The Thousand Roads to Mecca: 10 Centuries of Travelers Writing about the Muslim Pilgrimage*. Let's talk about that. Which of the travel pieces in this book are your favorites?
My favorite ones this morning (naturally, since I chose them, I like them all) are by women. I'll mention two of them. The first one is by a queen, or let's say, someone equivalent to a queen. She ruled over a vast area of India. Her name was Sikander and she was the Begum of Bhopal and lived at about the same time as Lincoln and Whitman, that is, our Civil War period. This is a woman who came as the ruler of a nation and performed the hajj along with a huge train of people, a whole retinue, including her mother, camels, et al, giving out presents everywhere she went. She clashed with the rulers of Mecca, a rather corrupt family that stretched back to the twelve hundreds, who were operating a graft-ridden hajj. She was repelled by the whole notion and in the conflict, the clash between the Mecca rulers who were milking the hajj and her moral outrage at what was happening to the religious festival, there's a very interesting something to be learned. She wrote a book and made just two copies, one for her own library and one for Queen Victoria.

Following Sikander by sixty years, along came an English-speaking woman from Australia who performed the hajj and wrote about it. She was at completely opposite ends of the spectrum from the Begum. She was a waif and did not know what her background was. Caucasian, green eyes, perhaps Australian British of Turkish background; one doesn't know. Her name was Winifred Stegar and she was on her own from the age of sixteen. She married an Indian nobleman and both of them were summarily thrown out of his family. They lived a hard, rough life as cameleers, the people who drove or rode camels, in Australia. There were a lot of them since camels were very popular in early-twentieth-century Australia. When she and her husband were in their thirties with several children, they decided to perform hajj, left the kids and traveled to Mecca all the way from Australia. It was 1927 and she wrote the book about it in the 1960s when she was in her eighties. It's a memoir, a very exciting book, let me tell you. It was just the time when the first cars were coming on and a shift from the days of the camel to the automobile was taking place. A big change in modern times.

How old were you when you wrote *The Hajj: An American's Pilgrimage to Mecca*?
I wrote it when I was forty-eight or forty-nine. When I finally became a Muslim, after twenty years of thinking about it, I wanted to make hajj and go to Mecca. It was an exciting prospect. I had been publishing books since I was in my twenties, so it seemed normal to write a book about it. It occurred to me that if the book was going to get the experience right, I should take it slow and acclimate myself a bit to what is, after all, quite a different pace of life.

Also, I had never celebrated Ramadan, the month-long fast, during which time, from sunrise to sunset, you don't eat, drink, smoke, have sex, drink water, anything. Nothing should pass your lips. Just becoming a Muslim at this point, I was trying to take on a few of the responsibilities of the faith. Ramadan is the Muslim Lent, you might say, and I realized I couldn't fast like that at home with the rest of society marching around in a completely different, consumer-oriented direction. If I was to get Ramadan right, I ought to go to a country where everybody was fasting. It would be a real Ramadan, without being more trying than it is.

So to combine the two big Muslim events, hajj and Ramadan, I went to Morocco for Ramadan, where I spent three months, one month before Ramadan, then the month of Ramadan, and a month afterward. From there I went to Mecca and prepared for hajj, the pilgrimage. For the book, I took little notebooks with me, the size of your palm, just for impressions. I did jot down some sort of notation every day, not *every* day, but more or less. Sounds, smells, what things looked like, and so on. Sometimes I was too busy to write notes, but I did keep some reminder, whatever reminder I could jot down. When I got back to California, I typed up the notes to see whether there actually was a book there, thought it over, and felt there was. And that is the book. It took me three years to write. It's essentially a book about Islam. Most Americans have their fingers in their ears about Islam. But it's a travel book, too. In the mainstream American community of readers, it has been well reviewed.

The title of another book you wrote, *Taking Back Islam, American Muslims Reclaim Their Faith*, is a bit puzzling. Does it refer to American Muslims who have spurned their faith?
No, not at all. What we meant by *reclaim their faith* is not that Muslims lost their faith but that the faith had been distorted, in the sense that Islam needed

to be distinguished by Muslims themselves from terrorist groups around the world that use Islam as a justification for violence. What they're reclaiming is Islam's true image from extremists, from corrupt regimes, from self-serving rulers, and from literalists who dismiss what religion is really about.

Religion is an invitation to improve your life. It's not a political program. American Muslims must reclaim Islam from people who use religion like a stick to beat people with. Like the Taliban. These people are sociopaths. They may consider themselves Muslims, but they're sociopaths. And it's up to Muslims to get the real image back. Nobody else is going to do it for them. Quite the opposite. Islam is drowning in a sea of myths. Some were created by other people. Some have been contrived by so-called Muslims who like to glorify violence and who glorify death. For them, violence is always easier and death is salvation. They contrive these myths about Islam because they want to duck the responsibility of working together to improve the world. They prefer to make it sound as if Islam is the only religion worth having, and the rest are lies. These people are a virus; they are not religious people. It's up to American Muslims to throw that virus off.

But why single out American Muslims as those who should reclaim Islam?

Because we're the ones who have freedom of speech. You can't ask people in most Islamic dictatorships to reclaim their faith. They'd be in prison in five minutes. So it's really up to people who have the freedom to speak, and these people are right here in America and can deal with this. It's our thing.

Few people know that more Muslims die of terrorism globally in this world than any other group. It is a fallacy to think of Muslims as the originators of terrorism. They're the victims of it more than anyone else. This association in our minds of terrorism and Muslim is something we've got to deal with. It's like the Italians and the Mafia, the Jews and money; it's the Muslims and bomb-throwers. The same process of stereotyping. Anarchy wasn't invented last year. Anarchy raged across Europe a hundred years ago. To pretend somehow that this is all new is sloppy and lazy thinking.

It's up to American Muslims, since no one else seems to care to do it, to distinguish themselves from this kind of activity. Islam is institutionally egalitarian. Its practice of worship is racially and ethnically integrated. When you go into a mosque, unlike most churches and synagogues in this country, except for a few perhaps, you invariably see blacks, whites, yellow, brown people, and hear all kinds of languages. They're there together, ethnically integrated. It's a model for our country that does not have ethnic integration without violence.

I grew up in Martin Luther King's day and watched those people being gunned down. We've made great strides but there's always the danger that history repeats itself. We're on the edge of screwing up again with our Bill of Rights. And I would like to see people think twice before they go off half cocked with a broad brush, and paint guilt by association over every Muslim in America.

Can you suggest a good English translation of the Koran? Faulty, misleading translations are a big problem. Is there a translation that preserves the Koran's integrity?

For years Muslims here have been handing out copies of the Koran, hoping to be better understood. But the most widespread English translation, the Khan translation, is the most misleading and full of errors. It is virtually installed in American mosques. TV pundits use it when they want to prove that Islam is violent, anti-Semitic, and oppressive.

What should Muslims like myself and any interested reader—both of whom can't read Arabic—do? Once I asked a Saudi citizen about this and his answer surprised me. *I grew up in Arab schools. But I never knew what the Koran was all about until I read an English translation. That brought me back to Islam.* The translation he read was Muhammad Asad's *The Message of the Qur'an.* Because of the footnotes, the size of the book is big and a bit unwieldy. One hopes a more portable edition will soon come along. Meanwhile, the closest I've come to discerning the Koran's content is through Asad. Incidentally, the purely sonoral splendor of the Arabic language, in which it is written, is accessible via numerous CDs.

Here's a *PS* to the above: Only a few months after September 11, the Los Angeles Unified School District removed three hundred copies of an English Koran from its school libraries for containing anti-Semitic statements in the appended commentary. The books were donated by a local mosque, in a well-meant effort to increase understanding of Islam among mainstream Americans. Alas.

As an American and as a Muslim, how did you react to 9/11?

As an American, I was horrified by the level of violence and by the coldness of its execution. Like many people, I felt angry. A handful of sociopaths, to make a point, had left in shreds the social contract by which an open society lives and breathes. Day by day, I also witnessed unparalleled heroics, performed without an ounce of rhetoric, in the service of other human beings. I'm suspicious of patriotism and of the pride it creates, but in the face of these heroics I felt proud to be living where I do.

As a Muslim, I had other, different feelings. The actions of the perpetrators appalled me, and especially their claim to be acting in Islam's name. Well before their actual identities emerged, many Muslims knew who these people were: political desperadoes wrapped in the flag of a peaceful faith. It wasn't difficult to disavow them. The principal Muslim advocacy groups, from the Council on American-Islamic Relations (CAIR) to the American Muslim Council (AMC) to Muslim Public Affairs Council (MPAC), all weighed in within hours against the perpetrators and on the side of the victims and democracy. And new organizations sprang up overnight, with names like Muslims Against Terrorism.

Some thoughtful Americans have looked for one small ray of hope resulting from the tragedy. Have you found any?
I notice a new openness on the part of American Muslims toward others. Since 9/11, mosques and Islamic centers across the country have engaged in more exchanges with people and institutions of other faiths than over the entire preceding decade. Every Sunday for months after the attacks, mosque parking lots in Detroit, Chicago, Los Angeles, Silicon Valley, and Atlanta were jammed with cars belonging to visitors from neighboring churches and synagogues. The interfaith open house became almost as regular an affair as the Muslim Friday congregational prayer. Everywhere one went, and in every mosque one heard about, Muslims were reaching out to soothe their shock, share their solidarity, and convey Islam's common ground with other faiths. Of all the ways the attacks on New York and Washington changed American Islam, this may be the most profound.

The events of September 11 ended years of Muslim isolation in America, as long pent-up desires to break the average Muslim's sense of otherness found expression in a natural urge to share communal grief and draw together in tragedy.

Are any Americans countering the anti-Muslim distrust?
The American Civil Liberties Union has become quite active. And I've met with quite a bit of healthy, intellectual curiosity about Muslims among mainstream Americans of all kinds. When I go to a university campus these days, I'm stunned to hear—and this is going on all over the country—that Arabic language classes are full to overflowing. The cultural classes on various aspects of Muslim history, the study of medieval Spain under Islam are packed, and ten years ago such classes were practically empty.

The focus of the media is on Islam as a bad thing, but people don't automatically buy it. They're curious, particularly the young people. Let's think back a bit. A similar phenomenon occurred after World War Two with the dreaded Japanese. We suddenly had an enormous interest in Buddhism. And in Japanese art.

In recent times America has had a big increase in Muslim immigration. Why?
American civil liberties and the Bill of Rights have opened our society to people, many of whom have fled very unpleasant situations. Many recently arrived Muslims know, just as well as you or I or better, what human rights are because they've had them taken away from them. They grew up without them. I'm

speaking of the thirty percent from Pakistan and India and of those from the Middle East. These are victims of the terrible dictatorships set up as the result of the withdrawal of the European powers from the colonial enterprise. Into the vacuum fell dictators who rose up and are still there. It has nothing to do with Islam. It has a whole lot to do with European politics. Those who could, fled to America, and that may be the reason.

What have American Muslims done to help themselves in American society?

Muslims have taken a busy hand in building their own institutions and societal requirements, such as churches, mosques, schools. Thirty or forty years ago, a Muslim living in the Midwest would have had to bury his mother or father by shipping the body to Washington, D.C., because there was only one Muslim cemetery and that was in Washington. The institutions for Muslims have been handmade here by themselves. Today there are thousands of mosques. Thirty years ago, only a handful existed and Islam was entirely associated with African-American liberation movements. This scared the hell out of everybody.

How do you explain the deportation of some Muslim immigrants?

We consider ourselves on a war footing, and as a result, many of the newly arrived have been pointed out as a potentially dangerous element in society. A few days ago an airplane took off with two hundred fifty Pakistanis who are being deported. These planes have been leaving America with some regularity after 9/11. Thirty percent of American Muslims are from South Asia and that translates into thirty percent of six to seven million people. These Muslims are being whisked off on what seem very flimsy reasons, like overstaying a visa by two days or students not having a sponsor. They fall through the cracks. It's scary. And the problem is that in a democracy, it could happen to you. If it happens to someone else, it could happen to you. All you need to do is show some allegiance to a person or group they would prefer you do not do, and the INS (Immigration Naturalization Service) can be at your door.

What good do Muslims bring to America?

One of the most valued things is that they've gotten Americans to appreciate what they (the Americans) have here. For me, the new Muslim immigrants are very invigorating and help remind me of all the wonderful things America offers. And seeing them, living alongside them, is like traveling without a passport. I can meet and talk and exchange views with people from all over the world. It's good for us. And it's good to have a world religion where the mosques are not divided up by color. *Only white people pray here, only African Americans pray there*, and so on. I love to watch the new generation, growing up here. I think it's good for our kids in public schools to meet children from somewhere else in the world besides Kansas. Muslim kids are attending schools all over the country. This new Muslim community is on the cutting edge of civil rights here, the way African Americans were in the sixties. Another thirty percent at least of American Muslims are African Americans. Thus we have sixty or seventy percent of people here who are very awake to civil rights. They know their value. If you're an African American or from the Middle East, you know the value of civil rights in a way that most of us don't think about. These new people are like reminders of what we've got here. I don't think Americans should be turning on them. Americans should be working with them, coexisting with them, honoring them.

CONCLUSION

In October 2004, the results of a six-year study financed by the Ford Foundation (under the auspices of Columbia University) were published in the *New York Times* and showed that New York City's Muslims have, since 9/11, identified more deeply with their religious roots and set aside the sectarian and linguistic differences that divided them. Professor Peter J. Awn of Columbia, who helped coordinate the study, is quoted as saying, "The general comfort level felt by most Muslims was truly jarred by September 11, and they became this threatening minority who would be defined mostly by their religion…That has caused serious soul-searching by the community." No doubt, these findings of the Columbia study reflect a similar situation throughout the United States.

But it is not only Muslims who are feeling a sense of confusion and soul-searching. Many Americans are undergoing a terrible period of readjustment following 9/11. Non-Muslims are fearful about the Muslims who are their neighbors and live in their midst. The most tragic result of this fear is the expanding extent of discrimination against Muslims, from job loss to crimes of hatred, several of which resulted in the victims' deaths. Over 80,000 men from essentially Muslim lands have been forced to register with the federal Department of Homeland Security, and 13,000 others, none of whom have been charged with terrorism-related offenses, are scheduled for deportation.

Much of the confusion and fear that Americans are experiencing may arise in part from the fact that many in this country know nothing about the vast majority of its American Muslim people, who do *not* comprise a like-minded mass of white-robed fundamentalists, as they do in some North African and Middle Eastern countries, but who are individuals in mostly Western dress, with diverse personal opinions, beliefs, and accomplishments. They are our doctors, police, teachers, grocery and restaurant owners, bureaucrats, taxicab drivers, construction workers, small-business owners, travel agents. They come from Ghana, Egypt, Bangladesh, India, and have always identified themselves by their culture of origin as well as their adopted culture as Americans. This book gives them a platform to introduce themselves and voice their patriotism and true feelings about the United States.

Because the subjects of my interviews are so varied and interesting, of different backgrounds and professions, I want to highlight some of the many incisive ideas they have expressed, which provide us with a better understanding of the Islamic world in America. My brief summaries cover such themes as the World Trade Center disaster, terrorists, our government policies, the question of responsibility, the Koran's attitude toward war, converts, intermarriage, an American expression of Islam, Islamic proselytizing—as well as patriotism and desire for peaceful coexistence. It is hoped that by keeping their comments and reflections in mind, American readers may draw new insights about their neighbors and form relationships based on facts, respect, and tolerance.

A common thread that runs through much of the text is the desire for a new Islam in America. Asma Hasan calls it a "New American Islam" or "New World Islam," and makes interesting points that relate mostly to younger Muslims educated in America. Omid Safi promotes a progressive Islam, which teaches that each human life has exactly the same worth. He hopes to see it universally adopted and speaks of Indonesia, where progressive Islam has catapulted the religion into the modern world and given women large opportunities in the professions. Shirin Devrim regrets that the worst thing that has happened to Islam in general is that it has never had a reformation.

The hackneyed Muslim images of long robe, *kaffiyeh*, and black beard for men, and the burka for women, draw heated rejections from several of our subjects. These images may be real in a fundamentalist country like Saudi Arabia, but they are hardly true of American Muslims in the United States. Dr. Zerhouni was particularly adamant on this score and said, "One size does *not* fit all."

On the salat, the five-times-a-day recital of prayer, there was a general acceptance and little disagreement. While it is made clear that not every Muslim observes salat *every* day, Aisha Kareem, a daily performer, says the prayers are a constant reminder to her throughout the day to stay on track. She recites them on the subway, for example, as she lives in space and time with other people.

Many have heard of hajj, the yearly gathering of Muslims in Mecca, Saudi Arabia, but have not read about it in such personal terms as presented on these pages. Two people interviewed actually made the trip. Dr. Elias Zerhouni sets the scene with his insightful comments on *why* hajj is such a powerful draw to Muslims. In the description voiced by Hamid Dana, an American convert, we get a glimpse of the magnitude of the event: so much of humanity in one spot. Michael Wolfe, also a convert, who made the journey and wrote a book on hajj, summons up the story of a princess from India who did hajj replete with entourage of servants, children, mother, and in-laws, and how she helped reclaim the holy event from charlatans and moneygrubbers.

One outstanding criticism of Islam, an idea that was expressed only once in all the interviews (and not elsewhere to my knowledge) was put forth by Dr. Zerhouni on the subject of Islam as a religion without clergy. Islam is based on the belief that there is a direct relationship between man and God, with no one in between. Zerhouni says there is a drawback in this because it can give rise to terrorist and fundamentalist movements, and to leaders like bin Laden who assume temporal powers in place of clergy and believe they represent religious truth.

Non-Muslim Americans have found that Muslims tend to proselytize, a quality they resent. Imam Omar Abu-Namous agrees that Muslims proselytize and provides a fascinating explanation for it. Dr. Faiz Khan claims proselytizing is not a tenet of Islam and gives his reasoning. Each presents forceful views on this controversial subject.

Mixed marriage is a subject that many of us in America have had to deal with, either in our own lives or the lives of friends and family. But usually such unions are between Protestant and Catholic, or Christian and Jew. With the increasing growth in the numbers of American Muslims, it will very likely become a more frequent decision to be made between Christian or Jew and Muslim. Safaa Zarzour, an educator and American-Palestinian Muslim, father of four daughters, relates the history of his successful marriage to a Midwestern Lutheran and how the decision of educating their girls found its own solution. Compare it with Professor Safi's account of his marriage to an American Catholic (wherein each spouse still observes his/her original faith), and the decision that couple made about the religious education of their children.

Most of the subjects who spoke on the treatment of women in Islam agree that it is not the religion, but the culture in which they live, that causes problems against women. Amira Al-Sarraf, Los Angeles housewife and mother, said that such treatment is rooted in a nation's fiber and no amount of study of the Koran, which condemns such treatment, will persuade people otherwise. The maltreatment of women was in place long before Islam entered the picture.

Whenever the subject of terrorism and the World Trade Center comes up, the reaction is usually one of horror. Imam Omar Abu-Namous says that 9/11 was devastating to the Muslim morale in this country. Zaki Hanafy declares those terrorists are not normal; they are sick in the head and do not understand Islam correctly.

Confronted with the commonly held belief that Islam promulgates war against non-Muslims, interviewees express resounding denial. After the interviews were completed, Professor Safi sent me the following sayings of the Prophet Muhammad on the subject of peace and love for others (selected and translated by Kabir Helminski). Regretfully, they were not part of the Safi interview, and I take the liberty of quoting them here. Despite the killings in the Middle East and the socio-political motivations behind them, these lines from Prophet Muhammad are clear:

> From morning until night and from night until morning
> Keep your heart free from malice towards anyone.

> A perfect Muslim is one from whose tongue and hands mankind is safe.

> You will not enter paradise until you believe,

And you will not believe until you love one another.
Let me guide you to something in the doing of which you will
love one another.
Give a greeting to everyone among you.

When it comes to placing blame for the disaster of the World Trade Center, a surprising thread runs through these narratives and that is that responsibility lies not only with the terrorists but also indirectly on America itself. Again it is an idea that is rarely touched in media coverage. Nurse Aisha Abdul Kareem, high-school student Yuseph Sleem, interfaith advocate Sharmin Ahmad, educator Ghazi Khankan, in good faith, all agree that America itself should assume part of the blame because of its handling of foreign affairs in recent times—especially as pertaining to the Middle East and South Asia. From the reasoning of these American Muslims, one deduces that the bombing was a retaliatory action, the type of retaliation that could be avoided in the future.

There is a thread of concern among Muslims over non-Muslim friends who have fallen away after 9/11 and in particular over contempt shown for Muslims after the disaster by such American fundamentalist preachers as Jerry Falwell, Pat Robertson, and Reverend Franklin Graham. Lobna Kronemer relates her own experience on this matter. Yuseph Sleem, among others, mentions the unfairness of blaming an entire race or religion for the terrorist acts of one or a few members. He refers to Timothy McVeigh, a Christian who perpetrated the Oklahoma City bombing. People do not call McVeigh's attack an act of "Christian" terrorism, and Sleem doesn't think we should call 9/11 an act of "Islamic" terrorism because it reflects wrongly on the entire Islamic religion.

To conclude: America represents the ideal country to Muslims, as it has to all immigrants who have arrived on these shores, past or present. This ideal is nowhere to my mind more forcefully expressed than in the life of Zaki Hanafy, a former lawyer in Alexandria, Egypt, who gave up his practice to come to America. He had read the U.S. Constitution and realized no other law gave people such freedom and security, and that America was where he wanted to live. For linguistic reasons, he could not pursue his profession in this country; to support his family, he now drives a cab, and seems happy to be doing so...because he is living in America.

GLOSSARY

abaya A long outer garment without sleeves, worn by women in Arab countries.

abla Older sister; a term of respect when used by a stranger to an older woman.

adhan The call to prayer announced by the muezzin (caller).

Aisha The Prophet Muhammad's third (and favorite) wife. She was an authority on medicine, poetry, and history, and an important source of the hadith.

Allah God.

Allahu akbar Translation: "God is most great." It is an important part of the Muslim call to prayer.

Ataturk, Kemal Turkish leader (1881–1938); the founder of modern Turkey. He abolished the caliphate, the rulership of Islam, which in effect abolished the religion in Turkey. He encouraged Western-style clothing and Westernized the country in many other ways.

ayatollah Translation: "sign of God." A Shiite religious leader, often one who takes an important political as well as religious role.

Bedouin Nomad Arab people of the Middle East; devout believers in Islam. Originally desert dwellers, they made their living by camel- and sheep-breeding. In the twentieth century, many were forced by local governments into a sedentary life.

bismillah First word of the phrase "Bismillah al-Rahman al-Rahin," that begins the Koran. The entire phrase means "in the name of God, the Merciful, the Compassionate," and is used by Muslims to begin letters, speeches, and official documents.

burka (also burqa) An all-over garment that leaves only the eyes visible, worn by some Muslim women. Under the Taliban, Afghan women were required to wear burkas.

caliph A title taken by Muslim rulers, such as the Turkish sultans, which asserts religious authority to rule derived from that of Muhammad.

chador A traditional dark garment worn by Muslim and sometimes Hindu women, which covers almost all of the head and body, leaving only the face, hands, and feet exposed.

Eid al-Fitr Translation: "feast of the breaking of the fast"; a Muslim festival that marks the end of Ramadan, the month-long period of fasting.

fatwa An Islamic decree; a formal legal opinion or religious decree issued by an Islamic leader.

fez A man's brimless felt cap in the shape of a flat-topped cone. It is similar to a tarboosh, which is taller.

Five Pillars of Islam These are the five requirements that are made of Muslims: a profession of faith (shahada), prayer recital five times a day, giving alms (zacat), fasting during Ramadan, and pilgrimage to Mecca (hajj)

hadith The collected traditions, teachings, and stories of the prophet Muhammad, accepted as a source of Islamic doctrine and law, separate from and second only to the Koran.

hajj The pilgrimage to Mecca, Saudi Arabia, that is a principal religious obligation of adult Muslims and required only once in a lifetime.

halal Meat for consumption by Muslims from animals that have been slaughtered in the ritual way prescribed by Islamic law.

Hashemites The Hashemites were the dynasty that ruled Mecca from 1343 to 1924. They claimed descent from Muhammad through the line that went back to his great-grandfather, from whom they derived their name. The Hashemites have provided the kings of Iraq and Jordan. Prince Zeid al-Hussein, brother of King Faisal of Iraq, was a Hashemite prince. He was the stepfather of Shirin Devrim, who was interviewed for this book.

hijab A scarf or veil covering the hair or head of women and girls. Hijab sometimes includes a long, flowing dress with sleeves.

imam A man who leads the ritual prayers in a mosque on Fridays.

jihad Translation: "struggle" or "exertion." A personal jihad is the struggle within oneself to live a good life and submit to the will of God. The term can also mean the defense of Islam and the Muslim people.

Kaaba A cube-shaped shrine in the center of the great mosque in Mecca. It contains the Black Stone, which according to Muslim belief was given to Abraham by the angel Gabriel and placed in the Kaaba by Abraham himself.

Koran (also Qur'an) Translation: "revelations"; it is the holy book of Islam that Allah revealed to Muhammad.

madrassa Place of study; a school or college usually used for religious education.

masjid Mosque.

Mecca The Saudi Arabian city visited by Muslims from all the world over, in a pilgrimage required only once in their lifetime.

maghrib The fourth prayer requirement of the Muslim day. It occurs around sunset.

meritocracy A system in which advancement is based solely on individual ability and achievement, not on family background. The Ottoman Empire is a good example of a meritocracy.

minaret Tower of a mosque, from which the muezzin announces the summons to prayer.

mosque (also masjid) Building where Muslims worship.

Muhammad The Prophet of the Muslims. He received from Allah the revelations of the Koran.

mullah Despite various past meanings, today the word denotes an Iranian religious leader.

Muslim Translation: "one who submits"; anyone who believes in the faith of Islam. Some Muslims argue that in view of the meaning of the word itself, anyone who submits his will to God is a Muslim.

Nation of Islam A movement of African Americans that produced a version of Islam that veered from the religion's original teachings and promoted a message of militancy, black supremacy, and separation. Later, in the 1990s, it came closer to Sunni Islam.

People of the Book A phrase used by Muslims to describe Christians and Jews. Like Muslim beliefs, the beliefs of Christians and Jews are based on revealed scripture, in a holy book. When Muslims speak of their holy books, they are referring to the Koran and the Bible.

rakah A unit of prayer comprising four alternating postures: standing, bending, kneeling, and bowing. Each of the five daily prayers is accompanied by one or more rakahs.

Ramadan The month of Muslim fasting.

salat One of the Five Pillars of Islam (the requirements for being Muslim). Salat comprises five daily prayers said at various times during the day: fajr at predawn; zuhr at noon; az-zuhr in the afternoon; maghrib at sunset; and isha in the evening.

shahada The first of the Five Pillars of Islam, shahada is the declaration of faith in Allah.

Shakirs An old distinguished family of Turkey that is known as having produced scholars, administrators, statesmen, soldiers, a general, and founders of madrassas. Shirin Devrim, an interviewee in this book, is descended from the Shakirs on her mother's side.

Shariah Islamic law as drawn from the Koran and hadith.

Sharifi In addition to the Hashemites (see page 275), the Sharifi are also members of the Prophet Muhammad's family. But the Sharifi, much larger in number, are not considered direct descendants.

sheikh This has several meanings: a person of knowledge and understanding; a teacher and guide; and, currently in the Middle East, is used as a form of address, such as Mister or Monsieur.

Shia's (also called Shiites) Muslims who believe that Muhammad's direct descendants, through his daughter Fatima and her husband Ali (the Prophet's cousin), should inherit the political and religious leadership of Islam. Shia's believe that the direct descendants are inspired by Allah and, therefore, infallible. Shia's comprise 15 percent of Muslims. Their main cleric is called an ayatollah.

Sufism, Sufi Islamic mysticism; Islamic mystic.

sunna The practice and example of Muhammad and the traditions coming from him. Many examples are set forth in the Hadith.

Sunni Muslims who believe that succession to Muslim leadership should not be hereditary but given to the most qualified and pious persons. The Sunnis consider such leaders as defenders of the faith and require that they must also be skilled politically. Divine inspiration is not a requisite. Sunnis comprise 85 percent of Muslims.

Turkomans A Central Asian people that began migrating westward in the seventh century A.D. Today, about 2 million live in Iraq. They speak Turkish and almost all are Muslims.

ulama A community of Muslim religious scholars who have jurisdiction over legal and social matters for the people of Islam. Various groups with a presence on the Internet have also claimed this designation.

umma The community of Muslim believers worldwide.

vizier A high officer in a Muslim government, especially in the Ottoman Empire.

Wahhabi Believers in an ultraconservative interpretation of Islam, practiced in Saudi Arabia, which rejects any innovation that occurred after the third century of Islam.

wali A Muslim "saint," but not in the Christian sense. The literal definition of the word is "helper," "patron," or "friend."

wudu Cleansing with water before starting salat, the prayer ritual. It is a symbol of purification.

zacat One of the Five Pillars of Islam: giving alms and charity. Muslims are asked to give 2.5 percent of their total wealth each year to charity.

INDEX

AUG 0 1 2005

Voices of American
Muslims.

24.95

DATE			

PELVIC PAIN EXPLAINED

PELVIC PAIN EXPLAINED

What Everyone Needs to Know

Stephanie A. Prendergast and Elizabeth H. Rummer

ROWMAN & LITTLEFIELD
Lanham • Boulder • New York • London

Published by Rowman & Littlefield
A wholly owned subsidiary of The Rowman & Littlefield Publishing Group,
Inc.
4501 Forbes Boulevard, Suite 200, Lanham, Maryland 20706
www.rowman.com

Unit A, Whitacre Mews, 26-34 Stannary Street, London SE11 4AB

British Library Cataloguing in Publication Information Available

Library of Congress Cataloging-in-Publication Data

Prendergast, Stephanie A., 1976–
Pelvic pain explained : what everyone needs to know / Stephanie A. Prendergast and Elizabeth H.
Rummer.
pages cm
Includes bibliographical references and index.
ISBN 978-1-4422-4831-1 (cloth : alk. paper) — ISBN 978-1-4422-4832-8 (electronic)
1. Pelvic floor—Diseases. 2. Pelvic floor—Diseases—Treatment. I. Rummer, Elizabeth H., 1976–
II. Title.
RG482.P74 2016
617.5'5—dc23
2015024826

∞ ™ The paper used in this publication meets the minimum requirements of
American National Standard for Information Sciences Permanence of Paper
for Printed Library Materials, ANSI/NISO Z39.48-1992.

Printed in the United States of America

CONTENTS

FOREWORD

If you suffer with pelvic pain, you need to read this book. Maybe several times. If you have a loved one with pelvic pain, both of you need to read this book. If you are a clinician who cares for patients with pelvic pain, you need to read this book. It is a down-to-earth, clearly written book that will educate and guide you in managing and relieving persistent pelvic pain.[1]

As you will learn when you read *Pelvic Pain Explained*, persistent pelvic pain is a common condition that affects people of every race, gender, socioeconomic group, and profession—it is a ubiquitous condition of all humans. It is as common as asthma, migraine, and low back pain. As is the case for all persistent pain conditions, it affects all aspects of the sufferer's life, but because of the location in the pelvis, it usually affects sexuality and intimacy far more than is the case with other pain conditions. For that reason, Liz and Stephanie devote a whole chapter to sex and pelvic pain.

Some may be concerned that the authors of this book are physical therapists, not physicians. You should not be. I am a physician who spent most of my clinical and academic career dedicated to caring for patients with persistent pelvic pain, doing research on pelvic pain, and teaching others about pelvic pain. I was one of the three founders of the International Pelvic Pain Society. This society has grown to be a premier organization dedicated to teaching about and care of patients with pelvic pain. It has more members who are physical therapists than physicians. When you read this book, you will have a clear understanding of why that is the case. I learned very early in my career that persistent pelvic pain, for all intents and purposes, always involves the musculoskeletal system, either as a primary or a secondary generator of pain. Physical therapists are ideal clinicians to deal with the musculoskeletal sources of pelvic pain, even when other bodily systems are also involved. They should always be part of the treatment team. So it is very appropriate that two physical therapists wrote *Pelvic Pain Explained*.

Stephanie and Liz are ideal physical therapists to be authors of this book. As they explain in their introduction, they have 30 years of combined experience both treating patients and educating providers. They have worked hard in their careers not only educating others, but also educating themselves. They have treated thousands of patients, male and female, and have a deep understanding of the approach to treatment that is needed if it is to be successful. This includes the strong involvement of the patient. Thus, they devote the whole third segment of their book to what the patient must do to stop being a patient, and return to being a "person." One of the most consistent frustrations during my 30 years treating women with persistent pelvic pain was the realization that if I was working harder than my patient to try to make her better, then we were both doomed to failure. Liz and Stephanie tell you in *Pelvic Pain Explained* what you need to do so that will not happen to you and your health care team. Additionally, they will help you navigate the complexities of our health care systems so you can find a team of clinicians that can educate, treat, and guide you to relieving your pain. Persistent pelvic pain is a complicated malady, and you will find that no one single provider will be able to help with you all the aspects of education and treatment that you will need.

So read this book if you are a patient, have a loved one, or are a clinician dealing with pelvic pain. Let it help you on your path to being well and pain-free, or having your loved one or your patient be pain-free.

Fred M. Howard, M.S., M.D.
Chairman of the Board
International Pelvic Pain Society
Professor Emeritus of Obstetrics and Gynecology
University of Rochester School of Medicine and Dentistry
St. John
United States Virgin Islands

ACKNOWLEDGMENTS

Thank you to Bonnie Bauman whom without her initiation, contributions, and support this book would not have been written. Thank you to Maria Lluberes for her wonderful illustrations.

We would like to thank the thousands of patients that trusted us with their health, providing us with the knowledge, experience, and passion to write this book. We would like to give a special thank you to Rhonda Kotarinos who paved the way for us as well as other physical therapists in this field. As the field grew, the International Pelvic Pain Society (IPPS) helped us further our education but also provided us with our first platform for teaching. We know this book would not have happened without each other and our extremely committed PHRC team. And, finally, we thank our supportive friends and family who are always there through our joys and successes.

INTRODUCTION

Anyone with persistent pelvic pain knows that getting on the right treatment path is often half the battle. The main reason for this is that persistent pain in general is a poorly understood medical condition compared to other diagnoses. So at the end of the day, many people with pelvic pain—while in the throes of dealing with symptoms that wreak havoc on their daily lives—are struggling to find answers. They're not alone in their frustration. Medical providers are often equally at a loss as they find themselves up against a lack of available research and education. The good news is that in recent years, a growing group of physicians, pelvic floor physical therapists, and psychologists are becoming actively involved in the research and management of pelvic pain syndromes. But while the landscape for treatment *is* improving, for many people with pelvic pain, getting a correct diagnosis and the appropriate treatment continues to be an uphill battle. We wrote this book to address that challenge. The purpose of this book is to act as a guide for patients and providers as they navigate the many complexities associated with the pelvic pain treatment process. As clinicians, we have a combined 30 years of experience both treating patients and educating providers. Over the years we've treated thousands of patients from one end of the pelvic pain spectrum to the other. As a result, we've learned what works (and what doesn't) in successfully treating pelvic pain. In the pages of this book we share that knowledge.

WHAT IS THIS BOOK ABOUT?

At its heart, *Pelvic Pain Explained* is an exploration of pelvic pain from how patients get it to the challenges both patients and providers face throughout the treatment process to a discussion of the impact that an "invisible" condition has on a patient's life and relationships, and much more. Patients will walk away from this book with a complete understanding of pelvic pain, from how it occurs to the variety of symptoms associated with it to how the impairments and contributing factors that are causing their symptoms are uncovered and treated. In addition, the book will provide patients with an understanding of all the current treatment options available to them. Those who develop pelvic pain can find the path to treatment frustrating and unsuccessful, oftentimes because they're attempting to work within the framework of recovery that they're used to; one in which they go to the doctor, maybe have some diagnostic testing done, then get a very specific diagnosis that dictates a very specific mode of treatment. This simply is not the path to recovery from pelvic pain. Pelvic pain is a health issue that often crosses the borders between medical disciplines because of the many different systems that can be involved. Gynecologists, urologists, gastroenterologists, orthopedists, pain management specialists, psychologists, and acupuncturists, among others, all have a role in treating the pelvic floor. In addition, for recovery to occur, the patient must be an active participant in the treatment process. This book provides patients with the guidance they need to navigate this unfamiliar treatment framework, thus placing them on the right path to recovery. For providers, the book demystifies pelvic pain. In addition, it contains information that will help them troubleshoot in situations where patients either cannot tolerate or are unresponsive to a particular treatment approach. As the information in these pages will prove, when a particular treatment doesn't work, another option exists.

The book is organized into three parts. The goal of the first part of the book is to give readers an overview of pelvic pain. Toward that end, the chapters in this section discuss the symptoms, causes, and factors that contribute to pelvic pain as well as explain the role of the neuromuscular system in the condition. Part II of the book lays out the path to recovery from pelvic pain. This part of the book provides guidance on how patients can assemble the best team of providers, takes readers through the pelvic pain PT process, and provides a complete overview of the many different treatment options available for the condition. In addition, part II covers pelvic pain–related issues concerning pregnancy and sexual health. Part III places patients in the driver's seat of their recovery by giving them actionable information. At-home self-treatment strategies, tips on communicating with providers and staying fit while in recovery, as well as practical tips for day-to-day living are among the topics covered in this section.

HOW WILL THIS BOOK HELP ME THROUGH TREATMENT?

This book aims to provide a stepping-off point for those with pelvic pain to begin to navigate the treatment process. Toward that end, it provides answers to the many questions they have as they stand on the threshold of their treatment journey, such as: *How did I get pelvic pain? What is the best way to treat pelvic pain? What are my treatment options? How do I find qualified and knowledgeable providers? How do I navigate day-to-day life with pelvic pain?* In addition, it guides patients through the many complexities that arise during the treatment and recovery process, such as what to do when treatments don't work; how to improve communication with medical providers; how to remain calm during a flare; and how to cope with the many emotional issues that crop up during the recovery process, among many others. Our main intention in writing this book is to streamline the treatment process for both patients and providers. Oftentimes patients fall into treatment traps, such as wasting time and money on unnecessary procedures that may make their condition worse. Just as often, they don't fully understand the treatment modalities they sign up for, so they're not compliant, and for that reason, they don't get better. For all of these reasons, in this book we don't just present information about pelvic pain; we combine it with the comprehensive assessment skills we've gained from our own experience as clinicians and educators. So by reading it, both patients and providers are not just informing themselves about pelvic pain, they're also beginning to think critically about the issues that surround the treatment process, thus better arming themselves for decision making along the way.

CAN READING THIS BOOK HELP ME GET BETTER?

Yes. For one thing, research shows that educating patients about the physiology behind their symptoms reduces stress, and in turn that reduces pain.[1] The information in this book will demystify pelvic pain for readers so they will have less stress and anxiety surrounding their pain. Also, the book will help patients get better by helping them to navigate the pelvic pain treatment process. It will help direct them to the right providers, allow them to make educated treatment choices, alert them to the right questions to ask, and, in general, enable them to be unintimidated by the treatment process. At the end of the day, all of this *will* help patients get better.

WHY DID PTS WRITE THIS BOOK?

Physical therapy is becoming the standout of the new interdisciplinary treatment approach to persistent pain. In fact, in her best-selling book on persistent pain, *The Pain Chronicles*, author Melanie Thernstrom advises readers to commit to giving PT a try. "Truly, if you take any advice from this book, take this one," she writes. And *New York Times* author Barry Meier, in his controversial article "The Problem with Pain Pills," passes along similar advice. PT, along with an interdisciplinary treatment plan, is the way to go, he writes. And to further validate the central role that PT now plays in the treatment of persistent pain, lawmakers in all 50 states and the District of Columbia have some form of "direct access" law in place, allowing patients to have direct access to PTs without a physician referral or prescription. This emphasis on PT is especially relevant when treating pelvic pain. That's because PT is a main line of treatment for the majority of pelvic pain patients. Therefore, it makes sense for *the* definitive book on navigating pelvic pain to be written by PTs.

When we met each other a decade ago, we instantly bonded over our shared passion for helping people with pelvic pain. Spurred on by our desire to improve the standard of care for this patient population, we ultimately partnered up and opened our physical therapy practice, the Pelvic Health and Rehabilitation Center (PHRC). From the outset, our goal with PHRC was to improve the standard of care for pelvic pain treatment. At this point, we believe we have developed a successful treatment model, one that stresses an interdisciplinary approach to treatment, and we're looking forward to sharing it in these pages.

All our best,
Stephanie and Liz

I

Pelvic Pain: A Road Map

1

PELVIC PAIN 101

Ben, age 31, a competitive cyclist, has been suffering from penile, scrotal, and perineal pain for nearly eight months. After the birth of her second baby, Holly, 28, can no longer have sex with her husband without experiencing severe vaginal pain. Annie, a 20-year-old college student, has been forced to take a semester off from school due to the intense vestibular burning she developed after a fall onto her tailbone. Paul, a high-powered attorney in his mid-forties, who spends countless hours sitting at a desk or on an airplane, has been suffering from anal and sit bone pain for nearly a year. Shortly after undergoing a hysterectomy, Veronica, 65, developed vulvar burning and clitoral pain.

This is a cross section of the millions of men and women dealing with pelvic pain in the United States. Most people don't even know they have a pelvic floor until they experience pain or dysfunction. For this reason, we decided that the best way to begin our task of explaining pelvic pain was with a chapter that explored the basics of this pain syndrome. Toward that end, we begin the chapter with an overview of the pelvic floor and its functions. Next, we move to a general explanation of the causes and symptoms of pelvic pain. Lastly, we wrap up with a discussion of the challenges involved for patients seeking treatment as well as an explanation of what we consider to be the best approach to treating pelvic pain.

WHAT IS MY PELVIC FLOOR FOR?

The pelvic floor is a hammock-like group of 14 thin muscles intertwined with nerves and surrounded by connective tissue that supports the abdominal organs while playing a key role in urinary, bowel, and sexual function as well as postural support. When you consider the many ordinary (and extraordinary) tasks the pelvic floor plays a role in—childbirth, sex, bowel movements, urination, continence, sitting, walking—it's difficult to understand why it's such an underrecognized part of our human anatomy!

PELVIC PAIN CAUSES

Now that you have a basic understanding of what the pelvic floor is, let's discuss what can go wrong with this swath of muscles, nerves, and

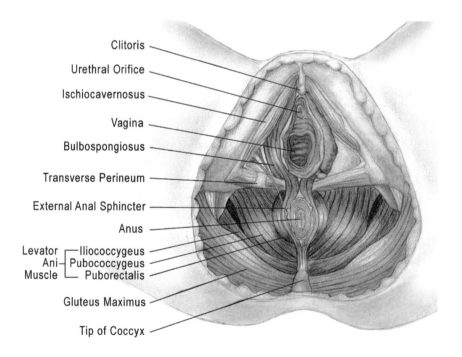

Figure 1.1. Female pelvic floor muscles and perineum. *Source: Pelvic Health and Rehabilitation Center*

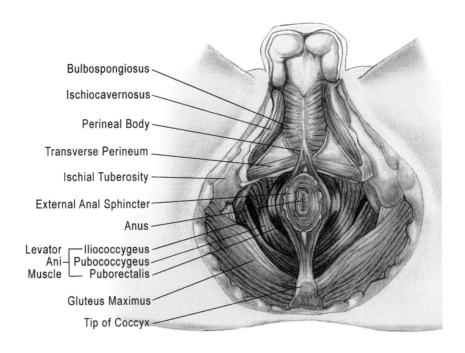

Bulbospongiosus

Ischiocavernosus

Perineal Body

Transverse Perineum

Ischial Tuberosity

External Anal Sphincter

Anus

Levator — Iliococcygeus
Ani — Pubococcygeus
Muscle — Puborectalis

Gluteus Maximus

Tip of Coccyx

Figure 1.2. Male pelvic floor muscles and perineum. *Source: Pelvic Health and Rehabilitation Center*

connective tissue to cause pelvic pain. In general, too-tight pelvic floor muscles, inflamed nerves of the pelvic floor, and/or restricted connective tissue are what ultimately will cause pelvic pain and urinary, bowel, and/or sexual dysfunction. *But how do these impairments occur?* The muscles, nerves, and connective tissue of the pelvic floor can become impaired in a number of ways. For example, childbirth; straining due to constipation; an injury, such as a fall on the tailbone; or repetitive activity, such as prolonged sitting, horseback riding, or cycling, can all lead to the development of a pelvic pain syndrome. In addition, any disease of the urinary, bowel, or reproductive systems, such as frequent urinary tract or yeast infections, bacterial prostatitis, or endometriosis can be the cause. More often than not, however, a combination of factors contributes to a patient's pain. Plus, it's common for symptoms to manifest after years of buildup with one incident serving as the proverbial "straw that broke the camel's back." For instance, a man works as a cashier at a grocery store, a job that requires him to repetitively rotate to the left as he scans groceries. As a result of this repetitive movement, the muscles on the left side of his body become tighter than those on the right. He then joins a gym to work out with the goal of becoming a better snowboarder. During his workouts he begins to do several sets of squats and sit-ups, which recruit the muscles on his right and left sides equally, but because the muscles on his left side are tighter from his job and therefore more vulnerable to injury, left abdominal trigger points develop. (A "trigger point" is a small, taut patch of involuntarily contracted muscle fibers within a muscle that can cause pain.) These trigger points begin to refer pain to the tip of his penis and perineum while he's working out at the gym. Finally, he falls on his tailbone several times snowboarding, so his penile and perineum pain becomes constant.

COMMON SYMPTOMS

Now that you have a general understanding of what causes pelvic pain, let's take a look at some of the more common symptoms associated with the condition. (This list is not meant to be definitive.)

In men symptoms may include:

- penile/scrotal/perineal or anal pain
- post-ejaculatory pain
- erectile dysfunction
- tailbone pain
- pain with sitting
- pain with exercise
- pain with urination, urinary urgency, frequency, hesitancy, and burning
- decreased force of urine stream
- constipation

In women symptoms can include:

- vulvar, vaginal, clitoral, perineal, or anal pain
- pain with sexual intercourse
- pain following sex
- interlabial, vulvar, or genital itching
- painful urination, urinary hesitancy, urgency, and/or frequency

- abdominal and groin pain
- sacroiliac joint pain/instability
- constipation
- painful periods
- pain with sitting
- pain with exercise

DIAGNOSIS AND TREATMENT CHALLENGES

Why is it so challenging to get a proper diagnosis and treatment for pelvic pain?

The answer to this question is multilayered. For one thing, persistent pain, which is commonly defined as pain that continues after tissue has healed, is poorly understood compared to other diagnoses. To be sure, until recently, clinical treatment for pain existed under the assumption that pain was a symptom of an underlying disease or trauma. The theory was that if you treated the underlying disease, the pain would go away. However, with persistent pain it often doesn't happen that way. Now researchers understand that pain in and of itself can be a diagnosis, and that left untreated, it has the potential to rewrite the central nervous system, causing changes to the brain and spinal cord, which can cause pain in the absence of an underlying cause. This represents a profound transformation in how those with persistent pain are evaluated. And it's only just in the past few years that it's trickled down into the treatment of pelvic pain.

Couple this with the fact that the treatment of pelvic pain diverges widely from the treatment of most medical conditions. Typically, when you have a medical problem, you go to the doctor, who perhaps runs a few tests, and then from there you get a diagnosis and treatment—usually some sort of medication. The diagnosis and treatment of pelvic pain simply does not work this way. For one thing, with pelvic pain, a "diagnosis" does not dictate treatment. Typically, pelvic pain ends up being a diagnosis of exclusion whereby other pathologies, such as an infection, must first be ruled out, and when symptoms persist, the patient is then given a descriptor diagnosis, such as "vulvodynia," which simply means "pain in the vulva." A second example is "interstitial cystitis/painful bladder syndrome" or "pudendal neuralgia," meaning pain in the bladder and the pudendal nerve distribution respectively. When a patient is given any one of these descriptor diagnoses, they're often confused and frustrated, mainly because none of them have specific, one-size-fits-all treatment protocols. *So if a diagnosis does not dictate treatment, what does?* What *does* dictate treatment for pelvic pain are the specific neurological, musculoskeletal, and psychological impairments that are uncovered and determined to be involved in a patient's symptoms. As already mentioned, pelvic pain is rarely caused by just one issue. Rather, more often than not, it's caused by a combination of factors, including impairments of the pelvic floor muscles, the central and peripheral nervous systems, and even behavioral issues, like poor posture or "holding in" one's urine. Therefore, a successful treatment approach involves identifying and treating all the different impairments contributing to a patient's symptoms. These impairments might be found in the muscles, joints, nerves, or connective tissue of the pelvic floor and girdle and/or the pelvic organs and the derma of the genitals. So we're not just talking about that hammock of 14 muscles described above. Therefore, the best course of action is to identify all the impairments that contribute to a patient's pelvic pain, and then treat each and every one of them individually while collectively treating the patient as a whole. But while a diagnosis does not dictate treatment for pelvic pain, oftentimes getting a specific diagnosis/diagnoses is necessary to work within our managed health care system. Take the point made by one of the readers of our blog:

> I've been given multiple diagnoses, and at least with the names, I'm getting treatment. For me, the different names to what is happening to my body do not matter except that the multiple doctors, PTs, etc. seem to treat just their specialty condition and without a name, it won't be treated. I strongly think that much of this is because our medical system is fragmented into so many specialties that don't interact, just refer. Now, I'm getting excellent care from my ob/gyn, pain doctor, gastroenterologist, and PT, but I wouldn't be getting treatment approved by our health insurance without a diagnosis, so for me the diagnosis equals treatment. Having a diagnosis seems to be a necessary evil in our fragmented, broken healthcare system.

Another departure from how most medical conditions are treated is that for the most part, a pelvic floor physical therapist will play the largest role in treating the impairments causing a patient's pain. That's because typically, those impairments are neuromuscular in nature, and physical therapy is the medical discipline that specializes in treating the neuromuscular system. So the typical scenario where patient visits doctor/patient gets diagnosis and treatment from doctor/patient gets well does not play out when it comes to pelvic pain.

The good news is that in just under a decade, tremendous strides have been made in the diagnosis and treatment of pelvic pain. For one thing, PTs have taken a solid leadership role in figuring out how to treat the condition. In addition, both physicians and PTs have embraced pelvic pain as a research topic. Also validating is the fact that at the time of this book's writing, a major initiative to improve the research and treatment of persistent pain includes pelvic pain as one of more than a dozen chronic pain syndromes that need an improved treatment approach.[1] Having solely treated the pelvic floor for more than 15 years, we understand the challenges involved with a pelvic pain diagnosis and treatment. We also know that it's possible for patients to navigate the current treatment landscape to get positive results. We see it every day in our clinics! And that's in essence what this book is about. After successfully treating thousands of patients, we know how to work within the current treatment landscape to get the best results.

PELVIC PAIN "DIAGNOSES"

While a diagnosis *should not* dictate treatment for pelvic pain, some diagnoses are *associated* with pelvic pain. Some of these diagnoses, such as endometriosis and interstitial cystitis, are disease processes where pelvic pain is a symptom. Others, such as pudendal neuralgia or vestibulodynia, fall under the category of "descriptor" diagnoses that we mentioned above and simply convey that pain is associated with a particular part of the body. We've provided a complete list of these diagnoses in the following list.

- vulvodynia, "primary/secondary" or "provoked/unprovoked": pain in the vulva
- dyspareunia: pain with sexual intercourse
- clitorodynia/genital pain: pain of the clitoris, genitalia
- penile pain
- anal pain
- perineum pain
- coccydynia: tailbone pain
- dysorgasmia: pain with orgasm
- pudendal neuralgia: pain in the distribution of the pudendal nerve
- vestibulodynia: pain of the vestibule
- vaginismus: severe pain upon attempted vaginal penetration or inability to achieve vaginal penetration
- orchialgia: pain in the testes

A BIOPSYCHOSOCIAL APPROACH TO TREATMENT

More and more, the medical community is moving toward treating the whole patient under a biopsychosocial model of care. Basically, this approach to medicine takes biological, psychological (thoughts, emotions, and behaviors), and social (socioeconomic and cultural) factors into consideration when treating a patient. We believe that a biopsychosocial model is the best approach to treating pelvic pain, and the way to put this model into practice is by taking an interdisciplinary treatment approach to treatment where all necessary medical disciplines are involved in a patient's recovery. Here's the reality: pelvic pain can cover many different systems of the body, including the musculoskeletal system, the urinary system, the reproductive system, the gastrointestinal (GI) system, the nervous system, and the endocrine system (hormones). On top of that, many of these systems have to be approached from different angles to successfully treat patients. For example, a patient who is having constipation issues may need to see a GI doctor, a nutritionist, and a PT to effectively treat his/her constipation. The GI doctor would rule out or treat any issues having to do with the patient's organs, a nutritionist might be needed to alter the patient's diet, and the PT will treat muscle dysfunction. So because pelvic pain can span so many different specialties in medicine, one lone specialty can't sufficiently evaluate and treat a complex pelvic pain case. The expertise of providers across disciplines is often required to effectively treat these cases. Gynecologists, urologists, gastroenterologists, orthopedists, pain management specialists, physical therapists, psychologists, and acupuncturists, among others, are all providers that have a role to play in treating pelvic pain syndromes.

THE ROLE OF THE PT IN TREATING PELVIC PAIN

The majority of pelvic pain cases will involve some kind of neuromuscular problem—a problem with the muscles, nerves, and connective tissue of the pelvic floor and adjacent areas. A PT is the medical provider who has the best understanding of these issues, and is therefore best equipped to treat them. Therefore, as mentioned above, a pelvic floor PT is going to play the largest role in treating a pelvic pain syndrome. But *what exactly is that role?*

In addition to uncovering and treating whatever neuromuscular impairments are driving a patient's symptoms, we believe that the best-case scenario is for the PT to take on the role of coordinator/facilitator of an interdisciplinary treatment plan, acting as a sort of patient "case manager." Here's why: an interdisciplinary treatment approach works best when one provider takes on the job of coordinating a patient's overall treatment plan. And with pelvic pain, it makes sense for the PT to take on the role of facilitator because number one, he/she will be spending the most time with the patient, and number two, he/she will be playing a major role in uncovering the patient's impairments. In our role as treatment facilitators, we not only uncover and treat whatever neuromuscular impairments exist, we also work with patients to figure out what other systems might be involved with their pain. If other systems do play a role, we help to get patients to the appropriate provider, acting as liaison with the assembled treatment team. We recognize that this puts a lot of responsibility onto PTs. To be sure, it's a big time commitment. But what we've observed in our practice is that if you want to successfully treat a person with pelvic pain, at the end of the day, it's what works.

In addition to facilitating a patient's interdisciplinary treatment plan, a PT often plays another, albeit less formal, role in treatment. While we're not psychologists and should never cross that line, the treatment we provide our patients has an emotional support component. Because we are often the provider who will spend the most time with patients, they have the opportunity to talk things through with us, to expose their fears and frustrations. Patients often apologize during their treatment session for "dumping" on us. Our response is always, "No apologies! That's what we're here for." As PTs, we work to encourage our patients and give them positive feedback throughout the recovery process. Sometimes this means giving them a nudge to go further in their recovery. For example, we may advise them to seek out other treatments, try intercourse for the first time after a break, or even to sit for 10 minutes longer than usual. So oftentimes a PT takes on the role of cheerleader during what can be a long treatment process.

JESSICA'S STORY

Since as far back as I can remember, I had on-and-off vestibule pain. In addition, all my life I've had bouts of constipation and hypermobile joints, meaning I am overly flexible (not a good thing). These are all factors that likely helped pave the way for my pelvic pain. One day when I was in my mid-twenties, I got a urinary tract infection that kicked off a downward spiral of constant vestibule and vaginal pain. That's when my search for answers began. Along the way, a urologist prescribed endless rounds of antibiotics. I underwent a cystoscopy, which is basically a bladder scope (ouch!), received an interstitial cystitis (IC) diagnosis, and got several more opinions from a variety of different doctors—a few of which concluded that my pain was caused by "stress." I read articles that convinced me that my symptoms were caused by "too much acid in my body" or "chronic yeast." These revelations resulted in some very extreme diets, including a "yeast cleanse." When all else failed, I spent hundreds of dollars on supplements, not because I necessarily thought they would help, but because I needed something proactive to do. Finally, months into my pain, I read about pelvic pain PT online, made an appointment to see Liz at PHRC, and started down the road to recovery. I won't lie and tell you that that road was an easy one. On the contrary, the ups and downs were crazy making. Along the way, I developed intense pain and fatigue. My joints even stopped working. I did nothing but lie around with my cat, go to doctor and PT appointments, and try my best to dress and feed myself. I had to take medical leave from school and work. I went on opiate painkillers, among other medications, including an antidepressant. I learned that chronic pain is a breeding ground for depression. It took about seven months of weekly PT for me to begin to feel better, and reach a turning point in my recovery. During my sessions with Liz, she worked internally on my tight pelvic floor, which she said was riddled with trigger points. In addition, she worked externally on my abdomen, thighs, and hips, where she found connective tissue restrictions. Besides my regular PT sessions, ice and heat helped, sitting on a cushion and not sitting too much helped, and using a foam roller to loosen tight muscles in my back and legs also helped.

It took about a year and a half of weekly PT for me to fully heal. Today, my vestibule and vaginal pain are completely gone. I have pain-free sex and normal orgasms. I can do any activity I want to and not experience pain. I wear underwear and jeans. (I wore wrap skirts with no underwear for more than a year.) And thanks to the education I received in PT, I am also super-aware of when and where I clench. I've learned that when I clench my abs, which I tend to do when I'm anxious or stressed, I feel pain in my pelvic floor. Therefore, deep breathing and relaxation exercises are a must for me during any stressful situation. I don't do yoga or sit-ups because they tense up my pelvic floor and abdomen. I bought an expensive office chair that I'll sit in for the rest of my working life. I no longer have the chronic fatigue (I was sleeping for more than 16 hours at a time at my worst). These days, I just think of myself as similar to someone with a bad back who shouldn't lift heavy things or overdo it. Lastly, I no longer wake up in the morning and think about pain. Instead, I think about what I'm going to eat that day (I love to eat!), who I'm going to see, and what I'm going to do. If you're in the midst of this condition, know that there is a way out, and as much as possible, have compassion for yourself. You're going through something hard, but you will get better.

CONCLUSION

In this chapter we've opened the door to the complex topic that is pelvic pain by taking a look at the basic anatomy of the pelvic floor, the causes of pelvic pain, and the many symptoms associated with the diagnosis. In addition, we've delved into the challenges involved with getting the appropriate treatment as well as what exactly constitutes that treatment. In the next chapter, we go into more detail about the factors that contribute to pelvic pain with the goal of answering a question that we get on a daily basis from patients: *How did I get this?*"

HOW COMMON IS PELVIC PAIN IN THE UNITED STATES?

Pelvic pain is every bit as common as back pain in the United States.[1] A look at the statistics shows just how common the condition is:

- Twenty percent of women will suffer from pelvic pain at some point in their lives.[2]
- Vulvodynia affects up to 16% of all women.[3]
- The estimated annual economic burden of vulvodynia in the United States is $31 billion to $72 billion.[4]
- Prostatitis is the third most common diagnosis of men under 50 presented to urologists annually, and 90% to 95% of all "prostatitis" diagnoses are actually male pelvic pain, showing the overdiagnosis of actual prostatitis and the underdiagnosis of male pelvic pain.[5]
- Up to 2 million *men* in the United States meet the diagnostic definition for persistent pelvic pain.[6]
- Chronic pelvic pain accounts for 10% of all visits to the gynecologist.[7]
- One in four women experience chronic vulvar pain (a symptom of pelvic pain) at some point in their lives.[8]
- Roughly 60% of sexually active women will suffer from painful sex at some point in their lives.[9]

- In a normal pregnancy, 13% to 36% of first-time moms show severe levator ani injury, one cause of postpartum pelvic floor dysfunction.[10]
- Pelvic girdle pain (a major cause of pelvic pain in pregnancy) occurs in 20% of pregnant women; for an estimated 7% to 8%, it results in severe disability.[11]
- Twenty-four percent of women have pain with intercourse 18 months after giving birth.[12]

Notes

1. KT Zondervan et al., "Prevalence and Incidence of Chronic Pelvic Pain in Primary Care: Evidence from a National General Practice Database," *Journal of Obstetrics and Gynecology* 106 (1999): 1149–1155.

2. G Apte et al., "Chronic Female Pelvic Pain: Part I: Clinical Pathoanatomy and Examination of the Pelvic Region," *Pain Practice* 12 (2012): 88–110.

3. *Ibid.*

4. LA Sadownik, "Etiology, Diagnosis, and Clinical Management of Vulvodynia," *International Journal of Women's Health* 6 (2014): 437–449.

5. J Bergman and S Zeitlin, "Prostatitis and Chronic Prostatitis/Chronic Pelvic Pain Syndrome," *Expert Review of Neurotherapeutics* 7 (2007): 301–307.

6. G Habermacher, J Chason, and A Schaeffer, "Chronic Prostatitis/Chronic Pelvic Pain Syndrome," *Annual Review of Medicine* 57 (2006): 195–206.

7. Gyang et al., "Musculoskeletal Causes of Chronic Pelvic Pain: What Every Gynecologist Should Know," *American College of Obstetrics and Gynecology* 121 (2013): 645–650.

8. *Ibid.*

9. *Ibid.*

10. N Schwertner-Tiepelmann et al., "Obstetric Levator Ani Muscle Injuries: Current Status," *Ultrasound Obstetrics and Gynecology* 39 (2012): 372–383.

11. A Vleeming et al., "European Guidelines for the Diagnosis and Treatment of Pelvic Girdle Pain," *European Spine Journal* 17 (2008): 794–819.

12. EA McDonald et al., "Dyspareunia and Childbirth: A Prospective Cohort Study," *British Journal of Obstetrics and Gynecology* 21 January 2015, doi: 10.1111/1471-0528.13263.

2

HOW DID I GET PELVIC PAIN? THE IMPORTANCE OF UNCOVERING CONTRIBUTING FACTORS

HOW DID I GET PELVIC PAIN?

This is a question that every person dealing with pelvic pain asks, and more so than the question *"What is my diagnosis?"* it's important to answer, because the information plays a key role in treatment. In general, the reality is that for most people with pelvic pain, it's not just one thing that caused their pelvic pain, but a handful of underlying causes that collectively provoked their symptoms. Remember, pelvic pain is often a muscle-driven pain syndrome, so when we talk about "contributing factors," what we're really talking about are the various events—childbirth, surgery, a fall on the tailbone, an infection, even repetitive activities like bicycling or sitting for long periods of time—that can cause the pelvic floor to become impaired. So *contributing factors* are what ultimately cause the *pelvic floor neuromuscular impairments* that in turn cause *the symptoms* of pelvic pain. Take Paul for example. Paul is a high-powered attorney in his forties whose job requires countless hours of sitting at a desk, in courtrooms, and on airplanes. Over the years, the contributing factor of sitting for long periods of time caused Paul's pelvic floor muscles to become overly tight. These too-tight muscles served as the impairment, which led to the development of his pelvic pain symptoms—anal and sit bone pain.

In this chapter, we're shining the spotlight on contributing factors. As mentioned above, it's an important variable of the pelvic pain equation to understand, because identifying all the factors that contribute to a patient's pelvic pain is a vital part of the treatment process. If the contributing factors, aka the underlying causes, of a patient's pelvic pain are not addressed, then the patient has less of a chance of getting better and/or more of a chance of recurring symptoms. Another reason it's important for patients to understand all the factors contributing to their symptoms is that it gives them the information they need to best advocate for their recovery. We'll start off the chapter with a basic explanation of how a contributing factor, whether it's a series of infections or a hormonal imbalance, actually evolves into a symptom-causing impairment. From there we'll take a look at the slew of contributing factors that can play a role in pelvic pain. What's so striking about this list is its variability; while some of the items on the list may seem obvious, others will come as a complete surprise to many readers. Lastly, we'll explore how, more often than not, it's a "perfect storm" of contributing factors that kicks off a pelvic pain syndrome.

HOW A CONTRIBUTING FACTOR BECOMES AN IMPAIRMENT

The straining that accompanies chronic constipation, the searing pain brought on by repetitive urinary tract infections (UTIs), the pushing that occurs with childbirth, the tissue compression that occurs with long hours of sitting; how can these events turn into the neuromuscular impairments that cause the symptoms of pelvic pain? While there are a few different ways, in this section we're going to focus on two of the most common ways. The first has to do with the way muscles work and the second has to do with the intimate relationship between organs and the tissue that surrounds them. Let's start with the former. Muscles are made up of fibers that either overlap to contract (shorten) the muscle or pull apart to stretch (lengthen) the muscle. Muscles that become too short because the fibers begin to overlap too much (as can occur with clenching) or too long because the fibers pull too far apart (as can occur with pushing during childbirth or constipation) become vulnerable to the development of trigger points. (As mentioned in a previous chapter, trigger points, a common impairment contributing to pelvic pain, are small, taut patches of painful, involuntarily contracted muscle fibers.) On top of the development of painful trigger points, muscles that become too short in and of themselves cause pelvic pain primarily because they restrict blood flow to the area.

The second main way a contributing factor becomes an impairment involves the intimate relationship between internal organs and the soft tissue surrounding them. As we discussed in chapter 1, the pelvic floor encapsulates a host of different organs, such as the uterus in women, the prostate in men, and the bladder and bowels in both men and women. When a problem arises with any of these organs, such as when the bladder and urethra are inflamed due to a UTI, pain from the organs can be referred to the surrounding neuromuscular tissue, namely the pelvic floor muscles and nerves, the abdominal muscles, and even the skin, such as the skin of the vulva or the penis. More familiar examples of organ-tissue referral patterns are when a person has a heart attack and pain is felt in the neck, shoulders, and/or back rather than the chest. Why does this pain referral happen? Researchers are not entirely sure, but an overriding theory is that at the level of the spinal cord there is crosstalk between the organs that are in trouble and the soft tissue and nerves located near them. Basically, the pain signal originating from the organ becomes jumbled, causing pain to be felt in areas other than where it stems. In addition to pain referral from organs, this crisscrossing of spinal cord signals can actually cause the pelvic floor muscles to contract. As a result, repetitive UTIs, for example, can cause the pelvic floor tissue and muscles to become too tight. On the flip side, impaired tissue of the pelvic floor can have this same reflexive effect on nearby organs. For example, tight pelvic floor muscles can cause pain in the urethra, bladder, or rectum. This in turn can create symptoms that mimic a urinary tract infection or gastrointestinal distress. None of these mechanisms are the patients' fault. We point this out because often we have patients who blame themselves for "clenching" in response to events, like a series of infections or endometriosis, wrongly believing that if only they'd been more "relaxed" and "less anxious" during these events, they wouldn't have gotten pelvic pain. This is simply not the case. These are physiological responses, which we have no conscious control over.

CONTRIBUTING FACTORS

Now that we've discussed how a contributing factor becomes an impairment, let's take a look at the varied list of factors that can contribute to pelvic pain. As we already touched on in the last chapter, the pelvic floor is a major hub of the body. Not only does it play a major role in daily movement, like walking and running, sitting, and standing, it also plays a starring role in many important bodily functions, including sexual activity, bowel movements, and urination. Is it any wonder then that so many different events can contribute to a pelvic pain syndrome? The list below covers the most common factors in pelvic pain, and while some of the items on it, like prolonged pushing during childbirth, might seem obvious, others, like having one leg that's shorter than the other, training for a marathon, or going through menopause, will likely come as a surprise to many readers.

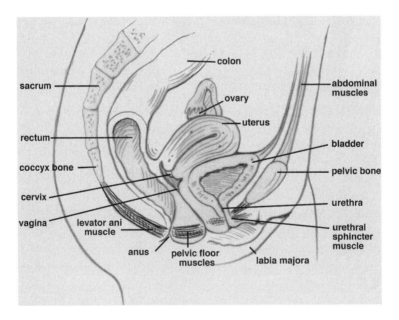

Figure 2.1. Urogynecological midsaggital view of the female pelvis. *Source: Amy Stein, DPT, BCB-PMD*

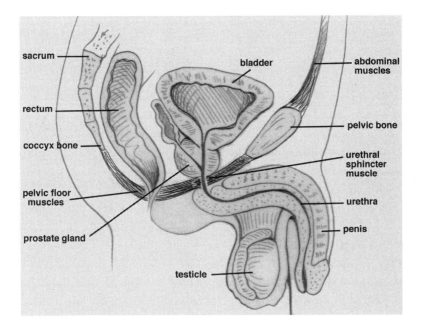

Figure 2.2. Urogenital midsaggital view of the male pelvis. *Source: Amy Stein, DPT, BCB-PMD*

Infections

A handful of different infections can contribute to pelvic pain. These include urinary tract infections (UTIs) and vaginal infections, such as those caused by yeast or bacteria. In addition, infectious agents can attack glands in the area, such as the prostate gland in men and the Bartholin's glands in women. (The Bartholin's glands are two pea-size glands located on either side of the opening of the vagina that secrete fluid to help lubricate the vagina for sex. These glands can become blocked and develop cysts, which can in turn become inflamed and infected.) Any of these infections can kick off any one or a combination of the mechanisms explained above, which then can lead to the neuromuscular impairments that cause pelvic pain. For example, a woman gets a UTI, which causes her bladder and urethra to become inflamed, causing urethral burning as well as pain in her lower abdomen. As a result, the connective tissue around her urethra as well as the muscles in her lower abdomen and groin become restricted, causing an additional source of pain. A UTI can also have symptoms of urinary urgency and frequency, which can cause a "holding" or clench response with the same outcome: muscles that become too tight, lack of blood flow, and vulnerability to trigger points. Another example is a man who gets chlamydia, a common sexually transmitted disease, and clenches his pelvic floor muscles because of the inflammation and pain from the infection. (This clenching is referred to as "guarding." Guarding is when we unconsciously clench our muscles to protect an area of the body that is inflamed or injured. Although it starts off as a protective mechanism, guarding ultimately causes muscles to become too tight—remember those overlapping muscle fibers—setting the stage for pain.)

Another way an infection can play a role in pelvic pain is when a woman gets multiple yeast infections. Here's how: over time, multiple yeast infections can cause neural irritation, either in major nerve branches of the pelvic floor, such as the pudendal nerve, or within the smaller, more superficial nerves that feed the skin of the vulva. This nerve irritation can cause pain in any of the areas these nerves innervate, such as the skin of the vulva, the skin of the clitoris, the perineum, the vagina, the urethra, and/or the rectum, as well as the guarding pattern described above.

In all the scenarios described above, even after the infection itself has cleared up, the resulting neuromuscular impairments can stick around, even mimicking the symptoms of the infection. While it's possible for one relatively normal infection to cause this outcome, more often than not, a severe infection that lasts a long time or a series of infections suffered over a period of years are the culprits. If it is determined that an infection is an underlying cause of a patient's pelvic pain, it's important that the infection be successfully treated by a doctor in order for recovery to occur. And if a patient is getting recurrent infections, such as recurrent UTIs after sex, it's important to work with a physician to figure out why this is happening and to take preventive measures.

Surgery

Dozens of different surgeries impact the pelvic floor. Some of the more common ones are hysterectomy, surgery to correct pelvic organ prolapse, hernia repair, and prostatectomy. So how can a surgery contribute to pelvic pain? The basic explanation is that an event can occur as a result of either the specific surgery itself (for example, the mesh used in a surgery to correct a pelvic organ prolapse can entrap a nerve) or the positioning of the patient during the surgery (such as the specific position of the hip joint during a hip labral repair). More often than not, when a surgery is behind pelvic pain symptoms, the patient will notice symptoms immediately after the surgical procedure. But sometimes there is a time lag. For instance, with mesh placement to correct a pelvic organ prolapse, problems might not arise until scarring starts to form around the mesh. Whatever the specifics of the case, if a patient believes that unresolved pelvic pain following surgery was caused by the surgery, we recommend that he/she consult with their physician as well as seek a second opinion. In these situations, it is possible that a follow-up surgery can decrease or eliminate the patient's pelvic pain, such as removal of mesh placement; therefore, it may be useful to consult a pelvic pain surgical specialist in this case.

Scar Tissue

Scar tissue is a common contributing factor to pelvic pain. Scar tissue is fibrous tissue that replaces normal tissue after an injury. It's made of the same stuff as the tissue it replaces—collagen. However, the quality of the collagen is inferior to the tissue it replaces. Plus, the tissue is usually not as elastic as the original. Scarring that affects the pelvic floor can happen as a result of any trauma to the area, including a C-section, perineum tear, or episiotomy during childbirth as well as a prostatectomy, a hysterectomy, a vasectomy, bowel surgery, endometriosis surgery, or a Bartholin's gland abscess removal. Scarring can also result from a skin disease called lichen sclerosis that can affect the vulva.

There are three major ways that scarring within or adjacent to the pelvic floor can cause problems. First, scar tissue is indiscriminate in what it attaches to. So it can adhere to skin, muscle, or connective tissue. Wherever it decides to hang out, it pulls on the surrounding tissue, making the area taut and restricting blood flow, which often results in pain. Another way that scar tissue can wreak havoc within the pelvic floor is as a result of referred pain. Remember, a network of nerves innervates the pelvic floor. If a scar is on top of or impinging on a nerve that innervates another part of the pelvic floor, then that area can also be affected. For example, if a man has a surgery to repair an inguinal hernia (a condition in which soft tissue bulges through the lower abdominal wall or groin), the mesh used in the surgery could entrap the ilioinguinal nerve located in the wall of the abdomen, causing pain in the root of the penis or the upper part of the scrotum. That's why it's important to remember that the pain and dysfunction caused by a scar is not always going to be in the area where the scar is. Another way scar tissue can cause problems within the pelvic floor is by impairing function in the area where it's located. For instance, if a muscle is torn and then a scar forms, as in an anal sphincter tear during a difficult childbirth, that muscle may lose some of its ability to contract, which can lead to a loss of control over urination, bowel movements, or sexual function.

Pregnancy/Childbirth

When a woman goes through a pregnancy and delivers a baby, her pelvic floor is put through the wringer. This is why we've decided to devote an entire chapter (chapter 4) to the topic of pregnancy and the pelvic floor. Common pelvic pain–related symptoms women can experience as a result of pregnancy and childbirth include back, groin, hip, vulvovaginal, tailbone, or pelvic floor pain; pain during sex; diminished or absent orgasm; urinary frequency, urgency, or retention (retention is difficulty starting the urine stream); constipation; and difficulty evacuating stool. Plus, vaginal tearing or an episiotomy during a vaginal delivery can also cause future issues with pelvic floor muscles.

Constipation

Constipation plays a major role in pelvic pain. But unlike some of the other contributing factors described in this chapter, it can either contribute to pelvic pain *or* be a symptom of other neuromuscular impairments. There are two different types of constipation. The first is general constipation, caused by a lack of motility in the large intestine. The large intestine, aka the colon, is designed to carry out a contracting and squeezing motion that propels stool through it. This action can become impaired, causing stool to move excessively slowly or not much at all. A variety of things can lead to this type of constipation, such as poor diet, lack of fluid intake, lack of exercise, or a sluggish colon. Also, many kinds of medication, like opiates or other pain meds, can cause general constipation. The second type of constipation is known as outlet constipation. Outlet constipation occurs when stool sits in the rectum and is difficult to eliminate. In other words, the train makes it to the station, but then gets stuck there. This can be due to pelvic floor muscle dysfunction, an overstretched rectum, or a situation in women where the tissue that separates the vaginal and rectal canals becomes weak. When stool becomes stuck, we tend to want to bear down and push in an effort to pass it. But straining only makes matters worse; the more we push, the more muscles and tissue become strained in both men and women. And in women, over time, the tissue between the vagina and rectum can even weaken, further exacerbating constipation. In this case, not only is stool having a hard time getting through the external sphincter, it's getting stuck and pocketing in weakened tissue.

Vulvovaginal/Anal Fissures

A vulvovaginal fissure is a tear or crack in the lining of the vulvovaginal tissue, while an anal fissure is a tear in the lining of the anal canal. Some of the more common reasons for vulvovaginal fissures are a lack of tissue integrity due to a drop in estrogen levels, frequent yeast infections, or decreased lubrication. As for anal fissures, more often than not, repetitive straining because of chronic constipation is the culprit. Fissures themselves can be very painful, causing sharp, stinging, burning pain as well as itching and bleeding. But as with any other contributing factor, they can also cause secondary pain due to their impact on the pelvic floor muscles. For instance, the pain from the fissure will cause guarding, which in turn will cause all the issues that come along with too-tight pelvic floor muscles. If vulvovaginal fissures are an underlying factor in a woman's pain, she should seek help from either a gynecologist or a dermatologist specializing in vulvovaginal skin issues (while these specialists are rare, they do exist). Anal fissures are treated by a colorectal doctor.

Anatomical/Biomechanical Abnormalities

A slew of anatomical/biomechanical abnormalities, such as having one leg that's shorter than the other, contribute to pelvic pain. (An anatomical abnormality is a problem with how the body is structured, whereas a biomechanical abnormality is a problem that affects how the body moves.) So why do anatomical/biomechanical abnormalities so often play a role in pelvic pain? The reason has to do with how the pelvic girdle (the "pelvic girdle" is all the pelvic floor muscles, the muscles that attach to the pelvis, and the basin-shaped unit of bones between the trunk and the legs) interacts with the rest of the body. The muscles of the pelvic girdle are always activated, whether it's to make sure we remain continent or to give us stability for standing up or walking. Therefore, a problem with another part of the body, such as when a person has poor posture, can actually affect the pelvic girdle. Whether or not it will ultimately contribute to pelvic pain depends on the severity and duration of the issue as well as the person's behavior. Some common anatomical/biomechanical abnormalities include sacroiliac joint dysfunction, spine dysfunction and/or pathology, postural dysfunction, limited or excessive joint mobility, and scoliosis (curvature of the spine). Plus, any orthopedic issue, such as a knee issue, also fits into this category. That's because a hip, knee, or back injury can change a person's anatomical structure in a way that can contribute to pelvic pain. One example is piriformis syndrome, which occurs when the sciatic nerve (a long nerve that begins in the low back and runs through the buttocks and all the way down to the lower limbs) is compressed or irritated by the piriformis muscle and other muscles that surround it in the buttocks. Because it's located in the vicinity of this problem, the obturator internus muscle (a thick, fan-shaped muscle within the pelvic floor) in someone with piriformis syndrome may become too tight, causing pelvic pain symptoms, such as tailbone or anal pain, or pain with sitting. Sometimes a patient has had a lifelong issue that suddenly becomes a problem. Oftentimes a patient will make the point that they've had the issue their whole life, so why is it a problem now? Our response is, "While it's existed for your whole life, in the past it hasn't caused you any problems. Now it's contributing to your pelvic pain, and in order to get you better, we have to work to normalize this anatomic issue." An anatomic deviation can become an issue over time or be provoked by something such as more time sitting or even getting a new car with a different type of seat. In addition, anatomical/biomechanical abnormalities can by themselves cause pelvic pain, or they can predispose someone to pelvic pain, if and when other factors come into play.

For example, let's say a woman has hypermobile joints, meaning her ligaments are too loose, and her muscles have to work harder to keep the joint the muscles surround together and functional. This woman gets a series of yeast infections, which make her pelvic floor muscles even tighter. Because of the hypermobility she has had her whole life, her pelvic floor muscles are already on the tight side, making her more likely to get pain from tight muscles than a woman who had the same series of infections but didn't already have tight muscles. So the series of yeast infections compound an already bad situation, causing an onset of pain. To treat this patient's pelvic pain, we'll have to work on the muscle dysfunction her hypermobility has caused over her entire life.

Overuse Injury

If a person is predisposed to pelvic pain due to an anatomical/biomechanical abnormality or any other issue, such as overly tight muscles from repetitive yeast infections, overuse injuries can occur, which in turn can contribute to the development of pelvic pain. The term "overuse" refers to any activity that exceeds a particular muscle's capabilities. For example, if someone has tight pelvic floor muscles, for whatever reason, and begins to do a popular high-intensity workout called Cross-Fit training, he/she might be susceptible to developing pelvic pain, whereas a person with a perfectly normal pelvic floor will have no problem with the workout. To be sure, often changes to a person's daily routine, which result in an overuse injury, act as the catalyst for pelvic pain. These changes can include taking up cycling, Pilates, or yoga; driving a new car; starting a long commute to work; or weathering a bad cough. But of course it doesn't have to be a new activity. It could be an activity a person has been doing for years, like a golfer who's had the same swing for years, a skateboarder who always pushes off with the same leg, or horseback riding or cycling that eventually catches up with his/her pelvic floor.

Hormonal Issues (in Women)

Because of their adjacency to the pelvic floor nerves and muscles, the vulvar and vaginal tissue, if compromised, can play a role in pelvic pain. And one of the things that can compromise vulvar/vaginal tissue is hormone fluctuation, specifically a drop in estrogen. For example, a drop in estrogen, as can occur either during perimenopause or menopause, can cause vulvar/vaginal tissue to have less skin integrity, which can result in skin tears (fissures) and/or pain with intercourse. As a result, pelvic floor muscle guarding can occur, setting the woman up for pelvic pain. In addition, an estrogen drop decreases a woman's ability to naturally lubricate, also causing pain with intercourse. Besides perimenopause and menopause, other hormonal issues that can contribute to pelvic pain include thyroid disease, starting a new birth control pill, and taking birth control for an extended period of time. For its part, thyroid disease is associated with all muscle pain, pelvic pain included. As for birth control pills and pelvic pain, generally, they can affect hormone levels, but to what extent they do so is very individual. However, we'd like to mention another issue surrounding birth control pills and pelvic pain. It involves an ongoing controversy in the pelvic pain arena. Here's the lowdown: aside from their obvious role in preventing unwanted pregnancy, birth control pills are the first-line treatment for several painful gynecologic diseases, such as endometriosis. This is because they suppress the hormones that perpetuate these diseases. However, this hormone suppression doesn't just have an effect on the reproductive tract; it also affects the tissue, muscle, or glands under its influence. Emerging research suggests that birth control pills can have a negative impact on vulvar and periurethral tissues and other glands in the pelvic region, and that this may actually cause pelvic pain. According to the theory, certain women may be more genetically susceptible to developing pelvic pain from oral contraceptives than others.[1] When it comes to the birth control pill as it may or may not relate to pelvic pain, our advice is if a woman develops pelvic pain after starting or stopping the birth control pill, hormonal deficiencies from the pill may be a factor in her pain, and she should definitely talk to her gynecologist about it. Or if she suspects that long-term birth control use may be contributing to her pain, she should also consult her gynecologist. And overall, if a hormonal issue is contributing to a patient's pain, it's important for her to see a physician, typically either a gynecologist or an endocrinologist, to get the problem under control.

Diseases/Syndromes

A handful of diseases/syndromes can have an impact on the pelvic floor, acting as contributing factors to pelvic pain. The most common of these are endometriosis, irritable bowel syndrome, fibromyalgia, polycystic ovarian syndrome, and interstitial cystitis. These conditions tend to cause symptoms that in turn create pain-causing impairments to the pelvic floor. For an example, let's look at how endometriosis can contribute to pelvic pain. Endometriosis is a condition where tissue like that which lines the inside of the uterus (known as endometrial tissue) grows outside of the uterus, most commonly in the abdominal cavity. This tissue can implant on any surface within the abdominal cavity, including the ovaries, bladder, rectum, and the abdominal/pelvic wall. Commonly reported symptoms of endometriosis are painful cramping prior to menstruation, pain during menstruation, pain with sex, bladder pain, and painful bowel movements. Endometriosis can impact the pelvic floor and cause pain in a variety of ways. First, endometrial tissue bleeds with menstruation, often leading to inflammation, scar tissue, and adhesion formation inside the abdominal and pelvic cavities. (Adhesions are fibrous bands of scar tissue that can attach to organs, muscles, and fascia.) These areas can become a source of pain. Furthermore, this can set up an unhealthy environment within the pelvic floor and pelvic girdle muscles because the decrease in pelvic and abdominal organ/muscle/connective tissue mobility can lead to decreased circulation, too-tight muscles, the development of painful trigger points, and connective tissue restriction. So on top of all the symptoms that already come with endometriosis, a patient can develop a host of pelvic floor–related impairments that cause pain on top of an already painful situation. In addition to the specific ways a particular disease process can contribute to pelvic pain, such as mentioned above in the case of endometriosis, in general, any painful symptoms that come along with a condition can lead to involuntary muscle contraction and guarding behaviors, further exacerbating the situation.

THE PERFECT STORM

As you can see after reading this chapter, a host of different factors can contribute to a pelvic pain syndrome. It's important for both providers and patients to have them on their radar in order to have all the information necessary to put together the best treatment plan. Equally important is fully understanding *how* a pelvic pain syndrome typically occurs. More often than not, it's not just one of the contributing factors discussed above that causes a full-blown pelvic pain syndrome; it's a handful of factors coupled with a timing component. Indeed, oftentimes several things have to happen at an exact moment in time for a person to develop pelvic pain. We call this a "perfect storm" scenario. Here's an example. Kathy, a 19-year-old college sophomore, gets mononucleosis, aka "mono." As a result of the virus, she develops a persistent cervical infection, which is treated with several rounds of antibiotics. Due to the antibiotics she gets thrush (a yeast infection in the mouth) as well as a vaginal yeast infection. Many rounds of antifungals later to treat what becomes a chronic vaginal yeast infection, she begins to have pain with intercourse. The pain with intercourse, along with the chronic yeast infections, causes Kathy to clench her pelvic floor muscles. On top of all that, Kathy is very hypermobile. So add tight pelvic floor muscles to pelvic girdle muscles that are already overworking to keep pelvic joints together, and what you get is even more pelvic floor muscle dysfunction. So what you end up with is a series of events—a virus that caused a yeast infection that kicked off muscle clenching that, when combined with an anatomical abnormality, caused muscle tightness— which ultimately created the perfect storm that left symptoms of pelvic pain in its wake.

TONY'S STORY

I've always been a super-athletic guy. When I wasn't chasing after my kids or helping to run my family's business, you could find me surfing, hunting, snowboarding, golfing, swimming, or playing basketball. But my active lifestyle came to a screeching halt when I was 29, and there was a period of time when I was sure I'd never participate in another activity I loved again, let alone be able to work or even have relations with my wife. It all started one unseasonably warm afternoon in February. On that day, as usual, I was in active mode, attempting to pull off the perfect handstand, when all of a sudden, I felt a sharp pinching pain in my lower abs. Three doctors later, I was diagnosed with an "abdominal strain" and prescribed core-strengthening exercises. The exercises only made my pain worse, and in a matter of weeks my symptoms exploded. The pain in my lower abdomen snowballed into pain with sitting, constant perineum and groin pain, and a burning pain at the tip of my penis as well as occasional anal pain. Unable to find any answers from the doctors I visited, I turned to the Internet. That's when the fear and panic set in. After spending hours online, I discovered that my symptoms were a match with a disorder called "pudendal nerve entrapment" or "PNE." After reading a litany of stories about PNE, I became convinced that I needed surgery as soon as possible to free an entrapped pudendal nerve. Otherwise, according to the information I was reading online, my symptoms would continue to get worse. I even contacted one of the doctors mentioned in the online forums who performed the surgery. The doctor encouraged me to fly out and schedule the surgery with him right away. I was terrified. I was reading all these horror stories, and I believed that if I didn't get surgery as soon as possible, I would end up impotent and incontinent. Even with surgery I was afraid of what my life was going to become. However, before I signed up for surgery, I decided to see one more doctor in San Francisco. Thankfully, that doctor was in the know about male pelvic pain. The doctor explained that trigger points and tight muscles in the pelvic floor and/or abdomen have the potential to cause all the symptoms I was experiencing. The doctor then prescribed pelvic floor PT. I admit at first I didn't believe PT was going to help me. But I decided I'd give it a try as a final effort before I got the surgery. After my first session with Stephanie, I felt a slight bit of relief, which was encouraging. What Stephanie found were trigger points throughout my rectus abdominus muscle, likely caused by the 200 crunches I did about four to five times a week. In addition, she found a great deal of external connective tissue restriction and pelvic floor muscle tightness as well as some irritation of my pudendal nerve. She also uncovered clues that my issues had been bubbling for some time before finally coming up to the surface. For one thing, I had a history of constipation and low back pain. For another thing, the urinary frequency I'd experience after long bike rides and the occasional post-ejaculatory burning I felt were signs that I had had underlying pelvic floor impairments for years. Ultimately, with regular PT sessions—at first twice weekly and then weekly—my pain and symptoms began to diminish, until eventually they were gone altogether. Today I have zero pain and I'm living an unrestricted, active life. But it didn't go away overnight. It took time, patience, and a lot of commitment to treatment.

CONCLUSION

Uncovering a patient's contributing factors and putting together the history of his/her "perfect storm" is one of the most important prerequisites of putting a treatment plan into action. It's a process that the patient and his/her PT, and other providers, must commit to together. Our hope is that this chapter will help with that process. In addition to our exploration of all the factors that can contribute to pelvic pain, we touched on the neuromuscular impairments that so often are in the driver's seat of a patient's pain. In the next chapter, we're going to take a closer look at those neuromuscular impairments by explaining exactly what can go wrong with the pelvic floor muscles, nerves, and connective tissue to cause the variety of symptoms that can make up a pelvic pain syndrome.

3

DEMYSTIFYING THE NEUROMUSCULAR IMPAIRMENTS THAT CAUSE PELVIC PAIN

When someone has back pain, knee pain, or shoulder pain, their mind immediately goes to the neuromuscular system. *Is it a muscular issue? A problem with the nerves of the area? Are joints or ligaments involved?* But when symptoms of pelvic pain arise—vaginal burning, anal pain, post-ejaculatory burning, testicular pain, pain with urination—the first stop on the thought train is rarely the neuromuscular system. And for many it can take a pretty long time to get there, with frustrating detours along the way. Even when it *is* put on the table as the possible driver of pain, some patients still have a hard time wrapping their heads around it. Take Mary for instance, a patient in her thirties who suffered from vulvar and urethral burning as well as urinary urgency/frequency. The first doctor Mary saw actually did tell her that he believed her muscles were tight and gave her a referral to a pelvic floor PT. However, she visited two more doctors and the emergency room before she finally decided to give the PT a call, and not because she really believed it was her answer. It was more a matter of needing to do something and figuring she might as well try a different route than the one she had already taken. When asked why she hesitated to see the PT, she simply said, "I just couldn't understand how PT, where you go when you need your knee or shoulder or leg fixed, was going to help with my burning vulva and urethra!" This is a completely understandable sentiment. The reality is that we simply aren't used to associating most of the areas of the body impacted by pelvic pain with muscles, nerves, and connective tissue. It just doesn't compute. This is why we've decided to devote an entire chapter to a discussion of how neuromuscular impairments can and do drive pelvic pain. In the previous chapter we talked about how different events can cause the neuromuscular impairments that in turn cause the symptoms of pelvic pain. In this chapter, we're drilling down a little deeper to take a look at exactly how these neuromuscular impairments translate into pelvic pain. Gaining this level of understanding is important, not only for the reasons we mention above, but also because it removes the mystery and sinisterness that so often surrounds persistent pelvic pain. For instance, when Mary learned that trigger points and too-tight muscles were the main drivers of her pain, she said it was a huge relief. "I wasn't crazy!" she said. "There wasn't some mysterious force causing my pain. There were actual physiological impairments at play, and they were treatable."

We'll begin the chapter with a discussion of what can go wrong with the muscles of the pelvic floor to cause pelvic pain. Next, we'll tackle the nerve issues that can come into play. From there we'll take a look at how connective tissue causes symptoms. Lastly, we'll end the chapter with an explanation of how the central nervous system enters into the mix. This chapter lays the groundwork for chapters 7 and 8, which go into detail on how all these impairments are treated.

MUSCLE IMPAIRMENTS

Too-Tight Muscles

As we've already explained, the hammock-like bundle of muscles that make up the pelvic floor support organs, assist in urinary and fecal continence, aid in sexual functioning, and stabilize connecting joints. And these muscles are always active, because if they were to completely relax, incontinence and organ prolapse would ensue. This constant state of contraction is actually what makes them more challenging to treat when they become impaired. As we've already touched on in previous chapters, two main impairments impact the muscles of the pelvic floor: too-tight muscles and trigger points.

Let's talk too-tight muscles first. In the last chapter we talked about what causes pelvic floor muscles to become too tight, but so far we haven't really delved into exactly why those tight muscles cause pain. The overriding reason is that when muscles become too tight, blood flow becomes restricted, meaning less oxygen reaches the tissue. This oxygen deficiency causes pain. In addition, too-tight muscles can actually cause other impairments that also cause pain. So you end up with pain on top of pain. For instance, tight muscles have a tendency to develop trigger points, a situation that also causes pain as well as dysfunction such as urinary urgency/frequency. This situation can also cause the compression of surrounding nerves, again, causing pain. On top of all that, tight muscles don't function efficiently, putting them at greater risk of incurring damage, like strains or tears, both of which, you guessed it, cause pain and dysfunction.

And tight muscles don't just cause pain where they lie; they also affect surrounding tissue. In the last chapter, we talked about how tight muscles can cause pain/dysfunction in adjacent organs, like when the muscles around the urinary sphincter become too tight, causing urgency, frequency, or pain with urination, but in addition to that, tight muscles can put the muscles they work closely with at risk. For example, neighboring muscles are going to have to compensate for a tight muscle that isn't "pulling its weight," so to speak. This in turn can cause pain in these muscles. To add insult to injury, too-tight pelvic floor muscles can also become weak muscles, meaning they aren't able to contract adequately. A consequence of this could be incontinence. Many pelvic pain symptoms are caused by too-tight muscles, including:

- Difficulty starting urine stream and interrupted urine stream
- Post-void "dribble"
- "Pinching" in the urethra after voiding
- Vulvar pain or burning
- Vulvar pain and/or deep vaginal pain with intercourse
- Perineal pain
- Pain at sit bones or tailbone when sitting
- Diminished or painful orgasm
- Trouble evacuating stool

WHY KEGELS ARE BAD FOR YOUR TIGHT PELVIC FLOOR

For decades doctors, PTs, trainers, therapists, you name it, have been hammering away at women—and men too—to do their Kegels to strengthen their pelvic floors. Preventing incontinence after childbirth and better sex are the promise for taking this advice. To be sure, it's advice that's seeped into mainstream culture. But the fact of the matter is Kegels are NOT for everybody, and for a certain population, doing them will actually do harm, not good. People with too-tight pelvic floor muscles and/or trigger points in their pelvic floor muscles should not do Kegels. Here's why: when you do a Kegel, you're doing a muscle contraction, and if you already have a tight pelvic floor, contracting it will only make it tighter, making your pelvic floor problems worse. Tight muscles do not like to be squeezed further. Not to mention that if you are predisposed to pelvic pain, perhaps your pelvic floor is tight but not yet symptomatic. Kegels could push you to develop symptoms. Remember, your pelvic floor muscles are the only group of muscles in the body that never get to rest, ever. They're working all the time to maintain continence, to support our pelvic organs, and to contribute to our posture and stability. Therefore, these muscles are "working out" all the time and don't follow the same rules as the other muscle groups in the body. Therefore, if you do get carried away with Kegels and over-strengthen your pelvic floor muscles, they can become too tight, which in turn can cause dysfunction and symptoms, such as pain and urinary urgency and frequency. So the pelvic floor muscles do not need extra strengthening from doing Kegels, unless something has overstretched them or injured them in some way that has made them truly weak (not weak *and tight*, but more on that in a bit). Your pelvic floor muscles can become overstretched and/or weak after childbirth, with age-related changes that are exacerbated by the hormonal changes during menopause, and after some gynecological surgeries. And this overstretching and weakening can lead to incontinence and pelvic organ prolapse. Kegels are appropriate when the pelvic floor is truly weak and/or over-stretched. We prescribe them all the time for this patient demographic. So tight muscles = Kegels bad. Weak and/or overstretched muscles = Kegels okay. If only we could end things here. But by now you're probably on to the fact that things are seldom simple with the pelvic floor. So here's the clincher: it's possible for a weak pelvic floor to also be a tight pelvic floor and/or to contain trigger points. In this situation, it's definitely NOT okay to do Kegels. So what does someone who has both a tight and a weak pelvic floor do, especially if he/she has other symptoms caused by the weakness? Well, the appropriate course of action in this situation would be to first work to clear up the tightness and trigger points with PT and whatever other treatments are appropriate. And then once the pelvic floor muscles are at a healthy tone—no longer too tight/all trigger points are gone—do Kegel exercises recommended by a trained PT to strengthen your pelvic floor. So to summarize: Kegels are not appropriate for folks with a tight pelvic floor or active trigger points or folks with a weak AND a tight pelvic floor. But it's okay to do Kegels to strengthen a weak pelvic floor.

TRIGGER POINTS

Before we talk about what causes trigger points or the role they play in pelvic pain, let's first take a closer look at what a trigger point is. As we've already mentioned, a trigger point is a small, taut band of involuntarily contracted muscle fibers within a muscle. But why do these contracted muscle fibers cause pain? The reason is that they affect blood supply to the nearby tissue (sound familiar?), which in turn makes the area hyperirritable, which will become even more uncomfortable/painful if compressed. They also cause referred pain to other areas. Two leading medical professionals, Drs. David Simons and Janet Travell, first coined the term "trigger point" in 1942. What they found in their research was that a handful of different kinds of trigger points exist. For instance, there are active trigger points, which as their name suggests, actively cause pain and other symptoms; latent trigger points, which are dormant but have the potential to cause trouble if they become activated; and satellite trigger points, which can crop up in another trigger point's referral zone.[1] (More on trigger point referral zones in a bit.) As we've already mentioned, muscles that are too tight, overlengthened, or weak are vulnerable to developing trigger points. Repetitive motions can lead to muscles that are too tight or overlengthened. For example, repetitively straining to have a bowel movement can lead to an overlengthening of the pelvic floor muscles. Also, when a checkout clerk regularly rotates to one side to scan items, muscles can become too tight on the side contracting to cause the rotation. In both scenarios the pelvic floor muscles are now vulnerable to developing trigger points because their ability to function properly becomes compromised and they become strained. In addition to repetitive behaviors/ movements, trigger points can crop up for other reasons. For example, local trauma can injure healthy muscles, causing trigger points to form. Examples of such trauma include a fall on the tailbone or childbirth. If muscles are already vulnerable due to an overshortening or overlengthening issue, seemingly benign things like a colonoscopy, laparoscopic surgery, or vaginal ultrasound can cause a trigger point. Plus, mechanical or organic stressors, like a hip labral tear or endometriosis, can also cause the development of trigger points.

Trigger points can be very misleading, and when dealing with them, it's a mistake to always assume the problem is where the pain is. For instance, they often refer pain elsewhere. For example, trigger points in the obturator internus muscle of the pelvic floor (a primary hip muscle that rotates the hip outward) can refer pain to the tailbone or the area above the opening of the anus. In addition to pain referral to these areas, a trigger point in the obturator internus muscle can cause pudendal nerve irritation because of its proximity to the pudendal nerve. On top of all that, trigger points can mimic joint pain and contribute to joint dysfunction because they cause altered movement patterns. For example, let's say you have trigger points in your gluteal muscles, specifically your gluteus maximus muscles, whose job it is to extend your hips. Because they have trigger points in them, these muscles are unable to function normally. Specifically, they are unable to recruit or activate normally when they need to during walking, causing your body to make adjustments. Indeed, in order to walk you have to be able to extend your hip to propel yourself forward. If your gluteus maximus isn't working correctly to do that, other muscles (for example, your iliotibial band, commonly referred to as the "IT band," which is a long, very tough muscle along the side of your leg that runs from your hip to your knee) are going to help out. Say this has been going on for months, or even years. The IT band will get tighter and tighter over time. Eventually it will start pulling on the kneecap, which can ultimately lead to knee pain. Trigger points can also refer pain to nearby organ systems and create connective tissue restrictions in overlying connective tissue.

Pretty much everyone will deal with trigger points at some point in their lives. The good news is that even though some 620 potential trigger points are possible in human muscle, they show up in pretty much the same location in everyone based on where nerves enter the muscles. Where they refer pain is also based on neurologic connections; therefore, trigger point maps exist, complete with referral patterns, and that goes for the pelvic floor too. This is great news, because as PTs undergo training to identify trigger points, they learn common trigger point locations that are associated with particular symptoms. This allows them to initiate a treatment plan that will likely start providing relief sooner rather than later. Trigger points play a role in the vast majority of cases of pelvic pain. Indeed, in some cases, they're the only culprits. For instance, we had a male patient, Ben, who had trigger points in his rectus abdominis muscle (the "six-pack" muscles of the abdomen) from doing too many sit-ups over a period of years. His main complaints were lower abdominal pain and penile pain. Initially he was misdiagnosed

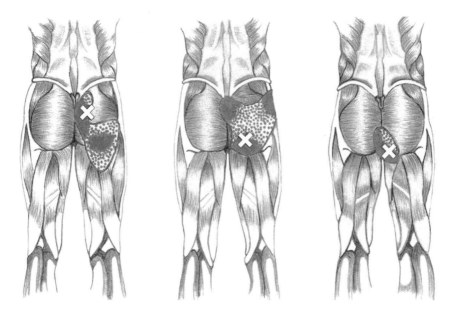

Figure 3.1.   Gluteus maximus muscle trigger points and their referral pattern. "**X**" indicates the trigger point, the solid shaded area indicates the primary referral zone, and the dotted area indicates the secondary referral zone. *Source: Pelvic Health and Rehabilitation Center*

with a hernia. He found his way to our clinic, and after about three months of working to release those trigger points, Ben's symptoms resolved. However, while it's possible for trigger points to be the sole cause of someone's pelvic pain, it's much more common for them to just be one layer of the pain. And here's another thing about trigger points: just about every symptom of pelvic pain can be caused by them! Vulvar burning, penile pain, vestibule burning, urethral burning, anal pain: trigger points in the pelvic floor and girdle muscles can be at the heart of each of these symptoms.

Whether too-tight muscles or trigger points or both are at play, when it's primarily caused by tightness, muscle pain is typically achy in nature; however, it *can* also be burny, especially when trigger points irritate nearby nerves. In addition, it tends to get worse as the day goes on. Commonly, pelvic MRIs or CT scans are ordered for patients with pelvic pain; however, while these tests can identify more sinister issues,

Table 3.1. Myofascial Trigger Point Referral Patterns

Muscle	Referral Pattern
Rectus abdominis	Mid and low back and viscerosomatic symptoms
Iliopsoas	Paravertebral and anterior thigh
Quadratus lumborum	Iliac crest, outer thigh, buttock
Gluteus maximus	Sacrum, coccyx, buttock
Gluteus medius	Low back, sacrum, buttock, lateral hip/thigh
Adductors	Groin and inner thigh
Hamstrings	Gluteal fold, posterior thigh, popliteal fossa
Piriformis	Low back, buttock, posterior thigh
Obturator internus	Coccyx and posterior thigh, fullness in rectum or vaginal pain
Coccygeus	Coccyx, sacrum, rectum
Pubococcygeus	Coccyx, sacrum, rectum
Iliococcygeus	Coccyx, sacrum, rectum
Ischiocavernosus	Perineal aching
Bulbospongiosus	Dyspareunia/impotence, perineal pain with sitting
Transverse perineum	Dyspareunia
External anal sphincter	Diffuse ache, pain with bowel movements, constipation
Urinary sphincter	Urinary retention, perineal urge, frequency

Source: Pelvic Health and Rehabilitation Center

like tumors, they will not diagnose tight muscles or the existence of trigger points. The best way to identify either is through an intravaginal or intrarectal exam, which a pelvic floor PT will do.

CONNECTIVE TISSUE RESTRICTION

Restricted connective tissue is another common impairment involved in pelvic pain. Most people aren't aware of the role connective tissue can play in pain. Not many people who are in pain will say, "My connective tissue hurts!" The job of connective tissue is to support, connect, or separate different types of tissue and organs. Ligaments, tendons, and cartilage are all considered connective tissue. However, the type of connective tissue that we're interested in when it comes to pelvic pain is known as "loose connective tissue." Loose connective tissue is aptly named, because its fibers are randomly arranged, and there's lots of space between the cells, which makes it the ideal tissue for cushioning and protecting. (For the sake of brevity, even though we're referring specifically to "loose connective tissue," going forward we'll be using the term "connective tissue.") Besides surrounding blood vessels and nerves, one of the biggest jobs of connective tissue in the body is to attach the skin to the muscles.

Connective tissue can become restricted as a result of dysfunction in underlying muscle, nerves, joints, and organs. When we talk about connective tissue as it relates to pelvic pain, we're talking about tissue in areas from the navel to the knees, back and front, and in certain cases also above and below these areas. The connective tissue that plays the largest role in pelvic pain includes the tissue of the abdomen, the inner and outer thighs, the hips, the buttocks, the tissue over the pubic bone and sit bones, and the tissue around the anus. When the connective tissue that attaches the skin to the muscle becomes restricted (think thickened or dense), it can and does cause pain. The main reason is that it causes decreased blood flow to the area. On top of all that, it's hypothesized that restricted connective tissue can cause referred pain—pain to organs (think bladder in the case of pelvic pain). Local symptoms of connective tissue restriction when it comes to pelvic pain include hypersensitivity (intolerance to clothing), itching (anal or vulvar itching in the absence of infection), visual changes (redness and/or darkened tissue), and/or impaired integrity (splitting of tissue). The severity of connective tissue restriction ranges. For example, a patient may have moderate connective tissue restriction, so when he is standing, it doesn't bother him. But when he sits, he compresses the too-tight tissue, further restricting blood flow and causing pain. Without treatment his symptoms may progress from provoked pain when sitting to unprovoked standing pain. Also, often women with vulvar pain and pain with sex have restricted vulvar connective tissue. Indeed, when this tissue is manipulated in PT, they often report that it reproduces their pain with intercourse. (Being able to reproduce symptoms in this way is always a good sign. As a general rule of thumb, when we can reproduce symptoms, we can often get rid of them.) In addition, restricted connective tissue in the vulva can cause itching or burning and restricted connective tissue in the abdomen can contribute to abdominal pain.

Peripheral nerves are the nerves outside the brain and spinal cord. When people think of peripheral nerves in relation to pelvic pain, they typically think of the pudendal nerve, but quite a few peripheral nerves can contribute to symptoms of pelvic pain. See table 3.2 for the names of these nerves as well as information on the areas they innervate.

Peripheral nerves can be injured or irritated for a number of different reasons. For one thing, they can become compressed. Nerves can become compressed by organs, scar tissue, behaviors/postures (sitting), activity (riding a bike or a horse), or placement of a foreign object (mesh). A particular kind of compression occurs when a nerve becomes "entrapped." For its part, entrapment occurs when a nerve's mobility is severely limited because it's stuck in tissue or some sort of anatomical tunnel, causing it to be severely compressed. Nerves can become entrapped by scar tissue, a foreign object (mesh), or an anatomic anomaly (someone could be born with a nerve that's entangled in a ligament, for instance). In the case of the pudendal nerve, for example, the two ligaments that surround the nerve can create a space that is too tight for the nerve, causing problems. In addition, nerves can get injured by stretch mechanisms such as a vaginal delivery, constipation, or deep and heavy squats. Lastly, infection can cause a nerve to become irritated. It's important to understand that an irritated nerve can cause dysfunction to whatever tissue it supplies. Muscles, organs, and skin can all be affected. *So how can a peripheral nerve issue translate into the symptoms of pelvic pain?* One example involves hernia surgery. During the

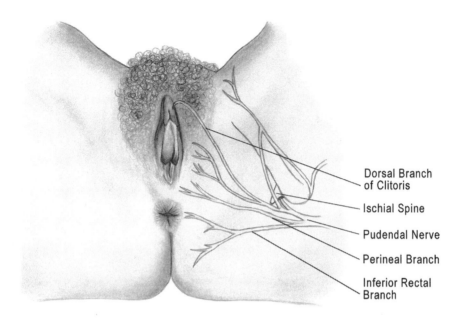

Dorsal Branch
of Clitoris

Ischial Spine

Pudendal Nerve

Perineal Branch

Inferior Rectal
Branch

Figure 3.2. Pudendal nerve and its branches. *Source: Pelvic Health and Rehabilitation Center*

surgery, the ilioinguinal nerve, which is located in the abdominal wall, can be affected and create penile and scrotal pain. Another involves impairment of the pudendal nerve, which can create burning vaginal or clitoral pain in women or penile, scrotal, or perineum pain in men. Lastly, the posterior femoral cutaneous nerve, which is located in the thigh, can cause pain with sitting and/or perineum pain. In addition to the major nerves of the pelvic floor, loads of tiny, superficial nerve branches can play a role in pelvic pain, in areas such as the vulva/vestibule, for instance. Indeed, vulvar/vestibule pain can be caused by an increase in nerve fiber density in the area. Nerve pain in the pelvis is typically sharp, shooting, stabbing, knife-like, burning, or itching anywhere in the distribution of the impacted nerves. Impaired nerves can also cause numbness.

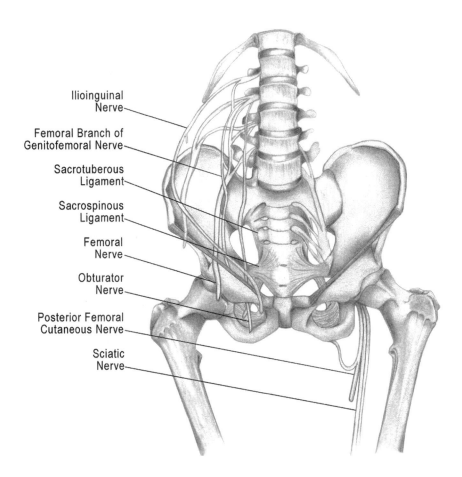

Ilioinguinal
Nerve

Femoral Branch of
Genitofemoral Nerve

Sacrotuberous
Ligament

Sacrospinous
Ligament

Femoral
Nerve

Obturator
Nerve

Posterior Femoral
Cutaneous Nerve

Sciatic
Nerve

Figure 3.3.   Peripheral nerves of the pelvis. *Source: Pelvic Health and Rehabilitation Center*

HOW THE CENTRAL NERVOUS SYSTEM FITS IN

With persistent pain, whether it's pelvic pain, knee pain, or back pain, we cannot ignore the role of the central nervous system (the brain and the spinal cord), because it's always involved. *What is that role?* Being in pain, including pelvic pain, can actually change how the brain and spinal cord receive input and produce symptoms. After tissues have healed from an injury, which is typically around 12 weeks, the brain can still create the *pain symptoms* of the initial injury, even though there is no longer a problem with the tissue. *So why bring this up now?* All the

Table 3.2.   Pelvic Nerves and the Structures They Supply

Nerve	Innervation
Pudendal	External genitalia, skin of the perineum and around the anus
Ilioinguinal	In men: skin over the root of the penis and upper part of the scrotum; in women: skin over the mons pubis and labia majora
Genitofemoral	Upper anterior thigh, skin of anterior scrotum in men, and mons pubis in women
Iliohypogastric	Skin over the lateral buttocks and above the pubis
Posterior femoral cutaneous	Posterior surface of thigh and leg and skin of perineum
Sciatic	Posterior portion of the thigh
Cluneal	Skin of the buttocks

Source: Pelvic Health and Rehabilitation Center

neuromuscular impairments we discussed above actually have the potential to modify the way our brain and spinal cord work, thereby, and unknown to the person dealing with the symptom-causing impairments, creating a perception of pain that's out of sync with the impairment or that hangs around once the impairment is cleared up. Specifically, someone with persistent pain can get to a place where they're actually having more pain with less or even no provocation. This phenomenon is called "central sensitization." Before we go into any more detail about how the nervous system can become sensitized in this way, we first want to talk a little about how pain works, including what it means to have "persistent pain" versus its counterpart, "acute pain."

Pain is a protective mechanism generated by the brain in response to a perceived threat, like burning your hand on the stove, which creates pain from the burned tissue. Oftentimes the degree of pain experienced is actually not directly in proportion to tissue damage. Consider this: a paper cut produces very little tissue damage yet can cause a lot of pain. Conversely, a soldier can get shot in battle yet not realize he's injured until he's off the battlefield. In some cases, pain may not be associated with tissue damage at all. For example, amputees may experience phantom limb pain in tissue that no longer exists, because the part of the brain that corresponded to the amputated limb can still generate the sensation of pain, even after the limb is gone. Plus, pain relies on context. For instance, athletes involved in vigorous sports ignore impacts that would send most of us screaming because it's all part of the game, and in that context the pain is expected and not threatening. "Catastrophic thinking," which is basically when a person ruminates about worst-case outcomes, can actually make pain worse. However, knowing pain is generated by the brain rather than by damaged tissues does not mean that pain is "all in your head" and should be ignored or dismissed. In fact, knowing that pain is the body's alarm system actually highlights the importance of treating it before the alarm system becomes wonky, overreacting to every perceived threat. So "acute pain" actually helps you avoid danger or more tissue damage. Persistent pain happens when pain occurs either in the complete absence of tissue damage or after the tissue damage has healed. (Persistent pain is typically considered pain lasting six months or more.) Central sensitization is the term used to describe that wonky pain loop. A sensitized nervous system is responsible for persistent pain. And what's happening is either the pain itself or other factors have modified the way the central nervous system works, so that a person actually becomes more sensitive and gets *more pain* with *less provocation or even no provocation*. This phenomenon involves changes to the central nervous system, in particular the brain and the spinal cord. So a sensitized nervous system not only makes people more sensitive to things that *should* hurt, but also to things that should not, like ordinary touch and pressure, for example. Patients tell us things like "my husband lightly touched my stomach and I jumped five feet" or "touching a cold floor with bare feet actually hurts." Other common examples of a sensitized nervous system that we see with our patients are intolerance to tight jeans and/or underwear and pain with sitting. In addition, when a sensitized nervous system is at play, any pain the person experiences might fade more slowly than it would in someone who doesn't have a sensitized nervous system. For example, a woman, let's call her Cynthia, who has had anal pain for a few years, and who has a sensitized nervous system as one element of her pain, gets a fairly normal vaginal yeast infection. In most cases, this kind of infection is treated with medication, clears up, and the pain stops. Life goes on. But in Cynthia's case, this little infection jacks up her anal pain (even though the infection has nothing to do with her anus), and the vaginal pain that is a symptom of the infection, instead of clearing up as soon as the infection does, lasts for weeks afterward. So in essence, a sensitized nervous system can cause a person to have more pain and for longer from something fairly benign versus someone whose nervous system is not sensitized. As providers who treat a persistent pain syndrome, we have to consider with each patient the role the central nervous system plays in their pain. Plus, as we've already mentioned, patients with pelvic pain are often initially misdiagnosed and don't get on the path to appropriate treatment right away. Oftentimes it can take six months to a year for them to get on that road, setting them up to develop a sensitized nervous system as one layer of their pain. We want to make it clear that we're not saying every person who has had pelvic pain for six months or more will develop a sensitized nervous system as a pain driver. That is simply not what we've seen in our years of treating pelvic pain. Time and again we have treated patients who have had symptoms for six months to a year and beyond, and after their tissue impairments are adequately treated, their pain has gone away. What we *are* saying is that with pelvic pain, providers must consider whether a patient's central nervous system is playing a role, and to what extent. And if they do believe the patient's pain has a strong central nervous system component, take steps to ensure that this layer of pain is dealt with, because doing so is every bit as important as working out a trigger point or loosening restricted connective tissue when it comes to a patient's recovery. That's why in chapter 5, we discuss how the central nervous system fits into our treatment approach and in chapter 6 we discuss other options for treating it.

In this chapter, we've taken a close look at exactly how neuromuscular impairments of the pelvic floor actually translate into the variety of symptoms associated with pelvic pain. A major takeaway is that these impairments can kick off a vicious cycle. A tight muscle causes a trigger point to form. A trigger point causes a nearby nerve to become irritated. An irritated nerve causes surrounding muscle to tighten, causing connective tissue restriction. These impairments cause pain, alerting the brain that something is wrong and ultimately changing the way the brain processes pain. A person becomes anxious, further increasing their pain. A vicious cycle has been set in motion. That's why in the next section of the book we will explore exactly how to go about breaking that cycle, beginning with a basic question: I have pelvic pain; now what do I do?

II

Getting on the Road to Healing

4

I HAVE PELVIC PAIN. WHAT DO I DO NOW?

Beth, a 31-year-old woman, woke up one morning with vulvar and vaginal burning. Assuming she had a yeast infection, a regular affliction for her, she self-treated with the usual over-the-counter medication. Three boxes of OTC medication later, she was still in pain. It was time to see a doctor. She made an appointment with her gynecologist. A barrage of tests came back negative. Fear set in. Seemingly overnight, things she had taken for granted like sitting, driving, and even wearing underwear and jeans became difficult because they exacerbated her pain. Sex was out of the question. So Beth did what millions of people with a health problem do: she logged on to the Internet. Googling "vaginal burning" and "vulvar burning" landed her in an online chat room for women diagnosed with "pudendal neuralgia." After reading horror story after horror story, her fear turned to terror and she was left wondering: *"Now what do I do?"*

Beth is one of many men and women with pelvic pain in the United States (and abroad) asking that question. We know this for a fact, because each day at our clinics, we get dozens of calls and e-mails, all different versions of the same question. As we've discussed in previous chapters, it's only in recent years that meaningful strides have been made in the understanding of chronic pain in general. And although there has been a momentum in research to study chronic pain, and pelvic pain specifically, it's still early days on both fronts. Therefore, when diagnosing and treating pelvic pain, there simply isn't a large body of time- *and* research-tested treatment options available for providers to draw from. As a result, it can still be difficult for pelvic pain sufferers to get an appropriate diagnosis and treatment. That's why we're devoting an entire chapter to providing a road map for patients to get on the right treatment path. Specifically, this chapter details three steps for patients to get on that path. They are:

1. Getting educated about pelvic pain.
2. Finding the right doctor.
3. Finding the right physical therapist (PT).

GETTING EDUCATED

Even though it can be a slippery slope, the Internet is a good place for those with pelvic pain to begin their education about the condition. Thankfully, today there are some fantastic pelvic pain–related blogs and online support groups. (See appendix A for a complete list of online resources that we have vetted and highly recommend.) Our advice to go online for information comes with a caveat, however. The Internet can be a terrifying place for a person in pain. Horror stories abound. So it's important to keep in mind that the majority of folks on the Internet are the ones struggling to get better; therefore, a disproportionate number of people online are not getting better versus those who are. Also, it's important for those who turn to the Internet for information to remember to *not* believe everything they read and to always consider the source. And even though their symptoms might seem exactly like someone else's that they read about, the underlying causes and circumstances are almost always going to be different, so what worked for one may or may not work for another. Bottom line: turn to the Internet to become an informed patient who can advocate for yourself, but always pay attention to the source of the information. Take what you need and leave the rest. And DO NOT linger in chat rooms filled with hard luck stories. Research shows that fear and anxiety absolutely, positively exacerbate pain. Lastly, do not use the Internet to glom on to a diagnosis. For instance, we regularly have people call, write in, and come to our clinics convinced that they have pudendal neuralgia or pudendal nerve entrapment because they've read about these particular diagnoses online.

FINDING A DOCTOR

When it comes to pelvic pain treatment, it's important to see a doctor to rule out infection or any other more serious pathology. But besides being able to rule out a serious pathology, a physician plays an important role in an interdisciplinary treatment approach to pelvic pain, namely, to manage any necessary medications and/or treat contributing factors, such as endometriosis, a Bartholin's abscess, dermatological issues, or hormone imbalances, just to name a few. Only a handful of physicians specialize in pelvic pain in the United States. Many people don't have the resources to travel to see one of these specialists, and as we'll explain, unless one of the few pelvic pain specialists is local to you, it's ultimately not necessary for your physician to be a specialist. Plus, it's important to remember that treating pelvic pain, more often than not, is going to be a longer-term process that involves PT. So at the end of the day, it makes sense to find a local physician to join your treatment team. The good news is, contrary to what most patients believe, a local physician, whether a gynecologist, urologist, or primary care physician, will more often than not be able to offer therapeutic options *even if they are not a pelvic pain specialist*. However, because many patients don't understand this treatment model from the outset, they're disappointed after they see a doctor because they expected to leave the appointment with a definitive diagnosis, treatment, and cure. We're hoping that the information provided in this chapter will spare patients that disappointment by explaining the role a local physician typically plays in an interdisciplinary treatment plan.

Typically the physician a female patient will visit is a gynecologist, unless her symptoms are mainly urological, in which case she'll see a urologist. Male patients usually start out going to a primary care physician, who may then refer them to a urologist. For the most part, treatment options these physicians can offer include medication to manage pain/other symptoms, topical creams, and/or possibly some sort of injection. (We will be going into much greater detail about these and other treatment options in chapter 8.) In addition, the physician can offer a referral to a pelvic floor PT as well as a pain management doctor.

So how do you know if a physician is a good fit to join your treatment team? Our advice is to explain your symptoms to the doctor, and if he/she looks perplexed or suggests a treatment that you've already tried, but that didn't work in the past, it's fair to ask the doctor if he/she feels comfortable treating your symptoms or if he/she has had experience with similar patients in the past. If the doctor says no or you are uncomfortable, then we recommend that you move on to the next doctor. Basically, you want a doctor who has an interest in learning about pelvic pain and with whom you can communicate comfortably. Another piece of advice is for you to share articles with the doctor that you believe pertain to your symptoms. (See appendix A for a list of blog posts from our blog and/or articles that may be appropriate to take to your doctor.)

When should you visit one of the few pelvic pain specialists practicing today? If you believe you have reached a plateau with your treatment plan, it might be worth seeing a pelvic pain specialist for a consultation to help modify, improve, or redirect your treatment in consultation with your local providers. But you always want to exhaust your local resources before traveling to a specialist and keep your local provider in the loop if you do. An exception to this rule is the few cases where a specialist is truly needed because of their expertise in a particular area, such as actual pudendal nerve entrapment, Tarlov cysts, or mesh removal.

At what point is it advisable to add a pain management doctor to your treatment team? Our thinking is that anytime a patient is going to take medication as part of his/her treatment plan, it's best for a pain management doctor to act as the prescribing physician, as medication management for persistent pain is their area of expertise. And bear in mind that a pain management doctor does not need to have expertise treating pelvic pain to be a valuable member of a treatment team. These physicians have experience treating all types of pain. We'd like to include the same caveat for visiting a pain management doctor that we brought up for a visit to a local physician. The pain management doctor's role in treatment is to help patients manage their symptoms, not to eradicate the problem. Besides asking your local physician if he/she has a trusted referral, a good resource for finding a pain management doctor is the International Association for the Study of Pain, a medical organization devoted to pain.

FINDING A PT

As already discussed in previous chapters, almost all pelvic pain syndromes involve some kind of neuromuscular issue, that is, a problem with the muscles, nerves, and connective tissue of the pelvic floor and adjacent areas. A PT is the medical provider who has the best understanding of the neuromuscular system and is therefore best equipped to treat it. It's important to see a PT who specializes in treating the pelvic floor. A decade ago qualified pelvic floor PTs were few and far between. Fast-forward to today. Marked progress has been made in pelvic pain PT education with more and more educational opportunities available to PTs. For example, when we graduated from PT school more than 15 years ago, we were not aware that pelvic floor rehabilitation was an available career path. Today PTs are graduating with an awareness that this specialty exists. Furthermore, today many postgraduate classes on pelvic pain treatment are available to PTs. In addition, medical institutions around the country have caught on to the demand for pelvic pain rehabilitation and have opened interdisciplinary pelvic pain clinics, many of which include on-staff pelvic floor PTs.

So how do you go about finding a knowledgeable and qualified pelvic floor PT? Fortunately, they are out there, and below is a list of resources for connecting with them:

American Physical Therapy Association

The APTA is a professional association for PTs in the United States. On its website, the organization offers a searchable database of "women's health" PTs. While pelvic pain does not discriminate between the sexes, the APTA is still working to iron out this discrepancy. In the meantime, many of the PTs listed in the APTA's "women's health" locator treat both men and women. You can find the APTA's women's health locator at www.womenshealthapta.org/find-a-physical-therapist/index.cfm.

Pelvic Floor Physical Therapy Classes

One great way to find a pelvic floor PT is to get in touch with the organizations that are teaching postgraduate courses in pelvic floor PT in cities around the United States. We teach such a class, so feel free to contact us, and if we know of a PT in your area that we are comfortable recommending, we will be more than happy to do so. Check out our website at www.pelvicpainrehab.com for our contact information. The Herman & Wallace Pelvic Rehabilitation Institute also teaches a variety of postgraduate pelvic floor PT courses. So a patient could contact the faculty members of Herman & Wallace and ask for a PT recommendation as well. You can find the Herman & Wallace website at http://hermanwallace.com.

The International Pelvic Pain Society

The IPPS has a "find a provider" option on its website at www.pelvicpain.org that includes a search for PTs.

Happy Pelvis

Happy Pelvis, a Yahoo support group, is a good resource for PT recommendations. The group was started specifically to support pelvic pain patients through the physical therapy process. Today Happy Pelvis has hundreds of active members who are always willing to recommend PTs. In addition, there is a searchable list of pelvic pain PTs in the group's archives. You can find Happy Pelvis at http://groups.yahoo.com/neo/groups/happypelvis/info.

Pelvic Pain Bloggers

The bloggers we include in our list of blogs in appendix A may be able to recommend a qualified PT. In fact, many of the bloggers are PTs themselves.

#pelvicmafia

The PTs in this Twitter group are always happy to recommend a PT if they can.

Above are all great resources to help you find a pelvic floor PT in your area. However, unfortunately, a few regions of the country have no qualified pelvic floor PTs . . . yet. *What do you do if you live in one of these areas?* Though it's not an ideal situation, patients will travel to see a qualified pelvic floor PT for a period of intensive treatment. *What do you do if you have to travel out of town for treatment but need it on a long-term basis, as so many pelvic pain patients ultimately do?* Some of our out-of-town patients arrange for a local PT who is not yet qualified to treat pelvic pain, but is willing to learn, to travel with them so we can show him/her how to best treat them, or they bring along their significant other to learn how to administer certain treatment techniques. The good news is that compared to even five years ago, the number of PTs treating pelvic pain has significantly increased and continues to do so thanks to new educational opportunities for PTs interested in pursuing this specialty. Plus, it's important to bear in mind that while treatment with a qualified pelvic floor PT is often an important component of an interdisciplinary treatment plan, there are several other avenues, as we will cover in great detail in upcoming chapters, which, when combined, can lead to recovery.

QUESTIONS TO ASK A POTENTIAL PT

Once you zero in on a PT, you can ask him or her a handful of questions to make sure he or she is a good fit. We've included that list of questions below.

1. *What is your approach to treating pelvic pain?* What you're looking for here is an approach that includes manual therapy techniques (connective tissue manipulation, trigger point therapies, joint mobilization, and nerve glides), delivered internally through the vagina or anus and externally to the pelvic floor and adjacent areas, such as the abdomen, hips, and inner/outer thighs. Other techniques used to treat pelvic pain include home exercises, neuromuscular reeducation, and central nervous system strate-

gies for decreasing pain. (The next chapter is a complete overview of pelvic pain PT and will give you a much clearer understanding of physical therapy techniques used to treat pelvic pain.)

2. *How long are your treatment sessions?* Treating pelvic pain can
   be time consuming because of the number of structures that are
   often involved in a pelvic pain syndrome. In an ideal setting, a
   treatment session should be an hour-long, one-on-one treatment
   session with the PT. Due to current health care constraints, however, this may not be possible, and the treatment times may be
   shorter.

3. *What percentage of your patients have pelvic pain?* In addition to
   pelvic pain, pelvic floor PTs are also trained to treat urinary and
   fecal incontinence, prepartum and postpartum dysfunction, and
   pelvic organ prolapse. While all these issues involve the pelvic
   floor, treatment for them is very different than treatment for
   pelvic pain. Therefore, it's important to find a PT with a specific
   interest in pelvic pain under the umbrella of pelvic floor disorders.

MOLLY'S STORY

One month after my thirty-second birthday, I woke up in excruciating
pain—it was as if someone had set me on fire while I slept—the focal
point of my pain was the left side of my vulva, but I also had extreme
vaginal and urethral burning. My first thought was that I had either a
yeast or bladder infection. I had just moved to California three weeks
before, so I had to find a doctor on the fly and hope for the best. Dr.
Number One took several tests and sent me home with a goody bag full
of creams, suppositories, and other meds. None of the remedies
worked, and all the tests came back negative. From there I began to see
the doctor regularly in an effort to get to the bottom of my pain. After
about the third visit, he told me he didn't know what was causing my
pain, but that my pelvic floor muscles were tight. He diagnosed me with
vulvodynia and recommended that I see a "vulvodynia specialist" as well
as a PT. At this point I was in a full-on state of panic—it felt like I had a
pile of burning coals inside me—it hurt to sit, it hurt to stand, it hurt to
urinate, sex was out of the question, I wasn't sleeping or eating—I was

truly in agony. In my state of anxiety I couldn't figure out how on earth a PT would be able to help me—wasn't a PT for a person who had broken his leg or been in a car accident? I honestly didn't understand how a PT could heal the kind of pain I was in. So I put the info away and concentrated on getting an appointment with Dr. Vulvodynia Specialist. To my utter dismay, his solution was to give me Capsaicin treatments, which consisted of me applying cream made from the hottest, reddest peppers on the planet to my already-on-fire vulva daily. Ugh, no. Check, please! After this incident I sought out two more opinions—one doctor, we'll call him Dr. Google, actually googled "vulvodynia" right in front of me. After scanning the info he came up with, he said, "Yep, you have vulvodynia." He also added that there was no way my pelvic floor muscles were too tight, and that getting PT for relief would be a waste of time. The next doctor told me that nothing whatsoever was wrong with me—great news, except for the part where I remained in terrible pain. Not long after, there came a day when I decided if I had to live life in such horrible pain, I'd rather not (just a little aside here—no one is more against death than me, so for me to even be thinking this way was incredible). That day I did what you do when you don't know what to do; I called my mom, and she told me to go straight to the hospital. At the time, a trip to the emergency room sounded like a wonderful idea to me. Truth be told, I had been harboring this fantasy of lying in a hospital bed surrounded by a team of doctors whose mission it was to figure out exactly what was wrong with me, and then cure me. But once again my hopes for getting to the bottom of my pain were dashed. It took a couple of doctors and an intern or two to tell me nothing showed up on any of the tests they ran on me, and they simply didn't know what was causing my pain. The day after the emergency room fiasco, I decided to call the PT that Dr. Number One had told me about and make an appointment. I was burned out on doctors, but I didn't want to give up. At least seeing a PT would keep me in the game. And that's when things began to turn around for me. The PT I saw was Stephanie. After working on the external connective tissue restrictions I had, Stephanie began to work on me internally. About five minutes into the session she found what she described as a "pea-size lump" on the left side of my vaginal wall. She referred me to a pelvic surgeon, who diagnosed me with a Bartholin's abscess. I was overjoyed that someone had finally found "the reason" for my pain. However, my happiness was short-lived, as two months after the surgery to remove the cyst, I was still in pain. Back to PT I went. What Stephanie found was that many of my pelvic floor muscles were tight, including the muscles surrounding my urethra, and that the muscle adjacent to where the cyst had been was riddled with trigger points. Apparently the muscle guarding I had done for the past year to "protect" my painful tissue had resulted in muscle tightening and trigger points. In addition to that, I had a great deal of connective tissue restriction on my inner thighs, sit bone area, abdomen, and bony pelvis. There was a lot of work to do. After six months of regular PT with Stephanie, I reached a place where I was about 90% pain-free. I do have urethral symptoms that fluctuate depending on how active I am, and the occasional bout of pain with sitting. But I manage both symptoms, and neither interferes with my ability to live my life to the fullest. I have pain-free sex, wear jeans, do yoga, and exercise. Recovery was a hard road, but once I got on the right path, with lots of patience and persistence I did get better, and if you're a patient reading this, you will too.

DIRECT ACCESS TO PHYSICAL THERAPY

While we recommend that patients see a physician prior to starting PT for all the above-mentioned reasons, there are situations where going straight to a pelvic floor PT without seeing a doctor first is an option. Indeed, at the time of this book's writing, all 50 states, including the District of Columbia, have some form of "direct access" law in place. Direct access is just what it sounds like. It allows patients to have direct access to PTs without a physician referral or prescription. However, some states have provisions tied to treatment without a physician referral, such as a time or visit limit. For example, in California, one of the states where we practice, after either 12 visits or 45 days, whichever comes first, patients must visit their doctor to have him/her sign off on the PT's plan of care, among other provisions. The direct access laws are often in flux, so if you have any questions about how the law applies in your specific state, we recommend that you contact the American Physical Therapy Association, the national professional organization for physical therapy. The organization publishes updated news on the direct access laws on its site at www.apta.org/directaccess, and you can contact the APTA directly as a consumer with questions at consumer@apta.org.

We believe patients can benefit from the direct access laws in a few specific situations. For example, it's not uncommon for patients to have long wait times before getting in to see their doctors. In this situation, it makes sense to start PT while they are waiting for the appointment, because then treatment can begin as soon as possible and the PT can communicate his/her findings to the physician. In addition, the PT can help the patient organize the information he/she will communicate to the doctor and help him/her formulate questions to ask during the appointment. Another example of the benefits of direct access is when a patient has seen a PT in the past and is just going in for a "tune-up" or because of symptom recurrence. A final example is when a patient has been to a physician/physicians who have ruled out other pathologies but did not know to refer the patient to PT. Patients can share their research regarding pelvic floor PT with their doctor and discuss their progress with him or her along the way. In these situations, physicians are often relieved that the patient has a solution when he or she may be at a loss. We have treated many patients in the past who found us without a physician referral. Typically we advise these patients to include at least one doctor in their treatment plan, and we help coordinate communication with this provider. This is actually how Beth, whose story kicked off the chapter, got to our office. After not getting answers from the doctors she saw, and encouraged by the members of the Happy Pelvis online group mentioned above, she made an appointment to see Liz. Fortunately Beth's impairments were pretty straightforward. She had severe tightness and trigger points in her pelvic floor as well as inner thigh connective tissue restrictions. After about five months of weekly manual internal and external PT, Beth was nearly pain-free.

It is our hope that this chapter has clearly explained the important first steps people dealing with pelvic pain must take to begin down the path toward healing. Armed from the outset with the knowledge that the path to recovery will be different from what they've experienced when seeking treatment for other conditions can remove much of the anxiety and frustration from the endeavor, leaving them to focus on what's important: getting better. Coming up in chapter 5, we're going to talk about a major component in the path toward recovery: pelvic floor physical therapy.

5

PELVIC PAIN PT: IN THE TREATMENT ROOM

HOW EXACTLY DOES A PHYSICAL THERAPIST TREAT PELVIC PAIN?

This is probably the most frequently asked question we get from patients and providers. It's understandable, as most people's experience with PT involves orthopedic PT following a surgery or injury, so it's hard for them to imagine how the physical therapy they're familiar with translates to treatment for pelvic pain. That's why in this chapter we're going to take you into the treatment room and show you exactly how we as pelvic floor PTs evaluate a patient and assess what is behind his/her symptoms. In addition, we take you through two important steps we take as we develop a treatment plan for patients—setting goals for treatment and coordinating with a patient's interdisciplinary treatment team. Lastly, we'll end the chapter with an explanation of where a sensitized nervous system fits into our treatment approach as well as a discussion of some specific issues that men with pelvic pain face as they navigate treatment.

EVALUATION: GETTING A HISTORY

At our clinic, treatment for pelvic pain begins with an evaluation. When we evaluate patients, our goal is to identify the contributing factors and impairments behind their pain. The bulk of the evaluation takes place at the first appointment, but it's not uncommon for it to take two to three appointments for us to get a complete picture of what's behind a patient's symptoms. Because no two cases of pelvic pain are the same, each patient evaluation is going to be different, but there are enough common notes that we can give you a general overview of how we evaluate a patient beginning with the first appointment. During the first appointment, the process of putting together the pieces of the puzzle of a patient's pain begins with a discussion of his/her history. Here we put our detective hats on and ask a series of questions about the history and onset of the patient's pain. Among the questions we ask are *What do you think caused your pain? Describe your symptoms? How long have you had symptoms? What exacerbates and alleviates your symptoms? What activities do your symptoms limit? What providers have you seen? What past treatments have you had, what has helped, and what has not? Describe the severity of your symptoms?* (For a complete list of the questions we ask our patients during their first appointment, see appendix B.) In addition to questions about the pain, we ask specific questions about urinary, bowel, and sexual function. For example, we ask patients if they experience urinary urgency, constipation, or pain with penetration or after ejaculation. Commonly the PT evaluation is the first time a patient has been asked these questions. And while some are surprised that we're asking them questions of such a personal nature, more often than not, they're relieved to finally be telling a medical provider things like how much sex hurts, that they're having trouble reaching orgasm, that they have to use their finger to assist in a bowel movement, or that they notice their urine stream doesn't sound as forceful as their counterpart's in a public restroom. This Q&A portion of the first appointment begins the process of gathering clues that we'll use to figure out why a patient is having pain and what needs to be done to address it. It also gives us the road map we use for the next part of the appointment—the hands-on examination. A patient's list of symptoms can be quite long, so during the interview, we work to suss out the symptoms that are the most bothersome for them. Because time is limited, we'll attack these symptoms first during the hands-on exam. What's more, information we get from patients at this point will guide us in approaching that exam. For example, as discussed in chapter 3, people suffering from persistent pain often develop a sensitized nervous system. This has to be considered before the examination, because it actually dictates our approach. For instance, we'll move more slowly through the exam, or we may not use certain evaluation techniques that have the potential to aggravate a sensitized nervous system. (We'll discuss more on how the central nervous system fits into our treatment approach below.) By the time the interview has come to a close, we've formulated a plan for the upcoming exam. After discussing it with the patient and asking if he/she has any questions, we leave the room to allow the patient to disrobe from the waist down, drape themselves, and get comfortable on the treatment table. From there the exam begins.

EVALUATION: HANDS-ON EXAMINATION

The goal of the evaluation exam is to begin uncovering a patient's symptom-causing impairments. In addition, we continue our search for all the factors contributing to a patient's pain. As already mentioned, during the exam we focus first on the areas we believe are causing the patient's most painful symptoms. But in general, during this hands-on portion of the exam, we're looking for the three common neuromuscular impairments we discussed in chapter 3: connective tissue restrictions, internal and external muscle impairments (too-tight muscles and/or trigger points), and peripheral nerve dysfunction. In addition, we're also going to check for any anatomical/biomechanical abnormalities (as discussed in chapter 2) by observing a combination of things, like posture and how the patient walks.

External Exam

We begin the exam externally. External structures we examine for possible impairments include the abdomen, hip muscles, inner/outer thighs, low back, and the sacroiliac and hip joints. When beginning the external exam, we'll always focus first on the structures we believe are the most relevant to the patient's symptoms. For example, if a patient complains of tailbone pain, we'll first examine his sacroiliac joint and the soft tissue around his tailbone, followed by a rectal examination. That's because impairments in these areas are commonly behind tailbone pain. Less important to this particular patient would be an evaluation of the abdominal wall, as it's typically not a generator of tailbone pain. In general, among other things, we're on the hunt for connective tissue restrictions, trigger points, or nerve dysfunction.

A major component of the external exam is our search for any possible connective tissue restrictions. Restricted connective tissue can cause symptoms such as pain with sitting or vulvar burning. As you'll recall from previous chapters, when we talk about connective tissue as it relates to pelvic pain, we're talking about tissue in the areas from the navel to the knees, back and front, and in certain cases, above and below these areas. Happy connective tissue is mobile, uniform in its density, and does not produce pain when touched. Restricted connective tissue is thick or "gummed up" and lacks mobility or is "sticky," and when examined, the patient will typically feel discomfort. Because of the referred pain patterns that can occur with connective tissue restriction, however, this discomfort may actually be felt elsewhere. Indeed, patients are often surprised when an area of connective tissue triggers their symptoms in another area. For instance, a female patient whose main complaint is pain with intercourse may have connective tissue restrictions in her abdomen around her belly button. While we're examining this area, it may cause vulvar discomfort or reproduce the vulvar pain she feels with intercourse. If we find that a patient's connective tissue is restricted in any of the areas we examine, we basically "pinch roll" the affected tissue below the skin and above the muscle between the thumb and four other fingers, with both hands. This is commonly referred to as "skin rolling." This technique is used to both evaluate and treat the tissue. What we're checking for when we evaluate connective tissue is how well it moves, its density, and its sensitivity. Treatment is aimed at loosening the tissue to improve blood flow, decrease thickness, and restore mobility. When tissue is restricted, manipulating it typically causes a sharp sensation and may even cause soreness or bruising in the days following treatment. As the patient's tissue normalizes over a series of appointments, however, the treatment becomes less painful.

Typically, after we examine a patient externally for connective tissue restrictions, we move on to areas that may harbor trigger points. External trigger points can be involved in a slew of different pelvic pain symptoms. For instance, if a patient has pain with sitting, we may find a trigger point in her obturator internus muscle, one of the pelvic girdle muscles that can be accessed externally. The majority of pelvic floor

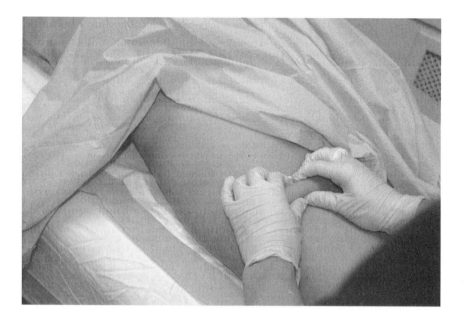

Figure 5.1. Connective tissue manipulation of the back of the thigh. *Source: Pelvic Health and Rehabilitation Center*

muscles can not be accessed externally, so for the most part, when we're examining a patient for external trigger points, we're examining the muscles attached to the outside of the pelvis, such as all the gluteal muscles, the hamstrings, and the abdominal muscles. When we find a trigger point (whether externally or internally), the patient will typically feel a sharp, stabbing pain. Palpation of the trigger point may also cause referred pain or reproduce one of his symptoms. (It's always a good thing when we can reproduce a patient's symptoms. That's because typically, if we can reproduce it, we can treat it.) For example, when we palpate a trigger point in the perineum of a male patient, it may reproduce the "golf ball" sensation he feels in his perineum when he sits. To us, a trigger point feels like a lentil, small and hard to the touch. In addition, it may twitch when compressed, and it often feels hotter than the surrounding tissue. We as PTs can use a variety of manual techniques to "release" (get rid of) a trigger point. Sometimes a trigger point can be successfully released in one treatment session, but more often than not, it takes place over multiple PT appointments. Other times, before we can get a trigger point to disappear, we must also work with the patient to clear up any ongoing contributing factors that caused the trigger point to form in the first place, like postural issues, for example.

Our next course of action in the external exam is to check for any impaired nerve mobility and/or nerve sensitivity. We use a few different techniques to evaluate and treat peripheral nerves. For example, we palpate, or lightly touch, peripheral nerves to determine whether they are involved in a patient's symptoms. If a nerve is tender when palpated, that's a clue that it may be part of the problem. Also, when appropriate, we can test whether the nerve has healthy mobility by moving the patient's extremities. For example, we'll bring the patient's knee toward his/her chest while gauging the nerve's reaction. Another way to test the nerve's mobility is to manipulate the connective tissue or muscles surrounding it. If a nerve has normal mobility, neither of these tests should cause pain or discomfort. If there is pain or discomfort, this is another clue that the nerve is likely involved. If a nerve *is* found to have impaired mobility or sensitivity, we use a number of different treatment strategies to resolve the muscle, tissue, and joint impairments contributing to the dysfunction. These treatment techniques involve manual therapy, exercise, and joint mobilizations.

Anatomical/Biomechanical Abnormalities

As we discussed in detail in chapter 2, a number of structural/biomechanical issues can play a role in pelvic pain. To review, some of the main ones are hip labral tears, sacroiliac joint dysfunction, leg length discrepancy, spine dysfunction, motor coordination issues, and dysfunctional posture. In the first evaluation appointment, if appropriate, we will work to figure out if any structural/biomechanical issues are driving the patient's pain. However, when evaluating a patient for structural/ biomechanical abnormalities, the line from impairment to symptom is not always as direct or obvious as with the other impairment groups, such as the defined pain patterns associated with trigger points. For example, say a patient has a symptom of pain in the tailbone and anus with sitting or transitioning from a standing to a sitting position. On the surface it would make sense to look for trigger points or connective tissue restrictions in the area as the culprits. But a structural/biomechanical abnormality could actually be at play, such as sacroiliac joint dysfunction (an SI joint that is "out of alignment") that is altering the mobility of certain branches of the pudendal nerve. Another challenge in connecting any structural/biomechanical abnormality to a patient's symptoms involves spine pathology. Spine pathology is often associated with weakness of the core and the small muscles of the back. If these muscles are weak, the muscles of the pelvic floor will have to overcompensate to provide stability, especially during complex movements, like playing sports or lifting. So say a patient has a disc herniation in his low back that causes him low back pain. If this patient continues to play sports, despite his back issues, some of his pelvic girdle muscles, such as his hip external rotators (obturator internus and piriformis), are going to overcompensate to give him stability during the activities. As a result, these muscles could become too tight or develop trigger points, causing the patient pelvic pain such as pain with sitting or tailbone pain. Assessing patients for any structural/biomechanical abnormalities is especially important if their history reveals things like he/she had a fall prior to the onset of pain or he/she has long-standing orthopedic issues. But it's less relevant for other patients, such as the patient who developed pelvic pain as a result of numerous infections. If the PT does determine that an anatomical/biomechanical issue plays a leading role in a patient's pain, treating it can be a delicate balancing act. That's because more often than not, strengthening exercises and stretches are the treatment techniques involved. And by the time a person presents with pelvic pain, typically he/she has symptom-causing impairments, like trigger points or a too-tight pelvic floor, which may actually become exacerbated as a result of these techniques. So more often than not, the PT may have to first treat the symptom-causing impairment before turning his/her attention to the structural/biomechanical abnormality.

Skin Inspection

Several areas of the skin can give clues about the underlying causes of a patient's pelvic pain. Specifically, we look for these clues on the skin of the perineum, scrotum, and anus in men and the vulva, perineum, and anus in women. We're looking for any number of abnormalities that may correlate with a patient's symptoms. For instance, we're noting whether the skin is red, pale, discolored, blotchy, swollen, fissured, or looks abnormal in any way. Hemorrhoids are another issue we're checking for. This information can give us different clues to what's contributing to a patient's pain. For example, hemorrhoids and anal fissures mean the patient likely has chronic constipation and does a lot of straining, clueing us in that the patient's motor control will likely need to be addressed in PT. Another example is pale vulvar tissue that feels thin or lacks elasticity. This tells us that a patient might have hormonal issues contributing to her pain. In addition to looking at the skin and feeling for any abnormalities, we test for vulvar sensitivity in our female patients by using a test called the "Q-tip" test. Here we use a Q-tip to gently touch areas of the vulva. In an asymptomatic patient, the touch of a Q-tip would be benign. A patient with pelvic pain, however, might have as one of her symptoms irritated vulvar tissue. For this patient, the touch of a Q-tip might be extremely painful. If this is the case, it tells us that nerve, muscle, or tissue dysfunction might be contributing to the hypersensitivity of the patient's vulvar tissue. Lastly, in some patients, it might be relevant to check the reflexes associated with these areas for clues. For example, one reflex associated with the anus is the so-called "anal wink." Indeed, when touched, the anal sphincter is supposed to contract, causing the anus to wink similar to how an eye winks. Another reflex associated with the area involves the clitoris. When touched, the clitoris is supposed to move due to a contraction of the bulbospongiosus and ischiocavernosus muscles. If either of these reflexes is impaired, it might indicate something is occurring with the patient's sacral nerves (the nerves that supply the muscles and tissue responsible for urinary, bowel, and sexual function) and that further diagnostic tests are in order, such as an EMG, nerve conduction velocity test, MRI, or CT scan.

Internal Examination

The final step in the exam is the internal pelvic floor evaluation. Here we're looking for insight into the state of the pelvic floor muscles, pudendal nerve, and the connective tissue that surrounds the urethra in female patients and the prostate in male patients. With the exception of the bulbospongiosus in men, all these muscles can be accessed internally via the vagina or the anus (although some of the muscles, such as the obturator internus and the bulbospongiosus in women, can also be accessed externally). When evaluating the internal muscles of the pelvic floor, we must first assess the patient's overall pelvic floor motor control. When we refer to "motor control" of the pelvic floor, we're talking about whether a person has the ability to perform certain pelvic floor movements when asked. Specifically, we're assessing the ability to contract, relax, and lengthen the muscles. A lack of motor control indicates that the muscles are impaired. Regaining proper motor control is important because it will help improve pelvic floor muscle function and reduce symptoms. From there we assess each muscle of the pelvic floor for tightness, trigger points, and/or tenderness. This is done through gentle palpation. Next, we examine the internal nerves of the pelvic floor. This primarily involves all the branches of the pudendal nerve. When evaluating the pudendal nerve, we want to assess the tenderness of each branch. However, if we find that any of the nerve branches are irritated, we take special care not to further irritate them when treating the surrounding muscles. In addition, we'll work to figure out what, if any, other impairments or contributing factors are causing the irritation. For example, a tight obturator internus muscle might be causing nerve irritation. By treating this muscle we can create a healthy environment for the nerve, causing the nerve irritation to subside. Finally, we examine the connective tissue around the urethra and vulvar tissue in women and the connective tissue near the prostate in men. We're looking for restricted connective tissue.

IF . . . THEN CHECK FOR . . .

At the end of the day, the patient's symptoms lead us in our evaluation, whether we're working externally or internally. And indeed, although each pelvic pain case is different as far as impairments go, patterns do exist. Often it's as straightforward as: if the patient is feeling A, then the PT should seek to rule out B, C, or D. For example, if a woman complains of urethral burning, we'll know to check for impairments in the following areas, because those impairments are often the culprits with this symptom:

- the abdomen, inner/outer thighs, and bony pelvis for connective tissue dysfunction
- the abdominal muscles for trigger points
- the pelvic floor muscles, particularly the pubococcygeus and the periurethral connective tissue for tightness and poor mobility

- the pelvic floor muscles for motor control problems

Below we've compiled a cheat sheet of additional impairment patterns:

If . . . perineal pain in men . . . then check for . . .

- connective tissue dysfunction along the pelvis and in the abdomen and perineum,
- trigger points in the urogenital diaphragm (bulbospongiosus, ischiocavernosus, transverse perineum), accessing the muscles both externally and internally when possible,
- and mobility of the perineal branch of the pudendal nerve.

If . . . pain with sitting . . . then check for . . .

- connective tissue dysfunction in the area of the pain, particularly the tissue around the sit bones, buttocks, and inner thighs and back of the thighs,
- trigger points and/or tightness in the pelvic floor muscles,
- trigger points (internally and externally) in the obturator internus muscle,
- and mobility of the perineal and/or rectal branch of the pudendal nerve.

If . . . pain upon vaginal penetration . . . then check for . . .

- trigger points or tightness in the urogenital diaphragm and adductors,
- connective tissue dysfunction in the vulvar tissue and the inner thighs,
- and mobility of the perineal and/or clitoral branch of the pudendal nerve.

If . . . pain post-ejaculation . . . then check for . . .

- connective tissue dysfunction in the inner thighs and lower abdomen,

- trigger points or tightness in the urogenital diaphragm,
- and mobility of the perineal and/or penile branch of the pudendal nerve.

If . . . tailbone pain . . . then check for . . .

- sacroiliac or sacrococcygeal joint dysfunction,
- trigger points or tightness in the iliococcygeus, pubococcygeus, and coccygeus muscles,
- connective tissue dysfunction in the buttocks, low back, and over the sacrum,
- trigger points in the obturator internus and piriformis muscles,
- and mobility of the inferior rectal branch of the pudendal nerve.

If . . . pain with bowel movements . . . then check for . . .

- trigger points or tightness in the puborectalis muscle and/or external anal sphincter,
- connective tissue dysfunction around the anus and in the buttocks,
- and mobility of the inferior rectal branch of the pudendal nerve.

If . . . urinary urgency/frequency . . . then check for . . .

- connective tissue dysfunction in the inner thighs and abdomen,
- trigger points and/or tightness in the pubococcygeus muscles,
- poor motor control of the pelvic floor muscles,
- and connective tissue dysfunction in the periurethral tissues.

MAKING A PLAN: MANAGING EXPECTATIONS AND SETTING GOALS

What we uncover during the patient evaluation gives us the information we need to start an effective treatment plan. An important part of embarking on a treatment plan with a patient is communicating expectations and goals. Toward that end, at the end of the first evaluation appointment, we give patients a clear idea of what we believe caused the onset of their symptoms, which identified impairments are causing their most bothersome symptoms, and how we're going to treat these impairments. In addition, we talk to the patient about what they can expect from PT, over the short term and over the long term. Obviously, a patient's ultimate goal with PT is to get better, but it's important to set more specific, attainable goals along the way, both long term and short term. For one thing, these goals give both PT and patient a benchmark to evaluate treatment progress. For another thing, setting *short-term* goals is one way to lay out reasonable expectations for the patient, and having reasonable expectations can play a major role in patient compliance and patience with the treatment process. For example, let's take the example of a female triathlete who has urinary urgency and frequency, pain with intercourse, vulvar itching, intolerance to pants, and inability to exercise without an increase in her bladder symptoms. Prior to coming to PT, her symptoms were present for three months following a series of urinary tract and yeast infections. Short-term goals (four to six PT visits) may be:

1. Patient will urinate no more than six to eight times in a 24-hour period.
2. Patient will be able to tolerate wearing loose pants.
3. Patient will not experience daily vulvar itching.

Layer by layer we address the impairments and reach goals. Every eight visits we note the patient's progress and reset the goals as well as the time frame surrounding them.

The set of goals for the next six to eight weeks might be:

1. Patient will be able to engage in intercourse without pain.
2. Patient will be able to run one mile without bladder symptoms.
3. Patient will be able to wear tight pants and jeans without discomfort.

Initially, we may see a patient one to two times per week for six to eight weeks. During this time we expect to see a change in their symptoms, as we are targeting the areas we believe play the largest role in their pain. Many patients reach their goals in three to six months of treatment, but some patients will need to be in treatment for longer, depending on the complexity of their case. Patients with more complex cases, meaning several different layers of contributing factors are involved in their pain, may take longer to reach their goals, like six months to one year. How long a patient has had pain, the severity of their symptoms, other medical issues happening concurrently, and whether a sensitized nervous system is a major component of their pain, all play a role in the rate at which patients improve.

MAKING A PLAN: AN INTERDISCIPLINARY APPROACH

In addition to setting goals with patients following their evaluation appointment, when necessary, we begin the process of making sure they have the right interdisciplinary treatment team in place. If they don't, we help them put one together. For example, if a patient already has providers on board who are helping them, we ask for their contact information so that we can send them our evaluation summary and call them if we have a question, need clarification on a component of their treatment plan, or want to discuss another treatment idea or strategy. Or if we believe a patient would benefit from interventions in addition to PT, we give them the necessary referrals. When suggesting additional treatment options for patients, like trigger point injections, Botox injections, or even medications, we always start with the most conservative treatments, meaning treatments that have the potential for maximum therapeutic benefit with the lowest risk. Once the patient has seen the referred provider or providers, we often get in contact with them to coordinate the best treatment strategy moving forward. Plus, it's always good to hear the other providers' impressions of the patient, so we can figure out if we need to change anything or add something to his/her treatment plan. As we've said before, when it comes to recovering from pelvic pain, working within an interdisciplinary treatment plan provides the greatest chance for our patients to meet their goals. Given that our role as providers is to tackle what is often one of the main drivers of a patient's symptoms and the fact that we'll see patients more frequently and for longer periods than other providers, we're more than willing to act as a facilitator of a patient's interdisciplinary plan.

WHERE THE CENTRAL NERVOUS SYSTEM FITS IN

Because we treat a persistent pain condition, we have to consider what role a sensitized nervous system plays in a patient's pain. Several clues can tip us off to whether a patient's sensitized central nervous system is behind his/her pain. For example, the patient may have a hard time describing the pain or where it's located. They may say something like, "It just kind of hurts all over." Another clue is if the patient's pain symptoms are spontaneous, meaning they seemingly occur without cause or an inciting activity. Lastly, the pain may be untrackable, meaning the patient can't really tell when it is going to flare up or why it happens. We begin uncovering what role the patient's central nervous system is playing in his/her pain during the initial evaluation interview. For example, a patient might tell us her pain started as pain with intercourse, then it evolved into constant vaginal pain, then the whole lower part of her body started to hurt, then she began having upper body pain, and now "everything" hurts. Now she can't even hold her partner's hand without increased vaginal pain, and any activity will increase it; six months ago, when her symptoms first started, she could still tolerate light exercise. When we're taking a patient's history, this kind of information indicates clearly that the nervous system is sensitized. In addition to altering the way we approach the patient's evaluation, if we determine a sensitized nervous system is heavily involved in a patient's pain, we work to figure out what other providers we can refer him/her to. Sometimes when patients hear that their pain might have a central nervous system component, they panic, wrongly believing it means nothing can be done for their symptoms. This couldn't be further from the truth! A number of treatment options are designed to treat a sensitized nervous system, from medication to acupuncture to a plethora of other techniques. (We provide more details about these in chapter 8.) While typically pain management doctors or psychologists have treated this issue, to date, a growing number of PTs are beginning to incorporate it into their therapy. Indeed, many pelvic floor PTs, us included, incorporate one particular technique into their treatment: pain education. To be sure, pain education has been proven to change the way patients perceive pain. In addition, it helps them overcome catastrophic thinking and fear avoidance behaviors, which in turn can alter their pain perception. At our clinics, we do a great deal of one-on-one pain physiology education with our patients during appointments. Not only do we ourselves discuss the information with them, we also refer them to a variety of well-vetted resources. Below is a list of a few of these resources:

- "Understanding Pain in Five Minutes," a video by the Body in Mind research team at the University of South Australia that's accessible at https://www.youtube.com/watch?v=4b8oB757DKc.
- "Why Things Hurt," a TED talk by neuroscientist Lorimer Moseley, Ph.D., of Samson Institute for Health Research at the University of South Australia, accessible at https://www.youtube.com/watch?v=gwd-wLdIHjs.
- *Explain Pain*, a book by David Butler, Australian physiotherapist and clinical researcher, and Lorimer Moseley (see appendix A).
- *Painful Yarns*, a book by Lorimer Moseley (see appendix A).
- *Understand Pain, Live Well Again* by Neil Pearson, which is available as a pamphlet as well as a PowerPoint presentation.

EVALUATION DAY: TAMRA'S STORY

Some might deem canceling a highly invasive surgery and deciding to fly out to San Francisco to see a PT recommended by online blog readers quite crazy. However, it turned out to be the best decision I ever made. I guess it makes sense to start at the beginning. I went to see Liz at PHRC because I had been suffering from unexplained vulvar and vaginal burning for several months. I immediately got a good feeling when I walked into the clinic because they had fancy cushions on their waiting room chairs. Imagine that—providing cushions for patients who have chronic pain problems! My appointment began with about 20 minutes of just talking about my medical history and previous symptoms. I basically filled Liz in on the past year and three months. In addition, she wanted to know my other medical history, like the fact that I was born with an inverted hip bone on my left side. After our talk she began the examination. The next hour she proceeded to do intense therapy on me. She began by doing external therapy, stimulating my muscles and connective tissue around the pelvic area. If you imagine the vagina as a triangle, she branched out on all three sides. "Massaging" isn't the proper word; it was harder than that. Liz called it "connective tissue manipulation" or "skin rolling." Certain parts were pretty painful, but tolerable. What is interesting is that I was in much more pain on the left side than the right. And indeed, Liz noticed my left side's muscles and tissue were much tighter. This point was further observed upon the inside examination and therapy. Her theory is that my left hip was never corrected when I was a child and may have initiated muscle imbalances, which my body compensated for so I could walk, but which have now evolved into pelvic floor dysfunction. The muscle imbalances cause my nerves to be hypersensitive, she said, and since a lot of nerves congregate around the pelvic floor, that's where I'm feeling the effects. The internal therapy hurt a lot in the beginning, but slowly I began to relax and not feel as much. Liz said she felt my muscles relax and respond to the treatment a few times, which is good news for my first PT appointment. The entire appointment took over two hours, and I learned a lot from Liz. She referred me to a PT in my city and she said she believed that with regular PT, in a year I would be fully recovered. To her, fully healed means "no cushion, bike riding, tampon using, sexually functioning, no pain ever again" recovered. Following my appointment, Liz e-mailed me an "evaluation summary," which listed all of her findings as well as her proposed treatment plan. I'm excited to pass this along to the PT I will see locally.

To wrap up, I just want to jot down some other points I took away from that first session:

- I've been wearing 100% cotton bikini underwear, but apparently the elastic is too tight for me. Elastic-less underwear will likely be less irritating.
- Liz said I would be sore a couple of days after therapy, especially externally. (She said it would feel like I had worked out really hard.) This was definitely true. It's been two days since therapy, and I'm still very sore. It seems to be worse along my two bikini lines and right below my top underwear line. But I like being sore, because I like feeling that progress is being made.
- PT is not a magic switch that's going to cure my pain in one day. Slowly my symptoms will begin to improve, and I will feel a decrease in pain levels.

A TYPICAL PELVIC PAIN PT TREATMENT SESSION

Now that we've covered the evaluation appointment, it's time to take a look at a typical pelvic pain PT session. At the beginning of a typical PT session, we walk into the room with the patient dressed and ask him/her pertinent questions to guide the treatment session. One important bit of information we want to get from patients is a description of their symptoms after their last treatment. We especially want to know how those first two or three days were after treatment. This is important for a few reasons. For one thing, oftentimes we'll focus our treatment for the day based on their response and what is bothering them the most. For another thing, it allows us to educate patients about reasonable expectations. For instance, if a patient is sore, we'll explain why that might be. (Soreness is common following PT, and while unpleasant, it is to be expected. Our patients often report that they feel "bruised.") On the other hand, an increase in their actual symptoms is obviously undesirable. When dealing with any pain syndrome, however, well-intended techniques can cause an increase in symptoms. These are typically transient and should resolve within 48 hours. If symptoms are better or worse after treatment, this tells us that we're targeting the right areas. Similar to the history, we want to know about the patient's most bothersome symptoms since the last appointment. For instance, if the patient has had pain with sex, we'll ask whether sex was possible. If it was, we'll want to know if anything was different about the experience. We'll want to know whether the pain was less in intensity, less in duration, or in a different area. A pelvic pain syndrome typically develops slowly over time, and the treatment process often follows suit. To be sure, a major symptom rarely goes away after one treatment. Rather, symptoms gradually become less bothersome after a series of treatments. And typically dysfunction changes before pain. For example, a patient with pudendal neuralgia may have burning perineal pain when sitting, and urinary hesitancy and frequency. The hesitancy and frequency may resolve completely as the burning pain with sitting declines over time. Clearly the burning pain is more bothersome, but the resolution of the urinary symptoms is a hint that things are improving. We typically spend the hour with a combination of manual therapy techniques, motor control exercises, and home program development. At the end of the appointment we review the overall game plan with the patient. For instance, we want them to know what changes to expect based on the techniques we used as well as the symptoms we expect to be unchanged based on what we didn't address. On the patient's end, their role is to comply with their home treatment program and lifestyle modifications we give them. And we encourage our patients to contact us immediately with any questions or concerns that come up between appointments.

MALE PELVIC PAIN: TREATING MEN RIGHT

As we've already made clear throughout the book, pelvic pain doesn't discriminate between the sexes. While it may be more prevalent in women for a variety of reasons—childbirth, vaginal infections, and hormonal fluctuations being the biggest—it is NOT a women's health issue! Men get it too. But when treating the condition, men with pelvic pain face their own set of challenges. For one thing, medical providers systematically misdiagnose any pelvic pain symptoms in men, including perineal pain, post-ejaculatory pain, urinary frequency, or penile pain, as a prostate infection, despite the absence of virus or bacteria. Typically the absence of a virus or bacteria simply means a switch in diagnosis from "prostate infection, or prostatitis" to "chronic nonbacterial prostatitis." And from there men are often prescribed antibiotics. In the beginning, because antibiotics have an analgesic effect, patients can actually feel a small improvement in symptoms. But before long, this effect wears off, and they're right back where they started. This situation exists despite the fact that in 1995, the National Institutes of Health (NIH) clearly stated that the diagnosis "chronic nonbacterial prostatitis" is incorrect for the symptoms of pelvic pain. To describe the symptoms, the NIH adopted the term "chronic pelvic pain syndrome." The symptoms the NIH listed for pelvic pain in men are painful urination, hesitancy, and frequency; penile, scrotal, anal, and perineal pain; and bowel and sexual dysfunction. On top of all that, despite the proven efficacy of PT for the treatment of pelvic pain, male patients as a whole have a harder time gaining access to a qualified pelvic floor PT. That's because not all pelvic floor PTs treat men. To date, the majority of pelvic floor PTs are women, and many female pelvic floor PTs are uncomfortable treating men. For some female PTs, it simply boils down to their not being comfortable dealing with the penis and scrotum. Among their qualms:

What if the patient gets an erection? How do I deal with that? Coming from a practice where about 30% of our patients are men with pelvic pain, here's our advice. If a male patient does get an erection, address it with a simple "Don't worry, it happens." And move on. But some female PTs are hesitant to treat male patients because they've received little to no training in treating the male pelvic floor. The good news is that in the past few years postgraduate-level classes (one of the main ways any PT receives education on pelvic floor rehabilitation) that focus on treating the male pelvic floor have become available for PTs, and more and more pelvic floor PTs are treating male patients. This is a big step in the right direction.

JUSTIN'S STORY

When I was 26, I woke up one day with urinary symptoms. Basically, I had a weak stream and felt as if I wasn't voiding completely. I also had a sensation in my urethra that's hard to describe. It wasn't pain, just a feeling of something being not quite right. Because the issue was urinary, I visited a urologist. The first doctor suspected either a prostate infection or a sexually transmitted disease. But all tests and cultures for either of those diagnoses came back negative. Nonetheless, the doctor diagnosed me as having "prostatitis," which is an infection of the prostate, and prescribed a course of antibiotics. When the medication didn't clear up my symptoms, I made an appointment with a second urologist, with the same outcome. In the course of a year, I saw about ten urologists, each of whom gave me a different course of antibiotics for "prostatitis" despite the fact that test after test came back negative for infection. After a year of urinary symptoms, the severity of which would wax and wane, I woke up one morning in the most pain I had ever been in in my life. It felt as if someone was stabbing me in the testicle with a knife. On top of that, I was having shooting pains in my anus and abdomen. The shooting pain was so severe, it literally sent me to my knees. I called two of the urologists I had the most faith in, and both said I was having "complications of prostatitis." At that point, I lost faith in these doctors' opinions as well as in the diagnosis of "prostatitis." Desperate for relief, I began searching online for answers. I focused my search on the prostate because I had never heard of pelvic pain, or the pelvic floor for that matter. In my search, I found an out-of-state doctor who was treating symptoms like mine by removing the prostate. Despite the possible side effects that come with that surgery—impotence, incontinence—I was in so much pain that I was seriously considering going that route. Eventually, the shooting pains disappeared, but I was left with constant testicular pain. Not knowing what was wrong was terrifying. Also, I had always been a very active person—very exercise conscious—but because of the pain and my fear of doing something to make it worse, I stopped working out completely. In fact, I stopped doing anything active and began to spend a lot of time either on the sofa or in bed. Thankfully, in the course of my research, I happened upon a pelvic pain online support group, and that's where I first learned about pelvic pain as well as pelvic floor PT. So I made an appointment with a PT on the East Coast, where I lived at the time, and began treatment. PT didn't help right away. Even though I was a super-compliant patient, it took about a year of regular PT and diligence with a home program for me to begin getting my life back. During that first year of PT, I lugged around a cushion everywhere I went for sitting and spent a lot of my time either on my sofa or in bed. I stopped drinking alcohol and caffeine, and I wasn't eating spicy foods because I was afraid all these things were contributing to my pain. And because of my pain and my anxiety surrounding it, I barely did anything social or that I enjoyed. My every waking moment became completely dictated by my pain. A big turning point came when I decided I needed to stop focusing on my symptoms and stop worrying that this would be something I would have for the rest of my life. That realization was life changing for me. That very week I went out with friends and had a couple of drinks, and thought, "Okay, I can have a normal life here." My mentality changed from that time forward. I found immediately that the less time I spent focusing on my pelvic pain, the better it got, and in turn the less I thought about it. I even began exercising again. I started swimming. It was an activity that allowed me to be active without flaring my symptoms. Then about a year into my pelvic pain, I moved to Los Angeles and began treatment with Stephanie at PHRC. By that time I was about 85% better, but I still had the testicular pain. It was improved, but was still there. What Stephanie found was that I lacked the motor control to relax my pelvic floor. Without the ability to do this, pelvic floor muscles will remain tight and become even tighter with exercise, thus continuing to produce pain. The first thing she taught me to do was relax my pelvic floor. Also, she found unresolved trigger points in several muscles that can cause testicular pain. So that's what we focused on in treatment. *So why did my symptoms start to begin with?* Stephanie's theory is that a combination of factors set off my pain. For one thing, I'm a super-active guy who's worked out hard with various trainers over the years. Add to that a history of low back pain, and voilà! Pelvic pain! After a few months of weekly PT with Stephanie, I am now pain-free. It was quite a journey! I learned a lot about myself along the way that I'll carry with me for the rest of my life. The benefits of relaxation and meditation are the most beneficial lesson I learned. I'm not really a spiritual person, but I now get how the mind-body connection works. I now have the tools to get stress out of my life, even if it's just for a few minutes a day. I know how to relax and be quiet, and I now understand that my mind has a huge impact on what happens with my body, and that I can work to control it. And another of the more interesting things that came out of my pelvic pain journey was learning just how common a problem it is. As soon as I began talking to others about what was happening with me, people I knew with pelvic pain issues or who knew someone who had pelvic pain issues began coming out of the woodwork, giving me a chance to share what I learned on my own journey. And basically that's number one: you need to see a qualified pelvic floor PT; and number two, recovery isn't going to be immediate, so you need to try your best to do whatever it takes to continue to live your life.

CONCLUSION

In this chapter, we've provided a look inside the PT treatment room. However, PT is but one treatment option available to those with pelvic pain. As we've already discussed in earlier chapters of the book, the most effective approach to treating pelvic pain is interdisciplinary, involving all appropriate providers. In the next chapter, we will discuss many of the treatment options offered by these other providers.

6

GUIDE TO NAVIGATING TREATMENT OPTIONS

Besides PT, a variety of treatment options exist for pelvic pain. Having options is always a good thing, but often, deciding what treatments to try, and at what point during recovery, can be challenging. Due to the multilayered nature of pelvic pain, more often than not, the best approach to deciding between treatment options is a nuanced one that takes many factors into consideration—factors such as timing and whether certain treatments are best undertaken in combination with others. However, often these nuances are overlooked, and patients fall into a trap of either throwing everything but the kitchen sink at their pain—never a good approach because trying too many different treatments at once can be costly and lead to feelings of hopelessness and despair if symptoms persist—or giving up on certain treatments too soon because their expectations were off the mark. To help avoid these and other treatment pitfalls, we're devoting an entire chapter to how best to navigate the variety of different options now available to treat pelvic pain. We begin the chapter with a survey of the other treatment options, besides PT. From there, we'll explore what we consider to be the best strategy for navigating these different treatments. Finally, we'll end the chapter with a discussion on handling conflicting treatment advice from providers.

PELVIC PAIN TREATMENTS: A GUIDE

Dry Needling

Dry needling is a technique whereby fine needles are introduced into trigger points. The introduction of the needle into the trigger point "disrupts" the trigger point, helping to eradicate it. Medication is not used in conjunction with the placement of the needle. We consider this a safe and effective treatment option to eliminate trigger points. If this option is available to you, we suggest working it into your treatment plan, as most people with pelvic pain have problematic trigger points. Several different medical providers can perform dry needling, such as acupuncturists, physicians, nurse practitioners, physician assistants, and in most states, PTs.[1]

Injections

A few different injections exist to treat pelvic pain. The most common are trigger point injections, Botox injections, and nerve blocks. See the list below for a brief description of each.

- Trigger point injections: an anesthetic or anesthetic/steroid combination solution is injected into a trigger point. The theory behind the effectiveness of trigger point injections is that the introduction of the needle into the trigger point "deactivates" the trigger point, helping to eradicate it. The anesthetic used in the injection doesn't make the treatment more effective, it simply makes it more comfortable for the patient by numbing the area after the injection. A growing body of research supports the use of trigger point injections in the treatment of trigger points for pelvic pain. Physicians, physician assistants, and nurse practitioners can administer trigger point injections.[2]

When working to decide if trigger point injections are right for your treatment plan, you should ask your PT and/or physician the following questions:

1. *Which of my muscles have trigger points, and which of these, if any, do you think are contributing to my symptoms?* As we discussed in previous chapters, trigger points are a common impairment behind the symptoms of pelvic pain. However, just because a trigger point is present, doesn't mean it's relevant for a patient's most bothersome symptoms. Your provider can help you figure out if an identified trigger point is likely affecting your symptoms and if so, whether trigger point injections are an appropriate treatment approach.

2. *Do you think I should first try PT or dry needling to treat my trigger points before trying trigger point injections?* We always encourage patients to approach treatment using more conservative options first, and then to move to more invasive procedures if the conservative treatments are not effective. Typically, if we identify trigger points in our patients that do not respond to manual PT techniques in four to six appointments, that's when we recommend trigger point injections.

- Botox injections: botulinum toxin type A (Botox), a toxin produced by the bacterium *Clostridium botulinum*, is injected into a muscle with the aim of decreasing "muscle spasm," aka muscle contraction. Here's how: Botox acts as a nerve impulse "blocker," which prevents the release of chemical transmitters in charge of activating the muscle. By blocking these transmitters, the message to contract doesn't get to the muscle; therefore, the muscle doesn't spasm or contract. After about three months the medication is no longer active. Botox is a treatment option for too-tight pelvic floor muscles. It's typically used when muscles don't respond to conservative treatment, such as PT, or in cases where when coupled with PT, it can help hasten recovery. The jury is still out on possible long-term and short-term side effects of Botox injections for pelvic pain. When deciding if Botox injections are right for your treatment plan, we've compiled a list of questions worth considering.

1. *Which of my muscles are "too tight," and which of these, if any, are contributing to my symptoms?* It's a good idea to ask your providers, either your PT or your physician, or both this question

to pinpoint if the muscles you're considering having Botoxed are indeed the muscles contributing to your symptoms.

2. *What are the risks of the injections?* In general, risks of Botox injections include urinary, gas, and fecal incontinence. This is especially the case when muscles around the urethral and anal sphincters are injected. When other muscles are injected, this potential side effect is not as much of a concern. A second potential side effect is that the muscles adjacent to the treated muscles may begin to compensate for the relaxation of their neighbors, causing new symptoms. Plus, there is the risk of the treatment causing an increase in pain.

3. *Is the therapeutic benefit worth the cost?* A limited number of providers offer Botox injections as a treatment for pelvic pain, necessitating travel. Also, most of the muscles injected for pelvic pain are not FDA approved; therefore, this procedure may not be covered by insurance. So when deciding whether to pursue Botox, patients often have to weigh financial factors into their decision.

4. *Am I going to have to keep getting these injections every three months to maintain the therapeutic benefits?* As mentioned above, the effects of Botox typically wear off after about three months. Typically, during that three-month window when the muscle/muscles are more relaxed, other treatments, such as PT, are administered, and the combination of treatments allows for expedited gains toward recovery. However, this is not always the case, and injections may need to be repeated in certain cases.

- Nerve blocks: medication is injected around a specific nerve for various purposes. These injections can contain an anesthetic (numbing medication) only or an anesthetic combined with a steroid (anti-inflammatory medication). In the context of treating pelvic pain, nerve blocks are typically used for three different purposes:

- as a therapeutic treatment to try to control acute nerve pain,
- as a diagnostic tool to try to determine the source of a particular symptom,
- or as a prognostic indicator to determine if a more permanent treatment (such as surgery) would be successful in treating symptoms.

If you have nerve-like pain (burning, stabbing, shooting) in a particular distribution of a specific nerve branch, a nerve block may be appropriate.

However, within the pelvic pain provider community, a wide array of opinions exist surrounding the effectiveness of nerve blocks as well as when and how they should be administered. For example, different opinions exist as to exactly what medications should be used in the blocks. And very little research is available to clear up these questions. So when deciding whether a nerve block is right for you, we recommend you ask the provider recommending the treatment exactly what he/she expects to achieve with the block. Specific questions to ask include:

- What is the exact purpose of the block? Is it to decrease symptoms or for diagnostic purposes?
- What are the potential side effects of the injection? Is it possible that it may increase my symptoms?
- If the purpose of the block is to lessen symptoms, to what degree and how long with the relief last?

Topical Options

A variety of topical medications are commonly prescribed for people dealing with pelvic pain. The majority of these medications are prescribed to female patients, as they are targeted to vulvar or vaginal tissue. One of the more common of these medications is topical estrogen, which is prescribed when estrogen levels are not at optimal levels, causing problems for a woman's vulvar tissue or vagina. Another common topical medication used to treat pelvic pain, particularly in women, is lidocaine. Lidocaine is an anesthetic, or numbing agent, which in ointment or cream form can be applied to areas of hypersensitivity or pain. For example, women with vulvar pain can apply it to the areas of their vulva that are painful or hypersensitive, enabling them to wear underwear or jeans with less discomfort. Some women with pelvic pain use it in place of, or in addition to, lubrication during intercourse to decrease the pain or hypersensitivity they feel during penetration. Other topical medications used to treat pelvic pain are compounded medications. A compounded medication includes several medications mixed together in one ointment or cream that can then be applied to the skin and/or vulvar tissue. These compounded medications can combine an anesthetic, like lidocaine; an anticonvulsant, like gabapentin; a muscle relaxer, like baclofen; a tricyclic, like amitriptyline; and/or a pain medication, like ketamine. However, these medications are not commonly prescribed by the average gynecologist or primary care physician, so seeking a consult with a pelvic pain specialist may be the best course of action if you want to try a compounded medication. Currently, research does not exist as to the efficacy of these compounded medications for treating pelvic pain symptoms.

Medications

Four categories of medications are commonly used to treat the various symptoms of pelvic pain. They are:

- neuropathic analgesics,
- anticonvulsants,
- N-methyl-D-aspartate (NMDA) antagonists,
- and benzodiazepines.

Neuropathic analgesics are antidepressant medications used to treat neuropathic pain. Examples are tricyclics and mixed reuptake inhibitors, or SNRIs. Tricyclic antidepressants are widely used for treating pelvic pain. Amitriptyline is the most commonly studied and has been shown to be an effective treatment for neuropathic pain.[3] Anticonvulsants have been used in pain management for many years. The two most common examples used to treat persistent pain are gabapentin (Neurontin) and pregabalin (Lyrica). Gabapentin has been reported to be well tolerated and an effective treatment in various pain conditions, particularly in neuropathic pain.[4] NMDA antagonists have also been useful in treating persistent pain conditions.[5] Ketamine is one example of this group of medications. Benzodiazepines are often used for treating symptoms such as anxiety, sleep difficulties, and muscle spasm. A commonly prescribed benzodiazepine is diazepam, or Valium. This medication can be taken orally, or as many people with pelvic pain take it, by vaginal or rectal suppository. In fact, several of the above-mentioned medications, such as neurontin and amitriptyline, can also be administered in suppository form either individually or as a compounded combination. A word about opiates to treat pelvic pain: according to the National Guideline Clearinghouse, a public resource for evidence-based clinical practice guidelines, the role of opiates for the treatment of pelvic pain is limited, and they should only be started in consultation with all parties involved (including the patient's family practitioner). National guidelines exist and should be followed. There is a growing understanding of the limitations of opioid use, and more recently, the paradoxical situation of opioid-induced hyperalgesia. Recent research shows that the above-mentioned classes of medications are more effective and safer for patients with nonmalignant pain.[6]

It's important for patients and their team to work together to figure out if and when certain medications are appropriate. In certain cases, the side effects or cost may outweigh the therapeutic benefit. What's more, although the medications discussed above have strong research to support their effectiveness for treating pain, exactly what this means will vary widely from patient to patient. For one patient, a certain medication will greatly impact his/her symptoms, but for another it may simply allow him/her to tolerate other treatments or prevent his/her nervous system from becoming more sensitized than it already is. Another important consideration is the therapeutic dose of the medication and the length of time needed to achieve that dose. For instance, it's possible that a medication appeared ineffective to a patient because he/she wasn't on a high enough dose and/or took the medication for too short a period of time, not giving it a chance to "kick in."

Neuromodulation

Neuromodulation is a technology that acts directly on nerves by altering or modulating their activity, delivering electrical stimulation to specific nerve distributions. The three kinds of neuromodulation most commonly used for the treatment of pelvic pain are tibial nerve stimulation, sacral neuromodulation, and pudendal nerve stimulation. Tibial nerve stimulation is done weekly on an outpatient basis for 12 weeks. It has been primarily used for urinary dysfunction, but emerging research suggests it may be a safe, minimally invasive, and inexpensive treatment option for pelvic pain.[7] While minimally invasive, tibial nerve stimulation is limited by patients needing to make weekly visits for treatment.

Sacral neuromodulation has been used successfully for many years for urinary dysfunction, and again, some promising research has supported its use for pelvic pain, but the jury is definitely still out on its effectiveness.[8]

Sacral neuromodulation is performed by implanting an electrical stimulating device on the third sacral nerve root, which carries information, including pain, to the brain. Pudendal nerve stimulation is a newer form of neuromodulation currently being studied and used experimentally. Instead of implanting the stimulating device onto the sacral nerve, the device is placed directly on the pudendal nerve, which also carries pain information from the pelvis to the brain. No determined protocol states when a person should consider neuromodulation. In most cases of both sacral and pudendal neuromodulation, a one-week trial is performed where the stimulator remains on the skin, but the patient can still determine if it causes pain relief. If relief is obtained, the device gets surgically implanted onto the nerve or nerve root. These procedures are often covered by insurance and may be worth considering if a patient's pain is not responding to more conservative treatments.

Continuous or Pulsed Radiofrequency

Continuous and pulsed radiofrequency use current to destroy tissue that carries pain signals. With continuous radiofrequency the current is applied continuously during treatment, whereas with pulsed radiofrequency it's applied using brief "pulses." The current is applied to the nerve itself through the skin via a needle. The theory is that eliminating fibers that cause pain will reduce symptoms for patients. Recent literature has shown that pulsed radiofrequency is safer than continuous radiofrequency.[9] However, to date, research regarding whether it's an effective treatment for pelvic pain is lacking.

Surgical Treatment Options

As we've discussed throughout this book, conservative treatment for pelvic pain is always the first and most desirable treatment approach. However, surgical intervention is necessary in some situations. As we've already discussed, many different contributing factors can be involved in pelvic pain. At times surgery is needed to treat a specific contributing factor. For example, surgery may be necessary to treat an underlying gynecological condition or an orthopedic issue. Because so many different surgeries are associated with the factors that can contribute to pelvic pain, it's impossible for us to cover all of them in this book; however, we would like to review a handful of the more commonly performed surgical procedures associated with pelvic pain, including pudendal nerve decompression surgery, a vestibulectomy, a laparoscopy, and surgical mesh removal. Below is a brief description of each.

Pudendal nerve decompression surgery

When the pudendal nerve becomes compressed or "entrapped," the condition is referred to as pudendal nerve entrapment or PNE, and the surgery used to release the nerve is called pudendal nerve decompression surgery. Symptoms of PNE are typically the same as symptoms of pudendal neuralgia and include stabbing, shooting, or burning pain anywhere along the trajectory of the pudendal nerve. The pudendal nerve can become entrapped in a variety of different ways; for example, as the result of surgery, such as when mesh is used to correct a prolapse, or as a result of scar tissue formation, such as from childbirth or a fall to the buttock area. Because there is no way to definitively diagnose PNE, it's a diagnosis of exclusion. In making the diagnosis, consideration of a patient's history is key. And the main indicator as to whether he/she has an entrapped nerve is whether a traumatic event or events have taken place. Besides the patient history, surgeons use several diagnostic tests to help them·determine, along with a patient history and evaluation, whether someone is a good candidate for surgery. However, at the end of the day, it's impossible for a physician to say with 100% certainty that a nerve is entrapped. And even when entrapment is suspected, often patients are initially steered toward more conservative treatments, such as Botox injections, nerve blocks, medication to reduce nerve hypersensitivity, PT, and lifestyle changes, such as limiting sitting or other physical activities that increase pain. If those treatments are unsuccessful and a patient opts for surgery, there is no guarantee that it will be successful. If a patient does go the surgery route, he/she will likely need to continue to pursue other treatments as well. In fact, the biggest impact of the surgery may be that it allows other treatments, like nerve blocks or PT, to be more successful by decreasing nerve irritation. For more detailed information about pudendal nerve decompression surgery, check out a Q&A on our blog with the two top surgeons who perform the operation in the United States: Dr. Mark Conway, attending gynecologist and pelvic surgeon at St. Joseph's Hospital in Nashua, New Hampshire; and Dr. Michael Hibner, the director of the Arizona Center for Chronic Pelvic Pain at St. Joseph's Hospital and Medical Center in Phoenix. (See http://www.pelvicpainrehab.com/pelvic-pain/1893/pne-your-questions-answered/ and http://www.pelvicpainrehab.com/pelvic-pain/1901/pne-your-questions-answered-part-ii/.)

Vestibulectomy

This is a surgical procedure indicated for certain women with localized provoked vestibulodynia (pain in the vestibule when touched or provoked) when more conservative treatment measures have failed. During the procedure, the surgeon removes the painful tissue. As with many of the surgical treatment options for pelvic pain, this procedure is rife with controversy within the medical community. What is most important in opting for this surgical treatment is determining whether or not you're an appropriate candidate. For the most part, that means that the patient's pain is coming from the inflamed vestibular tissue only and not from other contributing factors. Indeed, research has shown that for the right candidate, a vestibulectomy can be effective.[10] If you're a woman with provoked vestibulodynia and have failed conservative treatment, you may benefit from consulting with a pelvic pain specialist to determine if you are a good candidate for this treatment option.

Laparoscopy

Laparoscopy is a surgical procedure that uses a thin, lighted tube inserted through the belly to view or remove abdominal organs and/or female pelvic organs. The procedure is performed for many pelvic-pain-related reasons, such as removing organs like the uterus, removing abnormal growths like tumors or fibroids, or removing unwanted or pathological tissue like endometriosis. A decision on laparoscopy as a treatment option for a persistent pelvic-pain-related contributing factor needs to be carefully made under the guidance of a pelvic pain specialist.

Surgical mesh removal

Surgical mesh is a synthetic material that is commonly used in the surgical repair of hernias and some pelvic floor disorders. Mesh has received a lot of attention in the media lately for postsurgical complications associated with its use. Some of those complications can cause pelvic pain and therefore, a surgical procedure may be warranted to remove all or part of the mesh. One recent study examined the effects on pelvic pain after mesh revision or removal, and 73% of women reported an improvement in pain, 8% that their pain increased, and 19% reported that their pain was unchanged.[11] If you developed pelvic pain after a surgical procedure that involved mesh, we strongly encourage you to seek a consultation with a pelvic pain specialist to discuss your treatment options.

TREATING A SENSITIZED NERVOUS SYSTEM

In the past, when it was determined that a sensitized nervous system played a role in a patient's pain, the main line of treatment was medication. Fast-forward to today. While medication remains a viable option, these days a slew of other treatments are available to dial down a sensitized nervous system. These treatments are predicated on the fact that many cognitive processes play a role in how we perceive pain—processes like thoughts, emotions, and beliefs. So anxiety, stress, catastrophic thinking, fear avoidance—all these emotions/patterns of thinking—can impact how we perceive pain. Now that's not to say your pain is all in your head, and if you'll only "stop stressing and relax," it'll go away. If only it were that simple! No, what we're saying is that the brain is 100% responsible for how we perceive pain, and other things that go on in the brain—thoughts, emotions, beliefs—can impact that perception. By working to alter these cognitive processes, you can dial down a sensitized nervous system, and thus your pain. That's not to say it's an easy undertaking or it's a process that works overnight. Turning down the volume on a sensitized nervous system often takes time and commitment. And you don't have to figure it out on your own. Many patients turn to a psychologist to help them put a plan together. Plus, as we mentioned in the previous chapter, pelvic floor PTs can also play a role in the process, namely by educating patients on the physiology of their pain in order to remove some of the anxiety and fear surrounding it. In addition, they can identify certain thought patterns and behaviors, like catastrophic thinking or fear avoidance, and both address them with the patient and refer him/her to a psychologist or other appropriate provider. Below are some techniques commonly used to treat a sensitized nervous system. (Note: it's far from a definitive list!)

- Changing thought patterns, such as catastrophic thinking or fear avoidance around certain activities
- Relaxation training: these techniques are aimed at calming down the nervous system on a body-wide level with activities such as meditation, tai chi, yoga, deep breathing techniques, acupuncture, massage, and hypnosis.
- Guided imagery: this technique is designed more toward targeting the exact location of a patient's symptoms. Guided imagery directs thoughts and suggestions toward a relaxed and focused state. While a provider can walk you through guided imagery, you can also use tapes or a script. For instance, a DVD called *Guided Imagery for Women with Pelvic Pain, Interstitial Cystitis or Vulvodynia* is available for pelvic pain patients. For more information on this DVD, go to http://www.healthjourneys.com/Store/Products/Guided-Imagery-for-Women-with-Pelvic-Pain-Interstitial-Cystitis-or-Vulvodynia/527.
- Addressing sleep dysfunction: not getting enough rest is detrimental to a sensitized nervous system, so getting a good night's sleep regularly is a must.

COGNITIVE BEHAVIORAL THERAPY

Cognitive behavioral therapy (CBT) is a form of psychotherapy designed to treat problems by changing negative thinking, emotions, and thoughts. Those dealing with pelvic pain can often benefit from CBT. For one thing, it can help change their emotional responses to pain as well as any negative behavior patterns surrounding their pain. The desired outcome of CBT is to reduce distress for the patient while improving daily functioning by arming them with tools for coping and problem solving. Many of the treatment strategies used in CBT overlap with those for treating a sensitized nervous system. The main differentiator is that the goal with CBT is to improve a patient's outlook and daily functioning, while treating a sensitized nervous system is about changing how his/her brain is processing pain. However, ultimately, achieving the goals of the former will help toward achieving the goals of the latter.

Reprogramming My Sensitized Nervous System: Olivia's Story

My pain began after a routine gynecological surgery, which was followed by an undiagnosed vaginal bacterial infection that lasted for several months. My main symptoms were sit bone pain and pain down the back of my leg, plus an awful, prickly vulvar pain. About a year and a half into my symptoms, I traveled out-of-state to visit Stephanie, who found trigger points in my hip muscles and one in my right bulbospongiosus muscle, severe connective tissue restriction on my thighs and vulvar tissue, as well as some nerve irritation of my posterior femoral cutaneous nerve. When I got back home, I continued PT with a local therapist. In addition, I saw a chiropractor and used a topical nerve cream on my vulvar tissue and the back of my legs. As a result of these treatments, my sit bone pain and the pain down the back of my legs resolved. However, the awful prickly sensation I felt on my vulva persisted. I was two years into this pain, and it was really preventing me from living a normal life. Discouraged and frustrated, I began to research the central nervous system, chronic pain, and anxiety. I also started to see a health psychologist. (Health psychology is a specialty that focuses on how biological, social, and psychological factors influence health and illness.) My health psychologist confirmed what I was starting to figure out on my own. My fear of my symptoms was continuing my pain cycle, and in order to fully recover, I'd have to work to heal my nervous system. This was a huge breakthrough for me. But I knew it wasn't going to be easy. The first thing I did was take a break from PT and the chiropractor so that I could focus on my mental and emotional well-being. I knew I could always return to either at any time. My biggest problems from an emotional standpoint were that I had tremendous anxiety and hypervigilance around my symptoms. Even though I was feeling better and my day-to-day life had improved, I simply couldn't stop thinking about my pain. It was always in the back of my mind, affecting everything I did. The first thing I did to overcome this was to pick up a copy of a book titled *Hope and Help for Your Nerves* by Claire Weekes. The book helped me understand the nervous system and how to heal it. With the help of my therapist and the book, I began working to allow my symptoms to just be, without the tension and fear I invariably heaped on top of them. I had come to realize that this tension and fear was continuing my pain cycle by keeping my nervous system aroused. I also started wearing underwear, a pain trigger for me, every day, even if it was just for an hour. I needed my mind and body to remember that underwear was not a threat. Although it took several weeks, ultimately, wearing underwear began to feel normal again. I took the same approach to sitting. When I would have symptoms with sitting, I'd say to myself, "I feel this or that, and that's okay because there is no injury. It's just my nervous system." I also worked to keep myself busy and not focus on my pain while going about my day. Plus, I gave myself breaks to just relax. I even allowed myself at least one nap a day to make sure I was getting enough rest. After a few months, my plan began to pay off. I had about a two-and-a-half-month stretch of no pain! Encouraged, I began working out again. When I would notice symptoms as a result of my workout, I might back off a little, but I continued the activity. I knew I needed to expose myself to these situations to allow my nervous system to heal. Life became a lot easier, but for some reason, I still felt depressed, sad, and exhausted. The depression worsened, causing my nervous system to become worked up again. My prickly vulvar symptoms returned. I was so disappointed. After visiting my doctor for some blood work, it was uncovered that I had an overactive thyroid. Within two weeks of taking medication for the problem, I noticed an improvement in my mood. Eventually I began feeling well enough emotionally to once again begin allowing my symptoms to exist without reacting. Within a couple of months, I was again symptom-free. I'm fully aware that symptoms can return at any time, but if they do, I'll do my best to have less of a reaction to them and not get my nervous system aroused. I have tools in my toolbox now. I view my recovery as a remission. This remission could go on forever, or I could have a flare-up. The important thing for me to remember is if I do have a flare-up, my symptoms will go away.

DIAGNOSTIC TESTING

A slew of diagnostic tests can come into play when it comes to pelvic pain, such as bladder cystoscopy, vulvar biopsy, colonoscopy/endoscopy for IBS, or 3-Tesla MRI of the pelvis, to name a few. Certain diagnostic tests run the risk of causing pain flares and/or may be expensive, involving time and travel. Therefore, we advise patients to ask their providers exactly how the outcome of the test will change their treatment plan. Oftentimes the answer is that although it might give certain nuanced information to the provider, it may not have an impact on the patient's overall treatment plan. If the end result is not going to change and/or improve the patient's treatment plan, a particular test may not be the best use of patients' resources.

ALTERNATIVE MEDICINE

In addition to traditional Western medicine, certain alternative treatments can offer therapeutic benefit to those recovering from pelvic pain with relatively low risk. If our patients are having success with an alternative practitioner, we always encourage them to continue with that practitioner. And when referring patients to an alternative practitioner, as with any referral we give patients, we only refer to practitioners whom we've had experience with or whom we know well enough to feel confident that their services will benefit the patient. And we prefer to refer to practitioners who have some experience with and/or knowledge of pelvic pain. When we do refer patients to an alternative medicine practitioner, we do so for very specific services. Examples include:

- A naturopathic doctor may be beneficial for women who are struggling with chronic vaginal infections that have failed traditional treatment protocols or for patients who need help regulating their gastrointestinal, urinary, and vaginal balance to eliminate or prevent infections or to reduce symptoms of irritable bowel syndrome.
- A medical hypnosis practitioner may be helpful for a patient with a sensitized nervous system, or who is struggling with anxiety and is not interested in medication.

- An acupuncturist can administer dry needling for trigger points. Acupuncture may also help reduce overall pain and nervous system hypersensitivity and regulate sleep.

Alternative therapies can get costly, so we always advise patients to be very clear about what their goals and expectations are for treatment. A goal of "alleviating pain" is too broad. A more specific goal, such as "I'm hoping a naturopath can help me overcome my constipation so that I can eliminate it as a contributing factor to my pelvic pain," is much more on target. Having specific goals in place helps patients figure out if the treatments are helping and are worth continuing.

PUTTING IT ALL TOGETHER

Part of taking on the role of treatment facilitators for our patients is providing them with information and guidance when figuring out their interdisciplinary treatment approach. In doing so, we always suggest a "highest benefit with lowest risk" approach to choosing between different treatment options, meaning we counsel patients to first try more conservative treatments, such as PT, dry needling, or medication, before treatments that carry higher risk, such as Botox injections, nerve blocks, or surgery. Another consideration is timing. Oftentimes one layer of a patient's pain must be cleared up before another is targeted, such as a case where a patient's central nervous system must first be dialed down in order for manual PT techniques to be tolerated or effective. Plus, certain treatments work best in combination with others. For example, Botox or trigger point injections often work well in combination with PT and medication. Lastly, treatment for pelvic pain is a dynamic process that involves constant assessment and reassessment by all providers involved in a patient's treatment team. Regular reevaluations and discussions help a patient's treatment team determine the effects of current and past treatments as well as which therapeutic strategies to implement next as the patient improves.

HANDLING CONFLICTING INFORMATION FROM PROVIDERS

As we've already discussed throughout this book, when it comes to treating pelvic pain, an interdisciplinary approach is the way to go. However, at times patients may receive conflicting information from providers. Given the nature of pelvic pain—the fact that several contributing factors and impairments are often involved, requiring providers from across medical specialties to weigh in—differences of opinion among providers are bound to happen. Plus, even the best of medical specialists can get tripped up by a complex pelvic pain case and won't always know the best treatment approach to take. Lastly, it's worth bearing in mind that medical providers aren't always immune to the truth behind the saying "If all you have is a hammer, everything looks like a nail." But we understand how intimidating and challenging it can be for patients when their providers don't agree. Too often we have patients come to us with multiple diagnoses from multiple providers, for example. In fact, chances are if you're a female reader with pelvic pain, you've likely been diagnosed by a gynecologist with vulvodynia, by a urologist with interstitial cystitis, and by a gastroenterologist with IBS. Getting multiple diagnoses from physicians understandably leads to confusion and frustration. In addition, providers will on occasion offer conflicting opinions on treatment options. One fairly common example is when one provider recommends a nerve block while another tells the patient he/she should absolutely not get a nerve block. In such a scenario, it's best to ask each provider what his/her reasons are for their recommendations. Other questions to ask include: What is the desired effect of the treatment? What are the possible negative side effects? Are there alternative treatments to achieve the same goal? Once patients have all the information from each of their providers, they can then make a more informed decision. Another thing to keep in mind is that as we've discussed previously, not many providers have a lot of experience treating pelvic pain conditions. So if you get conflicting medical advice regarding your pelvic pain, consider your provider's experience treating pelvic pain specifically. He/she may be the world-renowned expert in another subset of medicine but have very little experience treating pelvic pain. And the specialists who treat pelvic pain will each have specific tests and treatments that they recommend and administer to patients. This is yet another reason we encourage patients to have one provider "driving" their care. This provider can help them sort through any different opinions they get from other members of their team. It is our philosophy, and we hope others adopt it, that if we cannot help our patient, we will help them get to the person or people that can.

In this chapter, we've provided a survey of the many treatment options available to treat pelvic pain. As the information above makes clear, no road map exists for putting together an appropriate treatment plan for a pelvic pain syndrome. Rather it's an exercise best approached with thoughtfulness and care and in consultation with your treatment team. Our hope is that the guidance we've presented above will help both patients and providers tackle the task.

7

THE PELVIC FLOOR AND PREGNANCY: TREATING NEW MOMS RIGHT

After her first pregnancy, Angela gave birth to a beautiful 7-pound, 3-ounce baby girl. More than six months after leaving the hospital, baby was healthy and thriving; however, the same couldn't be said for mom. Mentally, despite the sleep deprivation, she was full of joy over being a new mom, but physically . . . well, physically, she just didn't feel right. For one thing, every time she laughed or coughed, she leaked urine. And when she went for her first run after giving birth, she leaked and could not control gas. Before attempting the run, at her six-week post-partum follow-up appointment, she had told her ob-gyn about the leaking issue. Her doctor reassured her that a little leaking was normal after childbirth and instructed her to do Kegels. Then he cleared her for resuming sex and exercise, which brings us to the other reason Angela "wasn't feeling quite right." Before the baby, she and her husband had had a healthy sex life; now, post-baby, for Angela sex was painful. Any-time she and her husband would attempt intercourse, she would feel pain upon penetration. After a few more reassurances from her doctor that everything was fine, Angela figured that she'd better start getting used to her "new normal": painful sex, no more running, and occasional incontinence. *"Oh well, I guess it's all part of having kids,"* she thought. Angela is one of millions of new moms who believe that postpartum pelvic floor symptoms are all part of a new normal that they "just have to get used to." But Angela's symptoms and the host of other symptoms new moms can face after pregnancy and delivery, or during pregnancy for that matter, are far from "normal." In fact, the vast majority of common pregnancy and postpartum pelvic floor issues *are* treatable.

In this chapter we're going to take a close look at common pregnancy and postpartum pelvic floor issues that cause both pain and dysfunction. We'll begin the chapter with a discussion of the pelvic floor–related problems that can arise during pregnancy. Then we'll take a look at the problems that crop up after the baby is born. We'll end the chapter with a discussion of two common pregnancy/postpartum concerns we've heard time and again from new moms over the years: returning to exercise post-baby and navigating pregnancy if you're a woman with a history of pelvic pain.

PELVIC FLOOR PROBLEMS DURING PREGNANCY

Countless physical changes come with pregnancy, and not surprisingly many of those changes impact the pelvic floor. For one thing, pregnancy puts additional pressure on the muscles of the pelvic floor because of the added weight that inevitably comes along with it. So the pelvic floor muscles have to work even harder to hold/support everything in the abdomen as well as maintain continence. The pelvic floor muscles are designed for this amped-up role during pregnancy, however, so typically they'll bounce back to normal postpartum (but not always; more on this in the section below). But there are times when the muscles become so overtaxed during pregnancy that problems arise, such as urinary incontinence. Problems can also arise as a result of the postural changes that occur during pregnancy. Typically pregnancy causes a significant change in posture. Indeed, as the mom-to-be's abdomen and breasts become larger, her center of gravity is pushed forward, her low back becomes curved, her upper back becomes rounded, and her head is pushed forward to compensate for the new weight distribution. Hormonal changes during pregnancy are also behind pelvic floor–related problems. For example, a hormone called relaxin is released during pregnancy to soften and ultimately open the pelvic joints in preparation for delivery. This change can result in a feeling of instability as well as contribute to back pain and a loss of balance.

Below we've compiled a list of some of the more common problems that can crop up during pregnancy.

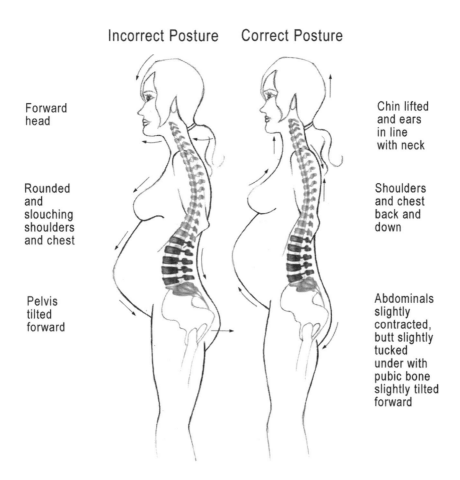

Incorrect Posture   Correct Posture

Forward
head

Rounded
and
slouching
shoulders
and chest

Pelvis
tilted
forward

Chin lifted
and ears
in line
with neck

Shoulders
and chest
back and
down

Abdominals
slightly
contracted,
butt slightly
tucked
under with
pubic bone
slightly tilted
forward

Figure 7.1.   Comparison of incorrect and correct posture during pregnancy.
Source: Pelvic Health and Rehabilitation Center

- Foot and back pain, specifically low back pain
- Neck pain and headaches due to changes in posture
- Sciatic, hip, sacral, pelvic girdle, and tailbone pain
- Urine leakage due to pelvic floor muscle dysfunction
- Round ligament pain: the round ligament supports the uterus as it grows

Women often talk to their ob-gyns about musculoskeletal pain during pregnancy. However, often they don't get referred to PT. The thinking is that their pain is caused by their pregnancy, which is only going to advance, so "why bother?" But while these problems are "common," they are not "normal," and a pregnant woman should not be left to power through the pain and discomfort she feels when solutions are available for help and relief. But the reality is that ob-gyns are not going to focus on a pregnant patient's musculoskeletal issues, so it may be best for an expectant mom to look to her primary care physician for counsel when she encounters any of the above-mentioned issues and to ask for a PT referral. Indeed, a pelvic floor PT can help with all the above-mentioned symptoms in part with manual therapy and therapeutic exercises aimed at decreasing pain, but also by educating patients on certain lifestyle modifications that can further help to decrease pain/discomfort/dysfunction. For example, a PT can make recommendations for more supportive footwear or shoe inserts or offer advice on how to support the low back and/or sacroiliac joint if there is instability. Plus, she can school expectant moms about shoulder- and neck-friendly ways to hold the baby during breastfeeding as well as back-friendly methods to hoist their new bundles of joy from the crib, floor, or stroller. More good news: in addition to treating pregnancy-related pain or discomfort, a pelvic floor PT can also deploy techniques that can actually better position a woman physically for delivery. For instance, a PT can work with an expectant mom to improve her pelvic floor motor control (improving motor control simply means to improve the strength, endurance, and ability to relax the pelvic floor muscles), which in turn will help her push more effectively during labor. Becoming a whiz at controlling your pelvic floor won't just help with pushing; it also has the potential to save you from encountering problems postpartum, such as leaking urine when laughing, sneezing, coughing, or exercising. A PT can further help prepare the pelvic floor muscles for a smooth delivery by assessing the muscles to make sure they're in the best possible shape. The pelvic floor muscles and core stabilizing muscles are intimately involved in the childbirth process. These muscles function at their maximum potential when they're lengthened, strengthened, and free of trigger points. Impaired muscles are not always symptomatic, so a mom-to-be can have a problem and not even realize it, a problem that has the potential to set her up for postpartum issues. A PT can examine each muscle individually, both internally and externally. If impairments are found, they can be treated with manual therapy and exercise. Lastly, a PT can teach an expectant mom techniques that may help prevent or lessen the degree of perineal tearing. (The perineum is the area of skin between the vagina and the anus.) This technique is called perineal massage, the practice of massaging a pregnant woman's perineum in preparation for childbirth. Typically the PT teaches both the mom-to-be and her partner this technique. The theory behind perineal massage is that massaging the tissue increases muscle and tissue elasticity, thus decreasing the likelihood of the perineum tearing (or if it does tear, decreasing the severity of the tear) during birth or during an instrument (forceps or vacuum extraction) delivery. In addition, the technique is aimed at lowering the need for an episiotomy.[1]

PELVIC GIRDLE PAIN

One of the more common pelvic pain–causing conditions that occurs during pregnancy is called pelvic girdle pain or PGP. PGP happens when pregnancy hormones cause the tendons and ligaments that secure and stabilize the pelvis to become more lax, leaving the bones susceptible to slipping out of place. The pelvis is made up of two bones joined to the base of the spine in two places, and then at the front to the pubic bone. It's designed to be strong enough to support the body but flexible enough to absorb the impact of the feet hitting the ground. PGP occurs when the bones become misaligned at the pelvic joints. Sometimes the joints can even lock up, leaving the woman temporarily unable to move one or both legs. According to research, PGP occurs in 50% of pregnant women.[2] Despite the high occurrence of the condition and the fact that it's treatable, more often than not, women either get no treatment at all or the wrong treatment, leaving them with pain in the back, leg, hip, buttock, and/or at the front of the pelvis as well as making them vulnerable to PGP during future pregnancies. The pain can be debilitating. Proper pelvic floor PT is the best treatment for PGP because it enables a woman to become more functional and experience less pain during the course of her pregnancy as well as during her labor and delivery. Here is a comprehensive list of all the strategies used by pelvic floor PTs to treat PGP:

- manual therapy techniques for soft tissue problems and joint dysfunction,

- stabilization exercises,
- stabilization tools such as orthotics and sacroiliac joint belts,
- and patient education for lifestyle and biomechanical modifications.

AFTER THE BABY: COMMON POSTPARTUM PELVIC FLOOR PROBLEMS

The pelvic floor takes a real beating during even a "normal" childbirth. Here's a play-by-play of exactly what happens to the pelvic floor during delivery: The skin layers of the vagina will stretch often to the point of tearing, requiring stitches. Also the pelvic floor muscles can become damaged during delivery, creating weakness, which in turn can cause symptoms like incontinence. During delivery, tissue damage like tearing can also occur either in the levator ani muscles (the bowl of muscles that form the floor of the pelvis and play a starring role in urinary and bowel function, organ support, and posture), which are severely stretched during delivery, or in the perineum or anus, which can cause postpartum pain and/or dysfunction. If tissue is torn (skin can tear without necessarily tearing muscle), the scar it forms can create pain upon compression or stretching, such as with sex or exercise. The pudendal nerve will also be stretched, resulting in a tension injury to the nerve. In most cases, these nerve injuries recover; however, some lasting effects are common and can contribute to both fecal and urinary incontinence. Whew! Knowing what happens to the pelvic floor during childbirth makes it a bit easier to grasp how problems can arise postpartum. These problems include incontinence, both urinary and fecal; back, groin, hip, vulvovaginal, perineal, tailbone, or pelvic floor pain; pain during sex; diminished or absent orgasm; urinary frequency, urgency, or retention (retention is difficulty starting the urine stream); constipation and difficulty evacuating stool; and difficulty with exercise. In addition, a very common abdominal issue that arises postpartum is a diastasis recti, which is a separation of the rectus abdominis or "six-pack" abdominal muscles from their central tendon. This causes abdominal weakness and has been linked to incontinence and back pain in postpartum women. (See below for more details about diastasis recti.) Plus, as was already touched on, vaginal tearing or an episiotomy performed during a vaginal delivery can also cause future pelvic floor muscle problems. (A third- or fourth-degree vaginal tear has gone deep enough into the tissue to tear pelvic floor muscles.)

Pelvic floor PT can easily treat many of the issues listed above. Just as a hamstring tear or rotator cuff tear needs PT, the pelvic floor muscles need proper rehab after pregnancy/delivery. And pelvic floor PT can help even if years have gone by since a woman has given birth. Ideally, however, if a problem has persisted for three months postpartum, it's time to get help. But sadly, the majority of new moms in the United States have no idea that PT can help them. Indeed, postpartum recovery/rehab has not completely caught on in the United States. Other countries, like France, Denmark, Australia, and the United Kingdom are much more attuned to this health issue. Consider France. In France, it's the standard of care for every new mom to receive PT after she delivers a baby. Specifically, after giving birth, women are prescribed 10 to 20 sessions of *la rééducation périnéale*. Translation: "PT designed to strengthen and rehabilitate the muscles of the pelvic floor." Toward that end, physical therapists, or as they're referred to in France, *kinésithérapeutes*, use both manual, internal techniques and biofeedback to strengthen and rehabilitate a new mom's pelvic floor. In addition to these initial appointments focused on the pelvic floor, 10 additional visits are prescribed that are primarily aimed at treating the abdominal wall for diastasis recti issues. The main goal of the program, which was instituted in 1985 and is paid for by French Social Security, is to prevent postpartum incontinence and pelvic organ prolapse and to restore sexual function. And indeed, the absence of postpartum pelvic floor rehab has been linked to long-term issues, such as incontinence and organ prolapse. Here in the United States, a pelvic floor evaluation and PT postpartum is not part of our labor and delivery culture. Typically, as was the case with Angela, once a new mom has been cleared to begin having sex again after her six-week follow-up appointment, she's simply advised to do Kegels. (Frustratingly, studies show that 40% of women who are told to do Kegels by their health care providers aren't doing them correctly, so it would seem that verbal instruction isn't enough. Women need someone to show them, not just tell them, how to do a Kegel.)[3] However, inroads are being carved out in the United States as more doctors are starting to prescribe postpartum PT, more women are starting to request it, and more PTs are starting to offer it.

POSTPARTUM PELVIC FLOOR REHAB

We believe it's beneficial for all new moms to have their pelvic floor evaluated after they've been cleared to resume sex and exercise. This kind of early intervention can help address any concerns and ultimately enable new moms to return to functional and active lives, while possibly preventing future pelvic floor dysfunction. At our clinics we treat not only incontinence but also the myriad of other postpartum problems that can crop up. So when we see a postpartum patient, whether it's for incontinence or another postpartum concern, we work to uncover any and all postpartum issues she may be having. Toward that end, the initial evaluation for the postpartum patient includes:

- Musculoskeletal examination: This includes a manual evaluation of the pelvic floor muscles, where we can identify problematic muscles and scar tissue and develop a treatment plan based on our findings.
- Diastasis recti examination: See below for a detailed look at how a diastasis recti is corrected with pelvic floor PT.
- Scar mobilization for C-section, episiotomy, and other vaginal scars: Scar tissue can cause persistent pain and lead to discomfort and pain with intercourse. (See below for an in-depth look at C-section scar problems and solutions.)
- Manual PT for concerns of pain with vaginal intercourse or pene-tration: operative or vaginal delivery can result in tissue hypersen-sitivity around the episiotomy scar and/or any scar tissue from perineal trauma or tearing as well as create trigger points or tight-ness in traumatized muscle in and around the pelvic floor. There-fore, the PT will work to normalize pelvic floor muscle tone, elim-inate trigger points, and decrease tissue hypersensitivity with manual techniques that can successfully resolve pain with vaginal intercourse or penetration.
- Pelvic floor muscle motor control exercises and training to treat urinary and/or fecal incontinence: Treating incontinence involves a host of exercises to strengthen the pelvic floor muscles as well as improve their motor control and endurance.

UNZIPPED: WHAT IS A DIASTASIS RECTI?

Most women seem to accept that pregnancy/childbirth changes their bodies. But what many don't realize is that some of these changes can be fixed. One of the "fixable" changes is a diastasis recti.

A diastasis recti is a separation of the rectus abdominis muscles, what many refer to as the "six-pack" muscles. This separation occurs along the band of connective tissue that runs down the middle of the rectus abdominis muscles. (This band of tissue is called the linea alba, but for our purposes, from here on out, we're going to refer to it as the midline.) During pregnancy, separation occurs down the midline because of the force of the uterus pushing against the wall of the abdomen coupled with the influx of pregnancy hormones that soften connective tissue.

A diastasis recti can occur anytime in the last half of pregnancy but most commonly occurs after pregnancy when the abdominal wall is lax and the thinner midline tissue no longer provides adequate support for the torso and internal organs. A small amount of widening of the midline happens in all pregnancies and is normal. Although some women's midlines spontaneously close after labor, for many, the tissue remains too wide. A midline separation of more than 2 to 2.5 finger widths, or 2 centimeters, is considered a problem. Predisposing factors for a diastasis recti include obesity, multiple births, and abdominal wall laxity from abdominal surgery.

What's the Problem with a Diastasis Recti?

A diastasis recti can lead to pelvic instability due to abdominal wall weakness. This instability can create a number of problems, including:

- Abdominal discomfort with certain movements, such as rolling over in bed, getting in/out of bed, and lifting heavy objects
- Umbilical hernia
- Pelvic girdle pain
- Sacroiliac joint pain
- Low back pain
- Pelvic floor dysfunction, such as urinary and fecal incontinence and pelvic organ prolapse

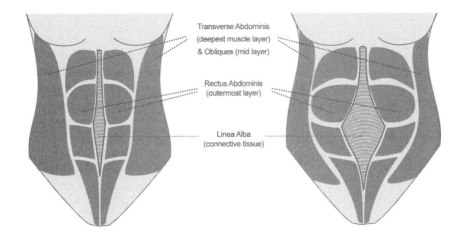

Transverse Abdominis
(deepest muscle layer)
& Obliques (mid layer)

Rectus Abdominis
(outermost layer)

Linea Alba
(connective tissue)

Figure 7.2.   Comparison of a normal abdomen verses an abdomen with a diastasis recti abdominus. *Source: MuTu System*

- Many new moms with a diastasis recti when they return to exercise might feel that they can't adequately perform certain exercises.
- In addition, a diastasis recti can change the appearance of the abdomen. The skin may droop, and some patients may even develop a hernia through the midline. Some postpartum patients with a diastasis recti complain of continuing to look pregnant.

Oftentimes patients want to know if they can do anything during pregnancy to prevent a diastasis recti. Our advice to them is to keep their abdominal muscles strong during pregnancy with appropriate exercises; maintain proper posture with sitting, standing, and activities such as pushing the grocery cart; avoid sit-up and double leg lift exercises; and avoid bearing down when doing activities such as lifting heavy objects and eliminating bowels. Aside from this, we teach patients proper techniques for getting up from a lying-down position as well as other general healthy body mechanics.

How Common Is a DR?

The reality is that about 53% of women have a diastasis recti immediately after delivery. This is because the tissues at the front of the abdomen are designed to allow the expansion of the belly in order to accommodate a growing baby. However, 36% of women will have a diastasis that remains abnormally wide at five to seven weeks postpartum.[4]

How Does One Check for Diastasis Recti?

The sooner a diastasis recti is caught, the easier it is to rehab. Here's how to check for a diastasis:

- Lie on your back with your knees bent and your feet on the floor.
- Place the fingertips of one hand at your belly button, and while your abdomen is relaxed, gently press your fingertips into your abdomen.
- Lift the top of your shoulders off the floor into a "crunch" position.
- Feel for the right and left sides of your rectus abdominis and take note of the number of fingers that fit into the gap.
- You will want to test this again approximately 1 to 2 inches above and below your belly button to determine the length of the gap.

If you find you have a diastasis, you will need to be cautious of the following activities, as they can create further separation of the abdominal muscles:

- abdominal sit-ups
- crunches
- oblique curls
- double leg lifts
- upper body twisting exercises
- exercises that include backbends over an exercise ball
- yoga postures that stretch the abs, such as "cow" pose and "up-dog" pose
- Pilates exercises that require the head to be lifted off the floor
- lifting and carrying heavy objects
- intense coughing without abdominal support

Basically, you will need to be cautious of any exercise that causes your abdominal wall to bulge out upon exertion. Once the diastasis is closed, you can gradually add these activities back in.

Diastasis Recti Correction

In general, correcting a diastasis includes core stabilization exercises, postural training, education on proper mobility techniques, and proper lifting techniques, as well as a fitting for an abdominal brace if needed (we will discuss this later on). In some cases, a self-guided program may be enough to correct a diastasis. But we recommend that postpartum women see a qualified pelvic floor PT if they believe they have a diastasis, because often other postpartum pelvic floor issues are at play. Here's a complete rundown of what we do to repair a patient's diastasis. During the first visit, we assess the length and width of the separation, the strength of the patient's abdominal muscles, the motor control of the pelvic floor, and the patient's posture. In addition, we assess hip, back, and sacral stability. Uncovering a patient's overall impairments is important in correcting a diastasis because only then can we put together a proper treatment plan. Since every patient is different, treatment plans are specifically tailored for each patient.

So how do we get down to actually closing the diastasis? Thankfully, closing a diastasis is not rocket science, and there are actually a few different methods for doing so. Here's our approach: the patient takes a towel or bedsheet, wraps it around her waist, and crosses it at the largest gap in the separation. For most people the largest gap is at the belly button. The patient must hold the sheet nice and tight, making sure the sheet is in between the ribs and hip bones, as they can hinder the sheet from being as tight as it needs to be. In that position, the patient does mini sit-ups. Patients need to do 30 to 60 daily repetitions of these sit-ups for a diastasis to close. Doing sit-ups without a towel or sheet could cause the gap to widen. But we'd like to stress that there are other approaches to closing a diastasis. Our advice to all new moms who believe they may have this issue is to seek out a health care professional for guidance. In addition to instructing patients on this exercise, we work to educate patients on what activities/exercises to do and not to do. For example, we'll tackle postural education, meaning we will show them how to sit and stand correctly; we teach them how to best carry heavy items (although this should be avoided if at all possible); how to lift objects correctly, including the baby; and how to correctly get into and out of bed, among other things.

As far as how long it takes for a diastasis to close, it all depends on the size of the gap, the amount of abdominal muscle strength, and other issues, such as obesity. The wider the gap, the longer rehabbing it will take. That said, although every patient is different, changes should start to occur within six weeks of rehab. But some patients do require surgery to correct a diastasis if it's not closing. If a patient doesn't see a sufficient closure in a 12-month time frame with consistent rehab efforts, then a surgical repair may be necessary. A general surgeon or a plastic surgeon can perform the surgery.

To Brace or Not to Brace

According to the social media/blogging world, *every* postpartum woman needs to wear a brace. This is simply incorrect messaging. So when is it appropriate to wear a brace? If a new mom can't reduce her diastasis through rehab and/or it's causing her significant daily limitations and pain, a brace may be useful. If a brace does provide comfort, it's a sign that the diastasis is a functional problem and should be addressed. In most cases it's okay to wear the brace for support while determining an effective course of treatment.

C-SECTION SCARS: PROBLEMS AND SOLUTIONS

A major issue that we treat for new moms involves C-section scarring. As of 2013, 32.7% of births ended in C-section.[5] "C-section" is short for cesarean section and is the delivery of a baby through an incision in the mother's abdomen and uterus. These days the most common incision used for a C-section is the "horizontal" or "bikini" incision. The incision is cut through the lower abdomen at the top of the pubic hair just over the hairline. Scarring from the incision builds up underneath the incision as well as in the uterus.

Now let's take a look at some potential problems caused by a C-section scar. A common complaint after a C-section is the sensitivity of the scar itself. For instance, it may hurt to lean over to pick up the baby or may cause pain with lifting or other positional changes. Standing up straight may be painful, as well as reaching over the head. In addition, the scar may cause a slight postural change, a sort of "pulling forward" that along with a decrease in the support of the back from the abdominal muscles could result in back pain. What's more, the round ligament that attaches from the sides of the uterus to the labia can be caught in scar tissue after a C-section because the incision is also right over the area where the round ligament crosses the pelvic brim. If this happens, a woman can experience labial pain, especially with transitional movements like going from a seated position to a standing position. Issues with lower digestion, such as irritable bowel syndrome or constipation, are also a possible consequence. This occurs because the scar tissue pulls within the abdominal cavity, affecting the organs. The good news is that the problems caused by a C-section scar can be treated with PT. *So how does a PT treat a C-section scar?* Most problems caused by C-section scarring can be improved or corrected altogether by making the scar more flexible by manipulating (moving and massaging) the scar tissue. The more scar tissue is moved and massaged, the softer and more similar to the tissue around it it becomes. This reduces tightness and breaks up adhesions (an adhesion occurs when scar tissue attaches to a nearby structure). Also, if a scar is pulled in all directions, the body will lay down the fibers of the scar tissue with more organization and in a similar alignment to the tissues around it. The scar blends in better and behaves more like normal tissue. So on the treatment table the PT will massage and manipulate your C-section scar and the area around it. Scars (internal and external) can be pushed, pulled, pinched, rolled, and rubbed. (Warning: manipulating a scar can be painful. That's because tissue that has restricted blood flow is super-sensitive to touch.) But this is a pain that comes with gain. Ultimately, scar mobilization promotes collagen remodeling, which increases pliability of the tissues and reduces uncomfortable sensations, such as itching or sensitivity. It's best to start C-section scar mobilization early in the healing process, usually six to eight weeks after the procedure. The reason early intervention is ideal is that the tissue will respond quickest during this period. However, the body remodels scar tissue constantly, so your tissues are being replaced with new tissue all the time, just at a much slower rate when scar tissue is older. A PT can also instruct a new mom how to perform the mobilization at home if appropriate.

"COMMON" BUT NOT NORMAL: INCONTINENCE AND PROLAPSE

Two of the most common postpartum problems new moms face either soon after giving birth or years later are incontinence and prolapse. First, let's take a look at incontinence. Postpartum women with urinary incontinence can leak urine when they sneeze, cough, laugh, or run. Some feel a frequent or sudden urge to urinate, even when their bladder isn't full. Others are unable to start the flow of urine at will or empty their bladder completely when urinating. Postpartum fecal incontinence is also possible. And many postpartum women have difficulty controlling gas or bowel movements. The main reason postpartum urinary incontinence occurs is damage to the muscles involved in continence. For example, muscle tearing during delivery or weakened, overstretched muscles can lead to incontinence. Also laughing, sneezing, coughing, jumping, running, or engaging in any activity that increases abdominal pressure places more pressure on the muscles that control continence, making them work harder. If they are weakened, they just can't do their job under increased pressure. Frustratingly, many women with incontinence postpartum do not seek help for their symptoms. That's because women often view urinary incontinence as either an unavoidable consequence of childbirth or a normal part of the aging process. Society validates these misconceptions in a number of ways; for instance, depicting new moms in all manner of media making light of how they "leak" every time they laugh or sneeze or by normalizing the condition with advertisements for "incontinence products." Plus, when a woman initially talks to her doctor about any problems she might be having with incontinence, she is simply told to "do Kegels." And as mentioned above, many women who do attempt to take this advice do the exercises incorrectly due to a lack of guidance. (Another issue with universally telling women with incontinence to "do Kegels" is that if the woman also has a tight pelvic floor, doing Kegels can cause pelvic pain. Plus, pelvic muscle weakness is not the only issue that causes incontinence, so muscle-strengthening exercises may be completely inappropriate.) In the case of postpartum women, muscle dysfunction or nerve injury causes incontinence; therefore, a PT would create an individualized program to correct whatever impairments are at play by increasing strength, coordination, and endurance of the pelvic floor and girdle muscles. In rare instances muscle tightness is contributing to incontinence, and a PT would normalize the tone of the muscles, then check motor control and teach strengthening if necessary.

Pelvic organ prolapse goes hand in hand with incontinence as a major postpartum-related pelvic floor issue caused by a weakening of the pelvic floor. Remember, one of the jobs of the pelvic floor is to support the organs of the pelvis. But for a variety of reasons, and pregnancy is a major reason, the muscle and connective tissue that offer that support can weaken. When they do, the organs can prolapse, descending into the vagina and causing a myriad of symptoms. This can happen immediately after childbirth or slowly over time and may not be apparent until a woman is older. (In women the pelvic organs include the cervix, uterus, bladder, urethra, intestines, and rectum.) There are five common types of prolapse into the vagina:

- Cystocele: the bladder descends into the vagina.
- Urethrocele: the urethra descends into the vagina.
- Rectocele: the rectum descends into the vagina.
- Enterocele: the small intestines descend into the vagina.
- Uterine prolapse: the uterus descends into the vagina.

While some prolapses can be asymptomatic, common complaints of women with prolapse are inability to wear a tampon; urinary and/or fecal incontinence; and pain with intercourse. As the pelvic organ prolapse gets worse, some women complain of:

- Pressure or a heavy sensation in the vagina that worsens by the end of the day or during bowel movements
- The feeling that they are "sitting on a ball"
- Needing to push stool out of the rectum by placing their fingers into or around the vagina during a bowel movement
- Difficulty starting to urinate or a weak or spraying stream of urine
- Urinary frequency or the sensation that they are unable to empty their bladder well
- Low back discomfort
- The need to lift up the bulging vagina or uterus to start urination
- Urinary leakage with intercourse

Like incontinence, prolapse is a common condition. Indeed, it's estimated that nearly 50% of all women between the ages of 50 and 79 have some form of prolapse.[6] In addition to childbirth, obesity and menopause are other factors that can contribute to developing a prolapse. *What are the treatment options for prolapse?* Lifestyle modifications and exercises for the pelvic floor muscles are typically the first line of treatment for the condition, both of which can be very effective. Lifestyle modifications include not straining with bowel movements and not lifting heavy items, and learning to avoid increasing abdominal pressure during daily activities. In some cases, wearing a pessary, which is a removable device that is placed into the vagina to help support the organ/organs from falling/bulging, is another nonsurgical way to manage a prolapse. Surgery is typically done only after a patient has tried conservative management first. In addition, a pelvic floor PT can help patients with prolapse by assessing the strength of the pelvic floor muscles and abdomen and also educating patients about specific strengthening routines that can help support the pelvic organs. Also, a PT can ensure that patients are not performing any lifting or other activities that will make a prolapse worse. Lastly, the PT can discuss whether a patient should see a physician for a surgical consult. *Can prolapse be prevented?* The answer to this is sometimes, but not always. That said, to attempt prevention, patients can avoid chronic straining, whether with exercise or when having a bowel movement; manage their weight; and maintain strength and stability in their pelvic floor and pelvic girdle muscles. Even if surgery is eventually needed to correct a prolapse, going into the surgery with a more normally functioning pelvic floor is only going to help matters. Look at it as the same as going into an ACL repair in the knee with strong surrounding muscles in the legs and hips versus weak muscles. However, when it comes to pelvic floor strengthening, we're hesitant to straight out advocate strengthening exercises, aka Kegels, because we are not in the business of recommending Kegels across the board for all the reasons we've already discussed. That said, if there is a true weakness (without muscle tightness or trigger points), then Kegels can help.

EXERCISE AFTER PREGNANCY

Most women are cleared for exercise at their six-week postpartum ob-gyn appointment. But as you've likely realized at this point in the chapter, postpartum recovery is complicated, and clearing every new mom for exercise six weeks after delivery perhaps isn't the best rule of thumb. That's because for a variety of reasons, not *all* new moms are ready to return to *all* exercise post-baby. For example, if there were any complications during delivery, or if a new mom isn't fully healed, which can mean many things, she may not be able to start exercising. Also, if a new mom still has a lot of hypermobility due to hormone changes and is feeling pain in her pelvis, pubic bones, or sacroiliac joint, she is probably not ready to jump back into exercise full force. Another example is a woman with a diastasis. As we've already explained, anyone with this issue should steer clear of core-heavy exercise, like Pilates, for instance. Factors that come into play when deciding whether a woman is ready to return to exercise after having a baby include:

- Her prior level of exercise. For instance, if the woman wasn't a runner prior to pregnancy, it's not a good idea to start running right after giving birth.
- What happened during delivery? For instance, did she have a vaginal delivery or a C-section? If she has an episiotomy scar or a C-section scar, she might have to wait longer than six weeks for the scar to heal.
- Are her joints still too mobile from all that relaxin that was released during pregnancy? Joints that are too mobile (a term we in the PT world refer to as hypermobile) can set someone up for injury.
- Is she breastfeeding? The hormones associated with breast milk cause ligaments to become lax (hypermobility).

In a perfect world, every postpartum woman would seek an evaluation from a PT to determine if/when and to what degree she is ready to return to exercise. But unfortunately we don't live in that world. So at the very least, it's our advice that if a new mom is having any pain, such as low back or pelvic girdle pain, or had any prepartum pain, musculoskeletal impairments are likely making postpartum exercise challenging, and a PT evaluation may be warranted. Frustratingly, we live in a society that puts an insane amount of pressure on new moms to get their pre-baby bodies back, fast! Not only are magazines filled with Photo-shopped images of postpartum celebs with headlines shouting how so-and-so LOST ALL THAT BABY WEIGHT! but the message is even doled out from our family and friends. We ourselves may even be guilty of it. How many times has the first thing you've said to a family member or friend who's just given birth been, "Wow, you look great!" If you think about it, it's a strange thing to say to a woman who's been through the baby-birthing mill. Unfortunately, so many new moms succumb to this societal pressure and push themselves too hard upon their return to exercise post-baby. We've seen this time and again with our patients. Our advice to all new moms when returning to exercise postpartum is to really listen to your body. If you feel like you're pushing yourself too hard to perform an exercise post-baby, then nine times out of ten, you are. This is an instance where "pushing through the pain" is the wrong thing to do. And as we've already mentioned, urine leakage during exercise postpartum is a sign that there is a pelvic floor impairment that needs to be checked out by a PT. In addition, many postpartum women who return to exercise complain of having a hard time getting back into the swing of things; they might say "they don't feel it" or "they can't do it right" when they're doing certain exercises. This might be a red flag that musculoskeletal impairments, such as a diastasis recti, need to be corrected.

PREGNANCY CONCERNS FOR WOMEN WITH A HISTORY OF PELVIC PAIN

So many women who develop pelvic pain do so in the midst of their childbearing years, so they're faced with the prospect of getting pregnant and giving birth while recovering from or managing a pelvic pain syndrome. Many questions crop up for them when tackling this major life decision, one that is rife with unknowns in the best of circumstances. Two of the most common considerations for women recovering from or managing pelvic pain are: *Do I need to come off all my medication before trying to get pregnant?* and *How will any hormonal fluctuations that come along with pregnancy or any necessary fertility treat-*

ments affect my pelvic pain? We put these questions to one of our colleagues in treating pelvic pain, Sarah D. Fox, M.D., an ob-gyn who serves as an assistant professor of obstetrics and gynecology at the Warren Alpert Medical School of Brown University. Here's what Dr. Fox had to say about trying to get pregnant while managing pelvic pain with medication:

> Typically, medications are not studied in pregnant women—fewer than 10% of FDA-approved medications have been studied in human pregnancy—so there is much uncertainty about medication safety in pregnancy. That said, a few medications are well studied and safe (category A) and a few medications are not well studied in humans, but there is no evidence of harm in animal studies (category B) and these medications may be taken in pregnancy. However, the greatest number of medications fall into "category C," where there is evidence of risk to the fetus in animal studies, but there is no data in humans. But in some cases, the benefits of treatment may outweigh the risk to the fetus. For example, many of the antidepressants are category C drugs, so there may be some risk involved; however, we know that women who experience untreated depression in pregnancy can have adverse outcomes related to their depression. In some cases, women may be able to manage depression with counseling and behavioral changes. But in others with more severe symptoms, it may be better to continue the medication. Category D medications show that they are associated with increased fetal risks, but there may still be a compelling reason to use such medications. For example, benzodiazepines, such as Valium, which are sometimes used vaginally to treat pelvic pain, would fall into this category. Lastly, "category X" indicates that there is significant fetal risk, and these medications should not be used in pregnancy. It is very important to call and ask your obstetrician about your medications as soon as you realize you are pregnant. It is also important to remember that 50% of pregnancies in the United States are unplanned, and by the time the pregnancy is recognized, there will already be fetal exposure. It seems that many women with pelvic pain feel that their pain will prevent them from getting pregnant. Although this may be the case, it's important to realize that if you are not using contraception, you may become pregnant. If you are taking medications that fall into categories C, D, or X, it's best to make sure you are using contraception and you speak with your pain management physician and your ob-gyn before trying to become pregnant. Here is a great source of informa-

tion on medications and pregnancy from the Centers for Disease Control: http://www.cdc.gov/pregnancy/meds/index.html. [7]

When asked about how the hormonal changes that occur during pregnancy or any necessary fertility treatments, Dr. Fox explained:

Hormonal changes that occur with pregnancy can certainly impact pelvic pain. For example, later in pregnancy there are elevations in the hormones estrogen and progesterone. For its part, the progesterone can actually be helpful in downregulating endometriosis, which may help make some women feel more comfortable during pregnancy. However, it also can be involved in causing laxity of the ligaments and joints. This is part of the mechanism by which women may experience pain in their pelvic girdle, SI joints, and pubic symphysis. In addition, progesterone levels (as well as the multivitamins and iron that many women take) can cause constipation that can worsen pelvic pain symptoms. And the mass effect of the pregnant uterus can cause worsening pain for many women, especially for those with bladder pain. Bladder pain may also worsen related to both the trauma of a vaginal delivery as well as after a C-section where the bladder is surgically manipulated. Also, with a 50% increase in blood volume during pregnancy, women experience more swelling, typically in the lower extremities. This swelling may worsen pelvic pain in some women. All that said, it is really challenging to predict how pregnancy will impact a woman's pelvic pain. Some women will feel better; others will feel worse during pregnancy and in the postpartum period. In any case, it is important not to get pregnant to improve pelvic pain, something that can backfire. For a pelvic pain patient who wants to have children, it is best to meet with your pain management physician before attempting pregnancy. This will allow you to determine all potential pain generators and examine which treatment options are available in pregnancy. It also allows you to set up resources for pregnancy, such as working with a pelvic floor PT to address the change in center of gravity, back pain, and pelvic girdle laxity. [8]

One question we as pelvic floor PTs get quite often from our patients who are considering getting pregnant is whether they should opt for a C-section or vaginal birth. Currently, no evidence exists to support whether one method of delivery is better than the other for a woman with pelvic pain. That said, if a woman has a pudendal nerve issue, is hypermobile, or suffered severe prolapse from a prior birth, a C-section may be recommended by a pelvic pain specialist. Our overall recommendation is for the patient to discuss this with her physician.

PHOEBE'S STORY

In the middle of the second trimester of my first pregnancy, I woke up one morning in terrible pain. It felt like I was being stabbed with a sharp knife in my bikini area. It hurt so badly that at times I could barely walk. Walking uphill or upstairs was extremely painful. I had to stop traveling for work. I actually got a handicap placard for my car because walking was so painful. Lying down was the only position that was comfortable. I had no idea what was happening, and I was terribly afraid I was going to have this pain for the rest of my pregnancy. I saw two doctors who diagnosed me as having "round ligament pain." They told me to take Tylenol and use a heating pad to help with the pain. It was my midwife who referred me to an orthopedic PT. The PT massaged my bikini area, and that helped to relieve the pain for short spurts of time; otherwise, I dealt with the pain for seven weeks, after which time it went away. But my relief was short-lived. In my third trimester, I began to notice that if I'd sit for long periods of time, my tailbone would begin to hurt. I remember being in the car during a long drive and being very uncomfortable. I found myself holding on to the bar on the roof of the car to ease the pressure on my tailbone area. At first I didn't really think much of the pain. I just figured it was a normal pregnancy issue. I went into labor about one month early. It was a pretty traumatic birth. I pushed for three hours. My son was eventually delivered via a vacuum-assisted vaginal delivery with an episiotomy. At about six weeks postpartum, I thought, "Oh my gosh! I'm still in a lot of pain down there!" It felt as if my pubic bone was bruised. It was pretty much in constant pain that would fluctuate in intensity. It especially worsened when I walked. And the tailbone pain I had noticed before my son was born was still there. Again, I turned to my midwife for advice. She referred me to PHRC for postpartum pelvic floor PT. In addition to focusing on my tailbone and pubic bone pain, Malinda, my PT at PHRC, also tackled the vaginal pain I was having as a result of my episiotomy and vacuum delivery. The scar tissue from the procedure was healing really hard and tough. It felt tight and sensitive down there. Sex was very painful. In addition, I was having some urinary incontinence. Malinda uncovered the impairments causing my pain, including a diastasis recti, a weak pelvic floor, hypersensitivity along my episiotomy scar, and connective tissue restrictions along my abdomen and pubic area. I gradually got better with twice-weekly PT sessions and with the help of the home treatment program Malinda prescribed, which included exercises to close my diastasis, self-massage with a tennis ball and foam roller for trigger points in my buttocks, episiotomy scar desensitization with dilators, and use of a support belt to help stabilize my pelvis. As we progressed in PT, she added exercises to strengthen my core and keep my hips in alignment. I went to PT for three months. It wasn't easy. The external work was pretty painful, although it did get less painful as time went on. That's where my history as an athlete really came in handy! I've been through hard training before, and I knew I could get through treatment. I wanted to have more children, so my goal was to fix my pelvic floor issues before my next pregnancy. After my experience, I've become a big advocate for pelvic floor PT for pregnancy. I tell my family members and friends who are pregnant that they should see a pelvic floor PT at least once to check things out with their pelvic floors. And to those who do have pain or other issues during pregnancy, I tell them they don't have to live with pain, and they shouldn't.

CONCLUSION

In this chapter we've covered the many issues associated with pregnancy and the pelvic floor, for women who are pregnant, new moms, and women with pelvic pain who are considering their reproductive options. In addition to pregnancy, another important function that is impacted by pelvic pain is sexual functioning. In the next chapter, we'll shine a light on exactly how pelvic pain can impact a person's sexual functioning.

8

PELVIC PAIN AND SEX: THE FACTS

As has already been discussed, the tissue, muscles, and nerves of the pelvic floor play a major role in sexual functioning. Therefore, it should come as no surprise that when impairments occur within the pelvic floor and surrounding tissue, sexual functioning is often impacted. To be sure, impaired sexual functioning is a common symptom of pelvic pain and can occur as a result of arousal, intercourse, orgasm, or post-orgasm. Symptoms of sexual pain and/or dysfunction can manifest in a number of different ways for someone with pelvic pain. For one thing, impaired tissue can be tender to the touch or can cause pain as a result of friction or compression. Pain can also occur as a result of orgasm or after orgasm due to the contraction of dysfunctional muscles or irritated nerves. Or sexual dysfunction can occur, such as erectile dysfunction in men due to too-tight muscles or restricted connective tissue or an inability to achieve orgasm in both sexes due to impaired muscles and/or nerves. Some of the more common symptoms of impaired sexual functioning with pelvic pain include vulvar/vaginal pain with vaginal penetration, pain in the genitals post-ejaculation, pain with orgasm, inability to orgasm, decreased lubrication in women, and erectile dysfunction. However, while many physiological mechanisms can cause sexual dysfunction, emotional issues also go along with pelvic pain and can also impact sexual functioning. For example, many people with pelvic pain become so used to viewing the pelvic floor as the source of their pain that they struggle to connect that part of their body with sexuality and pleasure. In this chapter, we're going to cover all these issues and more.

We'll begin the chapter with a brief overview of male and female sexual pain and dysfunction. Then we'll take a look at the role sexual function has in the PT treatment room. Finally we'll end the chapter with a discussion of some of the emotional issues that surround the impact of pelvic pain on sexual functioning.

MALE SEXUAL PAIN/DYSFUNCTION

For Billy, his sexual dysfunction was a symptom of a larger pelvic floor issue. At 32 he had been an avid cyclist for nearly 15 years. When he decided to compete in a triathlon, he upped his riding by 20 miles a week. Unfortunately, more time on his bike resulted in pelvic pain. Specifically, he began having right-side buttock pain and perineum pain. In addition, he developed erectile dysfunction that didn't respond to medication. Ultimately Billy made his way to PHRC for therapy with Stephanie. Stephanie found trigger points in his superficial pelvic floor muscles that were causing his perineum pain and erectile dysfunction, connective tissue restrictions in his buttocks causing his buttock pain, and lastly, a tight obturator internus muscle. Most likely a combination of all these impairments contributed to his erectile dysfunction. After about six months of PT, Billy's symptoms cleared up, including his erectile dysfunction.

Billy's case is but one example of the many ways pelvic pain can impact a male patient's sexual functioning. Below is a list of some of the other more common symptoms of sexual pain/dysfunction that can occur with pelvic pain along with a brief description of the possible physiological mechanisms behind each. Note: this is not meant to be a definitive list.

- perineal pain during intercourse or masturbation with thrusting due to perineal compression when there are trigger points in the perineum
- perineum or genital pain after sexual activity due to pelvic floor or girdle muscle trigger points or nerve irritation
- pain with ejaculation due to bulbospongiosus or ischiocavernosus trigger points or nerve irritation

- pain with touch anywhere on the genitals with manual stimulation or with a partner due to pudendal, sacral, or central nervous system irritation
- hypersensitivity (meaning light touch feels very irritating) at the tip of the penis due to pudendal, sacral, or central nervous system irritation
- lower abdominal, suprapubic, or bladder pain before, during, or after orgasm due to referred pain from the pelvic floor muscles, urethral irritation, or abdominal muscle trigger point
- decreased force of ejaculate due to tight pelvic floor muscles

Erectile Dysfunction and Pelvic Pain

A variety of things, such as cardiovascular disease, diabetes, obesity, or emotional issues can cause erectile dysfunction (ED). However, for a small percentage of men with ED, the pelvic floor may be the culprit. It's worth exploring the possibility that the pelvic floor is causing a man's ED in two situations. One, if the man's ED began around the same time as other pelvic floor symptoms/dysfunction, as was the case with Billy. And two, if all other possibilities and first-line treatments for ED have been tried and ruled out. To understand how the pelvic floor can cause ED, it helps to understand the role it plays in erection and ejaculation: First, blood rushes to the penis upon arousal. Then the ischiocavernosus (a pelvic floor muscle located at the base of the penis) contracts to keep the blood in the penis and maintain the erection. During sexual activity, the bulbospongiosus muscle (one of the superficial muscles of the pelvic floor) contracts and relaxes to push the ejaculate out.

If any of the aforementioned muscles are impaired, the process can be impacted. In addition, those muscles are innervated by part of the pudendal nerve. Therefore, if that nerve is impaired, it could negatively affect the performance of those muscles, again impacting the process. And in general, any pelvic floor impairment that affects healthy blood flow through the arteries involved in erection and ejaculation, like restricted connective tissue along the bony pelvis, can play a role in ED. On top of all that, painful contraction of those muscles during sex may also affect a man's ability to maintain an erection for psychological reasons.

FEMALE SEXUAL PAIN/DYSFUNCTION

Jessica, a 30-year-old patient of Liz, is an example of a patient whose sole symptom was pain with sex. She had been dating the same guy for seven years. The couple had never had intercourse because it was simply too painful for Jessica, not to mention that her muscles were so tight, her boyfriend's penis physically could not penetrate her vagina. Jessica was even unable to tolerate a gynecological exam with a speculum. Her condition is called vaginismus and is caused by involuntary spasming of the pelvic floor muscles surrounding the vagina. When Liz examined Jessica, she found that she did indeed have extremely tight pelvic floor muscles. Her approach to treating Jessica involved two main strategies: internal work to loosen Jessica's tight muscles and the use of dilators to desensitize the tissue. As a result of the manual treatment with Liz and the at-home dilator use, Jessica was ultimately able to have pain-free intercourse. Vaginismus is just one of many ways pelvic floor neuromuscular impairments can cause sexual pain/dysfunction in women. Below is a list of some other examples. Again, this is not meant to be a definitive list.

- vestibular/vulvar pain during intercourse or after intercourse, which can be caused by a number of neuromuscular issues, including too tight pelvic floor muscles or referred pain from pelvic floor muscle trigger points. It should also be pointed out that underlying causes besides neuromuscular impairments can play a role in vestibular/vulvar pain during intercourse, such as fissures and hormone imbalance. Additionally, the skin of the vulva and vestibule itself can be a source of pain. (Note: when the pain comes from the vestibule, the problem is referred to as provoked vestibulodynia.)
- vaginal pain during intercourse due to either too-tight pelvic floor muscles, pelvic floor muscle trigger points, or irritated pelvic floor nerves
- clitoral pain due to dermatological or hormonal issues, referred pain from pelvic floor muscles, or nerve hypersensitivity
- painful orgasm due to trigger points in the superficial pelvic floor muscles or nerve irritation

- Urinary urgency, frequency, and/or burning due to friction on the urethra and surrounding tissues or referred pain from the pelvic floor, pelvic girdle, or abdominal muscles

Persistent Genital Arousal Disorder

As you have realized by now, a number of different neuromuscular issues can impact a woman's sexual functioning; some, like vestibulodynia and vaginismus, have well-known diagnoses attached to them. Another diagnosis we would like to highlight in our discussion of female sexual pain/dysfunction is persistent genital arousal disorder, or PGAD. The International Society for the Study of Women's Health (ISSWSH) defines PGAD as "a persistent or recurrent, unwanted or intrusive, bothersome or distressing, genital dysesthesia (abnormal sensation) that is not associated with sexual interest." In other words, women with PGAD either constantly or periodically feel like they are on the verge of an orgasm in nonsexual places and times. They are unable to turn this feeling on or off. Normal sexual response has been defined as a four-stage cycle: excitement, plateau, orgasm, and resolution. People suffering from PGAD are thought to exist in the stages between excitement and orgasm, with no resolution. Symptoms can be associated with overactive bladder and restless legs syndrome, and for some sufferers achieving orgasm only further aggravates symptoms. (While the condition is thought to be more common in women, both men and women can suffer with PGAD.) An important thing to understand about PGAD is that the symptoms are not pleasurable, but painful. Although symptom severity varies among sufferers, this condition can be devastating for people. Patients we've treated who have PGAD have described the feeling as "extremely embarrassing, distracting, and painful." "It is impossible to interact socially and professionally with feelings of arousal. Medical professionals and well-intended friends and family members think it's funny or say they are 'jealous.' They have no idea what I am going through," explained one patient we have treated. It's only in the last few years that research has shed light on this perplexing problem. The current thought is that the symptoms of PGAD can be caused by excessive sensory peripheral information from irritated muscles, nerves, and/or genital tissues and/or a central sexual reflex that is under decreased inhibition from the central nervous system. *What causes a per-*

son to develop symptoms of PGAD? Exactly what causes PGAD is currently unknown. In a recent study of 15 women, symptoms of genital pain, depression, and interstitial cystitis were found in more than one-half of the patients. In addition, previous antidepressant use, restless legs syndrome, and pudendal neuralgia were found in a number of cases. Pelvic congestion syndrome and Tarlov cysts (fluid-filled sacs that most often affect nerve roots at the lower end of the spine) have been previously identified as possible contributors to PGAD, but these were not a common finding in this particular study.[1]

Currently PGAD is diagnosed based on a patient's symptoms, and a limited number of physicians in the United States have experience with PGAD. These physicians can be found through ISSWSH. As far as treatment goes, numerous interdisciplinary treatment combinations are considered reasonable options for people with PGAD. These include PT, TENS treatment, hypnotherapy, pharmaceutical management, hormonal regulation, pudendal nerve blocks, sympathetic nerve blocks, Botox, and neuromodulation.

PT AND SEXUAL HEALTH

As PTs, when we treat patients for pelvic pain–related symptoms, we pay attention to their sexual function. To be sure, when we interview patients in their first evaluation appointment, we always ask them questions about their sexual functioning, such as:

- *Is sex painful? If so, where exactly?*
- *When is it painful? (For instance, at the beginning during penetration or afterward or only during certain positions or only with intercourse or masturbation?)*
- *If it's a woman, is the pain superficial or deep?*
- *Has your ability to orgasm changed?*
- *If it's a woman, do you feel like you're producing adequate lubrication?*
- *If it's a man, is there pain during or after ejaculation?*
- *If it's a man, has the quality of your erection changed? Is it weaker now versus before your pelvic floor symptoms started?*

The responses to these questions can guide us as PTs in a myriad of ways. For example, if a male patient complains of pain with sitting or perineum pain, and he also has sexual dysfunction, we'll ask him if it started at the same time his pain started. If his answer is yes, that tells us his sexual dysfunction could be musculoskeletal in nature, so during our evaluation we'll home in on the pelvic floor muscles responsible for erection and ejaculation. For a female patient, if we uncover vulvar pain with penetration, we'll examine her more superficial muscles. Conversely, if she only complains of pain deeper with thrusting during sex, we'll focus on the deeper pelvic floor muscles, such as her levator ani muscle group or her obturator internus muscles. Two other important issues for us to consider when treating patients with sexual pain/dysfunction are hormones, especially for female patients, and what medications the patient is taking. Indeed, many different medications can affect sexual function. For instance, certain blood pressure medications cause erectile dysfunction. As for hormones, as we've already discussed in earlier chapters, for women, hormonal imbalance of estrogen and/or progesterone and/or testosterone can make sex painful or can interfere with the production of lubrication.

Will Sex Make My Pain Worse?

We often get this question from our patients, whether sex is painful for them or not, and the answer is not always a simple yes or no. For instance, we had a male patient whose penile pain, which was caused by trigger points in the ischiocavernosus and bulbospongiosus muscles, did intensify after sex and/or masturbation. So understandably, he was concerned that sexual activity was making his pain worse, and he wanted to know if he should discontinue having sex altogether. As a general rule, we rarely tell our patients to discontinue sexual activity, because the benefits can outweigh any negatives. For instance, the intimacy achieved with sex with a partner; the release of stress masturbation can achieve; and the overall endorphin rush sex produces all have benefits that can help someone with persistent pain. So it really is a personal decision for a patient to make: whether the benefit he/she gets from sexual activity is worth potentially slowing healing. All that said, there are two particular situations where a patient should be cautious. One, if a woman is experiencing vulvar tearing or fissuring every time she has penetration, it is important to treat whatever underlying problem is causing this prior to resuming intercourse. Also, patients should be aware that having sex "through the pain" may cause them to identify sex with pain, and that could set them up for avoidance issues that may interfere with sexual activity even after their pain resolves.

Lastly, a word on masturbation. When pelvic floor muscles become too tight, it's not uncommon for diminished orgasm to occur. As a result, it can be more difficult or take longer to achieve orgasm during masturbation. Therefore, patients report that they have to masturbate "more often" or "harder" to have an orgasm. Over the years, we've had quite a few patients who have told us they "over-masturbated" because their pain began shortly afterward and they feel guilty and ashamed. We always reassure them that they did not cause their pain by masturbating. We tell them that their impairments were lurking just below the surface and they would have become symptomatic eventually, whether they masturbated or not.

THE EMOTIONAL SIDE

Above we presented an overview of the physiological side of the impact pelvic pain has on sexual functioning; this section is devoted to a discussion of the emotional side. To present this side of the story, we thought it best to pick the brains of three top experts in sex therapy: Heather Howard, Ph.D., a board-certified sexologist and founder of the Center for Sexual Health and Rehabilitation in San Francisco; Rose Hartzell, Ph.D., a certified sex educator and therapist at San Diego Sexual Medicine; and Erica Marchand, Ph.D., a licensed psychologist specializing in couples and sex therapy in Los Angeles. In our discussions with these three experts, two major themes came up time and again. For one thing, many who deal with pelvic pain feel "broken" or "damaged." Secondly, oftentimes these folks end up avoiding intimacy altogether because of their pain.

Feeling "Broken"

A common emotional issue that comes up with pelvic pain patients around sex is feeling "broken" or feeling like less of a man or a woman.

"It's a loss of identity because so often people equate their manhood or womanhood with sexual functioning," explains Dr. Howard.[2] And with the societal weight placed on this part of the human anatomy, is it any wonder people can feel this way?

Getting Past Feelings of Brokenness

So what are some strategies that can help folks get past those feelings of "being broken"? One strategy is to "normalize" what is going on with the person and to work on overcoming feelings of isolation, says Dr. Howard. "One way of doing that is to explain that these are normal feelings for people with pelvic pain conditions," she says. Another big part of normalizing the situation is educating patients about exactly what's going on with their bodies from a physiological standpoint. In addition, if someone is in a partnered relationship and they fear their relationship will fail because of their "inadequacies," Dr. Howard reminds them "that all partnerships are going to hit stumbling blocks." Again, this helps the patient understand that they're not "broken" or "damaged" and that what they're going through with their partner is one of many challenges that can come up in a relationship.[3] Dr. Marchand agrees, explaining that all too often, people she works with take on an extraordinary amount of guilt for not being able to "satisfy their partners" sexually because of their pelvic pain issues, even going so far as to describe themselves as "freaks." The reality is, it's a pretty safe bet that all human beings will experience challenges in their sexual functioning, whether due to emotional issues, daily life stressors, health-related issues, or the normal results of aging. This is not to diminish what folks dealing with pelvic pain go through; it's simply a way to put the experience in perspective and help them feel less isolated and alone.

But for some, their feelings of being broken or damaged can shut down their sexuality. It's easy to understand why, says Dr. Marchand. So often, people begin to view the part of their body that once was an area of pleasure as an area that causes them pain and needs medical intervention. "So it becomes something that you don't associate with pleasure anymore," she says. "I don't want my patients to permanently associate their pelvic region with pain and medical intervention. So I think it's important to reclaim your genitals as an area of pleasure."

Some patients, such as women with vaginismus who have yet to have pain-free intercourse, might be doing this for the first time, points out Dr. Marchand. Toward this end, Dr. Marchand counsels patients to engage in masturbation or solo stimulation as a way to reconnect with this part of their body. "I will often counsel people to set aside some time and get comfortable, whether it's in your bed or on your couch or even on the floor on some pillows in front of a full-length mirror. I tell them not to answer their phones and to lock their doors. I ask them to get a mirror so they can see what they're doing. Then I ask them to use their fingers (skin on skin is better for this exercise than a vibrator) to explore their genitals. I want them to see what feels good to the touch, and what feels bad, both externally and internally. Having this level of awareness will not only help them reclaim this area of their body for pleasure, it'll also help them feel more in control when they're being intimate with a partner. To be sure, they'll be able to direct their partner on what to avoid and what kind of touch is pleasurable for them."[4]

TURNING OFF: INTIMACY AVOIDANCE

With pelvic pain, avoidance of sex or any intimacy at all is another common emotional issue. "For many of my patients, there is a fear that any type of physical touch will lead to intimacy or sexual intercourse; therefore, they'll close off all physical touch with their partner," explains Dr. Hartzell. "Ultimately, the physical distance will lead to emotional distance, and this can be disastrous for a relationship." And it can work both ways, she adds. She tells of a patient with vulvar pain who had a high sex drive, and on the days when she felt good enough to have sex, her partner was not interested because he had developed low sexual desire as a result of their complicated intimacy issues. His worry was always, "What if we are intimate, but she has pain, and there is a failed encounter?" Dr. Hartzell explained.[5] While everyone places a different weight on sex, and no one is saying that putting sex on the back burner is a good or bad thing, there can be negative consequences to turning off all physical touch, especially when you're in a relationship, points out Dr. Marchand. "It's possible for resentment or frustration to build up, which can be detrimental to the relationship," she says.[6] However, it's important, adds Dr. Howard, for those who go through this type of avoidance issue to understand that it's a "normal mechanism to back away from touch, because we as humans learn efficiently. And one of the first things that we learn is that pain is to be avoided. So it's really a functional response to someone's condition, not a dysfunctional one. The good news is that just as that behavior can be learned, it can be unlearned when a person with pelvic pain desires closeness and sexual contact with a partner. It is possible to break the association between pleasurable contact and pain."[7]

TURNING INTIMACY BACK ON

So how can someone dealing with pelvic pain overcome intimacy avoidance issues? "Because every patient/couple is unique, there is no standard," explains Dr. Hartzell. "Having said that, I will say that I always want to instill in my patients that there is no such thing as failed sex. Sex is not a performance, it's about having a connection, it's about fun, and it's about being intimate with your partner. And you can do that a lot of different ways. Often when I begin working with a couple I will try to take whatever activity is the most painful—and more often than not it's penetration—off the table. The goal is to get them to a place where instead of associating sex with pain, they begin to once again associate it with pleasure. The next step is to get them to be intimate again even if they can't have penetration or engage in other activities that are too painful. You would be surprised at how many people, especially women, are hung up on the idea that to have sex you must have penetration. The bottom line is sex does not equal penetration. There are so many other activities on the menu! For example, using a vibrator on the clitoris, oral sex, and clitoral stimulation without touching the vulva or the vagina, to name a few. I would like to add that this is also true for gay and lesbian couples dealing with sexual pain issues. *Penetration does not equal sex.*

"In addition, I'll often give my patients assignments to help them reestablish intimacy. One of my favorite assignments is for them to go to the dollar store to purchase $10 worth of items. Then each time they are intimate, they'll use one of the items. You would be surprised how much fun you can have with whipped cream or a spatula! Plus, I'm a big advocate of vibrators, so I have them go to a sex shop together and pick out one that they like, and begin experimenting with it. Also I ask them to participate in what is called 'sensate focus.' Here's how it works: the couple will set up their bedroom for intimacy—for example, lighting candles, putting on soft music—and then they'll get undressed, and each will spend 15 minutes or so giving the other pleasure, not orgasm, but exploring their partner's body. The partner on the receiving end is to give feedback as to what he or she likes/doesn't like. The communication is the key to this exercise. Oftentimes when you're caught up in the heat of sex, you're not going to 'spoil the moment' by telling your partner what's working or what's not working. But this way you're given the opportunity to really communicate what you like or don't like. Also, since the end goal is not about achieving orgasm, the pressure is off."[8]

EXPLAINING YOUR PAIN TO A POTENTIAL PARTNER

We've talked about how to communicate issues surrounding pelvic pain and sexual functioning with partners, but what about the impact your pelvic pain has on your sexual functioning as a single man or woman? How can you communicate your situation to a *potential* partner? Dr. Howard has some solid advice on this front. "My advice isn't so much concerning the words that you should use when you talk to a potential partner, it's more about coming from a place of self-worth when talking to that person. If you come into the conversation from an empowered space, as someone who sees him or herself in a positive light, who is a competent, successful person navigating a difficult health condition, you're less likely to overwhelm the person. Furthermore, it's important to come from a place of 'this is a part of me' as opposed to 'this is all of me' or 'this defines me.' So the more you approach it as a teacher, rather than someone begging for forgiveness, the greater the chance that the person feels like, 'Okay, I can learn something from you. You are clearly managing and living your life through this. You're moving along and you're doing okay, I guess I can be with you.' But if you speak as if you're not functioning, that's a lot for someone to want to take on."[9]

SUGGESTED READING FROM OUR THREE SEXUAL PAIN EXPERTS

- *Full Catastrophe Living* by Jon Kabat-Zinn is about a mind-body program for living with pain.
- *When Things Fall Apart* by Pema Chodron is about dealing with negative emotions without getting overwhelmed by them.
- *When Sex Hurts* by Andrew Goldstein and colleagues is great for information about sexual pain.
- *Guide to Getting It On* by Paul Joannides, *The New Male Sexuality* by Bernie Zilbergeld, and *The Elusive Orgasm* by Vivienne Cass all offer great insight and strategies for sexual exploration, especially when your sexual functioning has changed.
- Free sexual pain guides for patients and partners from the Center for Sexual Health and Rehabilitation can be found at http://sexualrehab.com/Additional-Resources.html.

SEXUAL PAIN: MELISSA'S STORY

I first noticed something was wrong when I tried to have sex with my boyfriend, now husband, for the first time and we were unable to have intercourse because it was extremely painful. I originally thought it was because I hadn't had sex in about a year—you know, "if you don't use it you lose it." But we tried a couple more times, and things didn't improve. After about a month, I began to realize I had a problem. Every time I would have sex, my perineum would tear, causing fissures. It was kind of like an unwanted episiotomy, but not as severe. First I went to my gynecologist, who I really loved. And her diagnosis was that I was having sex wrong. All my love for her faded in about 30 seconds, and I decided to leave her practice. When I went to see a second doctor, I brought photos I had taken of the tears. This second doctor allowed me to talk for less than a minute, looked at one of the pictures, and said that I had lichen sclerosus. I had actually come across this diagnosis in my research, so I knew what the symptoms were; therefore, I was doubtful, since they didn't sound like what I was experiencing. But she was con-vinced and proposed doing a biopsy to prove it. I agreed. So she did a biopsy of the tissue. But when I went in for my follow-up, she said she hadn't gotten enough tissue to confirm the diagnosis, but she was still positive that's what I had. At this point I'm thinking, "She's a doctor, she knows, and it's better to have a diagnosis rather than not know what's wrong with me." So I started steroid treatment, but deep down in my heart I knew I didn't have lichen sclerosus. Sex continued to be painful, and I could only tolerate it about once every one or two months. About a year later, a move caused me to have to switch doctors. I should also mention that I was going to the gynecologist rather frequently at this point because I was suffering from regular yeast and urinary tract infec-tions. This cycle had started when I came down with a UTI but mistook the symptoms for my normal pain issues. When I finally went to a doctor and was diagnosed with a UTI, the infection was extremely bad and set me up for a vicious cycle of further UTIs and yeast infections. The next doctor's proposed treatment for the pain I was having with sex was to surgically remove the offending tissue and see if healthy tissue would grow back in its place. I looked at her and I said, "Have you done this before?" And she said, "Only once, and it didn't work. But we can try it." I thanked her for her time, and in my mind I said, "You will never see me again." So now I'm on to Doctor Number Four. I saw this doctor for about two years, and while she didn't believe that I had lichens (a subsequent biopsy showed that I indeed did not), she didn't have an explanation for the tearing and my pain with sex. Even though she didn't have any answers for me, I liked that she didn't offer any crazy theories or treatment. Things got a little better with time. I'd still tear, and there'd still be pain, but it wasn't as intense. I felt like I was in a kind of holding pattern. During that time I also had begun to see a naturopath, which didn't impact the tearing and pain, but I do believe it helped with the yeast infections and UTIs. I got engaged but decided to put my marriage plans on hold. I just got to thinking, what's the point of getting married if I could barely consummate it? I was getting tired of the entire situation. And so was my fiancé. We were both frustrated by the lack of answers. So I began thinking about visiting an out-of-state specialist. Ultimately, I went to see Doctor Number Six, a vulvodynia specialist in-state, but in another city. Upon examining me, he said: "Wow! You're very tight!" Then he explained what he believed had been happening to me. He said I had extremely tight pelvic floor muscles, so tight that they were pulling the skin of my vulva taut—kind of like a rubber band—causing the skin to tear during sex. After hearing this I began to cry with relief. "OKAY!" I thought. "This is an explanation I haven't heard before!" The doctor prescribed PT. Prior to traveling to see the vulvodynia specialist, I had begun to have other symptoms. Specifically, my vulvar tissue had begun to get really red, irritated, and itchy. I had started seeing a dermatologist for these symptoms. She had diagnosed me as having "vulvar eczema" and had prescribed various creams. So at this point, my thinking was that between the treatments the vulvodynia specialist and dermatologist had prescribed, I was on the road to recovery. I was so relieved to finally have answers and a plan that seemed to make sense. About one year and two PTs (the first didn't help at all, and the second did help a bit) later, things began looking up. I started feeling better. Most importantly, the tearing had pretty much gone away. The pain with sex improved as a result. I had started seeing a therapist, so my mental health had also started to improve. So I was feeling like things were on the upswing. Although I still had some pain with sex and zero sex drive, I could go through the motions and tolerate sex more often than once every few months. I didn't flinch every time my husband touched me, and I could actually achieve orgasm. So even though sex wasn't great, it was okay. I was dealing with it. My husband was dealing with it. We were managing. Then it occurred to me after watching a motivational speaker on television one night that I had gotten complacent with my recovery. Suddenly I began to want more than just "okay" out of my sex life. I wanted "great"! That's when I started seeing Stephanie for regular PT. What Stephanie found were extremely tight pelvic girdle muscles and connective tissue restriction, which were not previously examined/treated by the other two PTs I saw. My pelvic floor muscles were not as impaired as these other two areas, because those had received attention from the other PTs. She believed that my lack of sex drive was possibly due to a lack of blood flow to my genitals due to my muscles being so tight as well as long-term birth control use. I didn't cry this time, but hearing this from Stephanie was another feeling of epiphany. The funny thing is, throughout my life I have had plenty of people tell me my body is tight, from my husband to masseuses to PTs. To address this overall tendency for my muscles to become tight, Stephanie helped me figure out a plan to do regular yoga. Now I have sex without pain and I can orgasm on a regular basis. For me the final roadblock was the lack of arousal. Ultimately, I chose to replace the birth control pill with an IUD. About a month later, my arousal returned.

CONCLUSION

In this chapter we've provided an overview of how pelvic pain can impact healthy sexual functioning, from both a physiological perspective and an emotional one. It's a part of the pelvic pain story that highlights the need for patients to be active members of their treatment teams, a theme that we go into in much further detail in the next section of the book, beginning with the next chapter, where we tackle at-home self-treatment as part of an overall treatment plan.

III

In the Driver's Seat: Taking Control of Your Healing

9

AT-HOME SELF-TREATMENT: TAKING MATTERS INTO YOUR OWN HANDS

Many people dealing with pelvic pain (and likely many that are reading this book) have tried the different do-it-yourself "protocols" out there for treating their pain without success or even to the detriment of their symptoms. But when it comes to self-treatment, like most things having to do with pelvic pain recovery, there is no "one-size-fits-all" approach. To be sure, what might help one could harm another, even if symptoms are identical. Case in point: two women, we'll call them Leah and Sue, both suffer from daily vulvar burning. It's determined by their PT evaluations that both have tight hamstrings and tight hip external rotators (the small muscles of the hip that rotate the femur in the hip joint). Stretching these muscles has the potential to be helpful, but it would be a mistake to prescribe those stretches to both Leah and Sue. Here's why: it turns out Leah also has trigger points in her hamstring muscles as well as irritation of her posterior femoral cutaneous nerve (a nerve distributed to the skin of the perineum and the back surface of the thigh and leg) as primary drivers of her symptoms. So hamstring stretches could irritate her trigger points and further irritate her angry nerve. As for Sue, she *can* stretch her tight hamstrings no problem, but stretching her hip external rotators could activate the trigger points she has in her obturator internus muscles. Case in point: therapeutic exercise intended to treat one impairment, in these cases a muscle, can irritate other muscles, nerves, and joints. However, while there is no one-size-fits-all approach to at-home self-treatment, what can be beneficial to a patient's recovery is an *individualized* home program that's developed and supervised by a PT. Think about it: typically, patients will see their PTs for one-hour appointments each week. That's four hours a month—four hours out of approximately 720 hours a month! The right home program, while it won't heal patients' pelvic pain, has the potential to make them feel better while hastening recovery. Lastly, an added benefit to establishing an individualized home program is that it gives patients lifelong tools to manage flare-ups.

Because home programs are important in pelvic pain recovery, we've decided to devote this chapter to the topic with the resounding caveat that *patients use the information in this chapter to further the dialogue with their PT about their home programs as opposed to trying any of the suggestions on their own.* We'll begin the chapter by taking a general look at how a home program can help with recovery. Then we'll discuss the importance of timing in putting a program into action. Next we'll give some general advice for home treatment. Lastly, we'll end the chapter by discussing the one activity, so-called "pelvic floor drops," that does have a place in every home treatment program.

HOW HOME TREATMENT CAN HELP

"Home treatment" means different things to different patients. For instance, some of our patients manually treat themselves either internally (using a dilator, handheld wand, or their finger), externally, or both. In addition, patients do an individualized combination of stretches and strengthening exercises at home. Others bring their partner to a PT session so he/she can learn how to administer appropriate techniques, either internally, externally, or both, between PT sessions. What all home treatment programs have in common is that they're designed to help a patient reach his/her treatment goals. For instance, if a PT identifies a muscle as tight or weak, the PT can recommend specific exercises to help strengthen or lengthen the muscle. For example, many of our male patients have tight hamstring muscles (in fact, male hamstrings are 15% tighter than those of females), and this can affect how they sit, which can in turn cause or exacerbate their pelvic pain symptoms. Once the PT determines that the hamstring muscles are free of trigger points, hamstring stretches may be appropriate for such a patient. In addition, patients can treat tight external muscles as well as external trigger points, like trigger points in the gluteal muscles or inner thighs, with different tools. For example, we often teach our patients how to use a foam roller to help loosen tight muscles early in their treatment. (More on home treatment tools below.)

TIMING MATTERS

When putting together a home treatment program for a patient, timing plays a key role. What we mean by this is that certain home treatment techniques need to be phased in at certain points in a patient's recovery, not before. For this phasing-in process, we'd like to share a few general rules of thumb:

1. Begin to stretch too-tight muscles only when any trigger points in those muscles are gone and any nerves involved in symptoms and particular exercise have regained normal mobility. For instance, if hamstrings are tight and need to be stretched but have active trigger points and/or the posterior femoral cutaneous nerve (a nerve that runs through the hamstrings) is irritated, stretching this muscle could both aggravate the trigger points and inflame the posterior femoral cutaneous nerve, causing further nerve irritation and more symptoms. For patients who have too-tight muscles with trigger points and/or nerve irritation that's preventing them from doing stretches, one option to loosen those too-tight muscles is foam rolling.

2. Begin to strengthen any pelvic floor muscles once trigger points are gone, muscles are no longer too tight, and they are actually weak. As we've explained in previous chapters, too-tight muscles and/or muscles with trigger points can also have a problem with weakness. These muscles will need to be strengthened, but not until after trigger points have been eradicated and too-tight muscles have been returned to a healthy tone. For example, if a woman presents postpartum with urinary incontinence, sacroiliac joint pain, and pain with intercourse, and her PT finds both internal and external trigger points (causing the pain with intercourse) as well as overall pelvic floor weakness (contributing to the incon-

tinence), the PT is going to tackle the trigger points first, then incorporate exercises aimed at improving the strength and motor control of her pelvic floor muscles.

3. Doing internal work to treat trigger points or too-tight muscles could be counterproductive if certain other impairments exist, such as fissures, tissue that is lacking in estrogen, or irritated vestibular tissue. While the internal work might help with the trigger points or too-tight muscles, the benefit is often undone if it further irritates the aforementioned impairments.

HOME TREATMENT TIPS

In addition to advice on timing, a few other general tips can help make a home treatment program successful.

Tools can help.

A handful of different tools can help with either external or internal home treatment work. Below is a list of tools we often recommend:

1. The TheraWand: This device was developed especially for internal pelvic floor work. With its curved shape and somewhat pointed tip, the TheraWand can help with trigger point release and the lengthening of too-tight muscles.
2. A foam roller: As mentioned above, foam rollers can be used to both stretch out too-tight muscles and release trigger points.
3. *The Trigger Point Therapy Workbook* by Clair Davies and Amber Davies: A helpful guide for patients who incorporate trigger point release into their home programs.
4. Tennis ball: Tennis balls are a great tool for working on pelvic girdle and trunk muscles.

A note on dilators: we don't recommend them across the board for at-home treatment of pelvic pain. (When we talk about dilators, we're referring to both the vaginal dilators that come in graduated sizes and any of the other handheld devices designed for internal pelvic floor work.) Dilator use is not therapeutic for all cases of pelvic pain and, in fact, can be harmful in some situations. For example, if a woman has vulvar pain that's caused by a dermatologic disease or referred pain from the pudendal nerve, home dilator use could irritate the tissue causing pain while not addressing its underlying cause. So while dilator use would be effective in many situations for male or female patients to treat internal trigger points and/or too-tight muscles, it's important to first ask your PT if it's appropriate in your particular case.

Pain is not gain.

As a general rule of thumb, if any home treatment technique makes a patient feel better, it's a keeper. However, the technique may cause discomfort at the time, typically because impairments exist in the targeted tissue. But if the technique is therapeutic, any discomfort felt in the beginning should dissipate, and symptoms should feel better afterward. If there is soreness afterward and the technique was therapeutic, the soreness will wear off, and the patient will feel better as a result of the treatment. But if the technique escalates pain or symptoms, patients should back off and discuss it with their PT.

Ice or heat?

Ice or heat can be helpful; however, for patients with nerve involvement, ice could exacerbate symptoms, often causing burning pain. If it does, discontinue. If either heat or ice is soothing, continue use.

Use the right lube.

For any type of internal work, a glycerin-free lubricant is the way to go. And if you use medical gloves, we recommend latex-free gloves. That's because both glycerin and latex can be irritating for some.

Do a test run with your PT.

We recommend that a patient test out any technique he/she plans to incorporate into a home treatment program with their PT first to make sure they're doing the technique correctly. For example, if any of our patients will be using a TheraWand or any other tool for internal self-treatment, we have them bring it into PT for a little guidance. What we'll do is actually palpate the muscles the patient is going to be working on at home with the TheraWand, while asking the patient to pay close attention to how the palpation feels. Then we have them do it themselves. After trying out the technique for one week, we ask them at their next appointment how they responded to the treatment and if they have any questions.

"Self-care" at home is just as important as "self-treatment."

Besides all the techniques we discuss above, like internal work and external work, another vital part of a home treatment program is self-care. By this we mean it's important to find certain activities, such as meditation, deep breathing, hot baths, tai chi (or inactivities: restful sleep is a must), that allow you to relax and calm your nervous system. As you've already learned, treating the nervous system is every bit as important as treating a trigger point or connective tissue restrictions.

PELVIC FLOOR DROPS

While every home treatment program should be individualized, every person dealing with pelvic pain can include one therapeutic activity in his/her home program, and we recommend it across the board. We call this exercise the pelvic floor drop. It's now common knowledge that people with pelvic pain usually have too-tight pelvic floor muscles. A pelvic floor drop helps to loosen those tight muscles. Basically, a drop is the opposite of a Kegel. When you do a drop, you're relaxing your pelvic floor. You achieve this relaxation by contracting a few of your pelvic floor's neighboring muscles (in this case your hip flexors, abductors, and external rotators), which in turn dial down the muscle activity of your pelvic floor. When we go through pelvic floor drops with patients during treatment, we initially ask them to lie on their backs with their hips flexed and externally rotated so that their knees are far apart and their feet are together. Basically, when you're in this position, you're doing a deep squat, just on your back, and a deep squat facilitates pelvic floor relaxation. (It's no coincidence that most of the world goes to the bathroom in this position or that a toddler still in diapers does.) Once they're in the desired position, we cue patients to do a pelvic floor drop by asking them to gently relax the area around the anus, as if they were going to pass gas or urinate. We then ask them to hold the position for five seconds on, five seconds off. At first, we have them do this with our finger inserted vaginally or anally in order to determine whether their pelvic floor muscles are achieving a relaxed state. If patients can achieve a drop, we give them positive feedback; if they're doing it incorrectly; we give them cues and/or hints on how to do it correctly. We don't assign patients drops for their home treatment program until they're able to do the exercise correctly in the treatment room. Two other positions help facilitate a drop besides the one described above: a standing deep squat and a child's pose. Both positions also mimic the deep squatting position. Doing a drop in a standing deep squat position has the added benefit of putting gravity and the person's body weight to work while lengthening the pelvic floor muscles. However, not all patients can get into this position because of limitations, such as hip or sacroiliac joint problems, pelvic organ prolapse, or pudendal nerve irritation. For these patients, the "flat back drop" or drops in child's pose are the best way to go. The pelvic floor drop is a first step toward teaching someone both how to relax the pelvic floor and how to regain control of their pelvic floor muscles. Drops can be done several times a day; the more the better! Ultimately we want patients to be able to relax their pelvic floors in any position—not just the three positions mentioned above. Indeed, the great thing about a drop is that it can be done anytime, anywhere. Once you get the hang of it, you can do it sitting at your desk, standing at the stove cooking dinner, or playing with the kids. We once had a patient who said she did them while walking her dog. As a cue, every time her dog would baptize a tree, mailbox, or fire hydrant, she would do a drop. (For instructions on how to do a pelvic floor drop, please click on our YouTube video at https://www.youtube.com/watch?v=K1I4Zu2SLXI.)

TAKE A DEEP BREATH: IT HELPS

Studies have shown that people with pain syndromes are "shallow breathers," meaning they're often in a stressed "fight or flight" state and don't breathe deeply and slowly. Diaphragmatic breathing, also known as "belly breathing," is carried out by contracting the diaphragm, the horizontal muscle between the chest cavity and the stomach cavity. This results in an expansion of the belly rather than the chest. Diaphragmatic breathing has the potential to help pelvic pain for a few reasons. For one thing, the diaphragm works in conjunction with the pelvic floor muscles, so when you inhale during a diaphragmatic breath, the pelvic floor muscles expand, allowing for greater pelvic floor muscle release, relaxation, and blood flow. Try it right now . . . we'll wait. Didn't you feel that nice pelvic floor expansion while you were taking in that big deep breath? This exercise has also been shown to decrease adrenaline and cortisol, two hormones that are often elevated in people with pain and stress. When cuing patients during diaphragmatic breathing, we tell them to place their hand on their belly to make sure it rises and falls with their breath. However, this isn't the only way to approach deep breathing; many safe, effective techniques exist, and we encourage you to find one or more that are a good fit for you.

HOW NOT TO FREAK OUT DURING A FLARE: MOLLY'S STORY

It's. Just. A. Flare. Four little words that pack a lot of power for me, because they instantly put the brakes on an impending panic attack. This wasn't always the case. Used to be that when I'd have a flare-up of my pelvic pain symptoms, it would devastate me, sending me into a panic-filled dark hole. But after some good communication with my PT, and frankly, getting to the other side of a handful of nasty flares, I had an epiphany, one that changed the course of my recovery, and one I'd like to share. As anyone who has gone through the treatment process for pelvic pain can attest to, it can be a complicated journey. No pill, surgery, set number of PT sessions, or any other secret sauce will get you better. What *does* get you better is an interdisciplinary treatment approach, and signing on to be an active member of the team. Throw in a heaping dose of persistence and patience, and that's how you heal from pelvic pain. At any given time, my treatment team has consisted of a pelvic floor PT, a physiatrist (pain management doctor), and a urogy-necologist. Treatments I have had include trigger point injections, Botox injections, epidural injections, nerve blocks, medication, and a home treatment program that included pelvic floor drops and internal pelvic floor muscle stretching with a TheraWand. I consider myself a pelvic pain success story. After a few years of regular PT and working my interdisciplinary treatment plan, I'd say I'm 90% better. Oftentimes, however, healing has felt a lot like taking one step forward and two steps backward. And flares happened. At the beginning they happened A LOT. Even as I write this, I can still recall the feeling of utter despair that would envelop me when I'd have an off-the-pain-scale flare-up. For me, a pain flare meant and continues to mean an intense urethral/vestibular/vulvar burning coupled with burning sit bone pain and urinary urgency/frequency. A flare would come unexpectedly. I would be having a good day, or a few good weeks, and then *BAM!* I'd feel as though I was back at square one. Sometimes I could connect a specific incident to the flare. A long car trip, sitting for too long, wearing the wrong pants, having sex, traveling, a urinary tract infection; all could set off a three-alarm flare. But other times, a flare would just seemingly come out of nowhere. Whatever was behind the flare, my reaction was always the same: I would hop on the catastrophizing train in my mind. *"All that progress out the window,"* I'd think. *"I'll never get better, I'll never enjoy [insert activity here] again." "My husband is going to leave me." "I'll never be able to have children." "My family and friends are going to abandon me." "I'm going to grow old alone." "Should I ask my doctor if I should try [insert name of drug or type of injection here]?" "I've got to make a plan!!!"* My anxiety would in turn feed the flames of my pain, and up up up my pain levels would go. It wasn't until I began getting regular PT with Stephanie and Liz, who began to educate me about what exactly was causing my symptoms as well as the recovery process, that I was finally able to develop tools that enabled me to stop the train on its tracks. With those tools, I was able to get to the other side of a flare without going into full-scale panic mode. Not only that, but the tools I developed helped me get through a flare *faster*. First, I want to share what I learned about flares: flares may happen as a result of very predictable things, such as a UTI or yeast infection, a bout of food poisoning, overdoing it at the gym, or even repetitive coughing from the flu. It's simply not always possible to avoid a triggering event, even when you know what your triggers are. For instance, stress, travel, and diet are common triggers that are often unavoidable. In addition, when a pain flare can't be tied to any tangible event, the central nervous system can be the culprit. This is because the central nervous system can generate pain without there being tissue damage. I also learned that on occasion a flare is your pelvic floor's way of telling you it's not ready for you to add a particular activity into the mix. For instance, when I began to wear pants again, I realized that there were certain kinds of pants, tight yoga pants for example, that would cause a flare. The pants were the triggering event because my tissues were still impaired. So I gave my cute new yoga pants to my coworker and went back to my looser-fitting yoga pants. Along those same lines, it often happens that as we begin to feel better, we start doing more, and sometimes flares are a reminder to pull back and to slow down. Lastly, it's important to remember that once you reach a level of healing, no matter the intensity of the flare, your body can and will get back to that level. These words of wisdom helped me because I could finally stop feeling as if I had gone backward every time I had a flare—that all the progress I had made had gone out the window. Instead, I realized that the flare was just a temporary bump on the road to recovery, and that made all the difference. It enabled me to keep the alarms in my brain from going off and to calmly take my bag of tools off the shelf and do what I needed to do to take care of myself. This was key for me, because I quickly learned that a negative response to flares could make the flares worse and further aggravate my nervous system. So for me, it was really important to remain calm and relaxed during a flare. "Easier said than done" may be your first response to this advice; however, trusting that my flare was temporary really made an enormous difference in my overall healing process. Since everyone's symptoms are different, what works for me may not be the thing for you. Yet I still want to share the contents of my "flare toolbox" to reflect how you can be proactive in overcoming a flare. I've already mentioned the first trick in my bag, but because it's so effective, it bears mentioning again. I literally take a deep breath and say these words either out loud or in my head: "It's. Just. A. Flare." I wasn't sure why this worked, so I asked Erica Marchand, Ph.D., a licensed psychologist in Los Angeles, to weigh in. "There's some evidence from neuroscience that naming or verbalizing difficult feelings decreases some of their emotional reactivity—'name it to tame it,'" Dr. Marchand explained. "Pain often provokes an automatic emotional reaction, but if we can name it and think about it (what to do about it, what has helped in the past, how long it will last, how to take care of ourselves), it gives us more choice about how to respond." Aside from "naming it to tame it," other tools in my flare toolbox include:

- Ice pack: "Ice." It sounds so simple, and it is, and to this day it still surprises me how effective icing is. It ALWAYS makes me feel better. What I usually do is call it an early night, line up a few of my favorite shows on Netflix or On Demand, and relax in bed with my trusty ice pack (a little chocolate helps too). Typically I'll apply the ice pack to my hot spots for 10 minutes or so. Take a break, repeat, and so on for a few hours until I fall asleep. And voilà! Not only will I feel better in real time, I'll wake up the next day feeling a remarkable improvement in my pain levels, especially my sit bone pain. (I want to acknowledge here that many people with nerve pain can't tolerate ice. These folks benefit more from heat. Also, for many chocolate is a bladder irritant.)
- Stretching: My TheraWand has long been a tool that I've used for self-treatment. When I flare, I find that a gentle stretch with my crystal wand (which I keep in the fridge, so it's always nice and cool) will make me feel better both during the stretching and the following day. I am careful to use an adequate amount of lubrication (which I also keep in the fridge). I find that the cool wand and lubrication help to cool the tissue.
- Medication: As I mentioned above, I have a physiatrist as a member of my treatment team, and she has given me specific medication to take in the event of a flare.

(Again, I want to reiterate that every patient with pelvic pain is different and while these tools work for me, they may not work for everyone. Except for the one below; that one is *universal*.)

- Boundaries: When you deal with a persistent pain issue, one of the things that happens is that you inevitably disappoint your family and friends. We all want to make the people we care about happy. It's part of being human. But when I slip into flare mode, I know from experience that just as important as the ice and the stretching and the medication are rest, relaxation, and keeping my stress levels as low as possible. So I've learned to be okay with turning down invitations or telling my husband that I need to have a quiet, relaxing day/night/weekend. E-mails and telephone calls will inevitably go unanswered, and I've learned to be okay with that, even knowing that the folks on the other end might not be.

CONCLUSION

In this chapter, we've provided some general guidelines to help navigate the at-home self-treatment process. A well-thought-out, individualized home treatment plan has the potential to greatly assist in a patient's recovery. In the next chapter we're going to tackle an issue that can be similarly beneficial—exercise.

10

HOW TO EXERCISE TO STAY FIT
WITHOUT FLARING SYMPTOMS

Our patients are typically very active, but when pelvic pain enters the picture, we often find that they'll stop moving altogether for fear of making themselves worse or after reading information online about what they should or shouldn't do. For those who do strive to remain active during recovery, exercising for fitness can cause a flare-up of symptoms, such as urinary urgency/frequency, perineal burning, or vulvar or anal itching, to name a few. Often this happens after patients have taken a break from their fitness routine, either because of their pain or due to that aforementioned fear of making their symptoms worse. When symptoms flare as a result of returning to exercise, patients understandably become frustrated, fearing they'll never be able to get back to the activities they enjoy. Many of our patients are very athletic, and having to stop exercising because of their pain can be devastating. Folks who were once athletes begin to feel "broken" when they can't do an activity seemingly as basic as restorative yoga. We always reassure these patients that it is possible to return to a high level of exercise, in time. And in the meantime, we work with them to put together a plan that allows them to stay active without inducing a flare of their symptoms. Plus, we reassure them that typically if symptoms increase from an activity, it's not because of tissue damage, and that the flare will resolve. Because regular exercise is so important for all-around good health, both physical and emotional, not to mention the proven benefits of exercise on persistent pain (see box below), we want our patients to establish a balance between staying fit and healthy and not exacerbating their symptoms. In doing so, we may need to ask them to modify exercise at first, but always with the goal of getting them back to their desired activities.

After years of working with patients on this issue, and armed with our knowledge of exercise anatomy and physiology, we've compiled a few general exercise tips for those recovering from pelvic pain. But at the end of the day, it's always best to discuss general exercise routines with your PT, who will be in the best position to know exactly what activities will/will not exacerbate your impairments.

GENERAL EXERCISE TIPS

1. Return to exercise slowly.

"When returning to activity, you always want to do more than the day before, but just a little more." This is a quote we borrowed from neuro-scientist and pain expert Lorimer Moseley. It embodies in a very practi-cal way the need to return to exercise slowly if you've been inactive for a period of time while in recovery from pelvic pain. Those recovering from pelvic pain are often eager to return to exercise once they're feeling better. Or they get carried away on "good days." We're always excited when patients are eager to return to activity, but we always advise them to temper their excitement with caution. Steady progress should always be the goal. The reason it's important to proceed with caution is that inactivity results in a loss of muscle strength. In addition to having to regain that lost strength, patients often need to regain coordination. To be sure, the coordination between the body and the brain weakens with disuse. Both strength and coordination do come back, but it takes time. So when returning to exercise after a period of inactivity, the best course of action is to scale back on the volume and intensity of whatever workout you did prior to pelvic pain. So if you're a runner who was benched for a bit while recovering from pelvic pain and you used to run 5 miles a day, it might be a good idea to start back at 1 mile a couple of days a week at a slower pace than you're used to, and see how it feels. The longer you've been out of the game, no matter what the exercise, the longer it will take to get back to your previous levels of activity. Another important piece of advice is to listen to your body. Our bodies always tell us when we've done too much.

2. Low-impact cardio is a great place to start.

While recovering from pelvic pain, low-impact cardio is a great activity, as it provides the benefits of getting the heart rate up and the endorphins flowing while not negatively impacting symptoms in the way high-impact activity may. For those with a history of pelvic pain, the best low-impact cardio exercise is walking. For those just starting out, we recommend walking without much of an incline. They can slowly increase their distance every week or so, and once they get to their goal distance, they can work to increase their pace. Then they can work to increase their elevation, but slowly. The key is to find a distance, pace, and incline that does not flare symptoms. If someone was a walker prior to pelvic pain, we tell him/her to start up again at a distance of about one-quarter of what they used to do, but at a slower pace. Once they've reached their goal distance, then they can begin slowly experimenting with pace and elevation. Another good choice for low-impact cardio is walking in water. Because the human body is practically weightless in water, muscles and joints are free of pressure when submerged. For the pelvic floor, this means less pressure bearing down on it as it supports the weight of the body/pelvic organs and maintains posture, so it can relax a bit more than it's used to doing, letting the buoyancy of the water do some of its work. Lastly, for those who like to go to the gym, we recommend the StepMill cardiovascular machine for low-impact cardio. This machine is great because at slower speeds—less than level 5 miles per hour—you get a great cardio workout with the added benefit of strengthening the gluteal muscles.

3. Engage in slower, low-impact exercise when doing strength training.

When getting back to strength training, either after recovering from pelvic pain or during recovery, as a general rule of thumb, slow, low-impact exercises are less likely to cause flare-ups, as they allow for the reprogramming of any faulty movement patterns (recruiting the wrong muscles for a movement) that developed while dealing with pelvic pain. Below are a few examples of these types of exercises:

- Shallow squats: Shallow squats are better because the deeper the squat, the greater the chance faulty movement patterns may creep back in.
- Shallow squats on a foam pad: This movement creates an unstable surface and therefore elicits a beneficial co-contraction of muscles. Plus, it's a safe and effective way to strengthen the gluteal muscles, thighs, and hips.
- Balancing on a Bosu ball or foam roller: If using the Bosu ball, first use the flat side down and progress to the round side down, moving from more stable to less stable.

4. If an exercise begins to hurt, stop.

When returning to exercise during or after recovery from pelvic pain, "no pain, no gain" couldn't be further from the truth! If an activity causes pain, either an increase in pelvic pain symptoms or any other pain, discontinue that exercise. Muscle soreness from a workout is often okay, but pain or an increase in symptoms is not. If you're on the fence about what constitutes "normal" muscle soreness versus pain, discuss it with your PT ASAP. That's his/her area of expertise, and he/she will be able to help you figure it out. Plus, he/she will be able to help you modify the activity or replace it with an entirely new one. All that said, there is one exception where "working through the pain" can be beneficial. That exception is when a patient needs to dial back an amped-up central nervous system. For example, Stephanie had a patient who noticed that using the elliptical machine resulted in symptoms of urinary urgency/frequency and hip pain afterward. After starting PT, the patient learned that a trigger point in her pubococcygeus and a labral tear in her hip were contributing to her symptoms. Although her symptoms improved in PT, the patient was afraid to try the elliptical machine again. When she did work up the nerve to try it, lo and behold, she felt the same discomfort she had prior to PT. She checked in with Stephanie about the matter. Stephanie assured her that her impairments were gone and encouraged her to work through the discomfort, concluding that the patient's central nervous system was at play, and that the fear and anxiety around using the machine were causing her discomfort. The patient took Stephanie's advice and was ultimately able to use the elliptical machine with no symptoms or discomfort.

5. Take care when working out your abdominal muscles.

1. The muscles of the abdominal wall and the pelvic floor are "synergists." This means they assist each other to accomplish movement. For instance, an abdominal muscle contraction will result in a pelvic floor contraction; therefore, some abdominal exercises can exacerbate pelvic pain symptoms if done too early in the recovery process. As a general rule of thumb, people recovering from pelvic pain can work their abdominal muscles once they (a) have no trigger points in any of the muscles activated during the exercise and (b) have regained motor control of their pelvic floor muscles and can relax them after they contract in response to the exercise. Below are the abdominal exercises we recommend to patients with pelvic pain. For a variety of reasons, these exercises typically don't negatively impact the pelvic floor.

- Planks: When you do a plank, pelvic floor activity will increase, but your pelvic floor is not going to contract as much as with a sit-up. Planks are also a better idea than sit-ups because they help to work muscles, specifically the transversus abdominis muscles, that are important in low back and pelvic girdle stability as well as urinary and bowel function. So not only are you doing an exercise that has less of an impact on the pelvic floor, you get more bang for your buck.
- Standing exercises that involve weights on a pulley: When you do these exercises, your abdominal muscles are going to help you remain upright, providing an abdominal workout with less stress on the pelvic floor compared to a sit-up.
- Knee raises sitting on a physio ball: The ball creates an unstable surface, so your abdominal and other pelvic girdle muscles contract to prevent you from falling off. Voilà! Instant workout! Moving the arms or raising the entire leg instead of just the knee can make this exercise harder.

6. Stay away from exercises that increase pelvic floor muscle tone during early symptom onset or early in the recovery process.

Certain exercises will increase pelvic floor tone (tighten muscles), and the majority of impairment-causing symptoms, like too-tight pelvic floor muscles, trigger points, and irritated nerves, can be made worse by increased pelvic floor tone. So these exercises are best avoided for those with a history of pelvic pain. Below is a list of such exercises:

- Activities that involve impact, such as single-leg or double-leg jumping
- Squatting in single-leg stance
- Gym machines versus free weights: Generally speaking, our patients have reported more issues with symptom flare-ups when using machines versus free weights. We theorize that the machines may not be at the proper height or the weights may actually be too heavy for the patient, resulting in more symptoms.
- Deep squats and lunges: When people with pelvic pain do squats or lunges, their hamstrings oftentimes take over instead of their gluteal muscles, which can be detrimental to a tight pelvic floor. Also, those with a history of pelvic pain often have too-tight hip rotators, and this prevents them from doing the exercise properly.
- Biking or spinning: Most people with pelvic pain have problems and pain in the muscles that are compressed on a bike seat, i.e., nearly the entire pelvic floor. So the pressure will aggravate the pelvic floor. In fact, we have had patients whose pain started as a result of biking in the first place. But that's not to say that if you're a passionate cyclist who develops pelvic pain, you'll never be able to ride again. This is definitely a goal we work toward with patients. However, while in recovery from pelvic pain, cycling will likely need to be temporarily put on hold.
- Sitting abduction/adduction machine: Many patients with pelvic pain have trigger points in the muscles these machines target—the inner/outer thighs—so using these machines will often aggravate the trigger points and therefore their symptoms. On top of that, these machines may actually cause pelvic pain and therefore should be avoided.

- Deep squats with heavy weights: Deep squats with heavy resistance are not a good choice. For one thing, it's common for those doing this exercise to recruit the wrong muscles for the movement, thus setting them up for injury. For another thing, this exercise lengthens the pudendal nerve and the pelvic floor muscles, making them both vulnerable to injury. In fact, this activity has actually been known to cause pudendal neuralgia.

ON-THE-FENCE EXERCISES

For some exercises, like biking, it's not hard to understand their potential to negatively impact a pelvic floor in recovery, but there are other, very common exercises, like running for instance, whose effect on a recovering pelvic floor is more nebulous. For these activities, it really does depend on the specifics of the person's case. The good news is that we do have some general guidelines for these workouts.

- Running: For patients who have trigger points in their pelvic girdle muscles or core weakness, running is going to bother their pelvic floor symptoms, but if they are clear in those areas, they can usually slowly get back into running.
- Swimming: Swimming is a great form of exercise. However, certain strokes may be problematic for those who have trigger points in areas that cause pelvic pain. For example, the breaststroke activates the obturator internus muscle, so patients with trigger points in this muscle should choose a different stroke, such as freestyle. Conversely, patients with psoas or hip flexor trigger points may get aggravated symptoms with the freestyle motion but feel comfortable using the breaststroke.
- Pilates and yoga: Yoga and Pilates have a wide range of exercise combinations, and not all are a good fit for a recovering pelvic floor. For example, mat Pilates classes are almost always a bad idea, because sit-ups, aka "100s," are very common in these classes. Certain yoga poses involve a lot of hip flexion, which could exacerbate irritated pelvic floor nerves, specifically the pudendal and posterior femoral cutaneous nerves, which are often involved in pelvic pain. We recommend that with either Pilates or yoga,

PTs and patients work together to figure out if a certain class is a good fit. Read these posts from our blog (http://www.pelvicpainrehab.com/alternative-treatment/815/can-yoga-help-my-pelvic-pain/) for more information on how yoga can be tailored to pelvic floor recovery, and remember timing is everything.

HOW EXERCISE ALTERS HOW WE EXPERIENCE PAIN

Exciting new research shows that regular exercise may alter how a person experiences pain. And the more exercise we do, according to the study, the higher pain tolerance becomes. Scientists have known for a long time that exercise can briefly dull pain. That's because as muscles begin to ache during exercise, our bodies release natural opiates, such as endorphins, that slightly dampen the ache. This is known as exercise-induced hypoalgesia, and it usually starts during the workout and hangs around for about 20 to 30 minutes afterward. But whether exercise can alter the body's response to pain over the long term has remained unclear. Now, thanks to research undertaken at the University of New South Wales in Australia, we're closer to getting an answer. Here's the lowdown: researchers recruited 12 inactive adults who expressed interest in exercising, and another 12 who were similar in age and activity levels but preferred not to exercise. The researchers first tested all the study participants to find out how they reacted to pain. Pain response is extremely individualized and depends on several factors, including pain threshold and pain tolerance. Basically, pain threshold is the point at which someone starts to feel pain, and pain tolerance refers to how much time he/she can put up with the pain before putting a stop to whatever is causing it. Once pain threshold and pain tolerance were noted, the participants were separated into two groups. One group began a program of moderate stationary bicycling for 30 minutes, three times a week, for six weeks. This group progressively became more fit. The other group went about their lives just as they had before signing on to the study. After six weeks, researchers tested the pain thresholds and pain tolerance of all the participants. This is what they found: the participants who did not exercise had no changes in their responses to pain; both their pain tolerance and pain threshold remained the same. As for the participants who exercised, while their pain threshold remained the same, they had a substantial increase in pain tolerance. And the participants who saw the greatest increase in fitness levels had the greatest jump in their pain tolerance. For those who deal with persistent pain, this may mean that moderate amounts of exercise can change their perception of pain, thus helping with daily functioning and leading to a higher quality of life.[1]

Note

1. MD Jones et al., "Aerobic Training Increases Pain Tolerance in Healthy Individuals," *Medicine & Science in Sports & Exercise* 46 (2014): 1640–1647.

TAMRA'S STORY

A Stabbing Pain

I was a busy college freshman only concerned with three things: my studies, tennis practice, and going out swing dancing with my boyfriend. I was young and eager to figure out my place in the world. Every day I would wake up early for tennis practice and hit for a few hours. Then I would quickly wolf down breakfast at the cafeteria and go to my classes before returning in the afternoon for weight lifting, conditioning, and more drills. I was known on the team for my mental toughness and my ability to do whatever it took to win.

That strength would disappear when I first had sharp pain with intercourse the summer after my freshman year. My boyfriend and I had been together for eight months, and up until that point, sex had been pain-free. Obviously concerned, I began seeing several gynecologists. The first told me I had a yeast infection, gave me some medication, and sent me on my way. The pain continued, so I saw another gynecologist on campus who told me I had a UTI, gave me some medication, and sent me on my way. The pain only worsened, and one night during my sophomore year, I felt such a stabbing pain, I found myself in an ambulance on my way to the emergency room. The doctor on call disregarded everything I told him and told me I must have an STD and tried to treat me for it. When I explained this was impossible, as I was in a committed relationship and practiced safe sex, and besides hadn't had intercourse in months, he shook his head and said I must be lying and there was nothing more he could do. I left the ER that night feeling ashamed and misunderstood.

I felt so alone in my pain—no one could see or understand I was hurting. I closed up emotionally for months, unable to tell anyone what I was going through. The pain continued to break me down, and I found it more and more difficult to make it through my schoolwork and daily tennis practices. I began skipping classes because I had difficulty sitting through lectures and placing pressure on my pelvis. If I had to attend class, I brought ice pack pads to put in my underwear and wore bulky sweatpants so no one would know. After continued frustration, I went to a fourth gynecologist, who mentioned vulvar vestibulitis for the first time to me. She explained this was a new diagnosis for women who felt sharp pain around their vulva and referred me to a specialist in Philadelphia for further treatment.

During my first visit to the specialist, I was prescribed an estrogen-based cream to build up the tissue around my vulva. I was also placed on an increasing dosage of an antidepressant as part of a pain control intervention. It had disastrous effects on me. Over the course of the next few months, I experienced extreme emotional swings. I would cry in the shower and found myself yelling at those closest to me. The medication also made me extremely groggy and made it even more difficult to focus on my schoolwork. My dad drove to my school several times a week to type my papers while I would dictate from bed. I no longer felt in control of my body or my mind. It was the furthest from myself that I have ever felt.

Not able to handle the side effects any longer, I returned to my specialist, and I remember sitting across from her in a small, cold room. I was frustrated that my treatments weren't working and wanted answers. She looked into my eyes and told me that vulvar vestibulitis is a chronic condition and that there would always be flare-ups, so I had better prepare myself to live with this for the rest of my life. I felt the last bit of hope in me shatter. I would never get better? How could I continue to live my life like this? The word "chronic" felt like a prison sentence. To me it meant both the certainty that I would have pain and the uncertainty of how it would affect me. I felt trapped. I sat motionless on the train back home that day, watching the world whirl by me. I felt as if my life was rushing past me and I was missing it. To make matters worse, this visit coincided with a bad breakup. We had been together for 2 years, but the weight of my illness became too much for him to handle. I believed no one would ever love me again, that I was cursed to go through this life alone. There was no sense in looking ahead to the future. I was now living day to day.

Since conservative treatment had failed, my specialist signed me up for a vestibulectomy. If the vulva were a clock, this surgery would essentially cut out 4 o'clock to 8 o'clock, the portions that were causing me the most pain, and would replace the tissue with internal vaginal tissue. The issue I had with this last-resort surgery was its narrowed focus. It would cut out the place I first felt pain, but what if there was more to the story? What if my pain came from elsewhere? These were questions I did not have enough knowledge to ask.

It was at this point that I turned to writing and started a health blog called *Sky-Circles* (http://sky-circles.blogspot.com/). The title was based on a poem by Rumi about having hope in the face of struggle. I had always been an avid reader, but I turned to poetry when I was sick—not as a hobby, but as a necessity. I sought solace in the words of Mary Oliver and Rumi. And eventually they inspired me to write. It had been seven long months of misdiagnosis, failed treatments, and continued pain, which I'd kept hidden from everyone but my immediate family. Writing was cathartic and allowed me to share my story. I found a nurturing online community where women could share their experiences and seek guidance. Only weeks before my vestibulectomy, a reader of my blog wrote to me and suggested that I see a women's health physical therapist, because something else could be referring pain to my vulva. She gave me the name of Liz and Stephanie's practice in San Francisco, and after researching what pelvic floor physical therapy entailed, I decided it was time to become proactive about my health. Up until then, I had been allowing my doctors to dictate my plan of care. It was time for me to become educated before making any more medical decisions. I booked an appointment and my flight, and two weeks later, my mom and I found ourselves driving up and down the hills of San Francisco. We would soon learn that up until that point, doctors had been looking at my pain through a narrowed lens. We were about to step back and see the bigger picture.

Finding Answers

It wasn't my first time seeing a women's health physical therapist. I had previously seen two in New Jersey who claimed expertise in the field, but in hindsight, had no idea what they were doing when it came to my case. The first only prescribed Kegel exercises and said I needed to strengthen my pelvic floor. The second used a biofeedback machine to show me I needed to relax my pelvic floor. Going to San Francisco was a completely different experience. Liz performed a comprehensive evaluation that included an internal pelvic and external orthopedic exam. She paid close attention to my hips, testing my flexibility and strength. She also asked extensive questions about my medical and athletic history. At the end of the visit she told me her findings, which included limited range of motion at the hip, indicative of labral tears. She explained that the asymmetrical rotation of tennis led to repetitive motion at the hips, causing stress to the musculature and joint. Liz also explained that hip trauma can refer pain to the pelvic floor. She recommended that I see a sports physician and have imaging done immediately. I flew back to the East Coast feeling more educated and more in control of my future. I was in the middle of my junior year and felt hopeful for the first time that I would make it to graduation pain-free.

Sure enough, I had tears in both my left and right labrum and spent the next two summers getting them repaired. They ended up being two of the biggest tears my surgeon had ever seen and required extensive rehabilitation. I found a new pelvic floor physical therapist in NYC, who did extensive internal and external manual physical therapy work. In addition, she worked to strengthen and stretch my hips. We discovered my pelvic floor was extremely tight, as well as my obturator internus and piriformis muscles. This explained why sitting had been so painful. Slowly I started improving and feeling more like myself. My hips became stronger, and I felt ready to get back to my life. When I became a senior, I was named captain of my university's tennis team. I put my patient identity to the side and became an athlete again. I played my heart out, but as the matches continued, the pain in my hips returned. I had to stop playing halfway through the year to focus more on my recovery.

Although my hip surgeries were successful, I was still having setbacks in my treatment. I continued to have pain throughout my body. I found a new pelvic health specialist and went through two years of Traumeel injections, a natural anti-inflammatory to help reduce pain. She would give them to me at certain trigger points around my vulva, vaginal opening, gluteal muscles, and hips. The injections only lasted a few minutes, but needle injections into your vagina and deep into your muscles is not an easy procedure to sit through. I would have to bring a pad for the walk home to prevent the blood from staining my underwear.

Around this time I finished my degree and accepted an exciting opportunity to work in environmental advocacy in Denver. I wasn't healthy yet, but I was tired of waiting to start my life. In many ways, I needed an escape. Unfortunately, after less than two months of working, I called home in tears and explained to my parents that I couldn't do it anymore. My parents, steadfast in their love and support, picked me up from the airport that weekend.

Back home with my parents, I went through yet another surgery, repairing tears along my pubic bone and surgically releasing my tight adductor muscles. I was infuriated and upset that yet again, my life was back on hold. I was still having difficulty sitting for longer than 15 minutes and dealt with constant, unshakable pain. But giving up wasn't an option for me. I went to physical therapy after my third surgery and was referred to a pain doctor for prolotherapy injections. These differed from my previous injections because they were more aggressive and required longer sessions.

Every month for the next year I went through trigger point injections in my hip, pelvic, and gluteal regions, the idea being that the irritant glucose solution would trigger the body's natural healing process and repair damaged areas. Each treatment was over an hour of repetitive injections with long needles. Out of all the things I went through, these treatments were undoubtedly the worst. During the first one, I was unprepared but managed to stay silent until I curled up in the back of the car while my mom drove me home. I cried and cried and cried. I cried out in pain, for going through something so awful, for not knowing when it would end. I cried because I wanted to be braver, stronger, better. I cried because it felt right and because I needed it and because I wanted to feel something other than pain.

And so, having been there myself, I want to tell you that it is okay to be at your worst. To cry your heart out because you feel defeated and alone and scared. It's okay to feel pain, to lose control and run away for a while. It's okay to lean on your friends and family. It's okay to be vulnerable and ask for help and see a therapist. It's okay to shut yourself down and lock yourself in your room. Just do whatever you can to make it through the day. Know that change is the only constant in life, and tomorrow always brings new possibilities. After six months of enduring the difficult prolotherapy treatments, I finally started to notice a decrease in my pain.

A New Calling

I continued to document my medical and emotional struggles online, since writing was so therapeutic. My blog began to grow in readership as more women searched for answers. It soon reached tens of thousands of readers from across the world. What had begun as a personal release became an avenue to spread awareness about an unknown and too-often-misunderstood topic. I unexpectedly became a confidant and mentor to others struggling with pelvic pain. I even appeared on an MTV *True Life* episode to further advocate for pelvic floor health, especially the intimate connection between the hips and pelvis. I received hundreds of e-mails from readers expressing their gratitude for my openness and asking for help in their own medical struggles. As I read more of these e-mails, I realized I could offer more than just an encouraging response or a referral. One day I was sitting in the exam chair at my specialist's office and suddenly realized that I should become a women's health physical therapist. Despite the barriers of going back to school and my continuing health problems, I wanted to help others find answers sooner than I had found mine. I wanted to offer comprehensive medical care that looked at the whole body, the whole person. I wanted to help others overcome struggle and hardships and help them persevere and make a meaningful life for themselves. And so I set off to give my own life more meaning.

In August 2012, I started at Thomas Jefferson University in Philadelphia. Since then, I have worked toward my doctorate degree in physical therapy and my dream of becoming a pelvic floor physical therapist. As I find myself mere months from graduation, I am excited and eager to begin and help my patients heal. My dream is to develop a practice that emphasizes holistic pelvic health, with a focus on female athletes. I want to develop protocols for this demographic to prevent injuries like mine from befalling others.

While working toward that goal, I've been able to focus on my health as well as my schoolwork. During the first year of my studies, I worked with a new pelvic floor PT in Philadelphia to manage my residual pain through aggressive manual work, strengthening exercises, and stretching. I'm happy to report that after that first year I've not been back to PT and have stopped all injection treatments. I've also fallen in love and now have pain-free sex for the first time in years. Plus, I'm beginning to love my body instead of seeing it as a battleground. I continue to live pain-free through preventive care, such as maintaining a healthy, balanced diet, stretching tight musculature, training with functional movement, strengthening my core and pelvic floor, and practicing healthy body mechanics. I also focus on emotional health, reducing stressors in my life with meditation, reading, and yoga.

People often ask what helped me the most during my recovery. With such a complicated medical history and trying so many different interventions simultaneously, it's difficult to pinpoint the exact medical impetus for my healing. After going through physical therapy school, I firmly believe in the strong connection between the pelvic floor and the hips. The surgeries I went through fixed my body's mechanical problems, while the proceeding physical therapy strengthened muscles that were weak and stretched muscles that were overcompensating. The most useful thing for me during this entire process was the attainment of knowledge. Self-education allowed me to take control over my own health care. As a physical therapist, it's a requirement to be a lifelong learner, but I urge everyone to actively seek information so that they can be proactive about their health.

Stronger than Ever

What began as a sharp, localized pain in June 2007 grew to encompass a mind-body seven-year journey. As I write this, I'm currently in the best physical shape of my life, even better than my years as a collegiate athlete. I go to the gym daily and especially love serious weight lifting. I have climbed Kilimanjaro, the tallest mountain in Africa, along with several other high mountain peaks in the United States. And on my 26th birthday, I ran my first marathon. It was a long journey, full of ups and downs. When I was in the midst of my pain, I would have done anything for someone to take it away from me. When I felt the most broken, a dear friend gave me a small Japanese pot with several gold lines. I thought it was an unusual gift until I read the card, which said it was a piece of Kintsugi pottery. It's a Japanese method of fixing cracked pottery with gold or silver and represents more than an art form. It's also a philosophy of life. The Japanese believe there is beauty in being broken, that cracks should be celebrated and not concealed. They also believe the gold fillings reinforce the pottery, making it stronger than it was before.

About Tamra: Tamra Wroblesky graduated from Thomas Jefferson University with a doctorate in physical therapy in 2015 and is currently focused on building her pelvic floor physical therapy practice in New Jersey. Prior to moving her pelvic pain advocacy to the treatment room, Tamra shared her experiences recovering from pelvic pain on her blog titled *Sky-Circles*. In addition, her pelvic pain story has been featured on MTV's mini-documentary show, *True Life*.

CONCLUSION

In this chapter we've offered guidelines intended to help those dealing with pelvic pain stay fit without flaring their symptoms. For so many reasons staying fit is important for those recovering from pelvic pain. But we know how tough it can be for a formerly active person to be faced with the pelvic pain recovery process. However, often they channel the drive and motivation they've acquired in sportsmanship to the task. Another challenge that those with pelvic pain face can be communicating with providers, especially when a team of providers from different specialties is involved in their treatment. This is the topic we cover in the next chapter.

11

TIPS FOR OPTIMIZING COMMUNICATION WITH YOUR PROVIDERS

For five years Kylee has been dealing with endometriosis. For the past year, her symptoms of abdominal, vaginal, and low back pain have gotten much worse. They've gone from intermittent pain just before and during her menstrual cycle to constant, 24/7 pain that has begun to interfere with her daily life. Believing that her pelvic floor muscles were most likely behind Kylee's uptick in symptoms as opposed to the disease process of her endometriosis, Kylee's doctor referred her to PT. And indeed, Kylee's PT found several impairments she believed to be the culprits behind Kylee's symptoms. Kylee made steady progress in PT, but after a few months, her PT suggested she try trigger point injections as a complementary treatment approach. The PT referred Kylee to a local physician for the injections. The trigger point injections were helpful, and Kylee was pleased with the way her treatment was progressing. It was wonderful to have so many nonsurgical options available to treat her symptoms. At the same time, however, she felt a bit overwhelmed having to juggle so many different providers. Not only was she seeing her PT weekly as well as the new physician for biweekly trigger point injections, she was also still under the care of the physician who had treated her endometriosis for the past five years, a pain management doctor, and an acupuncturist. She found herself struggling to keep everything straight with her different providers, not only in her own mind, but also between her treatment team. For example, she often had a hard time explaining what was happening in PT to her physicians. Kylee was motivated to do everything necessary to get better, and her gut told her that keeping all of her medical providers on the same page would help her reach her treatment goals sooner. But seeing multiple providers for one medical condition was new terrain for her, and she wasn't quite sure what steps were appropriate for her to take to ensure that she and her medical providers were all on the same page.

Kylee's experience is not unique. Many people with pelvic pain find themselves in a position where they have to work to coordinate care between multiple medical providers. The provider-patient relationship itself already comes fraught with its own communication challenges, especially in today's managed care environment where so many providers are pressed for time. Is it any wonder that patients can become overwhelmed? That's why we've decided to dedicate this chapter to providing advice to patients on how to best optimize communication— not only between themselves and their providers, but also between the providers who make up their interdisciplinary treatment team. We'll begin the chapter with some general tips for how patients can improve communication with each of their individual providers. Then we'll share advice on how they can best optimize communication with their PTs. Lastly, we'll reveal a few strategies patients can use to make sure their treatment team members are all on the same page.

TIPS FOR COMMUNICATING WITH PROVIDERS

Be proactive.

As you know by now, pelvic pain is a multilayered condition that crosses medical disciplines. In other words, it can be complicated. As you've also learned, there is no silver-bullet treatment for pelvic pain. It's simply not a condition where a doctor can "fix" the patient or where any one medical provider is likely to have all the answers. So patients have to be active participants in their treatment—a passive approach is just not going to cut it. What does this mean in the context of provider-patient communication? For one thing, it means that when you're at your appointment with your provider, make sure you're actively involved in the discourse. Ask questions if you don't fully understand what your provider is saying. And if you process information better by reading it, feel free to ask your provider if he/she has any articles or other written information you can take home with you or if he/she can recommend any resources for you to check out. Also, don't be afraid to suggest treatment options to your providers based on your own research. Some patients may feel it's not their place to suggest treatment options. Rest assured, living in the Internet age, where so much information is available to patients, means medical providers understand that patients are better informed today than ever before. Therefore, at this point, they're used to patients suggesting options for treatment. But here's a tip nonetheless: a great way to approach any provider about whether a particular treatment option might be worth trying out is to bring in research on the treatment. If you do this, you're speaking the language of your medical providers, and chances are they'll be more comfortable trying something new that they hadn't thought of themselves.

Be prepared.

The majority of medical providers, physicians especially, are overloaded with patients, and their time with you is limited. So to maximize the time you have with them, be extra prepared for your appointments. For example, arrive at your first appointment with any provider with a concise history of your symptoms. It's a good idea to write it down beforehand complete with any pertinent dates, such as when you had a particular surgery or other intervention. Also, for each successive appointment, take some time, even if it's on the drive to the office, to prepare your thoughts beforehand. You know your provider will ask you how your symptoms have been since the last time he/she saw you. So be sure and have your response to this question ready to go. And be as specific as possible about your symptoms. If your pain increased, be specific about exactly what symptom worsened, exactly how it feels, and where the pain is located. The same goes for any interventions you may have tried since the last time you saw a provider. Explain exactly what your reaction was to the intervention, whether it was medication, injections, or even your first round of PT appointments. And also have any questions for the provider at the ready. Again, jot them down if it helps you remember. Lastly, if you communicate with your provider via e-mail, make sure any e-mails you send are clear and concise, and instead of sending several e-mails, try your best to limit the number of e-mails you send.

Be honest.

It's human nature for patients to want to please their medical providers. But it's important that you're always completely honest with them. For example, never minimize your symptoms for fear of disappointing a provider. You won't hurt his/her feelings if a particular treatment didn't work (or even flared your symptoms). The provider's goal is to help you get better, and in order to do this, he/she needs all the information you can give him/her about your condition. If you think about it, medical providers who treat a persistent pain condition rely heavily on what patients tell them. There simply aren't barrages of tests they can do to determine how a patient's treatment is progressing. For that reason, what you report to your providers is key to allowing them to give you the best care possible. So be honest with them, even if that means telling them your symptoms haven't improved since the last time you saw them or that you actually feel worse. It's also human nature for patients to want to present themselves in the best possible light to their providers for fear of being judged. But again, a provider must have an accurate picture of your condition in order to make the best decisions possible for your treatment. So for example, if your PT prescribed a home exercise program for you to do between appointments, and you didn't do it for whatever reason, be honest about it. That way, the PT won't think that the therapeutic exercises simply were not helpful. Also, some people with pelvic pain are embarrassed to share certain details with their providers that are relevant to their recovery—details about their urinary, bowel, or sexual function. This is understandable, but again, it's vital for providers to have all the facts of your case in order to make the best decisions possible. So if you're one of these folks, remind yourself that most medical providers have heard it all, and the details you find embarrassing are likely pretty run-of-the-mill for the provider.

OPTIMIZING COMMUNICATION WITH YOUR PT

When we're evaluating or treating patients, we're constantly explaining to them what we're doing and why. On top of explanations throughout the appointment, at the end of every appointment we give our patients a brief verbal summary of what we did, what we found, and what our expectations are for the progression of their recovery. While it's the job of a PT to keep patients in the loop about the therapeutic techniques they're using during PT, for a variety of different reasons, patients may not get all the information they need to fully grasp what's going on with their treatment. Plus, the dynamic between PT and patient can sometimes be tricky. Oftentimes patients are hesitant to question their PTs for fear of insulting them or disrespecting their expertise. Therefore, they may feel too intimidated to speak up when they have questions or concerns about their treatment. This lack of communication can be detrimental to pelvic floor PT for many reasons, not the least of which is that for some patients, successful treatment will require a major time and emotional commitment. So if a patient is confused or frustrated about treatment, he/she might ultimately decide to throw in the towel and discontinue PT, even though in the long run it's the best treatment option for them. For another thing, a full understanding of the treatment process results in less anxiety. And remember, when anxiety levels go down, it's possible for pain levels to follow suit. Therefore, when it comes to PT for pelvic pain, it's vital that patients be kept in the loop. So at any time during the process, if you as a patient have a question or concern, don't hesitate to bring it up with your PT. He/she wants you to be an active member of your treatment team and will welcome your desire to understand what's going on. Another important area of communication between patient and PT involves patient feedback. Patients must be sure that during their treatment they are providing their PTs with necessary and important feedback. For example, if what the PT is doing is providing relief, it's important that the patient communicate that to the PT. Conversely, if treatment is causing increased pain, it's important for patients to speak up and to describe in as much detail as possible exactly what they're experiencing. This type of feedback helps PTs evaluate their patient's progress and helps them determine if they need to make any treatment adjustments. Lastly, it's important that patients inform their PT of any relevant occurrences between appoint-

ments and that they answer their PT's questions to the best of their
ability. Again, this information enables the PT to evaluate and modify
his/her treatment approach throughout the treatment process. A good
tip for making sure you remember exactly how you responded to treatment is to jot down a quick note one, two, or even three days after
treatment. That way, when you see your PT again after an entire week
has gone by, you'll have those notes to help you recall details you otherwise might forget.

It's important to understand that the information you need to communicate with your PT will change as you progress in treatment. To be
sure, you'll want to discuss certain topics with him/her at the beginning
of PT, when you reach mid-treatment, and then when it comes time for
you to be discharged. For example, at the beginning of treatment, ask
your PT what his/her findings were, how the impairments he/she found
are causing your symptoms, and what he/she plans to do to try and
resolve those symptoms. Then mid-treatment, it's a good idea to ask
him/her how you're progressing and if there is anything you should be
doing to expedite your treatment. Upon discharge, good questions to
ask are how you can maintain the gains you've made in PT and what, if
any, signs you should look for if you have to come in for a tune-up. For
instance, should you come in if you have a one-day relapse of symptoms, or should you wait until you've had a few symptom relapses before calling to make an appointment?

TIPS FOR KEEPING YOUR INTERDISCIPLINARY TEAM ON THE SAME PAGE

- Pick the member of your treatment team you're the most comfortable with and ask him/her if they are willing to take a leadership role
  in your case and to act as a facilitator. As we've said in earlier chapters, this provider will often be the PT simply because he/she spends
  the most time with the patient and he/she is dealing with the neuromuscular system, which is so often a main driver of pelvic pain.
  However, other providers may be willing to take on this role as well.
  The patient will have the best sense of which member of his/her
  team is the best fit for the job.

- Ask providers to write down any technical information you need to update the other providers on your team. For instance, Liz had a patient who was receiving regular trigger point injections from a physician. Because it was hard for the patient to remember the names of the different muscles where Liz found trigger points that might benefit from injections, he had her write them down on a sticky note at each appointment. He asked the doctor to do the same each time he injected the muscles.

- Ask providers to send a copy of their notes to other providers. When we evaluate a patient for the first time, we write up an evaluation summary. In the summary we include a list of our objective findings along with our assessment and treatment plan. We repeat this exercise several times along the way as we reassess patients, and in each instance, we send these treatment summaries to the other providers on the patient's treatment team. This way, the necessary providers are kept abreast of exactly how patients are progressing in PT.

- Ask a provider to give another provider a call to talk. In our role as PTs, we often call other providers to confer on a patient. For example, if we come across a contributing factor that falls under the bailiwick of the provider or if we have an idea for treatment that the provider can carry out, such as administering injections or adding a certain medication to the patient's treatment plan, we simply give him/her a call to discuss it.

- If you gauge that your provider may be interested, ask him/her if he/she would be interested in co-treating you with another provider. For example, we've had many instances in our practice where physicians, other PTs, and/or acupuncturists have come to our clinic to co-treat a patient in order to collaborate in person about his/her treatment. This is beneficial because it allows both providers to evaluate the patient at the same time, giving each insight into how the other examines the patient. For instance, we've found it helpful to hear the questions that other providers ask our patients as well as the patients' responses. This gives us invaluable insight into how the other provider assesses the patient. Gaining this level of understanding of another component of a patient's treatment plan can help providers fine-tune their own treatment strategy. Additionally, if two providers get the opportunity to work on a particular impairment together during an appointment, the hope is that the impairment will be more successfully treated. For example, if the patient has a trigger point in one of her hip muscles that the PT thinks would benefit from dry needling, but the patient's acupuncturist is having problems locating the trigger point, the PT can provide guidance as to where to place the needle.

In this chapter we've given patients some tips we believe will enable them to better navigate an interdisciplinary treatment plan, which many folks dealing with pelvic pain have little to no experience with. In fact, so many people in the midst of recovering from pelvic pain have never been in a situation where they've had to focus so many resources—mental, emotional, financial, the list goes on—on their recovery. That's why in the next chapter, we offer some tips for navigating day-to-day living while in recovery for pelvic pain.

12

TIPS FOR DAY-TO-DAY LIVING

In this book, we've covered at length all the different treatment options available for pelvic pain, but so often, recovery from a persistent pain condition isn't just about what goes on in a doctor's office or in the PT treatment room; it also involves a great deal of day-to-day self-care. When we talk about day-to-day self-care, we're talking about the every-day measures folks take to further their recovery. And that's what this chapter is about. In it, we'll discuss a few general self-care tips that we frequently pass along to patients. In addition, we include some tried-and-true tips in the words of former patients. Lastly, because it's not just normal, day-to-day living that can pose challenges to patients, we're going to wrap up the chapter with a discussion of how to survive the holidays, advice that can be easily applied to any special occasion.

A FEW TIPS FOR DAY-TO-DAY LIVING

Cushions

For many who are in recovery from pelvic pain, sitting is a pain trigger. For that reason, we often have to help patients develop strategies that will make sitting more tolerable. Using a cushion when sitting can be helpful. When shopping for a cushion in the marketplace, we advise patients to look for one that will provide pressure relief to the areas that are painful for them when they sit, such as the perineum, tailbone, or vulva, or cushions that distribute their weight more evenly when they sit, thus reducing pressure on certain areas of the pelvis, such as the sit bones or tailbone. But at the end of the day, the best cushion is the one that makes sitting the most comfortable. Our patients have used a handful of commercially available cushions in the past, such as the Thera-Seat (http://www.theraseat.com/) cushion. Two other companies, Cushion Your Assets (www.cushionyourassets.com) and WonderGel (https://wondergel.com/), manufacture cushions that might be helpful to those in recovery from pelvic pain. Sometimes, however, finding the right cushion takes a bit of creativity. For instance, we've had patients who have used padded or gel-covered medical toilet seat covers as cushions, often covering them with homemade slipcovers. Patients have also reported success using more than one type of cushion throughout the day—for example, they might use a different cushion in the car versus when sitting at a desk. Also, replacing a desk chair with a physio ball has been helpful for some of our patients. Unfortunately, finding the "right" cushion for you may turn out to be a lengthy and expensive endeavor. To be sure, we've had patients who've had to keep trying (and buying) cushions until they found the one that worked best for them. However, our thinking is that if your pain increases with sitting and your daily routine involves a lot of sitting (long commute in the car, sitting at a desk), it's worth investing the time and money in finding the right cushion for you.

Clothing

For some patients, clothing is a pain trigger. For example, many women with vulvar pain can't wear jeans or pants because they find the inseam irritating. Some of our patients have found that wearing jeans can be made tolerable if they use a product called the Go Commandos patch (http://www.gocommandos.com/), an adhesive underwear alternative that will cover the inseam. In general, if clothing is a trigger, we advise patients to wear loose clothing that doesn't put pressure on painful areas. For our female patients this often means forgoing underwear, jeans, and pants until they feel better and opting for skirts and dresses instead. And for our male patients, this typically means wearing no underwear and baggier pants and/or shorts with lower inseams.

Shoes

Because so many people with pelvic pain have pain with sitting, they end up standing a great deal longer day in and day out than the average person. For this reason alone, wearing supportive footwear is important to minimize fatigue and/or discomfort in the back, feet, and/or legs when standing. Wearing supportive footwear could mean simply wearing good, supportive sneakers or it could mean using shoe inserts. Patients often ask us if store-bought shoe inserts are sufficient or if custom orthotics are necessary. There is no cut-and-dried answer to this question. Typically we tell patients to start with inexpensive, store-bought orthotics and to use them on a trial basis to see if they are comfortable and lessen lower body fatigue and/or discomfort. If they don't do the trick, then we refer them to a trusted podiatrist for custom-fitted orthotics. Another bit of advice regarding shoes is that flip-flops and high heels should be worn only on rare occasions! That's because for their part, flip-flops do not provide arch support, which can be detrimental from a musculoskeletal perspective. And heels change a person's center of gravity in a way that puts pressure on the low back and pelvic floor. As with many things concerning treatment for pelvic pain, consulting your PT about what sort of footwear is best for your particular situation is always the best way to go.

LIFE HACKS FROM PATIENTS

When we talk to patients recovering from pelvic pain about challenges they face in their everyday lives, the discussion inevitably turns to three topics: communicating an "invisible" condition to family and friends; finding a helpful support system; and the challenge of setting limits with others. Below is some wise advice from folks who have faced these challenges head-on.

A PAIN TO EXPLAIN: CORA'S STORY

In December 2006 my life came to a butt-numbing, crotch-burning halt. My husband and I were on a flight to California. Halfway through the flight, I started to go numb in the "down there" region. I squirmed in my seat in fear, praying that we were close to landing. I leaned over and whispered to my husband that I was losing feeling in my crotch and thighs. Being an emergency medicine doctor, he went straight into ER mode. He thought I might be having a spinal cord emergency and that as soon as we landed, we may need to get to a hospital for a stat MRI scan. Although I made it through that weekend without an ER visit, a few weeks later I had another episode, which in the famous words of my husband "bought me a ticket to the ER." At the hospital, I learned I had injured some delicate muscles I didn't even know I had, and apparently one of my nerves was a little ticked off too. The more formal diagnoses: pelvic floor dysfunction (PFD) with pudendal neuralgia (PN). Ah, such a clinical name for "pain in the ass." I later learned that *pudendal* is the Latin word for "shame." "Great," I thought, "I have a shameful, painful condition. How do I explain that?" It didn't take long for family and friends to hear that I had an injury and was in bed on pain medication. Lots of pain medication. I called my dog-training students and canceled sessions and made arrangements to have the house cleaned and the farm chores done. Like it or not, I was down for the count and closed for business. When family and friends suddenly see an active, healthy woman flat in bed and unable to sit, they ask questions. "What did you do, exactly?" "Can it be fixed?" "Why can't you sit?" What hurts?" "How could this happen to you? You're so healthy!" The questions were endless. How you choose to respond to such questions is a very personal decision. I found with some family members, there was the "too much information" factor. For instance, for my older brother, just hearing "back pain" was plenty. Then there are the old soul friends with whom I was able to share many details. With them I've been able to talk about the dark, scary, sleepless nights. I've whined about the lack of sex in my marriage. I've also shared with them the private details of PT and the more humorous spin I tend to put on this whole deal. When thinking about whom you tell and what you tell them, it is important to think about the motivation of the person asking. Is this a close friend with genuine concern? Is this person a snoopy neighbor or colleague? Is this person really a friend? I've given all sorts of responses, and some have been more tactful than others. I remember one male acquaintance who kept asking for more details. Finally I said to him, "If I tell you any more details, I'm certain you'll blush!" He never asked me another question again. For a while I was telling people that I have a back injury with some muscle and nerve trauma. But that explanation was met with numerous recommendations about back cures, which became tiresome. Now I am more relaxed about the whole thing. If someone asks me, I give a brief and vague response. This usually happens when I am in a public place and some chivalrous man will offer me his seat. Really, they still do that! I politely reject the offer, and if they persist, I say, "Thanks, I'm more comfortable standing. I have an injury." My PT gave me some incredible advice. I asked her how to respond to inquiries regarding my sudden need to stand up all the time and all the other lifestyle changes that accompany the spectrum of PFD. She said that I might ask, "What is it that you'd like to know?" I love that response. It allows for a gentle pause, and time for the other person to respectfully reframe their question or change the subject. I don't think there are any easy ways to communicate what PFD truly is to others in our everyday lives. Even our doctors and PTs have trouble at times. What I think is most important is that as we work toward healing, we do our best to surround ourselves with a caring support system. I have shed many tears in my horse's fur on a quiet night in the barn. And ya know, he never asked "Why?"

SETTING UP A SUPPORT SYSTEM

Cora's Story

Pelvic pain is not something we run marathons for or distribute ribbons for. On the contrary, it's an invisible condition, and for that reason, those dealing with it can feel isolated and alone at a time when they need support more than ever. One of the things I did to make sure I had a strong support system in place during my recovery is I began seeing a therapist. I wanted to maintain as much normalcy as possible, but I knew I needed someplace to vent, and I discovered early on that talking to family worried them, and I didn't want to worry them. Plus I knew they didn't get it. Seeing a therapist provided me with a safe outlet where I could unload. It was so helpful to know I had a standing appointment each week with someone who would help me work through the many ups and downs that come along with a persistent pain condition.

Justin's Story

The best support I got was from another guy around my own age who also had pelvic pain. My therapist put me in touch with him. He was a high-powered lawyer, and it was really encouraging for me to meet someone who had been through what I was going through. It made me feel less isolated. Also, I got some amazing advice from him, which helped me to change my attitude about my own situation. For one thing, he stressed how important it was for me to comply with treatment. It was inspiring to me to see how he worked PT and his home treatment plan into his busy schedule. For another thing, he helped me to realize that during recovery, flare-ups happened, and that they were only temporary setbacks. He said when he would have a flare, instead of giving in to depression and discouragement, he would simply view them as a reminder to continue to be vigilant about his treatment plan. But perhaps most important of all, he was integral in helping me realize that while I was in recovery, I still needed to live my life. For instance, he swam, and maybe that was a little painful, but it was better than being inactive. Also, he'd go out to dinner, and maybe sitting would cause him discomfort, but the social interaction was worth it.

SETTING LIMITS

Georgia's Story

Going through life, it's normal to want to please others. It's just human nature. But when you have to deal with a persistent pain condition (or any major health issue for that matter), your well-being has to become your priority. And a major part of focusing on your own well-being is to learn to set limits and to say, "No, I'm sorry, but I can't." This is not always easy. Pelvic pain is an invisible condition, and so often those who are dealing with it look perfectly healthy and robust. Therefore, the people in their lives struggle to understand why they can't make firm plans or keep commitments. When my pain first started and I found myself having to turn down invitations or when I simply couldn't show up for the people in my life in all the ways I had before, I spent a lot of time stressing myself out about it or even worse, pushing myself to do things that hindered my recovery for fear of disappointing others. Eventually I began to realize that setting limits was an important part of taking care of myself, and that by working so hard to not let others down, I was ultimately letting myself down. A couple of things helped me deal with the repercussions that sometimes came along with setting limits and boundaries with the people in my life. For one thing, I realized (with the help of a therapist) that disappointment is a part of life and that I needed to be okay with disappointing others in situations where my intention was to take care of my health. Second (again with the help of a therapist), I realized that by setting limits and taking care of myself I was actually taking care of the people in my life who depended on me, my husband and son. This resonated with me, because like so many people dealing with pelvic pain, it was important to me that I continue to be there for my family. Reframing limit setting as taking care of my family as well as myself really helped put things into perspective for me, allowing me get past a lot of unnecessary guilt and anxiety.

PELVIC PAIN HOLIDAY SURVIVAL GUIDE: MOLLY'S STORY

"It's the most wonderful DREADFUL time of the year!" A few years ago, that's how I felt about the holidays. It was not always thus. Used to be I was the holidays' biggest fan. As soon as the Halloween candy hit the grocery store shelves, I'd feel a pang of excitement that lasted right up until my hangover on New Year's Day. Turkey. Stuffing. Green bean casserole. Gaudy Christmas lights. Johnny Mathis's velvety voice on the radio. Watching *A Christmas Story* on a loop. Frenzied Christmas shopping! Presents! Christmas cookies! I loved it all! But when I began dealing with a persistent pelvic pain issue, my holiday joy turned to holiday dread. At the first whiff of Halloween candy a cloud of anxiety would settle over me. What was once a thrilling time of the year became a time of stress, frustration, disappointment, and resentment. Not to mention jacked-up pain levels. The good news is that with some trial and error, I've come to once again embrace the holiday season. In fact, my holiday love affair is stronger than ever now *because* of all the lessons I was forced to learn. Before I get into how I learned to embrace the holiday season again, let me first explain my reasons for sour-ing on it to begin with. Managing a chronic pain condition forces you to take care of yourself. Toward that end, my regimen included weekly PT sessions, taking my meds on time, self-treatment, frequent icing, wear-ing clothes that didn't irritate my hot spots (living in Southern Califor-nia meant I could wear comfy skirts and dresses practically year-round), getting enough rest and exercise, and eating well. Once the holidays rolled around, much of that went out the window. For me, the holidays required travel and prolonged family visitation. For both Thanksgiving and Christmas my husband and I would spend a week or so with either his family or mine. And while it was wonderful to be among family, the travel, having to veer off my self-care routine, and the marathon social-izing was tough, and not only caused my pain to flare, but a great deal of anxiety to boot, which exacerbated the flare.

Turns out I was not alone. "A lot of people with chronic pain go into the holidays with free-floating anxiety on how it's going to go," said Dr. Erica Marchand, Ph.D. and licensed psychologist. "So it colors the whole experience." Dr. Marchand asks her patients who are in this predicament to pinpoint the things they're worried about the most. "Because it's usually not everything, even though it feels like every-thing." Once patients pinpoint the things they're most worried about, she helps them develop "survival strategies" for getting past their anxie-ty. In addition to asking patients to pick out what they're most worried about, she asks them to name the things they're looking forward to most. "Realize that these are the activities you really want to do, so that if need be, you can cancel or not accept other invitations. That way you'll have the energy to feel good enough to do the things that lift you up during the holiday season. Because it's not just about making your family happy, it's also about enjoying yourself." For my part, when I sat down to really figure out what it was about the holiday season that I dreaded most, I realized it was the pressure to be the perfect wife, daughter, daughter-in-law, aunt, sister, friend, etc. I hate disappointing people, and during the holidays, especially during family visits, there were a lot more people to potentially disappoint. For example, If I was in too much pain or too tired to join in on some activity or needed some time alone to ice after a long day of sitting and wearing not-so-comfort-able clothes (sundresses don't fly everywhere in December), family and friends didn't always get it. "Often we set perfectionist standards for ourselves," said Dr. Marchand. "I think it's important to realize this and to then cut ourselves some slack. You just need to be a *good enough* wife, daughter, mom, sister, friend." "Not to mention," she added, "that usually we ourselves think about our perceived shortcomings so much more than whomever we're worried we've offended. So I think it's important to ask 'Am I allowing myself to feel too guilty about this? Am I allowing a family member/friend to make me feel too bad about this? Is it perhaps okay that I had to cancel plans, and that someone is disappointed because of it?'" And to remember that everybody cancels plans sometimes, and not everyone always feels well. For me, once I realized this—that it was okay if someone was disappointed, and that typically they'd just process it, get over it, and still love me at the other end—it was a life changer. I realized I didn't have to manage everyone's reactions or emotional responses.

That led me to understand that I myself had my own issues with being disappointed with my family and friends around the holiday season. I realized that when I thought they weren't being understanding enough about my limitations, I became resentful, and nothing can dampen holiday cheer like good old-fashioned resentment! It was then that I realized that I myself had to be more empathetic. It occurred to me that it is extremely difficult to really *get* what someone dealing with persistent pain is going through. "It's an invisible condition," explained Dr. Marchand. "It's not like you have a cast on your arm or a bandage to remind people that there's pain involved. Empathy is a difficult thing, and humans have a really difficult time empathizing with something they cannot see or have not experienced themselves." For me, this reality hit home when my husband began dealing with chronic back pain. This is a guy who is super-active and athletic. He's one of those human energy machines who do more in a day than most people do in a week. But when he started experiencing his own invisible pain issue, I had to constantly remind myself why he wasn't doing all the stuff he normally did or why he wasn't up for doing something I wanted us to do together. Or worse yet, *he* had to remind *me* that he was in pain, and when he did, I realized it had completely slipped my mind. And I'm someone who has dealt with a persistent pain issue. Once I really understood how challenging it is to empathize with an invisible health condition, I was able to bypass those feelings of resentment that would crop up during holiday visits. But I'd like to stress that understanding that empathizing with those with a persistent pain condition isn't always easy, doesn't mean you shouldn't expect any to come your way. "It's reasonable to expect empathy from the people in your life, but we sometimes have an idea what a supportive response is, and when people don't respond in those exact ways, but their intentions are good, we feel hurt and resentful. Instead of going down that road, it helps to try to understand what their intentions are, and give them a chance to respond in a better way later. Also, it's worth keeping in mind that it's hard to see someone you love in pain. To be in a situation where you're powerless to make their pain go away. We want the people we love to be well and happy. For their sake, and frankly, for ours too. We want them to feel good, so we ourselves don't have to feel bad, so we don't have to feel guilty, or worry, or take care of them, or any of that. It's human nature."

Another strategy that helped me to get past my anxiety around the holidays was learning to be okay with setting boundaries. For example, I stopped saying yes to every activity on the agenda. Or if it was still early in the evening but I was ready to leave a party or get-together, I learned to not give in to entreaties to "stay a little longer." It became easier to set these boundaries when I realized doing so actually made me a team player. "Think about why you're trying to be accommodating during the holidays," said Dr. Marchand. "Usually it's so that the people in your lives will feel good and have a positive experience. If you are comfortable and having a good experience, chances are greater that those around you will too. So it really is in everyone's best interest for you to feel good and happy. It allows you to be the best host/guest and gives you the best possible outcome."[1]

But what about the people in your life who are just never going to get it no matter what? Like Aunt Edna or Cousin Eddie who complain about you leaving the party early or hassle you for your lousy Christmas shopping efforts (gift cards for everyone!). To deal with these situations, what I do is envision myself in a bubble where I can observe that person's reaction and my reaction, but there is some distance. They don't get to get into my bubble. And from there I sort of narrate the process, like Aunt So-and-So is being rude again, now she's frowning, now she's complaining about me in some way. Narrating the process places me at an observational distance from the situation. And from there, I don't feel that I have to either fix it or control it.

Appendix A

PELVIC PAIN RESOURCES

BOOKS

Explain Pain by David Butler (NOI Group, 2nd edition, 2013)

Explain Pain resources aim to give clinicians and people in pain the power to challenge pain and to consider new models for viewing what happens during pain.

The Pain Chronicles by Melanie Thernstrom (Farrar, Straus and Giroux, 1st edition, 2010)

In *The Pain Chronicles*, Melanie Thernstrom traces conceptions of pain throughout the ages—from ancient Babylonian pain-banishing spells to modern brain imaging—to reveal the elusive, mysterious nature of pain itself.

The Anxiety and Phobia Workbook by Edmund J. Bourne (New Harbinger Publications, 4th edition, 2005)

Exercises and worksheets to overcome problems with anxiety and phobic disorders.

The Trigger Point Therapy Workbook: Your Self-Treatment Guide by Clair Davies (New Harbinger Publications, 2nd edition, 2004)

Clair Davies creates a highly effective form of pain therapy that anyone can learn. This book is a valuable contribution to the field of self-applied therapeutic bodywork.

Painful Yarns by Lorimer Moseley (Orthopedic Physical Therapy Products, 1st edition, 2007)

A collection of stories that provides an entertaining and informative way to understand modern pain biology.

Stop Endometriosis and Pelvic Pain by Andrew Cook (Femsana Press, 1st edition, 2012)

"I'm writing this book for women who have endometriosis, to help you realize you're not alone, and, above all, to offer hope." —Dr. Andrew Cook

Wild Creative (Atria Books/Beyond Words, 2014)

Through stories, visualizations, and other creative exercises, Wild Creative reveals groundbreaking tools for realigning the creative field and actively designing your life.

The Better Bladder Book by Wendy Cohan (Hunter House, 2010)

Wendy Cohan, RN, empowers readers to master effective self-help tools such as stress reduction, pelvic floor relaxation, and herbal remedies to conquer bladder symptoms and pelvic pain.

Healing Painful Sex by Deborah Coady (Seal Press, 2011)

Both Deborah Coady's (MD) medical expertise and Nancy Fish's (MSW, MPH) personal experience with sexual pain and her extensive professional experience as a psychotherapist provide readers with an all-inclusive understanding of the medical causes of these complex conditions as well as multidimensional medical and psychological treatments.

Secret Suffering by Susan Bilheimer and Robert J. Echenberg (2010)

Secret Suffering is the first book to open the floodgates to expose the issue of chronic sexual pain, which tears couples apart and destroys both partners' quality of life, and present in-depth interviews of suffering couples.

Heal Pelvic Pain by Amy Stein (McGraw-Hill Education, 1st edition, 2008)

Discusses stretching, toning, and relaxation exercises for pelvic pain, plus healing massages and a specialized nutrition plan for men, women, and children of all ages.

Healing Pelvic Pain and Abdominal Pain by Amy Stein

A DVD that tackles pelvic and abdominal pain, including IC/PBS, IBS, vulvodynia, endometriosis, nonbacterial prostatitis, and unexplained back, pelvic, tailbone, abdominal, bladder, bowel, genital, and sexual pain and dysfunction.

A Headache in the Pelvis by David Wise and Rodney Anderson (National Center for Pelvic Pain, 6th revised edition, 2012)

A Headache in the Pelvis adds new research recently published in the *Journal of Urology* done by the Wise-Anderson team describing the relationship of painful trigger points that refer and re-create specific symptoms of pelvic pain.

When Sex Hurts by Andrew Goldstein, Caroline Pukall, and Irwin Goldstein (Da Capo Lifelong Books, 2011)

Director of the Centers for Vulvovaginal Disorders Dr. Andrew Goldstein and leading researcher Dr. Caroline Pukall tackle the stereotypes, myths, and realities of dyspareunia, addressing its more than 20 different causes and offering the most up-to-date research. This book provides the long-awaited answers to so many women's questions.

PRODUCTS

Dilators (https://www.vaginismus.com/products/dilator_set)

Simply better products, these medical-grade dilators are smooth and comfortable, easy to control, lightweight, and safe.

Vmagic (http://www.vmagicnow.com/)

Vmagic skin cream is a 100% natural and organic solution for vulvar discomfort from irritation, dryness, and inflammation.

Pelvic Therapy Hot/Cold Pad (http://pelvicpainsolutions.com/cart/index.php?main_page=index&cPath=355)

Targets the abdomen, hips, pubic bone, pelvic floor/crotch, tailbone, and low back simultaneously with natural hot/cold therapy.

LifeStyles® SKYN® Intense Feel (http://www.lifestyles.com/category/condoms/)

SKYN is the first premium condom made from polyisoprene—a scientifically formulated non-latex material that delivers the ultimate sensitivity that is the closest thing to wearing nothing.

Restore Pressure Point Massager (http://www.gaiam.com/product/restore-pressure-point-massager/05-58255.html)

Target pressure points, increase circulation, and alleviate sore muscles with this convenient massager. Includes a downloadable massage guide to rejuvenate tired and sore muscles throughout your body.

MuTu System (http://mutusystem.com/download-the-mutu-system-coaching-programme.html)

The complete body makeover for every mom who wants to lose the baby belly, improve pelvic floor function, and strengthen her core to get strong, fit, and body confident.

Pelvic Floor Relaxation CD for Pelvic Pain (https://www.pelvicexercises.com.au/pelvic-exercise-products/)

Thirty minutes of guided pelvic floor muscle and whole body relaxation with breathing exercises, in two versions for men and women.

GoCommandos (http://www.gocommandos.com/)

GoCommandos all-cotton patches stick securely in your pants and jeans, eliminating conventional underwear. Now worn by many women suffering from pelvic pain and vulvar and bladder conditions who claim they are extremely soothing and comfortable.

Slippery Stuff (http://www.cmtmedical.com/index.php?main_page=product_info&products_id=473)

Slippery Stuff is a hygienic, water-based and water-soluble, odorless, long-lasting, and latex-compatible product and is formulated to match the body's own natural lubrication.

Kolorex Intimate Care Cream (http://www.swansonvitamins.com/natures-sources-kolorex-intimate-care-cream-1-76-oz-cream)

Soothing herbal cream free from synthetic preservatives, mineral oils, synthetic fragrances, and parabens.

Gabrialla Abdominal Binder (http://www.itamed.com/Abdominal-Binders.html)

Decreases pressure and provides excellent support to the abdomen, waist, and lumbosacral areas.

DVD: *The Pelvic Floor Piston: Foundation for Fitness* (https://www.juliewiebept.com/products/)

Physical therapist Julie Wiebe guides you step-by-step through new concepts, exercises, movement strategies, and body awareness tips easily integrated into your day.

DVD: *Your Pace Yoga "Relieve Pelvic Pain"* by Dustienne Miller

This DVD was created by Dustienne Miller, a board-certified women's health physical therapist and Kripalu yoga teacher. This yoga home program was specifically designed for men and women who are healing chronic pelvic pain. The DVD weaves together breath work, meditation, body awareness, and gentle yoga postures. This stress-relieving program can be practiced in as little as 20 minutes, making it possible to fit into daily life.

TheraWand (http://www.therawand.com)

TheraWand has been found by physical therapists to be indispensable in pelvic floor treatments, including but not limited to trigger point (myofascial) release, painful intercourse, scar tissue, sensitivity, tight vaginal opening, vaginismus, anorgasmia, prostate massage, and more.

Reduce Sexual Pain Guides **(http://sexualrehab.com/Additional-Resources.html)**

PDF guides that provide a new way to look at sex for couples, as well as more information on pleasurable products, and activities.

Cushions

Cushion Your Assets (http://www.cushionyourassets.com/)
TheraSeat (http://www.cmtmedical.com/in-dex.php?main_page=product_info&products_id=415)
WonderGel Cushion (http://www.bedbathandbeyond.com/1/1/197992-wondergel-extreme-seat-cushion.html)

BLOGS/VIDEOS

Dr. Jen Gunter, https://drjengunter.wordpress.com/
Julie Wiebe, PT, https://www.juliewiebept.com/blog/
Blog About Pelvic Pain, http://www.blogaboutpelvicpain.com/
Sexual Healing
Body in Mind, http://www.bodyinmind.org/
IC Network, http://www.ic-network.com/
The Pelvic Guru, http://pelvicguru.com/
Understanding Pain: What to do about it in less than five minutes? https://www.youtube.com/watch?v=4b8oB757DKc&feature=player_embedded
Pain Management Meditation Video, https://www.youtube.com/watch?v=2kVKx-6uzsE
Pelvic Floor Part 1—The Pelvic Diaphragm—3D Anatomy Video Tutorial, http://anatomyzone.com/tutorials/musculoskeletal/pelvic-floor/
Pelvic Floor Part 2—Perineal Membrane and Deep Perineal Pouch, https://www.youtube.com/watch?v=q0Ax3rLFc6M

SUPPORT GROUPS

Happy Pelvis, https://groups.yahoo.com/neo/groups/happypelvis/info
Pelvic Pain Support Network, https://healthunlocked.com/pelvicpain
Endometriosis Groups, http://endometriosis.org/support/support-groups/
Baby Center, http://community.babycenter.com/
Golden Gate Mothers Group, http://www.ggmg.org/
IC Network, http://www.ic-network.com/forum/forum.php
Pelvic Organ Prolapse Support, http://www.pelvicorganprolapsesupport.org/
Women's Health Foundation, http://womenshealthfoundation.org/

Appendix B

EVALUATION INTERVIEW: COMPLETE LIST OF QUESTIONS

SYMPTOMS INFORMATION:

- What do you think caused your symptoms?
- When did your symptoms begin?
- Describe the quality of the symptoms—itching, burning, aching, etc.
- What makes your symptoms worse?
- What makes your symptoms better?
- Are your symptoms intermittent or constant?

URINARY INFORMATION:

- Do you have difficulty initiating your urinary stream?
- Is the stream weak or interrupted?
- How many times per day do you void?
- How many times per night do you void?
- Do certain foods, beverages, positions, or activities change your urinary function?
- Do you experience pain or burning before, during, or after voiding? If so, where?
- Do you leak urine when you cough, sneeze, or laugh?
- Do you leak urine when you feel the urge to void?
- Do you leak urine without realizing it?

BOWEL INFORMATION:

- Do you have a history of constipation and/or IBS? If yes, is it currently controlled?
- How often do you have a bowel movement?
- Do you have a history of anal fissures or hemorrhoids?
- Do you experience pain or burning before, during, or after a bowel movement?
- Do you have difficulty evacuating stool?
- Has the shape or quality of your bowel movements changed recently?

SEXUAL AND GENITAL INFORMATION:

Men:

- Are you able to obtain an erection?
- Are you able to ejaculate?
- Do you experience pain before, during, or after ejaculation?
- Have you noticed a change in the quality of your erection and/or ejaculate?
- Do you have genital or pelvic itching?

Women:

- Do you experience pain with penetration?
- Do you experience pain with deep thrusting or certain positions?
- Do you have painful menses?
- Are you able to achieve an orgasm?
- Do you have pain before, during, or after intercourse and/or orgasm?
- Do you experience genital or pelvic itching?
- Do you have a history of urinary tract infections?
- Do you have a history of yeast infections?
- Do you feel the presence of a foreign body in the vagina or as if things are falling out of the vagina?

NOTES

FOREWORD

1. There is some debate regarding the use of the terminology "persistent pelvic pain" or "chronic pelvic pain." Currently, the thinking is that pelvic pain is not always chronic, that in many cases it can be cured or at least very well controlled. Thus, "chronic" is thought by many experts to be an inappropriate name and "persistent" more appropriate to the condition.

INTRODUCTION

1. T Jackson et al., "The Impact of Threatening Information about Pain on Coping and Pain Tolerance," *British Journal of Health Psychology* 10 (2005): 441–451.

I. PELVIC PAIN 101

1. R Fillingim et al., "The ACTTION-American Pain Society Pain Taxonomy (AAPT): An Evidence-Based and Multidimensional Approach to Classifying Chronic Pain Conditions," *Journal of Pain* 15, no. 3 (March 2014): 241–249.

2. HOW DID I GET PELVIC PAIN? THE IMPORTANCE OF UNCOVERING CONTRIBUTING FACTORS

1. I Goldstein and L Burrows, "Can Oral Contraceptives Cause Vestibulodynia?" *Journal of Sexual Medicine* 7 (2010): 1585–1587.

3. DEMYSTIFYING THE NEUROMUSCULAR IMPAIRMENTS THAT CAUSE PELVIC PAIN

1. D Simons et al., *Travell and Simons' Myofascial Pain and Dysfunction: The Trigger Point Manual* (LLW, 1998).

6. GUIDE TO NAVIGATING TREATMENT OPTIONS

1. RM Moldwin and JY Fariello, "Myofascial Trigger Points of the Pelvic Floor: Associations with Urological Pain Syndromes and Treatment Strategies Including Injection Therapy," *Current Urology Report* 14, no. 5 (October 2013): 409–417.

2. *Ibid.*

3. SH Richeimer et al., "Utilization Patterns of Tricyclic Antidepressants in a Multidisciplinary Pain Clinic: A Survey," *Clinical Journal of Pain* 13 (1997): 324–329.

4. A Beydoun et al., "Gabapentin: Pharmacokinetics, Efficacy, and Safety," *Clinical Neuropharmacology* 14 (1995): 469–481.

5. DJ Hewitt, "The Use of NMDA-Receptor Antagonists in the Treatment of Chronic Pain," *Clinical Journal of Pain* 16, no. 2 (2000): S73–S79.

6. D Engeler et al., "General Treatment of Chronic Pelvic Pain: Guidelines on Chronic Pelvic Pain," European Association of Urology (February 2012): 122–130.

7. P Gupta et al., "Percutaneous Tibial Nerve Stimulation and Sacral Neuromodulation: An Update," *Current Urology Report* 16, no. 2 (February 2015): 4.

8. KM Alo and J Holsheimer, "New Trends in Neuromodulation for the Management of Neuropathic Pain," *Neurosurgery* 50 (2002): 690–703.

9. D Byrd and S Mackey, "Pulsed Radio Frequency for Chronic Pain," *Current Pain and Headaches Report* 1 (January 12, 2008): 37–41.

10. CL Swanson et al., "Localized Provoked Vestibulodynia: Outcomes after Modified Vestibulectomy," *Journal of Reproductive Medicine* 59, no. 3–4 (March–April 2014): 121–126.

11. JM Danford et al., "Postoperative Pain Outcomes after Transvaginal Mesh Revision," *International Urogynecology Journal* 26, no. 1 (January 2015): 65–69.

7. THE PELVIC FLOOR AND PREGNANCY: TREATING NEW MOMS RIGHT

1. M Beckmann and O Stock, "Antenatal Perineal Massage for Reducing Perineal Trauma," *Cochrane Database of Systemic Reviews* 4 (2013).

2. WH Wu et al., "Pregnancy Related Pelvic Girdle Pain: Terminology, Clinical Presentation, and Prevalence," *European Spine Journal* 13 (2004): 575–589.

3. K Bo, "Evaluation of Female Pelvic Floor Muscle Function and Strength," *Physical Therapy* 85 (2005): 269–282.

4. JS Boissonnault and MJ Blaschak, "Incidence of Diastasis Recti Abdominis during the Childbearing Years," *Physical Therapy Journal* 68 (1988): 1082–1086.

5. J Martin et al., "Births: Final Data for 2013," *Centers for Disease Control and Prevention National Vital Statistics Reports* 64 (2015).

6. K Bo, "Evaluation of Female Pelvic Floor Muscle Function and Strength," *Physical Therapy Journal* 85 (2005): 269–282.

7. Sara Fox, e-mail message to author, February 14, 2015.

8. Mark Conway, e-mail message to author, February 16, 2015.

8. PELVIC PAIN AND SEX: THE FACTS

1. L Pink, V Rancourt, and A Gordon, "Persistent Genital Arousal in Women with Pelvic and Genital Pain," *Journal of Obstetrics and Gynaecology Canada* 36, no. 4 (April 2014): 324–330.

2. Heather Howard, Ph.D. (board certified sexologist) in discussion with the author, March 6, 2015.

3. *Ibid.*

4. Erica Marchand, Ph.D. (psychologist specializing in couples and sex therapy) in discussion with the author, March 3, 2015.

5. Rose Hartzell, Ph.D. (certified sex educator and therapist) in discussion with the author, March 11, 2015.

6. Marchand, March 3, 2015.

7. Howard, March 6, 2015.

8. Hartzell, March 11, 2015.

9. Howard, March 6, 2015.

12. TIPS FOR DAY-TO-DAY LIVING

1. Dr. Erica Marchand, Ph.D. (licensed psychologist), in discussion with the author, November 15, 2014.

BIBLIOGRAPHY

Alo, KM and J Holsheimer. "New Trends in Neuromodulation for the Management of Neuropathic Pain." *Neurosurgery* 50 (2002): 690–703.

Apte, G et al. "Chronic Female Pelvic Pain: Part I: Clinical Pathoanatomy and Examination of the Pelvic Region." *Pain Practice* 12 (2012): 88–110.

Beckmann, M and O Stock. "Antenatal Perineal Massage for Reducing Perineal Trauma." *Cochrane Database of Systemic Reviews* 4 (2013).

Bergman, J and S Zeitlin. "Prostatitis and Chronic Prostatitis/Chronic Pelvic Pain Syndrome." *Expert Review of Neurotherapeutics* 7 (2007): 301–307.

Beydoun, A et al. "Gabapentin: Pharmacokinetics, Efficacy, and Safety." *Clinical Neuropharmacology* 14 (1995): 469–481.

Bo, K. "Evaluation of Female Pelvic Floor Muscle Function and Strength." *Physical Therapy Journal* 85 (2005): 269–282.

Boissonnault, JS and MJ Blaschak. "Incidence of Diastasis Recti Abdominis during the Childbearing Years." *Physical Therapy Journal* 68 (1988): 1082–1086.

Byrd, D and S Mackey. "Pulsed Radio Frequency for Chronic Pain." *Current Pain and Headaches Report* 1 (January 12, 2008): 37–41.

Danford, JM, DJ Osborn, WS Reynolds, DH Biller, and RR Dmochowski. "Postoperative Pain Outcomes after Transvaginal Mesh Revision." *International Urogynecology Journal* 26, no. 1 (January 2015): 65–69.

Engeler, D, AP Baranowski, S Elneil, J Hughes, EJ Messelink, P Oliveira, A van Ophoven, and AC de C Williams. "General Treatment of Chronic Pelvic Pain: Guidelines on Chronic Pelvic Pain." European Association of Urology (February 2012): 122–130.

Fillingim, R, S Bruehl, and R Dworkin et al. "The ACTTION-American Pain Society Pain Taxonomy (AAPT): An Evidence-Based and Multidimensional Approach to Classifying Chronic Pain Conditions." *Journal of Pain* 15, no. 3 (March 2014): 241–249.

Goldstein, I and L Burrows. "Can Oral Contraceptives cause Vestibulodynia?" *Journal of Sexual Medicine* 7 (2010): 1585–1587.

Gupta, P, MJ Ehlert, LT Sirls, and KM Peters. "Percutaneous Tibial Nerve Stimulation and Sacral Neuromodulation: An Update." *Current Urology Report* 16, no. 2 (February 2015): 4.

Gyang et al. "Musculoskeletal Causes of Chronic Pelvic Pain: What Every Gynecologist Should Know." *American College of Obstetrics and Gynecology* 121 (2013): 645–650.

Habermacher, G, J Chason, and A Schaeffer. "Chronic Prostatitis/Chronic Pelvic Pain Syndrome." *Annual Review of Medicine* 57 (2006): 195–206.

Hewitt, DJ. "The Use of NMDA-Receptor Antagonists in the Treatment of Chronic Pain." *Clinical Journal of Pain* 16, no. 2 (2000): S73–S79.

Jackson, T, L Pope, T Nagasaka, A Fritch, T Iezzi, and H Chen. "The Impact of Threatening Information about Pain on Coping and Pain Tolerance." *British Journal of Health Psychology* 10 (2005): 441–451.

Jones, MD, J Booth, JL Taylor, and BK Barry. "Aerobic Training Increases Pain Tolerance in Healthy Individuals." *Medicine & Science in Sports & Exercise* 46 (2014): 1640–1647.

Martin, J, B Hamilton, M Osterman, S Curtin, and T Mathews. "Births: Final Data for 2013." *Centers for Disease Control and Prevention National Vital Statistics Reports* 64 (2015).

McDonald, EA, D Gartland, R Small, and SJ Brown. "Dyspareunia and Childbirth: A Prospective Cohort Study." *British Journal of Obstetrics and Gynecology* 21 January 2015, doi: 10.1111/1471-0528.13263.

Moldwin, RM and JY Fariello. "Myofascial Trigger Points of the Pelvic Floor: Associations with Urological Pain Syndromes and Treatment Strategies Including Injection Therapy." *Current Urology Report* 14, no. 5 (October 2013): 409–417.

Pink, L, V Rancourt, and A Gordon. "Persistent Genital Arousal in Women with Pelvic and Genital Pain." *Journal of Obstetrics and Gynaecology Canada* 36, no. 4 (April 2014): 324–330.

Richeimer, SH et al. "Utilization Patterns of Tricyclic Antidepressants in a Multidisciplinary Pain Clinic: A Survey." *Clinical Journal of Pain* 13 (1997): 324–329.

Sadownik, LA. "Etiology, Diagnosis, and Clinical Management of Vulvodynia." *International Journal of Women's Health* 6 (2014): 437–449.

Schwertner-Tiepelmann, N, R Thakar, AH Sultan, and R Tunn. "Obstetric Levator Ani Muscle Injuries: Current Status." *Ultrasound Obstetrics and Gynecology* 39 (2012): 372–383.

Simons, D, J Travell, L Simons, and B Cummings. *Travell and Simons' Myofascial Pain and Dysfunction: The Trigger Point Manual.* (LLW, 1998).

Swanson, CL, JA Rueter, JE Olson, AL Weaver, and CR Stanhope. "Localized Provoked Vestibulodynia: Outcomes after Modified Vestibulectomy." *Journal of Reproductive Medicine* 59, no. 3–4 (March–April 2014): 121–126.

Vleeming, A, HB Albert, and HC Ostgaard et al. "European Guidelines for the Diagnosis and Treatment of Pelvic Girdle Pain." *European Spine Journal* 17 (2008): 794–819.

Wu, WH, OG Meijer, K Uegaki, JM Mens, JH van Dieen, PI Wuisman, and HC Ostgaard. "Pregnancy Related Pelvic Girdle Pain: Terminology, Clinical Presentation, and Prevalence." *European Spine Journal* 13 (2004): 575–589.

Zondervan, KT, PL Yudkin, MP Vessey, MG Dawes, DH Barlow, and SH Kennedy. "Prevalence and Incidence of Chronic Pelvic Pain in Primary Care: Evidence from a National General Practice Database." *Journal of Obstetrics and Gynecology* 106 (1999): 1149–1155.

INDEX

ABOUT THE AUTHORS

Stephanie Prendergast and **Elizabeth Rummer** are the founders of the Pelvic Health and Rehabilitation Center (PHRC), a physical therapy practice that focuses solely on the treatment of pelvic pain/dysfunction for men and women. With four locations in California (Los Angeles, San Francisco, Berkeley, and Los Gatos) and one East Coast location in Waltham, Massachusetts, PHRC is the premier pelvic floor rehabilitation clinic in the country. Stephanie and Liz are well-recognized experts and thought leaders in the treatment of pelvic pain/dysfunction. They lecture worldwide and have been interviewed by and/or contributed articles to publications such as the *New York Times* and the *Los Angeles Times* along with several medical textbooks, including *Chronic Pelvic Pain and Dysfunction: Practical Physical Medicine; Abdominal and Pelvic Pain: From Definition to Best Practice;* and *Fascia: The Tensional Network of the Human Body*. In addition, they hold leadership roles in numerous pelvic pain–related organizations. Stephanie was the first physical therapist to be elected as president of the International Pelvic Pain Society in 2013 after serving on their board of directors for 10 years. They are also involved in the Global Society for Endometriosis and Pelvic Pain Surgeons, and Stephanie was a cofounder, lecturer, and scientific program chair for the World Congress on Abdominal and Pelvic Pain in Amsterdam in 2013, in Nice in 2015, and in Washington, DC, in 2017.